BELIEF REVISION

Cambridge Tracts in Theoretical Computer Science

Managing Editor   Professor C.J. van Rijsbergen, Department of Computing Science, University of Glasgow

Editorial Board

S. Abramsky, Department of Computing Science, Imperial College of Science and Technology
P.H. Aczel, Department of Computer Science, University of Manchester
J.W. de Bakker, Centrum voor Wiskunde en Informatica, Amsterdam
J.A. Goguen, Programming Research Group, University of Oxford
J.V. Tucker, Department of Mathematics and Computer Science, University College of Swansea

Titles in the series

BELIEF REVISION

Edited by
PETER GÄRDENFORS
Department of Philosophy
Lund University

CAMBRIDGE
UNIVERSITY PRESS

PUBLISHED BY THE PRESS SYNDICATE OF THE UNIVERSITY OF CAMBRIDGE
The Pitt Building, Trumpington Street, Cambridge, United Kingdom

CAMBRIDGE UNIVERSITY PRESS
The Edinburgh Building, Cambridge CB2 2RU, UK
40 West 20th Street, New York NY 10011–4211, USA
477 Williamstown Road, Port Melbourne, VIC 3207, Australia
Ruiz de Alarcón 13, 28014 Madrid, Spain
Dock House, The Waterfront, Cape Town 8001, South Africa

http://www.cambridge.org

First published 1992
First paperback edition 2003

A catalogue record for this book is available from the British Library

ISBN 0 521 41260 9 hardback
ISBN 0 521 54564 1 paperback

CONTENTS

Belief Revision: An Introduction

PETER GÄRDENFORS

Cognitive Science, Department of Philosophy,
Lund University, S-223 50 Lund, Sweden

1 THE PROBLEMS OF BELIEF REVISION

1.1 An Example

Suppose that you have a database that contains, among other things, the following pieces of information (in some form of code):

α: All European swans are white.

β: The bird caught in the trap is a swan.

γ: The bird caught in the trap comes from Sweden.

δ: Sweden is part of Europe.

If your database is coupled with a program that can compute logical inferences in the given code, the following fact is derivable from α - δ:

ε: The bird caught in the trap is white.

Now suppose that, *as a matter of fact*, the bird caught in the trap turns out to be black. This means that you want to add the fact $\neg\varepsilon$, i.e., the negation of ε, to the database. But then the database becomes *inconsistent*. If you want to keep the database consistent, which is normally a sound methodology, you need to *revise* it. This means that some of the beliefs in the original database must be retracted. You don't want to give up all of the beliefs since this would be an unnecessary loss of valuable information. So you have to *choose* between retracting α, β, γ or δ.

The problem of belief revision is that logical considerations alone do not tell you which beliefs to give up, but this has to be decided by some other means. What makes things more complicated is that beliefs in a database have *logical consequences*, so when giving up a belief you have to decide as well which of the consequences to retain and which to retract. For example, if you decide to retract α in the situation described here, α has as logical consequences, among others, the following two:

α':   All European swans except the one caught in the trap are white

and

α'':   All European swans except some of the Swedish are white.

Do you want to keep any of these sentences in the revised database?

1.2 The Methodological Problems of Belief Revisions

When trying to handle belief revisions in a computational setting, there are three main methodological questions to settle:

(1)   How are the beliefs in the database *represented*?

Most databases work with elements like *facts* and *rules* as primitive forms of representing information. The code used to represent the beliefs may be more or less closely related to standard logical formalism. A mechanism for belief revision is sensitive to the formalism chosen to represent the beliefs.

(2)   What is the relation between the elements explicitly represented in the database and the beliefs that may be *derived* from these elements?

This relation is to a large extent dependent on the *application area* of the database. In some cases the elements explicitly formulated in the database have a special status in comparison to the logical consequences of these beliefs that may be derived by some inference mechanism. In other cases, the formulation of the beliefs in the database is immaterial so that any representation that has the same logical consequences, i.e., the same set of implicit beliefs, is equivalent. As will be seen in several papers in this volume, the nature of the relation between explicit and implicit beliefs is of crucial importance for how the belief revision process is attacked.

(3)   How are the choices concerning what to retract made?

Logic alone is not sufficient to decide between which beliefs to give up and which to retain when performing a belief revision. What are the extralogical factors that determine the choices? One idea is that the information lost when giving up beliefs should be kept minimal. Another idea is that some beliefs are considered more important or entrenched than others and the beliefs that should be retracted are the least important ones. Within computer science the use of *integrity constraints* is a common way of handling the problem. Again, the methodological rules chosen here are dependent on the application area.

1.3 Three Kinds of Belief Changes

A belief revision occurs when a new piece of information that is *inconsistent* with the present belief system (or database) is added to that system in such a way that the result is a new consistent belief system. But this is not the only kind of change that can occur in a belief system. Depending on how beliefs are represented and what kinds of inputs are accepted, different typologies of belief changes are possible.

In the most common case, when beliefs are represented by *sentences* in some code, and when a belief is either *accepted* or *rejected* in a belief system K (so that no degrees of belief are considered), one can distinguish three main kinds of belief changes:

(i) *Expansion*: A new sentence ϕ is added to a belief system K together with the logical consequences of the addition (regardless of whether the larger set so formed is consistent). The belief system that results from expanding K by a sentence ϕ will be denoted $K+\phi$.

(ii) *Revision*: A new sentence that is inconsistent with a belief system K is added, but, in order to maintain consistency in the resulting belief system, some of the old sentences in K are deleted. The result of revising K by a sentence ϕ will be denoted $K \dot{+} \phi$.

(iii) *Contraction*: Some sentence in K is retracted without adding any new facts. In order for the resulting system to be closed under logical consequences some other sentences from K must be given up. The result of contracting K with respect to ϕ will be denoted $K \dot{-} \phi$.

Expansions of belief systems can be handled comparatively easily. $K+\phi$ can simply be defined as the logical closure of K together with ϕ:

(Def +) $$K+\phi = \{\psi : K \cup \{\phi\} \vdash \psi\}$$

As is easily shown, $K+\phi$ defined in this way will be closed under logical consequences and will be consistent when ϕ is consistent with K.

It is not possible to give a similar explicit definition of revisions and contractions in logical and set-theoretical notions only. The problems for revisions were presented in the introductory example. There is no purely logical reason for making one choice rather than the other among the sentences to be retracted, but we have to rely on additional information about these sentences. Thus, from a logical point of view, there are several ways of specifying the revision $K \dot{+} \phi$. Though $K \dot{+} \phi$ cannot be characterized uniquely in logical terms, the *general properties* of a revision function can be investigated, and – in some cases, at least – *algorithms* can be found for computing revision functions. These two goals will be handled technically by using the notion of a *revision function* "$\dot{+}$" which has two arguments, a belief system K and a sentence ϕ, and which has as its value the revised belief system $K \dot{+} \phi$.

The contraction process faces parallel problems. To give a simple example, consider a belief system K which contains the sentences ϕ, ψ, $\phi \wedge \psi \rightarrow \chi$ and their logical consequences (among which is χ). Suppose that we want to contract K by deleting χ. Of course, χ must be deleted from K when forming $K \dot{-} \chi$, but also at least one of the sentences ϕ, ψ, or $\phi \wedge \psi \rightarrow \chi$ must be given up in order to maintain consistency. Again, there is no purely logical reason for making one choice rather than the other. Another concrete example is provided by Fagin, Ullman and Vardi (1983, p. 353).

The common denominator in both this example and the introductory one is that the database is not viewed merely as a collection of logically independent facts, but rather as a collection of axioms from which other facts can be derived. It is the interaction between the updated facts and the derived facts that is the source of the problem.

In parallel with revision we can introduce the concept of a *contraction function* "$\dot{-}$" which has the same two arguments as before, i.e., a belief system K and a sentence ϕ (to be retracted from K), and which produces as its value the belief system $K \dot{-} \phi$. In Section 3.3, I shall show that the problems of revision and contraction are closely related – being two sides of the same coin.

1.4 Two Approaches to Describing Belief Revisions

When tackling the problem of belief revision there are two general strategies to follow, namely, to present explicit *constructions* of the revision process and to formulate *postulates* for such constructions. For a computer scientist the ultimate solution to the problem about belief revision is to develop *algorithms* for computing appropriate revision and contraction functions for an arbitrary belief system. In this volume several proposals for constructions of revision methods will be presented. These methods are not presented as pure algorithms, but on a slightly more general level.

However, in order to know whether an algorithm is successful or not it is necessary to determine what an 'appropriate' revision function is. Our standards for revision and contraction functions will be various *rationality postulates*. The formulations of these postulates are given in a more or less equational form. One guiding idea is that the revision $K \dot{+} \phi$ of K with respect to ϕ should represent the minimal change of K needed to accommodate ϕ consistently. The consequences of the postulates will also be investigated.

Much of the theoretical work within belief revision theory consists of connecting the two approaches. This is done via a number of *representation theorems*, which show that the revision methods that satisfy a particular set of rationality postulates are exactly those that fall within some computationally well defined class of methods.[1]

---

[1]For further discussion of the two strategies cf. Makinson (1985, pp. 350-351).

2 MODELS OF BELIEF STATES

2.1 Preliminaries

Before we can start discussing models of belief revision, we must have a way of modelling belief states since a revision method is defined as a function from one belief state into another. The most common models of belief states in computational contexts are *sentential* or *propositional*, in the sense that the elements constituting the belief systems are coded as formulas representing sentences. This kind of model will be the focus of this introduction, but some alternative types of models will be encountered in the volume.

But even if we stick to propositional models of belief systems, there are many options. First of all, we must choose an appropriate *language* to formulate the belief sentences. For example, databases include some form of *rules*, and there are many ways of formalizing these: as quantified sentences in first order logic, as PROLOG rules (corresponding to Horn-clauses), as default statements (e.g., in the style of Reiter (1980)), as probability statements, etc.

In this introduction, I shall work with a language L which is based on first order logic. The details of L will be left open for the time being. It will be assumed that L is closed under applications of the *boolean operators* $\neg$ (negation), $\wedge$ (conjunction), $\vee$ (disjunction) and $\rightarrow$ (implication). We will use ϕ, ψ, χ, etc. as variables over sentences in L. It is also convenient to introduce the symbols $\top$ and $\bot$ for the two sentential constants "truth" and "falsity."

What is accepted in a formal model of a belief state are not only the sentences that are explicitly put into the database, but also the *logical consequences* of these beliefs. Hence, the second factor which has to be decided upon when modelling a belief state is what *logic* governs the beliefs. In practice this depends on which theorem-proving mechanism is used in combination with the database. However, when doing a theoretical analysis, one wants to abstract from the idiosyncrasies of a particular algorithm for theorem proving and start from a more general description of the logic. If the logic is undecidable, further complications will arise, but we will ignore these for the time being.

I shall assume that the underlying logic includes *classical propositional logic* and that it is compact.[2] If K logically entails ϕ we will write this as $K \vdash \phi$. Where K is a set of sentences, we shall use the notation Cn(K) for the set of all logical consequences of K, i.e., Cn(K) = $\{\phi : K \vdash \phi\}$. All papers in this volume presume classical logic, except the one by Cross and Thomason where a four-valued logic is used instead.

---

[2] A logic is compact iff whenever A is a logical consequence of a set of sentence K, then there is a *finite* subset K' of K such that A is a logical consequence of K'.

2.2 Belief Sets

The simplest way of modelling a belief state is to represent it by a *set* of sentences from L. Accordingly, we define a *belief set* as a set K of sentences in L which satisfies the following *integrity constraint*:[3]

(I)   If K logically entails ψ, then $\psi \in K$.

In logical parlance, (I) says that K is *closed under logical consequences*. The interpretation of such a set is that it contains all the sentences that are *accepted* in the modelled belief state. Consequently, when $\phi \in K$ we say that ϕ is accepted in K and when $\neg\phi \in K$ we say that ϕ is rejected in K. It should be noted that a sentence being accepted does not imply that it has any form of justification or support.[4] A belief set can also be seen as a *theory* which is a partial description of the world. "Partial" because in general there are sentences ϕ such that neither ϕ nor $\neg\phi$ are in K.

By classical logic, whenever K is *inconsistent*, then $K \vdash \phi$ for every sentence ϕ of the language L. This means that there is exactly one inconsistent belief set under our definition, namely, the set of all sentences of L. We introduce the notation $K_\perp$ for this belief set.

2.3 Belief Bases

Against modelling belief states as belief sets it has been argued (Makinson 1985, Hansson 1990, 1991, Nebel 1990, Fuhrmann 1991) that some of our beliefs have no independent standing but arise only as inferences from our more basic belief. It is not possible to express this distinction in a belief set since there are no markers for which beliefs are basic and which are derived. Furthermore, it seems that when we perform revisions or contractions we never do it to the belief set itself which contains an infinite number of elements, but rather on some finite *base* for the belief set.

Formally, this idea can be modelled by saying that B_K is a *base for a belief set* K iff B_K is a finite subset of K and $Cn(B_K) = K$. Then instead of introducing revision and contraction functions that are defined on belief sets it is assumed that these functions are defined on bases. Such functions will be called *base revisions* and *base contractions* respectively. This approach introduces a more finegrained structure since we can have two bases B_K and C_K such that $Cn(B_K) = Cn(C_K)$ but $B_K \neq C_K$. The papers by Nebel and Hansson in this volume concern base revisions. They will be presented in Section 3.5.

---

[3]Belief sets were called *knowledge sets* in Gärdenfors and Makinson (1988).

[4]For further discussion of the interpretation of belief sets cf. Gärdenfors (1988).

There is no general answer to the question of which model is the best of full belief sets or bases, but this depends on the particular application area. Within computer science applications, bases seem easier to handle since they are explicitly finite structures. However, it has been argued in Gärdenfors (1990) that much of the computational advantages of bases for belief sets can be modelled by belief sets together with the notion of *epistemic entrenchment* of beliefs (cf. Section 4.1).

2.4 Possible Worlds Models

An obvious objection to using sets of sentences as models of belief states is that the *objects* of belief are normally not sentences but rather the *contents* of sentences, that is, propositions. The characterization of propositions that has been most popular among philosophers during recent years is to identify them with *sets of possible worlds*. The basic semantic idea connecting sentences with propositions is then that a sentence expresses a given proposition if and only if it is true in exactly those possible worlds that constitute the set of worlds representing the proposition.

By taking beliefs to be beliefs in propositions, we can then model a belief state by a set W_K of possible worlds. The epistemic interpretation of W_K is that it is the narrowest set of possible worlds in which the individual being in the modelled belief state is certain to find the actual world. This kind of model of a belief state has been used by Harper (1977), Grove (1988), among others and in a generalized form by Spohn (1988) (also cf. the comparisons in Gärdenfors (1978)). In this volume, Katsuno and Mendelzon, and Morreau use this way of modelling belief states.

There is a very close correspondence between belief sets and possible worlds models. For any set W_K of possible worlds we can define a corresponding belief set K as the set of those sentences that are true in all worlds in W_K (assuming that the set of propositional atoms is finite). It is easy to verify that K defined in this way satisfies the integrity constraint (I) so that it is indeed a belief set. Conversely, for any belief set K, we can define a corresponding possible worlds model W_K by identifying the possible worlds in W_K with the *maximal consistent extensions* of K. Then we say that a sentence ϕ is *true* in such an extension w iff $\phi \in$ w. Again it is easy to verify that this will generate an appropriate possible worlds model (for details cf. Grove (1988)).

From a computational point of view, belief sets are much more tractable than possible worlds models. So even though possible worlds models are popular among logicians, the considerations here show that the two kinds of models are basically equivalent. And if we want to implement belief revision systems, sentential models like belief sets, and in particular bases for belief sets, are much easier to handle.

2.5 Justifications vs. Coherence Models

Another question that has to be answered when modelling a state of belief is whether the *justifications* for the beliefs should be part of the model or not. With respect to this question there are two main approaches. One is the *foundations* theory which holds that one should keep track of the justifications for one's beliefs: Propositions that have no justification should not be accepted as beliefs. The other is the *coherence* theory which holds that one need not consider the pedigree of one's beliefs. The focus is instead on the *logical* structure of the beliefs – what matters is how a belief coheres with the other beliefs that are accepted in the present state.[5] The belief sets presented above clearly fall into the latter category.

It should be obvious that the foundations and the coherence theories have very different implications for what should count as rational *changes* of belief systems. According to the foundations theory, belief revision should consist, first, in giving up all beliefs that no longer have a *satisfactory justification* and, second, in adding new beliefs that have become justified. On the other hand, according to the coherence theory, the objectives are, first, to maintain *consistency* in the revised epistemic state and, second, to make *minimal changes* of the old state that guarantee sufficient overall coherence. Thus, the two theories of belief revision are based on conflicting ideas of what constitutes rational changes of belief. The choice of underlying theory is, of course, also crucial for how a computer scientist will attack the problem of implementing a belief revision system.

Doyle's paper in this volume deals with the relations between justification theories and coherence theories of belief revision. In an earlier paper (Gärdenfors 1990), I presented some arguments for preferring the coherence approach to the foundations approach. Doyle argues that I have overemphasized the differences between the two approaches. He also wants to show that the foundations approach represents the most direct way of making the coherence approach computationally accessible.

Galliers' theory of autonomous belief revision, also in this volume, suggests in another way that the choice between coherence and foundational theories may not be exclusive; her theory in fact represents a blend between the two approaches. In a sense, also the belief base models presented in Section 2.3 show traces of justificationalism – the beliefs in the base are thought of as more foundational than the derived beliefs.

---

[5]Harman (1986) presents an analysis of the epistemological aspects of the two approaches.

3 RATIONALITY POSTULATES FOR BELIEF REVISION

3.1 The AGM Postulates for Revision

In this section, it will be assumed that belief sets (that is sets of sentences closed under logical consequences) are used as models of belief states. The goal is now to formulate postulates for rational revision and expansion functions defined over such belief sets.

The underlying motivation for these postulates (which are taken from Alchourrón, Gärdenfors, and Makinson (1985), hence the name) is that when we change our beliefs, we want to retain as much as possible from our old beliefs – we want to make a *minimal change*. Information is in general not gratuitous, and unnecessary losses of information are therefore to be avoided. This heuristic criterion may be called the criterion of *informational economy*.

However, it turns out to be difficult to give a precise quantitative definition of the loss of information (see, e.g., the discussion of minimality in Gärdenfors 1988, pp. 66-68). Instead we shall follow another line of specifying 'minimal change': We assume that the sentences in a belief set have different degrees of *epistemic entrenchment*, and when we give up sentences when forming a revision or a contraction, we give up those with the lowest degree of entrenchment. The idea of epistemic entrenchment will be presented in greater detail in Section 4.1.

It is assumed that for every belief set K and every sentence ϕ in L, there is a *unique* belief set $K \dotplus \phi$ representing the revision of K with respect to ϕ. In other words $\dotplus$ is a *function* taking a belief set and a sentence as arguments and giving a belief set as a result. This is admittedly a strong assumption, since in many cases, the information available is not sufficient to determine a unique revision. However, from a computational point of view this assumption is gratifying. In Doyle (1991) and Galliers' paper in this volume this assumption is not made.

The first postulate requires that the outputs of the revision function indeed be belief sets:

(K$\dotplus$1)   For any sentence ϕ and any belief set K, $K \dotplus \phi$ is a belief set.

The second postulate guarantees that the input sentence ϕ is accepted in $K \dotplus \phi$:

(K$\dotplus$2) $\phi \in K \dotplus \phi$.

The normal application area of a revision process is when the input ϕ contradicts what is already in K, that is $\neg\phi \in K$. However, in order to have the revision function defined for all arguments, we can easily extend it to cover the case when $\neg\phi \notin K$. In this case, revision is identified with expansion. For technical reasons, this identification is divided into two parts:

(K∔3) $K \dot{+} \phi \subseteq K + \phi$.

(K∔4)   If $\neg\phi \notin K$, then $K + \phi \subseteq K \dot{+} \phi$.

The purpose of a revision is to produce a new *consistent* belief set. Thus $K \dot{+} \phi$ should be consistent, unless ϕ is logically impossible:

(K∔5) $K \dot{+} \phi = K_\perp$ if and only if $\vdash \neg\phi$.

It should be the *content* of the input sentence ϕ rather than its particular linguistic formulation that determines the revision. In other words, belief revisions should be analysed on the *knowledge level* and not on the syntactic level. This means that logically equivalent sentences should lead to identical revisions:

(K∔6)   If $\vdash \phi \leftrightarrow \psi$, then $K \dot{+} \phi = K \dot{+} \psi$.

The postulates (K∔1) - (K∔6) are elementary requirements that connect K, ϕ and $K \dot{+} \phi$. This set will be called the *basic* set of postulates. The final two conditions concern *composite* belief revisions. The idea is that, if $K \dot{+} \phi$ is a revision of K and $K \dot{+} \phi$ is to be changed by a further sentence ψ, such a change should be made by expansions of $K \dot{+} \phi$ whenever possible. More generally, the minimal change of K to include both ϕ and ψ, that is, $K \dot{+} \phi \wedge \psi$, ought to be the same as the expansion of $K \dot{+} \phi$ by ψ, so long as ψ does not contradict the beliefs in $K \dot{+} \phi$. For technical reasons the precise formulation is split into two postulates:

(K∔7) $K \dot{+} \phi \wedge \psi \subseteq (K \dot{+} \phi) + \psi$.

(K∔8)   If $\neg\psi \notin K \dot{+} \phi$, then $(K \dot{+} \phi) + \psi \subseteq K \dot{+} \phi \wedge \psi$.

When $\neg\psi \in K$, then $(K \dot{+} \phi) + \psi$ is $K_\perp$, which is why the proviso is needed in (K∔8) but not in (K∔7).

We turn next to some consequences of the postulates. It can be shown (Gärdenfors, 1988, p. 57) that in the presence of the basic set of postulates (K∔7) is equivalent to:

(1) $K \dot{+} \phi \cap K \dot{+} \psi \subseteq K \dot{+} \phi \vee \psi$.

Another principle that is useful is the following 'factoring' condition:

(2) $K \dot{+} \phi \vee \psi = K \dot{+} \phi$ or $K \dot{+} \phi \vee \psi = K \dot{+} \psi$ or $K \dot{+} \phi \vee \psi = K \dot{+} \phi \cap K \dot{+} \psi$.

It can be shown that, given the basic postulates, (2) is in fact equivalent to the conjunction of (K∔7) and (K∔8).

Furthermore (K∔7) and (K∔8) together entail the following identity criterion:

(3) $K \dot{+} \phi = K \dot{+} \psi$ if and only if $\psi \in K \dot{+} \phi$ and $\phi \in K \dot{+} \psi$.

The postulates (K+1) - (K+8) do not uniquely characterise the revision K+ϕ in terms of only K and ϕ. This is, however, as it should be. I believe it would be a mistake to expect that only logical properties are sufficient to characterise the revision process.

3.2 The AGM Postulates for Contraction

The postulates for the contraction function '$\doteq$' will, to an even larger extent than for revisions, be motivated by the princple of informational economy. The first postulate is of a familiar kind:

(K$\doteq$1)   For any sentence ϕ and any belief set K, K$\doteq\phi$ is a belief set.

Because K$\doteq\phi$ is formed from K by giving up some beliefs, it should be required that no new beliefs occur in K$\doteq\phi$:

(K$\doteq$2)   K$\doteq\phi \subseteq$ K.

When $\phi \notin$ K, the criterion of informational economy requires that nothing be retracted from K:

(K$\doteq$3)   If $\phi \notin$ K, then K$\doteq\phi$ = K.

We also postulate that the sentence to be contracted not be a logical consequence of the beliefs retained in K$\doteq\phi$ (unless ϕ is logically valid in which case it can never be retracted because of the integrity constraint (I)):

(K$\doteq$4)   If not $\vdash \phi$, then $\phi \notin$ K$\doteq\phi$.

From (K$\doteq$1) to (K$\doteq$4) it follows that

(4)   If $\phi \notin$ K, then (K$\doteq\phi$)+$\phi \subseteq$ K.

In other words, if we first retract ϕ and then add ϕ again to the resulting belief set K$\doteq\phi$, no beliefs are accepted that were not accepted in the original belief set. The criterion of informational economy demands that as many beliefs as possible should be kept in K$\doteq\phi$. One way of guaranteeing this is to require that expanding K$\doteq\phi$ by ϕ should take us back to exactly the same state as before the contraction, that is K:

(K$\doteq$5)   If $\phi \in$ K, then K $\subseteq$ (K$\doteq\phi$)+ϕ.

This is the so called *recovery postulate*, which enables us to 'undo' contractions. It has turned out to be the most controversial among the AGM postulates for contraction.

The sixth postulate is analogous to (K+6):

(K$\doteq$6)   If $\vdash \phi \leftrightarrow \psi$, then K$\doteq\phi$ = K$\doteq\psi$.

Postulates $(K \dot{-} 1)$ - $(K \dot{-} 6)$ are called the *basic set* of postulates for contractions. Again, two further postulates for contractions with respect to conjunctions will be added. The motivations for these postulates are much the same as for $(K \dot{+} 7)$ and $(K \dot{+} 8)$.

$(K \dot{-} 7)$ $K \dot{-} \phi \cap K \dot{-} \psi \subseteq K \dot{-} \phi \wedge \psi$.

$(K \dot{-} 8)$ If $\phi \notin K \dot{-} \phi \wedge \psi$, then $K \dot{-} \phi \wedge \psi \subseteq K \dot{-} \psi$.

It is interesting to note that $(K \dot{-} 7)$ is in fact equivalent, given the basic postulates, to the seemingly weaker

(5) $K \dot{-} \phi \cap Cn(\{\phi\}) \subseteq K \dot{-} \phi \wedge \psi$.

In parallel with (2) it can be shown that $(K \dot{-} 7)$ and $(K \dot{-} 8)$ are jointly equivalent to the following condition:

(6) $K \dot{-} \phi \wedge \psi = K \dot{-} \phi$ or $K \dot{-} \phi \wedge \psi = K \dot{-} \psi$ or $K \dot{-} \phi \wedge \psi = K \dot{-} \phi \cap K \dot{-} \psi$.

A useful consequence of (6) is the following which says that $K \dot{-} \phi \wedge \psi$ is 'covered' either by $K \dot{-} \phi$ or by $K \dot{-} \psi$:

(7)   Either $K \dot{-} \phi \wedge \psi \subseteq K \dot{-} \phi$ or $K \dot{-} \phi \wedge \psi \subseteq K \dot{-} \psi$.

The postulates for revision and contraction and their consequences are dicussed further in Chapter 3 of Gärdenfors (1988).

3.3 From Contractions to Revisions and vice versa

We turn next to a study of the connections between revision and contraction functions. In the previous two sections they were characterized by two sets of postulates. These postulates are *independent* in the sense that the postulates for revisions do not refer to contractions and vice versa. A natural question is now whether either contraction or revision can be defined in terms of the other. Here we shall present two positive answers to this question.

A revision of a knowledge set can be seen as a composition of a contraction and an expansion. More precisely: In order to construct the revision $K \dot{+} \phi$, one first contracts K with respect to $\neg \phi$ and then expands $K \dot{-} \neg \phi$ by ϕ. Formally, we have the following definition which is called the *Levi identity*:

(Def $\dot{+}$) $K \dot{+} \phi = (K \dot{-} \neg \phi) \dot{+} \phi$

That this definition is appropriate is shown by the following result:

Theorem 1: If a contraction function '$\dot{-}$' satisfies $(K \dot{-} 1)$ to $(K \dot{-} 4)$ and $(K \dot{-} 6)$, then the revision function '$\dot{+}$' obtained from (Def $\dot{+}$) satisfies $(K \dot{+} 1)$ - $(K \dot{+} 6)$. Furthermore, if

(K$\doteq$7) also is satisfied, (K+7) will be satisfied for the defined revision function; and if (K$\doteq$8) also is satisfied, (K+8) will be satisfied for the defined revision function.

This result supports (Def +) as an appropriate definition of a revision function. Note that the controversial recovery postulate (K$\doteq$5) is not used in the theorem.

Conversely, contractions can be defined in terms of revisions. The idea is that a sentence ψ is accepted in the contraction K$\doteq\phi$ if and only if ψ is accepted both in K and in K+$\neg\phi$. Formally, this amounts to the following definition which has been called the *Harper identity*:

(Def $\doteq$) $K\doteq\phi = K \cap K+\neg\phi.$

Again, this definition is supported by the following result:

Theorem 2: If a revision function '+' satisfies (K+-1) to (K+6), then the contraction function '$\doteq$' obtained from (Def $\doteq$) satisfies (K$\doteq$1) - (K$\doteq$6). Furthermore, if (K+7) is satisfied, (K$\doteq$7) will be satisfied for the defined contraction function; and if (K+8) is satisfied, (K$\doteq$8) will be satisfied for the defined contraction function.

The two theorems show that the defined revision and contraction functions have the right properties. Hence, the two sets of postulates for revision and contraction functions are interchangeable and a method for constructing one of the functions would automatically, via (Def +) or (Def $\doteq$), yield a construction of the other function satisfying the desired set of postulates.

3.4 Representation Theorems

This section will introduce a first kind of explicit modelling of a contraction function for belief sets. Via the Levi identity (Def +) and Theorem 1, such a model can be used to define a revision function as well.

The problem in focus is how to define the contraction K$\doteq\phi$ with respect to a belief set K and a proposition ϕ. A general idea is to start from K and then give some recipe for choosing which propositions to delete from K so that K$\doteq\phi$ does not contain ϕ as a logical consequence. According to the criterion of informational economy we should look at as large a subset of K as possible.

The following notion is useful: A belief set K' is a *maximal subset of K that fails to imply* ϕ if and only if (i) K' $\subseteq$ K, (ii) $\phi \notin$ Cn(K'), and (iii) for any K" such that K'$\subset$ K"$\subseteq$ K, $\phi \in$ Cn(K"). The last clause entails that if K' were to be expanded by some sentence from K-K' it would entail ϕ. The set of all belief sets that fail to imply ϕ will be denoted K$\perp\phi$. Using the assumption that $\vdash$ is compact it is easy to show that this set is nonempty, unless ϕ is logically valid.

A first tentative solution to the problem of constructing a contraction function is to identify $K \dot{-} \phi$ with one of the maximal subsets in $K \perp \phi$. Technically, this can be done with the aid of a *selection function* γ that picks out an element $\gamma(K \perp \phi)$ of $K \perp \phi$ for any K and any ϕ whenever $K \perp \phi$ is nonempty. We then define $K \dot{-} \phi$ by the following rule:

(*Maxichoice*) $K \dot{-} \phi = \gamma(K \perp \phi)$ when not $\vdash \phi$, and $K \dot{-} \phi = K$ otherwise.

Contraction functions determined by some such selection function were called *maxichoice contraction functions* in Alchourrón, Gärdenfors and Makinson (1985).

A first test for this construction is whether it has the desirable properties. It is easy to show that any maxichoice contraction function satisfies $(K \dot{-} 1) - (K \dot{-} 6)$. But it will also satisfy the following *fullness* condition:

$(K \dot{-} F)$ If $\psi \in K$ and $\psi \notin K \dot{-} \phi$, then $\psi \to \phi \in K \dot{-} \phi$ for any belief set K.

We can now show that $(K \dot{-} 1) - (K \dot{-} 6)$ and $(K \dot{-} F)$ characterizes maxichoice contraction function in the sense of the following *representation theorem*. Let us say that a contraction function '$\dot{-}$' can be *generated* by a maxichoice contraction function iff there is some selection function γ such that '$\dot{-}$' is identical with the function obtained from γ by the maxichoice rule above.

Theorem 3: Any contraction function that satisfies $(K \dot{-} 1) - (K \dot{-} 6)$ and $(K \dot{-} F)$ can be generated by a maxichoice contraction function.

However, in a sense, maxichoice contraction functions in general produce contractions that are *too large*. A result from Alchourrón and Makinson (1982) is applicable here: Let us say that a belief set K is *maximal* iff for every sentence ψ, either $\psi \in K$ or $\neg \psi \in K$. One can now show the following discomforting result:

Theorem 4: If a revision function '$\dotplus$' is defined from a maxichoice contraction function '$\dot{-}$' by means of the Levi identity, then, for any ϕ such that $\neg \phi \in K$, $K \dotplus \phi$ will be maximal.

In a sense, maxichoice contraction functions create maximal belief sets. So a second tentative idea is to assume that $K \dot{-} \phi$ contains only the propositions that are *common to all* of the maximal subsets in $K \perp \phi$:

(*Meet*) $K \dot{-} \phi = \cap(K \perp \phi)$ whenever $K \perp \phi$ is nonempty and $K \dot{-} \phi = K$ otherwise.

This kind of function was called *full meet contraction function* in Alchourrón, Gärdenfors, and Makinson (1985). Again, it is easy to show that any full meet contraction function satisfies $(K \dot{-} 1) - (K \dot{-} 6)$. They also satisfy the following *intersection* condition:

$(K \dot{-} I)$ For all ϕ and ψ, $K \dot{-} \phi \wedge \psi = K \dot{-} \phi \cap K \dot{-} \psi$.

We have the following representation theorem:

Theorem 5: A contraction function satisfies $(K \dotminus 1)$ - $(K \dotminus 6)$ and $(K \dotminus I)$ iff it can be generated as a full meet contraction function.

The drawback of of full meet contraction is the opposite of maxichoice contraction – in general it results in contracted belief sets that are far *too small*. The following result is proved in Alchourrón and Makinson (1982):

Theorem 6: If a revision function '$\dotplus$' is defined from a full meet contraction function '$\dotminus$' by means of the Levi identity, then, for any ϕ such that $\neg\phi \in K$, $K \dotplus \phi = Cn(\{\phi\})$.

In other words, the revision will contain only ϕ and its logical consequences.

A third attempt is to use only *some* of the maximal subsets in $K \perp \phi$ when defining $K \dotminus \phi$. Technically, a *selection function* γ can be used to pick out a nonempty *subset* $\gamma(K \perp \phi)$ of $K \perp \phi$, if the latter is nonempty, and that puts $\gamma(K \perp \phi) = K$ in the limiting case when $K \perp \phi$ is empty. The contraction function can then be defined as follows:

(Partial meet): $K \dotminus \phi = \cap \gamma(K \perp \phi)$.

Such a contraction function was called a *partial meet contraction function* in Alchourrón, Gärdenfors, and Makinson (1985). The following representation theorem shows that $(K \dotminus 1)$ - $(K \dotminus 6)$ indeed characterizes the class of partial meet contraction functions:

Theorem 7: For every belief set K, '$\dotminus$' is a partial meet contraction function *iff* '$\dotminus$' satisfies postulates $(K \dotminus 1)$ - $(K \dotminus 6)$.

So far we have put no constraints on the selection function γ. The idea of γ picking out the 'best' elements of $K \perp \phi$ can be made more precise by assuming that there is an *ordering* of the maximal subsets in $K \perp \phi$ that can be used to pick out the top elements. Technically, we do this by introducing the notation $M(K)$ for the *union* of the family of all the sets $K \perp \phi$, where ϕ is any proposition in K that is not logically valid. Then it is assumed that there exists a *transitive and reflexive* ordering relation $\leq$ on $M(K)$. When $K \perp \phi$ is nonempty, this relation can be used to *define* a selection function that picks out the top elements in the ordering:

(Def γ) $\gamma(K \perp \phi) = \{K' \in K \perp \phi : K'' \leq K'$ for all $K'' \in K \perp \phi\}$

A contraction function that is determined from $\leq$ via the selection function γ given by (Def γ) will be called a *transitively relational partial meet contraction function*. This way of defining the selection function constrains the class of partial meet contraction functions that can be generated:

Theorem 8: For any belief set K, '$\dot{-}$' satisfies (K$\dot{-}$1) - (K$\dot{-}$8) iff '$\dot{-}$' is a transitively relational partial meet contraction function.

Thus we have found a way of connecting the rationality postulates with a general way of modelling contraction functions. The drawback of the construction is that the computational costs involved in determining the content of the relevant maximal subsets of a belief set K are so overwhelming that we should take a look at some other possible solutions to the problem of constructing belief revisions and contractions.

3.5 Contraction and Revision of Bases

As a generalization of the AGM postulates several authors have suggested postulates for revisions and contractions of *bases* for belief sets rather than the belief sets themselves. In this volume the papers by Hansson and Nebel (see also Fuhrmann 1989, Hansson 1989, 1991, Makinson 1987, Nebel 1990) use this kind of model. As Hansson writes in his paper, "this model is based on the intuition that some of our beliefs have no independent standing but arise only as inferences from our more basic beliefs."

Hansson and Nebel analyse various forms of base revision and base contractions. Nebel evaluates his models, in a number of theorems, in relation to the AGM postulates, but Hansson also introduces some postulates that are special for base revision. For example, his postulate of *relevance* can (slightly simplified) be written as follows in my terminology:

(8)   If $\psi \in H$, but $\psi \notin H\dot{-}\phi$, then there is some H' such that $H\dot{-}\phi \subset H' \subseteq H$ and $\phi \notin Cn(H')$, but $\phi \in Cn(H' \cup \{\psi\})$.

Here H denotes a *finite base* for a belief state consisting of sentences from L. The logical closure of H, that is Cn(H), will be a belief set. The intuition behind this postulate is that if a sentence ψ is retracted from H when ϕ is rejected, then ψ plays some role in the fact that H but not $H\dot{-}\phi$ logically entails ϕ. On the basis of relevance and other postulates for base contraction, Hansson proves several representation theorems (and further results can be found in Hansson (1991)).

An interesting feature of Nebel's paper is that he investigates the *computational complexity* of different belief revision procedures. As far as I know, he is the first one to attack these issues. An initial problem is that already the trivial case of deciding whether $\psi \in Cn(\emptyset)\dot{+}\phi$ is co-NP-complete so that a more finegrained set of complexity classes are needed than just saying that belief revision is NP-hard. Nebel solves this problem by using the polynomial hierarchy of complexity classes (Garey and Johnson 1979). On the basis of this hierarchy, he is then able to prove a number of results concerning the complexity of various revision methods. The analysis shows that all base revision methods analyzed in his paper that satisfy the full set of AGM postulates turn out to be no harder than ordinary propositional derivability.

4 CONSTRUCTIVE MODELS

4.1 Epistemic Entrenchment

Even if all sentences in a belief set are accepted or considered as facts (so that they are assigned maximal probability), this does not mean that all sentences are are of equal value for planning or problem-solving purposes. Certain pieces of our knowledge and beliefs about the world are more important than others when planning future actions, conducting scientific investigations, or reasoning in general. We will say that some sentences in a belief system have a higher degree of *epistemic entrenchment* than others. This degree of entrenchment will, intuitively, have a bearing on what is abandoned from a belief set, and what is retained, when a contraction or a revision is carried out. This section begins by presenting a set of postulates for epistemic entrenchment which will serve as a basis for a constructive definition of appropriate revision and contraction functions.

The guiding idea for the construction is that when a belief set K is revised or contracted, the sentences in K that are given up are those having the lowest degrees of epistemic entrenchment. Fagin, Ullman and Vardi (1983), pp. 358 ff., introduce the notion of "database priorities" which is closely related to the idea of epistemic entrenchment and is used in a similar way to update belief sets. However, they do not present any axiomatization of this notion. Section 5 of Nebel's paper in this volume provides a precise characterization of the relationship between epistemic entrenchment and database priorities.

We will not assume that one can quantitatively measure degrees of epistemic entrenchment, but will only work with *qualitative* properties of this notion. One reason for this is that we want to emphasise that the problem of uniquely specifying a revision function (or a contraction function) can be solved, assuming only very little structure on the belief sets apart from their logical properties.

If ϕ and ψ are sentences in L, the notation $\phi \leq \psi$ will be used as a shorthand for "ψ is at least as epistemically entrenched as ϕ." The strict relation $\phi < \psi$, representing "ψ is epistemically more entrenched than ϕ," is defined as $\phi \leq \psi$ and not $\psi \leq \phi$.

Postulates for epistemic entrenchment:

(EE1)	If $\phi \leq \psi$ and $\psi \leq \chi$, then $\phi \leq \chi$	(transitivity)
(EE2)	If $\phi \vdash \psi$, then $\phi \leq \psi$	(dominance)
(EE3)	For any ϕ and ψ, $\phi \leq \phi \wedge \psi$ or $\psi \leq \phi \wedge \psi$	(conjunctiveness)
(EE4)	When $K \neq K_\perp$, $\phi \notin K$ iff $\phi \leq \psi$, for all ψ	(minimality)
(EE5)	If $\psi \leq \phi$ for all ψ, then $\vdash \phi$	(maximality)

The justification for (EE2) is that if ϕ logically entails ψ, and either ϕ or ψ must be retracted from K, then it will be a smaller change to give up ϕ and retain ψ rather than to give up ψ, because then ϕ must be retracted too, if we want the revised belief set to satisfy the integrity constraint (I). The rationale for (EE3) is as follows: If one wants to retract $\phi \wedge \psi$ from K, this can only be achieved by giving up either ϕ or ψ and, consequently, the informational loss incurred by giving up $\phi \wedge \psi$ will be the same as the loss incurred by giving up ϕ or that incurred by giving up ψ. (Note that it follows already from (EE2) that $\phi \wedge \psi \leq \phi$ and $\phi \wedge \psi \leq \psi$.) The postulates (EE4) and (EE5) only take care of limiting cases: (EE4) requires that sentences already not in K have minimal epistemic entrenchment in relation to K; and (EE5) says that only logically valid sentences can be maximal in $\leq$. (The converse of (EE5) follows from (EE2), since if $\vdash \phi$, then $\psi \vdash \phi$, for all ψ.)

It should be noted that the relation $\leq$ is only defined *in relation to a given K* – different belief sets may be associated with different orderings of epistemic entrenchment.[6]

We mention the following simple consequences of these postulates:

Lemma: Suppose the ordering $\leq$ satisfies (EE1) - (EE3). Then it also has the following properties:

(i) $\phi \leq \psi$ or $\psi \leq \phi$ (connectivity);
(ii)   If $\psi \wedge \chi \leq \phi$, then $\psi \leq \phi$ or $\chi \leq \phi$;
(iii) $\phi < \psi$ iff $\phi \wedge \psi < \psi$.
(iv)   If $\chi \leq \phi$ and $\chi \leq \psi$, then $\chi \leq \phi \wedge \psi$.
(v)   If $\phi \leq \psi$, then $\phi \leq \phi \wedge \psi$.

The main purpose of this section is to show the connections between orderings of epistemic entrenchment and the AGM contraction and revision functions presented in Sections 3.1 and 3.2. We will accomplish this by providing two conditions, one of which determines an ordering of epistemic entrenchment assuming a contraction function and a belief set as given, and the other of which determines a contraction function assuming an ordering of epistemic entrenchment and a belief set as given. The first condition is:

(C$\leq$) $\phi \leq \psi$ if and only if $\phi \notin K \dot{-} \phi \wedge \psi$ or $\vdash \phi \wedge \psi$.

The idea underlying this definition is that when we contract K with respect to $\phi \wedge \psi$ we must give up ϕ or ψ (or both) and ϕ should be retracted just in case ψ is at least as epistemically entrenched as ϕ. In the limiting case when both ϕ and ψ are logically valid, they are of equal epistemic entrenchment (in conformity with (EE2)).

The second, and from a constructive point of view most central, condition gives an explicit definition of a contraction function in terms of the relation of epistemic entrenchment:

_____

[6]Rott (1992) has developed a generalized notion of epistemic entrenchment which is not dependent on a particular K.

(C$\doteq$) $\psi \in K\doteq\phi$ if and only if $\psi \in K$ and either $\phi < \phi \vee \psi$ or $\vdash\phi$.

Condition (C$\doteq$) provides us with a tool for explicitly defining a contraction function in terms of the ordering $\leq$. An encouraging test of the appropriateness of such a definition is the following theorem proved in Gärdenfors and Makinson (1988):

Theorem 9: If an ordering $\leq$ satisfies (EE1) - (EE5), then the contraction function which is uniquely determined by (C$\doteq$) satisfies (K$\doteq$1) - (K$\doteq$8) as well as the condition (C$\leq$).

Conversely, we can show that if we start from a given contraction function and determine an ordering of epistemic entrenchment with the aid of condition (C$\leq$), the ordering will have the desired properties:

Theorem 10: If a contraction function '$\doteq$' satisfies (K$\doteq$1) - (K$\doteq$8), then the ordering $\leq$ that is uniquely determined by (C$\leq$) satisfies (EE1) - (EE5) as well as the condition (C$\doteq$).

These results suggest that the problem of constructing appropriate contraction and revision functions can be *reduced* to the problem of providing an appropriate ordering of epistemic entrenchment. Furthermore, condition (C$\doteq$) gives an explicit answer to which sentences are included in the contracted belief set, given the initial belief set and an ordering of epistemic entrenchment. From a computational point of view, applying (C$\doteq$) is trivial, once the ordering $\leq$ of the elements of K is given.

The comparison $\phi < \phi \vee \psi$ in (C$\doteq$) is somewhat counterintuitive. Rott (1991) has investigated the following more natural version of the condition:

(C$\doteq$R) $\psi \in K\doteq_R\phi$ if and only if $\psi \in K$ and either $\phi < \psi$ or $\vdash\phi$.

He then shows that the contraction function '$\doteq_R$' defined in this way has the following properties:

Theorem 11: Let '$\doteq_R$' be the contraction function defined in (C$\doteq$R). If $\leq$ satisfies (EE1) - (EE5), then '$\doteq_R$' satisfies (K$\doteq$1) - (K$\doteq$4) and (K$\doteq$6) - (K$\doteq$8), but not (K$\doteq$5).

Since '$\doteq_R$' does not satisfy the controversial 'recovery' postulate (K$\doteq$5), it follows that '$\doteq_R$' defined by (C$\doteq$R) is in general not identical to '$\doteq$' defined by (C$\doteq$).[7] However, let '$\dotplus_R$' and '$\dotplus$' be the revision functions defined from '$\doteq_R$' and '$\doteq$' by the Levi identity. Rott proves:

Theorem 12: '$\dotplus_R$' and '$\dotplus$' are identical revision functions.

A consequence of this theorem is that if we are only interested in modelling revisions and not contractions, we can use the extremely simple test (C$\doteq$R) when computing the revision functions, without having to bother about the disjunctions in (C$\doteq$).

---

[7] '$\doteq_R$' is a 'withdrawal function' in the sense of Makinson (1987).

4.2 Safe Contraction

Yet another approach to the problem of constructing contraction functions was introduced by Alchourrón and Makinson (1985) and is called *safe contraction*. Their contraction procedure can be described as follows: Let K be a belief set, and suppose that we want to contract K with respect to ϕ. Alchourrón and Makinson postulate a "hierarchy" < over K that is assumed to be acyclical (that is, for no ϕ_1, ϕ_2 ..., ϕ_n in K is it the case that $\phi_1 < \phi_2 < ... < \phi_n < \phi_1$). Given such a hierarchy, we say that an element ψ is *safe* with respect to ϕ iff ψ is not a minimal element (under <) of any *minimal* subset K' of K such that K' $\vdash \phi$. Equivalently, every minimal subset K' of K such that K' $\vdash \phi$ either does not contain ψ or else contains some χ such that $\chi < \psi$. Intuitively, the idea is that ψ is safe if it can never be "blamed" for the implication of ϕ. Note that, in contrast to the earlier constructions, this definition uses *minimal* subsets of K that *entail* ϕ rather than maximal subsets of K that do *not* entail ϕ.

Rott's paper in this volume concerns the relation between orderings of epistemic entrenchment and the hierarchies over K used in the definition of safe contraction. He presents ways of translating between the types of orderings and proves that they are equivalent. This is in contrast to what was conjectured by Alchourrón and Makinson (1985) and Gärdenfors (1988). In this way, he completes the map of correspondences between (1) the AGM postulates for contractions, (2) the AGM postulates for revisions, (3) relational partial meet contractions functions, (4) epistemic entrenchment contractions, and (5) safe contractions.

4.3 Possibility Theory

Apart from the five areas mentioned in the previous paragraph, *possibility theory* can be added as a sixth area which can be connected to epistemic entrenchment relations, in the first place, and thereby also indirectly with belief revisions and contraction. This is the topic of Dubois and Prade's contribution to the volume.

Perhaps the best way of relating possibility theory to the theory of belief revision is to start with the *qualitative necessity relation* (Dubois 1986) which is an ordering $\geq_c$ (and the corresponding strict relation $>_c$) of sentences satisfying the following axioms:

(A0) $\top >_c \bot$

(A1) $\phi \geq_c \psi$ or $\psi \geq_c \phi$

(A2) $\phi \geq_c \psi$ and $\psi \geq_c \chi$ imply $\phi \geq_c \chi$

(A3) $\phi \geq_c \bot$

(C)   if $\phi \geq_c \psi$, then, for all χ, $\phi \wedge \chi \geq_c \psi \wedge \chi$

A qualitative necessity relation can be generated from a *necessity measure* N so that $\phi \geq_c \psi$ if and only if $N(\phi) \geq N(\psi)$, where N satisfies the following characteristic property:

(9) $N(\phi \wedge \psi) = \min(N(\phi), N(\psi))$

Dually, one can define a possibility measure Π as a function satisfying:

(10) $\Pi(\phi \vee \psi) = \max(\Pi(\phi), \Pi(\psi))$

Indeed, possibility measures are related to necessity measures through the relationship $N(\phi) = 1 - \Pi(\neg\phi)$. The dual qualitative possibility ordering $\geq_\Pi$ can be related to $\geq_c$ by the following equivalence:

(11) $\phi \geq_\Pi \psi$ if and only if $\neg\psi \geq_c \neg\phi$.

It has been shown by Dubois and Prade (1991) that a qualitative necessity ordering is almost identical to an epistemic entrenchment relation. The exception is that for epistemic entrenchment it is requested that $\top >_c \phi$ instead of (A0).

This connection between possibility theory and epistemic entrenchment forms the starting point for the paper by Dubois and Prade in this volume. They represent belief states by necessity measures and rewrite the rationality postulates for revision and contraction accordingly. They also show how this model of a belief state can be used to describe updating with *uncertain* pieces of evidence. They make some interesting comparisons with Spohn's (1988) *ordinal conditional functions*, which form a different way of introducing degrees of belief.

4.4 Updates vs. Revisions

Katsuno and Mendelzon present an interesting alternative to revision in their contribution to this volume. This alternative method is called *updating* and is also used by Morreau in his paper on planning. The basic idea is that one needs to make a distinction between two kinds of information and the corresponding changes. On the one hand there is new information about a *static* world. For this kind of information the revision process, as it has been described is appropriate. On the other hand, there is new information about *changes* in the world brought about by some agent. For both types, the new piece of information may be inconsistent with the current state of belief. However Katsuno, Mendelzon and Morreau argue that the revision process is inadequate as a model of rational belief change caused by the second type of information. For this kind of change an *updating* procedure is appropriate

To illustrate their argument, let me borrow an example from Winslett (1988). Suppose that all we know in K about a particular room is that there is a table, a book and a magazine in it, and that either (β) the book is on the table, or (μ) the magazine is on the table, but not both, i.e., the belief state K is essentially $Cn((\beta \wedge \neg\mu) \vee (\mu \wedge \neg\beta))$. A robot is then ordered to put the book on the table, and as a consequence, we learn that β. If we change our beliefs by revision we should, according to (K+4), end up in a belief state that contains $\beta \wedge \neg\mu$ since β is consistent with K. But why should we conclude that the magazine is not on the table?

In order to describe how updating works, we must present their version of a possible worlds model for belief states. Let L be the language of standard propositional logic and let P be the set of propositional letters in L. An *interpretation* of L is a function I from P to the set {T,F} of truth values. This function is extended to L recursively in the standard way, so that $I(\phi \wedge \psi) = T$ iff $I(\phi) = T$ and $I(\psi) = T$, etc. A *model* of a sentence φ is an interpretation I such that $I(\phi) = T$. A model of a set of sentences K is an interpretation I such that $I(\phi) = T$, for all $\phi \in K$. Mod(K) denotes the set of all models of K.

Instead of using an ordering of $K\perp\neg\phi$ (the maximal consistent subsets of K that don't entail $\neg\phi$) when determining $K+\phi$, Katsuno and Mendelzon (and several other researchers; see Katsuno and Mendelzon's (1989) survey) have proposed to look at an *ordering of the set of all interpretations* and then use this ordering to decide which interpretations should constitute *models of* $K+\phi$, and thus indirectly determine $K+\phi$ in this way. The intended meaning of such an ordering is that some interpretations that are models of φ (but not of K) are *closer* to models of K than other interpretations. Such an ordering of interpretations should, of course, be dependent on K.

Technically, we assign to each belief set K a pre-ordering $\leq_K$ over the set of interpretations of L (and a corresponding strict ordering $<_K$).[8] Following Katsuno and Mendelzon we say that $\leq_K$ is *faithful*[9] if these conditions hold:

(i) $\leq_K$ is transitive and reflexive.
(ii)   If I, J $\in$ Mod(K), then I $<_K$ J does not hold.
(iii)   If I $\in$ Mod(K) and J $\notin$ Mod(K), then I $<_K$ J.

If M is a set of interpretations of L, we let Min(M,$\leq_K$) denote the set of interpretations I which are minimal in M with respect to $\leq_K$. $K+\phi$ can now be determined from $\leq_K$ as the belief set which has exactly Min(Mod({φ}),$\leq_K$) as its set of models. Katsuno and Mendelzon (1989) prove the following general result:

Theorem 13: A revision function $+$ satisfies (K+1) - (K+8) if and only if there exists a total faithful ordering $\leq_K$ such Mod($K+\phi$) = Min(Mod({φ}),$\leq_K$).

---

[8]To be precise, Katsuno and Mendelson only consider belief sets that can be represented by a *single* sentence from L (i.e., the conjunction of all the beliefs in K).

[9]This condition is called 'persistent' in Katsuno and Mendelzon (1989).

This theorem gives a representation of belief revision in their terminology. Using this terminology the difference between revising and updating can be described as follows: Methods for revising K by ϕ that satisfy (K+1) - (K+8) are exactly those that select from the models of ϕ that are 'closest' to the models of K. In contrast, update models select, for each model I of K, the set of models of ϕ that are *closest to I*.[10] The update K+ϕ is then characterized by the union of all such models.

The difference between the methods may seem marginal at a first glance, but the properties of updating are, in general, quite different from those of revision. In connection with the example above, we have already noted that updating violates (K+4). On the other hand, updating satisfies the following postulate, which is violated by revision:

(12) $(K \vee K')+\phi = (K+\phi) \vee (K'+\phi)$

This postulates presumes that belief states are modelled by single sentences so that disjunctions of belief states are well defined.

Morreau's paper in this volume is an application to *planning* of the updating procedure. Using this method he presents a framework for modelling reasoning about action. The language he uses includes a conditional operator > which is used to represent statements of the form 'If the agent were to do α, this would result in ϕ being true.' The conditionals are analyzed both semantically and axiomatically. By nesting conditionals of this kind he can describe the content of sequences of actions, and in this way obtain an elegant way of representing planning.

4.5 Autonomous Belief Revision and Communication

Postulate (K+2) requires that an input ϕ given to a belief state K *must* be accepted in the revision K+ϕ. Galliers argues in her paper in this volume that this is in conflict with the *autonomy* of the agents having the various belief states. In *communication*, one agent informs another about something, aiming at changing the receiver's belief state. It remains, however, the decision of the autonomous receiver whether the information should be accepted or not. As Gallier's puts it, "Autonomous agents may or may not comply with the recognised intended effects of an utterance on their cognitive states. There are no specialised rules dictating what is a cooperative response. Rational communicative action must therefore be planned not only as purposive, but as *strategic*."

So in order to model belief revisions in a communicative setting one must be able to specify *whether* to accept the contents of an utterance from another agent, as well as *how* to perform the possible revisions caused by the utterance. The underlying principle for

---

[10]This method is essentially equivalent to 'imaging' as introduced in a probabilistic context by Lewis (1976) and generalized to the context of belief sets in Gärdenfors (1988).

Galliers is that the acceptability of a new utterance is dependent on the degree of coherence of the belief state that would result if the utterance were added. Her model of revision is essentially determined by such a coherence ordering, where the degree of coherence is defined as maximal derivability of *core beliefs*. It is not required that there be a unique revision, and, furthermore, it is not required that any preferred revision incorporate the communicated information.

Galliers then adds a foundational aspect to the belief revision model by working with *assumptions* of various kinds and *justifications* for the assumptions. For example, the endorsement of an assumption depends on whether it is communicated by a reliable source or a spurious source. In this way, her model model of autonomous belief revision is a mixture of coherence and foundationalism. The model has been implemented as a component of a strategic planner for cooperative dialogue.

4.6 Conditionals and the Ramsey Test

There is a close connection between belief revisions and the meaning of *conditional sentences*. The carrying hypothesis is that conditional sentences, in various forms, are about changes of states of belief. The form of conditional sentence that is central is "if ϕ were the case, then β would be the case" or "if ϕ is the case, then β is (will be) the case," where ϕ may or may not contradict what is already accepted in a given epistemic state K. If ϕ contradicts what is accepted in K, the conditional is called a *counterfactual* (relative to K), otherwise it is called an *open conditional* (relative to K).

The epistemic semantics for counterfactuals and open conditionals will be based on F. P. Ramsey's test for evaluating a conditional sentence. His test can be described as follows: In order to find out whether a conditional sentence is acceptable in a given state of belief, one first adds the antecedent of the conditional hypothetically to the given stock of beliefs. Second, if the antecedent together with the formerly accepted sentences leads to a contradiction, then one makes some adjustments, as small as possible without modifying the hypothetical belief in the antecedent, such that consistency is maintained. Finally, one considers whether or not the consequent of the conditional is accepted in this adjusted state of belief.

Given the analysis of belief revisions in Section 2, we see that it is very natural to reformulate the Ramsey test in a more condensed way:

(RT) $\phi > \beta \in K$ iff $\beta \in K \dotplus \phi$

This test has attracted a great deal of attention as a possible starting point for a formal semantics of conditionals. Ginsberg (1986) argues that a formal semantics for counterfactuals is of great value for many problem areas within AI, in particular since they form the core of nonmonotonic inferences.

Note that the formulation of (RT) presupposes that sentences of the form $\phi > \beta$ belong to the object language and that they can be elements of the belief sets in a belief revision model. Let us call this extended object language L'.

Some results in Gärdenfors (1978) seem to justify the claim that the Ramsey test can be used as a basis for an epistemic semantics of conditionals. However, the list of conditions that were used to generate the logic of conditionals does not include (K+4) (or the full strength of (K+8)). An interesting question is whether it is possible to use (RT) together with (K+4) when analysing the logic of conditionals. With minor qualifications, the answer turns out to be *no*. In order to put the result as strongly as possible, one can start from the following *preservation* condition:

(K+P)   If $\neg\phi \notin K$ and $\psi \in K$, then $\psi \in K+\phi$

It is easy to show that the preservation criterion is essentially equivalent to (K+4).

The Ramsey test and the preservation criterion are each of considerable interest for the analysis of the dynamics of belief. Unfortunately, it can be proved that, on the pain of triviality, the Ramsey test and the preservation criterion are inconsistent with each other (Gärdenfors 1986).

Let us formulate this result with some care. A background assumption is that the revision function is defined for all belief sets.[11] Note that in L', sentences containing the conditional connective '>' will be treated on a par with sentences without this operator. The Ramsey test (RT) is, of course, dependent on this assumption. A consequence of (RT) that is crucial is the following *monotonicity* criterion:

(K+M)   For all belief sets K and K' and all ϕ, if $K \subseteq K'$, then $K+\phi \subseteq K'+\phi$.

The conditions on the revision function that will be needed for the proof are (K+2) and the following very weak criterion, which is one half of (K+5):

(K+5w)   If $K \neq K_\perp$ and $K+\phi = K_\perp$, then $\vdash \neg\phi$.

The final assumption that will be needed for the inconsistency result is that the belief revision system is non-trivial. As usual, two propositions ϕ and ψ are said to be disjoint iff $\vdash \neg(\phi \wedge \psi)$. A belief revision system will be said to be non-trivial iff there are at least three pairwise disjoint sentences ϕ, ψ, and χ and some belief set K which is consistent with all three sentences, i.e., $\neg\phi \notin K$, $\neg\psi \notin K$, and $\neg\chi \notin K$.

---

[11]What is needed for the proof is only the assumption that if K is in the domain of the revision function, so are all *expansions* K+ϕ.

Theorem 14: There is no non-trivial belief revision system that satisfies all the conditions (K+2), (K+5w), (K+M) and (K+P).

It should be noted that the conditional connective '>' is used neither in the formulation of the theorem nor in its proof. If (K+P) is replaced by (K+4), then (K+2) is not needed for the proof of the theorem.

Corollary: There is no non-trivial belief revision system that satisfies all the conditions (K+2), (K+5w), (RT) and (K+P).

The theorem and its corollary show that the Ramsey test (RT) and the preservation condition (K+P) (or, equivalently, (K+4)) cannot both be rational criteria for belief revisions. However, the Ramsey test has a great deal of appeal, and several ways of getting around the impossibility result have been tried. In his paper in this volume, Morreau uses *updating* instead of revision in formulating the Ramsey test (as was noted above, updating does not satisfy (K+4)) and it is easy to show that this combination is consistent.

Another approach is taken by Cross and Thomason in their paper in this volume. They also retain the Ramsey test, but they work with a different logical framework than what has been used above. Firstly, they use a four-valued logic which changes the accompanying proof theory. Secondly, they restrict revision to *atomistic* inputs, i.e., the only sentences for which the revision process is defined are either atomic sentences or negated atomic sentences.

By restricting the revision procedure in this way, Cross and Thomason show that it is now possible to work out a theory of conditionals that satisfies the Ramsey test. Furthermore, they show that the theory of nonmonotonic *inheritance* from Horty, Thomason, and Touretzky (1990) can be interpreted as a special case of their logic of conditionals. In this way we find yet another connection between the theory of belief revision and other areas of computer science.

Acknowledgements

I wish to thank Hirofumi Katsuno, Michael Morreau, Bernhard Nebel, Richmond Thomason and Hans Rott for helpful comments on an earlier version of this paper.

REFERENCES

Alchourrón, C. E., P. Gärdenfors, and D. Makinson (1985): "On the logic of theory change: Partial meet contraction and revision functions," *The Journal of Symbolic Logic 50*, 510-530.

Alchourrón, C. E. and Makinson, D. (1985): "On the logic of theory change: Safe contraction," *Studia Logica 44*, 405-422.

Doyle, J. (1991): "Rational belief revision (Preliminary report)," *Principles of Knowledge Representation and Reasoning,* ed. by J. Allen, R. Fikes, and E. Sandewall, Los Altos, CA: Morgan Kaufmann, 163-174.

Dubois, D. (1986): "Belief structures, possibility theory and decomposable confidence measures on finite sets," *Computers and Artificial Intelligence 5*, 403-416.

Dubois, D. and H. Prade (1991): "Epistemic entrenchment and possibility logic," to appear in *Artificial Intelligence*.

Fagin, R., Ullman, J. D., and Vardi, M. Y. (1983): "On the semantics of updates in databases," *Proceedings of Second ACM SIGACT-SIGMOD*, Atlanta, pp. 352-365.

Fuhrmann, A. (1991): "Theory contraction through base contraction," *Journal of Philosophical Logic 20*, 175-203.

Gärdenfors, P. (1978): "Conditionals and changes of belief," in *The Logic and Epistemology of Scientific Change*, ed. by I. Niiniluoto and R. Tuomela, *Acta Philosophica Fennica 30*, 381-404.

Gärdenfors, P. (1986): "Belief revisions and the Ramsey test for conditionals," *The Philosophical Review 95*, 81-93.

Gärdenfors P. (1988): *Knowledge in Flux: Modeling the Dynamics of Epistemic States,* Cambridge, MA: The MIT Press, Bradford Books.

Gärdenfors, P. and D. Makinson. (1988): "Revisions of knowledge systems using epistemic entrenchment," in *Proceedings of the Second Conference on Theoretical Aspects of Reasoning about Knowledge,* M. Vardi ed., Los Altos, CA: Morgan Kaufmann.

Garey, M. R. and Johnson, D. S. (1979): *Computers and Intractability – A Guide to the Theory of NP-Completeness*, San Francisco: Freeman.

Ginsberg, M. L. (1986): "Counterfactuals," *Artificial Intelligence 30*, 35-79.

Grove, A. (1988): "Two modellings for theory change," *Journal of Philosophical Logic 17*, 157-170.

Hansson, S. O. (1989): "In defense of base contraction," to appear in *Synthese*.

Hansson, S. O. (1991): *Belief Base Dynamics*, Uppsala: Acta Universitatis Upsaliensis.

Harman, G. (1986): *Change in Viev: Principles of Reasoning*, Cambridge, MA: The MIT Press, Bradford Books.

Harper, W. L. (1977): "Rational conceptual change," in *PSA 1976*, East Lansing, Mich: Philosophy of Science Association, vol. 2, 462-494.

Horty, J. F., Thomason R. H., and Touretsky, D. S. (1990): "A skeptical theory of inheritance in nomonotonic semantic networks," *Artificial Intelligence 42*, 311-348.

Katsuno, H. and Mendelzon, A. O. (1989): "A unified view of propositional knowledge base updates," *Proceedings of the 11th Internationsl Joint Conference on Artificial Intelligence*, San Mateo, CA: Morgan Kaufmann, 269-276.

Lewis, D. K. (1976): "Probabilities of conditionals and conditional probabilities," *The Philosophical Review 85*, 297-315.

Makinson, D. (1985): "How to give it up: A survey of some formal aspects of the logic of theory change," *Synthese 62*, 347-363.

Makinson, D. (1987): "On the status of the postulate of recovery in the logic of theory change," *Journal of Philosophical Logic 16*, 383-394.

Nebel, B. (1990): *Reasoning and Revision in Hybrid Representation Systems*, *Lecture Notes in Computer Science*, vol. 422, Berlin: Springer

Reiter R. (1980): "A logic for default reasoning," *Artificial Intelligence 13*, 81-132.

Rott, H. (1991):"Two methods of constructing contractions and revisions of knowledge systems," *Journal of Philosophical Logic 20*, 149-173.

Rott, H. (1992): "Preferential belief change using generalized epistemic entrenchment", to appear in *Journal of Logic, Language and Information*.

Spohn, W. (1988): "Ordinal conditional functions: A dynamic theory of epistemic states," in W. L. Harper and B. Skyrms, eds, *Causation in Decision, Belief Change, and Statistics*, *vol. 2*, Dordrecht: Reidel, 105-134.

Winslett, M. (1988): "Reasoning about action using a possible models approach," *Proceedings of the Seventh National Conference on Artificial Intelligence*, 89-93.

Reason Maintenance and Belief Revision
Foundations vs. Coherence Theories

Jon Doyle

Laboratory for Computer Science
Massachusetts Institute of Technology

In memory of Norma Charlotte Schleif Miller, 1898-1991

1 INTRODUCTION

Recent years have seen considerable work on two approaches to belief revision: the so-called *foundations* and *coherence* approaches. The foundations approach supposes that a rational agent derives its beliefs from justifications or reasons for these beliefs: in particular, that the agent holds some belief if and only if it possesses a satisfactory reason for that belief. According to the foundations approach, beliefs change as the agent adopts or abandons reasons. The coherence approach, in contrast, maintains that pedigrees do not matter for rational beliefs, but that the agent instead holds some belief just as long as it logically coheres with the agent's other beliefs. More specifically, the coherence approach supposes that revisions conform to minimal change principles and conserve as many beliefs as possible as specific beliefs are added or removed. The artificial intelligence notion of *reason maintenance system* (Doyle, 1979) (also called "truth maintenance system") has been viewed as exemplifying the foundations approach, as it explicitly computes sets of beliefs from sets of recorded reasons. The so-called AGM theory of Alchourrón, Gärdenfors and Makinson (1985; 1988) exemplifies the coherence approach with its formal postulates characterizing conservative belief revision.

Although philosophical work on the coherence approach influenced at least some of the work on the foundations approach (e.g., (Doyle, 1979) draws inspiration from (Quine, 1953; Quine and Ullian, 1978)), Harman (1986) and Gärdenfors (1990) view the two approaches as antithetical. Gärdenfors has presented perhaps the most direct argument for preferring the coherence approach to the foundations approach. He argues that the foundations approach involves excessive computational expense, that it conflicts with observed psychological behavior, and that the coherence approach subsumes the foundations approach in the sense that one can sometimes reconstruct the information contained in reasons from the information about "epistemic entrenchment" guiding conservative revision.

In this paper, we examine Gärdenfors's criticisms of the foundations approach. We argue that the coherence and foundations approaches differ less than has been supposed, in that the fundamental concerns of the coherence approach for conservatism in belief revision apply in exactly the same way in the foundations approach. We also argue that the foundations approach represents the most direct way of mechanizing the coherence approach. Moreover, the computational costs of revisions based on epistemic entrenchment appear to equal or exceed those of revisions based on reasons, in the sense that any entrenchment ordering from which information about reasons may be recovered will be at least as costly to update as the reasons it represents. We conclude that while the coherence approach offers a valuable perspective on belief revision, it does not yet provide an adequate theoretical or practical basis for characterizing or mechanizing belief revision.

2 THE COHERENCE APPROACH TO BELIEF REVISION

The coherence approach to belief revision maintains that an agent holds some belief just as long as it coheres with the agent's other beliefs, independent of how they may have been inferred or adopted. In other words, the coherence approach focuses on logical and psychological relations among beliefs rather than on inferential pedigrees. While one belief may be related to more beliefs than another, no belief is more fundamental than another. Indeed, when the set of beliefs contains sufficiently many of the consequences of these beliefs, one can usually derive any single belief from the others. A deductively closed set of beliefs represents the extreme case in which each belief follows from all the others.

One arrives at different coherence theories by choosing different ways of making the notion of "coherence" precise. Typical theories require that belief states should be *logically consistent*, and that changes of state should be *epistemologically conservative* in the sense that (roughly speaking) the agent retains as many of its beliefs as possible when it accommodates its beliefs to new information. (Quine (1970) calls epistemological conservatism "minimum mutilation"; Harman (1986) also calls it "conservativity.") Some authors, for example Harman (1986), supplement or supplant consistency with other relations of implication and explanation among beliefs, but these just indicate additional connections among beliefs rather than reasons stating why some beliefs are held. The requirement of consistency reflects a concern with the logical content of the agent's beliefs: inconsistent beliefs describe no world, and so cannot be useful. The requirement of conservatism reflects a concern with the economics of reasoning: information is valuable (costly to acquire), and so loss of information should be minimized.

A precise coherence approach must spell out just what these two requirements mean.

Logical consistency has an accepted definition, so the most pressing task is to provide a precise notion of conservatism. Two of the simplest ways of comparing the sizes of changes in beliefs compare the sets of added and subtracted beliefs or the cardinality of these sets. But measures of the size of changes need not be as simple as counting the number of beliefs adopted or abandoned.

2.1 The AGM formalization

In order to formalize the essence of conservative revision independent of particular choices of measures, Alchourrón, Gärdenfors and Makinson (1985) developed an axiomatic approach to belief revision that avoids commitment to any particular measure. (Gärdenfors (1988) treats this approach along with related materials by the authors.) We summarize their approach using an adaptation of the notations of (Alchourrón *et al.*, 1985). We suppose that $\mathcal{L}$ is a propositional language over the standard sentential connectives ($\neg$, $\wedge$, $\vee$, $\rightarrow$, $\leftrightarrow$), denote individual propositions by α, β, and γ, and denote sets of propositions by K and K'. We write $\vdash$ to mean classical propositional derivability, and write Cn to mean the corresponding closure operator

$$Cn(K) \stackrel{\text{def}}{=} \{\alpha \in \mathcal{L} \mid K \vdash \alpha\}.$$

The AGM approach models states of belief by sets of propositions. In some treatments, such as that of Gärdenfors (1988), states of belief are modeled by deductively closed (but not necessarily consistent) sets of propositions, that is, propositional *theories* $K \subseteq \mathcal{L}$ such that $K = Cn(K)$. The intent is to capture the import of the agent's beliefs, not necessarily what the agent will explicitly assent to or represent. Many of the theoretical results about belief revision concern this case of closed belief states. In other treatments, however, states of belief are modeled by sets of propositions that need not be deductively closed. These sets, called *belief bases*, represent the beliefs contained in their deductive closure. Formally, we say that K' is a base for K whenever $K = Cn(K')$ (even when $K = K'$). Naturally, a given theory can be represented by many different belief bases. The case of greatest practical interest is when the belief base K' is finite (and small), but not every theory has a finite basis.

The AGM approach considers three types of operations on belief states. For each belief state K and proposition α we have:

Expansion: Expanding K with α, written $K + \alpha$, means adding α to K and requiring that the result be a (possibly inconsistent) belief state.

Contraction: Contracting K with respect to α, written $K \dot{-} \alpha$, means removing α from K in such a way to result in a belief state.

Revision: Revising K with α, written $K \dot{+} \alpha$, means adding α to K in such a way that the result is a consistent belief state.

Expansion is naturally defined in terms of the union of the set of beliefs and the new proposition. In the belief base model, we may take the expansion of K by α as this union itself

$$K + \alpha \stackrel{\text{def}}{=} K \cup \{\alpha\},$$

while for closed belief states, we take the expansion to be the closure of this union

$$K + \alpha \stackrel{\text{def}}{=} Cn(K \cup \{\alpha\}).$$

Contraction and revision, on the other hand, have no single natural definitions, only the standard requirement that the change made be as small as possible so as to minimize unnecessary loss of knowledge. This requirement does not define these operations since there are usually several ways to get rid of some belief. In the case of contraction, for example, there is generally no largest belief state $K' \subseteq K$ such that $K' \nvdash \alpha$. For example, if α and β are logically independent, $K = \{\alpha, \beta\}$, and we wish to determine $K \dotminus (\alpha \wedge \beta)$, neither $\{\alpha\}$ nor $\{\beta\}$ entails $\alpha \wedge \beta$, but neither is one a subset of the other.

Prevented from identifying unique natural contraction and revision operations, Alchourrón, Gärdenfors, and Makinson formulate and motivate sets of rationality postulates that these operations should satisfy. We do not need to review these postulates here, other than to mention that the postulates for contraction and revision are logically equivalent if the revision $K \dotplus \alpha$ of a theory K is defined by means of the *Levi identity*

$$K \dotplus \alpha \stackrel{\text{def}}{=} (K \dotminus \neg\alpha) + \alpha,$$

so that revision by α is equivalent to contracting by $\neg\alpha$ to remove any inconsistent beliefs and then expanding with α. Alternatively, one can define contractions in terms of revisions by means of the *Harper identity*

$$K \dotminus \alpha \stackrel{\text{def}}{=} (K \dotplus \neg\alpha) \cap K,$$

so that the contraction by α is equivalent to taking those beliefs that would be preserved if $\neg\alpha$ were now believed.

2.2 Epistemic entrenchment

Gärdenfors (1988) views the behaviors described by the AGM postulates as arising from a more fundamental notion, that of *epistemic entrenchment*. Epistemic entrenchment is characterized by a complete preorder (a reflexive and transitive relation) over propositions which indicates which propositions are more valuable than others. This ordering influences revisions by the requirement that revisions retain more entrenched beliefs in preference to less entrenched ones. It may change over time or with the state of belief.

If α and β are propositions, we write $\alpha \leq \beta$ to mean that β is at least as epistemically entrenched as α. We write $\alpha < \beta$ (the strict part of this order) to mean that β is more entrenched than α, that is, that $\alpha \leq \beta$ and $\beta \not\leq \alpha$. We write $\alpha \sim \beta$ (the reflexive part of the order) to mean that $\alpha \leq \beta$ and $\beta \leq \alpha$. The following postulates characterize the qualitative structure of epistemic entrenchment.

($\leq$1) If $\alpha \leq \beta$ and $\beta \leq \gamma$, then $\alpha \leq \gamma$; *(transitivity)*

($\leq$2) If $\alpha \vdash \beta$, then $\alpha \leq \beta$; *(dominance)*

($\leq$3) Either $\alpha \leq \alpha \wedge \beta$ or $\beta \leq \alpha \wedge \beta$; *(conjunctiveness)*

($\leq$4) If K is a consistent theory, then $\alpha \leq \beta$ for all β iff $\alpha \notin K$; *(minimality)*

($\leq$5) If $\alpha \leq \beta$ for all α, then $\vdash \beta$. *(maximality)*

Postulate ($\leq$1) just says that $\leq$ is an ordering relation, while the other postulates all concern how the logic of propositions interacts with the ordering. Postulate ($\leq$2) says that α entails β, then retracting α is a smaller change than retracting β, since the closure requirement on belief states means that β cannot be retracted without giving up α as well. Postulate ($\leq$3) reflects the fact that a conjunction cannot be retracted without giving up at least one of its conjuncts. Taken together postulates ($\leq$1)-($\leq$3) imply that $\leq$ is a complete ordering, that is, that either $x \leq \beta$ or $\beta \leq \alpha$. Propositions not in a belief state are minimally entrenched in that state, according to ($\leq$4), and according to ($\leq$5), the only way a proposition can be maximally entrenched is if it is logically valid.

The influence of epistemic entrenchment on belief revisions is characterized by two conditions relating entrenchment orderings and contraction functions over theories. The first condition,

$$\alpha \leq \beta \text{ iff either } \alpha \notin K \dotminus (\alpha \wedge \beta) \text{ or } \vdash \alpha \wedge \beta, \tag{1}$$

says that in contracting a theory K with respect to a conjunction, we must give up the conjunct of lesser epistemic entrenchment, or both conjuncts if they are equally entrenched. It says, roughly speaking, that $\alpha < \beta$ is the same as $\beta \in K \dotminus (\alpha \wedge \beta)$. The second condition,

$$\beta \in K \dotminus \alpha \text{ iff } \beta \in K \text{ and either } \alpha < \alpha \vee \beta \text{ or } \vdash \alpha,$$

explicitly characterizes contraction functions in terms of epistemic entrenchment orderings. Using the contraction condition (1), Gärdenfors and Makinson (1988) prove that the postulates ($\leq$1)-($\leq$5) characterize the same class of belief revision operations as do the AGM postulates for contraction and revision.

3 THE FOUNDATIONS APPROACH

Where the coherence approach seeks to view all beliefs as held independently, related only by coherence requirements, the foundations approach divides beliefs into two classes: those justified by other beliefs, and those not justified by other beliefs. The former constitute derived beliefs, while one may view the latter as "self-justifying" beliefs or basic postulates. In contrast to the way beliefs provide each other with mutual support in the coherence approach, and so provide little help when it comes to giving explanations of why one believes something, the foundations approach provides explanations of beliefs by requiring that each derived belief be supportable by means of some noncircular arguments from basic beliefs. This noncircularity also allows one to use the arguments to determine changes to the overall set of beliefs; one should retain a belief, even after removing one of its justifications, as long as independent justifications remain, and one should abandon a belief after removing or invalidating the last of its justifications. In other words, one should hold a derived belief if and only if it has at least one noncircular argument from foundational beliefs.

3.1 Reason maintenance

Harman (1986) and Gärdenfors (1990) view reason maintenance systems as prime exemplars of the foundations approach. A reason maintenance system acts as a subsystem of a more general system for reasoning. It helps revise the database states of the overall system by using records of inferences or computations to trace the consequences of initial changes. By keeping track of what information has been computed from what, such it reconstructs the information "derivable" from given information. Although we find it convenient to think of these bits of information and derivations as beliefs and arguments, one may apply reason maintenance more generally to all sorts of computational or mental structures.

For concreteness, we follow Harman and Gärdenfors and focus on RMS, the particular reason maintenance system developed by the author (Doyle, 1979). We may formalize its essential features as follows, simplifying its complex actual structure in ways that do not matter for the present discussion. (See (Doyle, 1983a; Doyle, 1983b) for more detailed discussions.)

States of RMS contain two types of elements: *nodes* and *reasons*. We write N to denote the set of possible nodes, and R to denote the set of possible reasons. RMS uses nodes to represent information (beliefs, desires, rules, procedures, database elements, etc.) of significance to the overall reasoning system, but those "external" meanings have no bearing on the "internal" operation of RMS. RMS uses reasons to represent inferences, or more precisely, specific inference rules. Because nodes need not represent beliefs, RMS imposes no logic on nodes. Instead, the only relations among nodes are those indicated explicitly by reasons. These may, if desired, encode logical relations directly. For simplicity, we assume no nodes are reasons, so that each state consists of a set $N \subseteq \mathcal{N}$ of nodes and a set $R \subseteq \mathcal{R}$ of reasons.[1] We say that each node in N is *in* (the set of beliefs), and that each node in $\mathcal{N} \setminus N$ is *out* (of the set of beliefs).

The original RMS provided two types of reasons: *support-list* reasons and *conditional-proof* reasons. For simplicity, we will ignore conditional-proof reasons and assume that all reasons are support-list reasons. Each support-list reason takes the form (I, O, c) where $I, O \subseteq \mathcal{N}$ and $c \in \mathcal{N}$. The components I, O and c are called the *inlist*, the *outlist*, and the *consequent*, respectively. We call the reason *monotonic* if O is empty, and *nonmonotonic* otherwise. Each reason is interpreted as a rule stipulating inferences the RMS must make, according to which the consequent holds if all of the nodes in the inlist are held and none of the nodes in the outlist are held.

A state (N, R) is a *legal* state of RMS just in case N consists exactly of the *grounded* consequences of the reasons R. Formally, (N, R) is a legal state just in case

1. If $(I, O, c) \in R$, $I \subseteq N$, and $N \cap O = \emptyset$, then $c \in N$; and

2. If $n \in N$, then there is a finite sequence $\langle n_0, \ldots, n_m \rangle$ of elements of $N \cup R$ such that $n = n_m$ and for each $i \leq m$, either $n_i \in R$, or there is some $j < i$ such that

   (a) $n_j = (I, O, n_i)$,

   (b) for each $x \in I$, $x = n_k$ for some $k < j$, and

   (c) $x \notin N$ for each $x \in O$.

In other words, (N, R) is a legal state if the set of nodes *satisfies* every reason in R and if every node in N is supported by a noncircular argument from the *valid* reasons in R. Each set of reasons supports 0 or more legal states. For example, $\{(\{\alpha\}, \{\alpha\}, \alpha)\}$ supports none, $\{(\{\}, \{\}, \alpha)\}$ supports one, and $\{(\{\}, \{\alpha\}, \beta), (\{\}, \{\beta\}, \alpha)\}$ supports two if $\alpha \neq \beta$.

Whenever the reasoner adds or deletes reasons, RMS updates the set of nodes to produce a new legal state. Because a single set of reasons may support any of several sets of nodes, these updates involve choices. The RMS update algorithm was designed to attempt to update states conservatively. That is, if one takes the current state (N, R) and modifies R to obtain R', RMS should choose a new legal state (N', R') with a set of nodes N' as close as possible to the current set N. More precisely, RMS should choose N' so that for any other legal state (N'', R'), neither

---

[1]It is easy to construct theories in which reasons are nodes themselves, and so may support other reasons. In such theories, one may express all reasons as defeasible reasons and express all changes of belief through addition of reasons. See (Doyle, 1983b) for details.

$N \triangle N'' \subseteq N \triangle N'$ nor $N \triangle N' \subseteq N \triangle N''$ holds, where $\triangle$ denotes symmetric difference $(X \triangle Y = (X \setminus Y) \cup (Y \setminus X))$. Due to the difficulty of quickly computing this form of conservative updates, however, RMS only approximates conservative updates. Reason maintenance systems developed later use simpler notions of conservatism which may be computed more rapidly. For updating beliefs based on monotonic reasons, for example, McAllester's (1982; 1990) efficient so-called "boolean constraint propagation" technique maintains orderings of the premises generating belief sets. As Nebel (1989; 1990) points out, this ordering is analogous to an entrenchment ordering, and permits rapid conservative updates.

The belief revision operations of expansion and contraction correspond to the operations of adding or deleting reasons. Expansion corresponds to adding a reason of the form $(\{\}, \{\}, \alpha)$, which makes α a premise or basic belief. Contraction corresponds to removing all reasons for a node. Addition of other sorts of reasons does not correspond directly to any belief revision operations, as these reasons specify part of the (possibly nonmonotonic) logic of beliefs. Adding a monotonic reason with a nonempty inlist corresponds to adding an ordinary argument step, while adding a nonmonotonic reason lets RMS adopt a belief as an assumption.

3.2 Dependency-directed backtracking
The operation of revision has no direct realization in changes to the set of reasons. It instead corresponds to the operation of the *dependency-directed backtracking* (DDB) system, which we have omitted from the formalization of RMS above.

Unlike the operations of expansion and contraction, the operation of revision involves the notion of logical consistency in an essential way. Consistency does not matter to RMS in adding or deleting reasons; instead, the basic operations of RMS only maintain coherence of reasons and nodes. (Many discussions of reason maintenance misrepresent the truth by claiming that RMS maintains consistency of beliefs. This misrepresentation may stem from the somewhat misleading role of logical consistency in nonmonotonic logic (McDermott and Doyle, 1980).) RMS contraction, moreover, works only for beliefs explicitly represented as nodes, as it depends on removing all explicitly represented reasons for the belief. The operation of revision, in contrast, seeks to resolve a conflict among beliefs rather than to add or subtract reasons from the reason set, and so requires a notion of explicit inconsistency among beliefs.

Since RMS has no knowledge of the meanings of nodes, the reasoner must tell it which nodes represent contradictions. RMS, in turn, informs DDB whenever a contradiction node becomes believed, at which point the backtracker attempts to defeat the arguments supporting the contradiction node by defeating assumptions underlying those arguments. DDB never attempts to remove reasons or premises, only to defeat nonmonotonic assumptions. If the argument for the contradiction node does not depend on any of these (i.e., it consists entirely of monotonic reasons), DDB leaves the contradiction node in place as a continuing belief.

Just as RMS seeks to minimize changes through its incremental update algorithm, DDB seeks to effect minimal revisions in choosing which assumption to defeat. Specifically, the backtracker defeats only "maximal" assumptions that do not depend on other assumptions. This means, in effect, that DDB topologically sorts the beliefs supporting the contradiction node by viewing the reasons comprising the supporting argument as a directed hypergraph. The maximally-positioned assumptions in this ordering of beliefs then constitute the candidates for defeat. The backtracker then chooses one of these assumptions and defeats the reason supporting the chosen assumption by providing a new reason for one of the nodes in its outlist. The new defeating reason is entirely monotonic, and expresses the inconsistency of the chosen assumption with the other maximal assumptions and with other maximally-ordered beliefs in the contradiction node's support. The actual procedure is fairly complex, and we do not attempt to formalize it here. But it is not too misleading to say that the topological sorting process corresponds to calculating an entrenchment ordering, and that DDB revision corresponds to abandoning enough minimally entrenched assumptions to restore consistency. (Cf. (Nebel, 1990, pp. 183-185).)

4 COHERENTIST CRITICISMS OF FOUNDATIONS APPROACHES

Virtually all artificial intelligence approaches to belief revision have been based on some form of reason maintenance, but Harman (1986) and Gärdenfors (1990) reject such foundations-like approaches on a variety of grounds: as psychologically unrealistic (Harman and Gärdenfors), unconservative (Harman), uneconomic (Gärdenfors), and logically superfluous given the notion of epistemic entrenchment (Gärdenfors). We briefly summarize each of these critiques.

4.1 The psychological critique
Experiments have shown that humans only rarely remember the reasons for their beliefs, and that they often retain beliefs even when their original evidential basis is completely destroyed. Harman (1986) interprets these experiments as indicating the people do not keep track of the justification relations among their beliefs, so that they cannot tell when new evidence undermines the basis on which some belief was adopted. Gärdenfors (1990) follows Harman in concluding that the foundations approach cannot be the basis for a psychologically plausible account of belief revision, since it presupposes information that seems experimentally absent.

4.2 The conservativity critique
According to Harman (1986, p. 46), "one is justified in continuing fully to accept something in the absence of a special reason not to", a principle he calls the "principle of conservatism". Harman faults foundations approaches because "the foundations theory rejects any principle of conservatism" ((Harman, 1986, p. 30)), or more precisely,

"the coherence theory is conservative in a way the foundations theory is not" ((Harman, 1986, p. 32)). Since Harman views his principle of conservatism as a hallmark of rationality in reasoning, he views the foundations approach as producing irrational behavior.

4.3 The economic critique

According to Gärdenfors (1990), storing derivations of beliefs in memory and using them to update beliefs constitutes a great burden on the reasoner. In the first place, restricting revisions to changing only the foundational beliefs seems too limiting, since nothing in the foundations approach ensures that the foundational beliefs are more basic or valuable in any epistemological or utilitarian sense than the derived beliefs they support. But more importantly, the expected benefit of ensuring that states of belief are well-founded does not justify the cost.

> It is *intellectually extremely costly* to keep track of the sources of beliefs and the benefits are, by far, outweighed by the costs. (Gärdenfors, 1990, p. 31) (his emphasis)
>
> After all, it is not very often that a justification for a belief is actually withdrawn and, as long as we do not introduce new beliefs without justification, the vast majority of our beliefs will hence remain justified. (Gärdenfors, 1990, p. 32)

That is, if a belief has been held and has not caused trouble, there seems to be no good reason to abandon it just because the original reason for which it was believed vanishes or is forgotten. In short, the global extra computations needed to record and ensure proper foundations for belief seems unwarranted compared with a simple approach of purely conservative updates of belief states.

4.4 The superfluity critique

On the face of it, the foundations approach provides reasons for beliefs while the coherence approach does not. For example, in a deductively closed set of beliefs, every belief follows from all the rest, so the coherence approach seems lacking when it comes to providing reasonable explanations of why one believes something. But Gärdenfors (1990) claims that this supposed advantage misconceives the power of the coherence approach, in that the coherence approach can also (in some cases) provide reasons for beliefs.

Gärdenfors observes that any coherence approach involves not only the set of beliefs but also something corresponding to the ordering of epistemic entrenchment, and that while the belief set itself need not determine reasons for beliefs, the entrenchment ordering can be examined to reveal these reasons. For example, let r stand for "it rains today" and h stand for "Oscar wears his hat", and suppose that a deductively closed state of belief K contains r, $r \to h$, and h. Consider now the result of removing r from K. Superficially, conservatism says that we should retain as many current beliefs as possible, including the belief h. But the result of this contraction depends on how entrenched different beliefs are, and Gärdenfors shows that whether h is retained in $K \doteq r$ depends on whether $r \vee \neg h$ is more entrenched than $r \vee h$. If rain is the *only* reason for Oscar to wear his hat, then $r \vee \neg h$ will be more entrenched than $r \vee h$, and we will have $h \notin K \doteq r$. If Oscar wears his hat even if it does not rain, then $r \vee h$ will be the more entrenched, and we will have $h \in K \doteq r$.

Gärdenfors generalizes from this example to suggest that it may be possible to give a general definition of reasons in terms of epistemic entrenchment. He discusses one possibility for such a definition due to Spohn (1983). Reformulated in the AGM framework, this definition just says that α is a reason for β in K if $\alpha, \beta \in K$ and $\alpha \vee \beta \leq \alpha$; that is, if β is also removed whenever α is. This reconstruction of reasons from epistemic entrenchment does not fully reproduce the foundations approach, however. As Gärdenfors points out, according to this criterion we may have α is a reason for β is a reason for γ is a reason for α, which shows that this particular construction does not correspond to tracing beliefs back to foundational, self-justifying beliefs. Nevertheless, Gärdenfors hopes that a better definition may be possible, and concludes that "representing epistemic states as belief sets together with an ordering of epistemic entrenchment provides us with a way to handle most of what is desired both by the foundations theory and the coherence theory" (Gärdenfors, 1990, p. 45). He thus concludes that the ability to distinguish reasons does not constitute a true advantage of the foundations approach.

4.5 A closer look
While the coherentist critiques certainly give one cause to hesitate before embracing reason maintenance, one may also wonder why artificial intelligence researchers have adopted it so frequently if it has so many defects and no offsetting advantages. To understand better the relative attractions of these approaches, we take a closer look at the issues raised by these critiques. We find, in fact, that these critiques do not stand.

5 ASSESSING THE PSYCHOLOGICAL CRITIQUE

Harman and Gärdenfors correctly observe that the foundations approach, at least as embodied in systems like RMS, corresponds poorly to observed human behavior. But the force of this observation is not at all clear, since psychological accuracy need not be the only aim of a theory of belief revision. In particular, the aim of most artificial intelligence work on belief revision has been to construct computationally useful reasoning mechanisms. One might be pleased if the most useful mechanisms turn out to be psychologically plausible, but computational utility does not depend on that. Indeed, humans might prefer to use a computational system that reasons differently than they do if they find they do better using it than relying on their own abilities.

Moreover, it seems unreasonable to criticize the foundations approach on both psychological and economic grounds. If psychological accuracy is the aim, it matters little if alternative means provide greater efficiency. Efficiency and psychological accuracy bear particularly little correlation when different underlying embodiments (machines or brains) are considered, since humans may not be able to exploit the most efficient computational techniques in their own thinking.

But even if one does take the aim of the theory to be psychological accuracy, recording and using reasons in belief revision does not entail producing unnatural behavior. RMS ensures only that all beliefs enjoy well-founded support, not that all arguments are well-founded. Nothing prevents one from supplying RMS with a circular set of reasons, such as $\{(\{\}, \{\alpha\}, \beta), (\{\}, \{\beta\}, \alpha)\}$. Indeed, most problems yield circular sets of reasons quite naturally simply by reflecting logical relationships among beliefs. As in coherence approaches, which beliefs RMS (or the reasoner) takes as basic may change, at least in principle, with the task at hand.

More fundamentally, however, the recording and using of reasons to revise beliefs does not presuppose a foundations approach. Recent work continues to borrow from coherence approaches by recognizing that recording reasons does not commit one to actually using them, or to making them accessible when reporting on one's reasons. For example, where the original RMS used recorded reasons compulsively in updating beliefs, as prescribed by the foundations approach, the theories of reason maintenance developed in (Doyle, 1983b) make the degree of grounding variable, so that beliefs may be either "locally" or "globally" grounded. Similarly, the rational, distributed reason maintenance service described in (Doyle and Wellman, 1990) uses reasons to revise beliefs only as seems convenient, so that the effective foundations of the belief set change due to further processing even without new information about inferences. This system therefore violates the foundations requirement that beliefs hold only due to well-founded arguments for them. This suggests that one clearly separate the foundations requirement from the more general notions of recording and using reasons as aids to explanation and recomputation, since the latter roles for reasons make sense in both foundations and coherence approaches.

6 ASSESSING THE CONSERVATIVITY CRITIQUE

Addressing the conservativity critique requires recognizing that discussions of belief revision employ two senses of the term "conservatism". Harman uses the term to mean that beliefs *persist* and do not change without specific reasons to disbelieve them. Using this sense of the term, we may agree with his claim that foundations approaches reject conservatism, for the foundations approach calls for abandoning beliefs when one no longer has specific reasons for believing them. But this criticism takes a narrow view of what constitutes a reason for belief. One may take Harman's principle of conservatism as stating a general reason for belief: namely, a lack of past indications that the belief is false constitutes a reason for continuing belief. Such reasons can be respected by a foundations approach simply by adding explicit defeasible reasons for each belief. That is, one might reproduce the coherence approach within the foundations approach simply by adding a reason

$$(\{\}, \{\text{“}\alpha \text{ has been directly challenged”}\}, \alpha)$$

for each node α the first time the α becomes *in*.

Gärdenfors, on the other hand, uses the term "conservatism" to mean *minimal change*, that beliefs do not change more than is necessary. This sense corresponds to the notions of contraction and revision captured by the AGM postulates, according to which one does not abandon both α and β when abandoning α would suffice. This sense of the term seems somewhat more general than the alternative persistence sense, since the persistence interpretation seems to cover only the operation of revision, ignoring the operation of contraction. (Harman, of course, also endorses minimal changes for revision operations, even if his principle of conservatism seems to rule out contraction operations.) But, as the preceding description of RMS makes clear, reason maintenance involves conservative updates in this sense, as its incremental revision approach minimizes the set of changed beliefs. This same behavior can apply to any foundations approach, so that this sense of conservatism does not distinguish coherence and foundations approaches at all.

7 ASSESSING THE ECONOMIC CRITIQUE

Gärdenfors (1990) makes the claim that reason maintenance entails excessive costs, but provides no support for this claim. He describes the reason maintenance system of (Doyle, 1979) as an exemplar of the foundations approach, but presents no analysis of costs of either that specific system or of the foundations approach more generally. More to the point, he makes no attempt to compare the cost of the foundations approach with the cost of the AGM approach he favors. We do this now, and see that the situation is considerably different than that implied by the economic critique.

7.1 Logical costs
Both the coherence and foundations approaches have as their ideal deductively closed states of belief. Unfortunately, practical approaches must abandon this ideal since it entails infinite belief states. Practical approaches must instead be based on finite versions or representations of these theories. Fortunately, restricting attention to finite cases poses no insurmountable problems for either approach. The AGM postulates for contraction, for example, apply perfectly well to finite belief bases, and RMS revises finite belief bases together with finitely many of their conclusions.

Deductive closure, however, is not the only logical property one must abandon to achieve a practical approach, for the requirement that states of belief be logically consistent also entails considerable computational costs for both the coherence and foundations approaches in the usual philosophical conception. Since we model beliefs as sentences in a logical language, determining the consistency or inconsistency of a set of sentences will be undecidable for even moderately expressive languages, and will require time exponential in the size of the sentences in the worst case for sentences of propositional logic. To obtain a realistic theory in accord with the observed ease of human belief revision, it may be necessary to weaken or drop the consistency requirement, as is done in many artificial intelligence approaches. RMS, for example, lacks any knowledge of the what its nodes mean, depends on the reasoner to tell it when some node represents a contradiction, and leaves the conflicting beliefs in place if they do not depend on defeasible assumptions.

Problems remain for the economic critique even if we drop the requirements that beliefs be closed and consistent. In the first place, the AGM approach requires, in postulate (≤ 2), that logically more general beliefs must also be more entrenched. Postulates (≤ 3)-(≤ 5) also involve logical dependencies among beliefs. Since determining entailment is as difficult as determining consistency, it would seem that practical approaches must also drop these restrictions on entrenchment orderings. For example, Nebel's (1989; 1990) theory of belief base revision employs orderings of *epistemic relevance*, which are like entrenchment orderings, but which need not respect any logical dependencies among beliefs. Nebel shows that revision according to epistemic relevance orderings satisfies the AGM postulates when lifted to deductively closed states of beliefs. As another example, the theory of *economically rational* belief revision presented in (Doyle, 1991) replaces epistemic entrenchment orderings with arbitrary preference orderings over beliefs and belief states. Like epistemic relevance orderings, these preference orderings need not respect any logical dependencies. But because contraction and revision are defined differently in this theory (as choices rational with respect to the preferences), economically rational belief revision need not satisfy the AGM postulates except when preferences do respect logical dependencies (that is, when one prefers logically more informative states of belief to less informative states).

We conclude that to obtain a practical approach to belief revision, we must give up both logical closure and the consistency and dependency requirements of the AGM approach. If we do not, AGM belief revision is manifestly more costly than more logically modest approaches like reason maintenance.

7.2 Computational costs

To get to the underlying question of whether revising beliefs via epistemic entrenchment costs less computationally than revising beliefs via foundations approaches, we must place the approaches on equal footings and ignore the logical structure of propositions. This means considering arbitrary propositional orderings in the coherence approach, and nonlogical systems like RMS in the foundations approach.

One may easily determine upper bounds on the computational costs of reason maintenance. Updating beliefs after adding or removing a reason costs little when all reasons are monotonic: the time required is at worst cubic in the number of beliefs mentioned by reasons in R, and typically is much less. Updating beliefs apparently costs more when nonmonotonic reasons are used: in the typical system, the time required is at most exponential in the number of beliefs mentioned by reasons in R.

The costs of revising beliefs via epistemic entrenchment are, in contrast, much harder to analyze. To begin with, one must first recall that the AGM approach permits the entrenchment ordering to change with the belief state. To assess the total cost of revision, therefore, one must take the cost of updating this ordering into account. Since the AGM approach never specifies anything about how entrenchment orderings change, we must make assumptions about these changes to conclude anything at all about the cost of entrenchment-based belief revision.

If the ordering of epistemic entrenchment never changes, the cost of belief revision is at worst exponential in the size of the belief base. Gärdenfors and Makinson (1988) show that one can represent the entrenchment ordering in a size linear in the set of dual atoms of a finite belief base. Since these dual atoms are generally of a size exponential in the size of the belief base, examining this representation requires time exponential in the size of the belief base. Comparing this with the cost of reason maintenance, we see that fixed entrenchment revision costs more than reason maintenance with only monotonic reasons, and costs no less than reason maintenance with nonmonotonic reasons.

The economic critique, however, does not seem compatible with the assumption of fixed epistemic entrenchment orderings. Given the emphasis in (Gärdenfors, 1990) on how epistemic entrenchment can represent information about what beliefs justify others, it seems reasonable to assume that the entrenchment ordering must change at least as frequently as does information about justifications. Any application characterized by an ordering that remains constant throughout reasoning is analogous to belief revision given a fixed set of reasons, changing only premises. As just noted, these revisions can be computed as quickly using reason maintenance as when using the dual-atom representation of the entrenchment ordering. Thus to complete the comparison we must determine the cost of updating epistemic entrenchment orderings.

We cannot offer any precise analysis of the cost of updating entrenchment orderings. But if entrenchment orderings do in fact capture all the information in reasons, then updating entrenchment orderings must be roughly as costly as updating reasons. In this case, translating reasons to entrenchment orderings and then using the orderings to compute revisions provides an algorithm for computing revisions from reasons. Any lower bound on the cost of computing revisions from reasons thus provides (ignoring the costs of translation) a lower bound on the cost of computing revisions from entrenchment orderings. Updating entrenchment could cost less only if entrenchment orderings cannot capture all the content of reasons, or if the cost of translating between reasons and orderings is comparable to the cost of revision. Thus if reasons do reduce to entrenchment orderings, then revision using entrenchment may be at least as costly as revision using reasons. This is, of course, just the opposite of the conclusion of the economic critique.

7.3 Practical convenience

Any practical assessment of belief revision and reason maintenance must take into account the human costs of the approach in addition to purely computational costs. One may prefer to use a somewhat more computationally costly approach if it offers much greater convenience to the user. We consider two issues connected with the practical convenience of coherence and foundations approaches.

In the first place, the practical utility of a revision method depends in part on how hard the user must work to give the system new information, in particular, new reasons or new entrenchment orderings. An entrenchment ordering consists of a sequence of sets of equivalently entrenched beliefs, and one might well think this a simpler structure than a set of reasons that this ordering might represent. But if the typical update to this ordering stems from new inferences drawn by the reasoner, then reasons offer the simpler structure for describing the new information, since they correspond directly to the structure of the inference. If the entrenchment ordering is to be updated with every new inference, it seems plausible that the underlying representation should be a set of reasons, from which entrenchment orderings are computed whenever desired. Indeed, we expect that foundations approaches like reason maintenance provide the most natural way of representing and updating entrenchment orderings, particularly when there may be multiple reasons for holding beliefs.

In the second place, the practical utility of a revision method depends in part on how hard the user must work to represent specific information in the system's language. The complete orderings used to describe epistemic entrenchment and epistemic relevance offer limited flexibility in expressing the revision criteria that prove important in practice. Voting schemes, for example, appear often in common methods for choosing among alternatives, but no fixed complete ordering of propositions can express majority voting. In particular, fixed orderings cannot express conservative revision principles like minimizing the *number* of beliefs changed during revision (i.e., Harman's (1986) "simple measure"). Achieving any dependence of ordering on the global composition of the alternatives means revising the linear propositional order to fit each set of alternatives, which hardly seems a practical approach if the user must supply these reorderings. Requiring one to express revision information in the form of entrenchment orderings may therefore impede construction of useful revision systems when the task calls for criteria beyond those easily expressible.

The need for flexibility in specifying contraction and revision guidelines becomes even more apparent if we look to the usual explanations, such as those in (Quine and Ullian, 1978), of why one revision is selected over another. Many different properties of propositions influence whether one proposition is more entrenched than another; one belief might be more entrenched because it is more specific, or was adopted more recently, or has longer standing (was adopted less recently), or has higher probability of being true, or comes from a source of higher authority. As we may expect to discover new guidelines specific to particular tasks and domains, we might expect a practical approach to belief revision to provide some way of specifying these guidelines piecemeal and combining them automatically.

Three problems with these specific guidelines complicate matters, however. The first problem is that these revision criteria are often partial. For example, there are many different dimensions of specificity, and two beliefs may be such that neither is more specific than the other. Similarly, probabilities need not be known for all propositions, and authorities need not address all questions. Thus while each of the guidelines provides information about entrenchment orderings, each provides only partial ordering. In formal terms, each guideline corresponds to a preorder in which not all elements are related to each other.

The second problem is that none of the specific guidelines constitute a comprehensive criterion that takes all possible considerations into account. A comprehensive picture of the entrenchment ordering, all things considered, comes only by combining all of the specific guidelines. Moreover, the overall ordering may be partial, just like the specific guidelines.

The third problem is that the specific guidelines may conflict in some cases. To borrow an example from nonmonotonic logic, one guideline might order beliefs that Quakers are pacifists more entrenched than beliefs that Quakers are not pacifists, and another guideline might order beliefs that Republicans are not pacifists more entrenched than beliefs that Republicans are pacifists. These orderings conflict on cases like that of Nixon, and a guideline ordering more specific rules more entrenched than more general ones does not help since "Quaker" and "Republican" are incomparable categories. Indeed, as argued in (Doyle and Wellman, 1991), other ordering criteria can conflict as well, including very specific criteria corresponding to individual nonmonotonic reasons and default rules. Constructing a global ordering thus means resolving the conflicts among the specific guidelines being combined.

Thus if we seek truly flexible contraction and revision, we need some way of modularly combining and reconciling partial, conflicting, noncomprehensive orderings of propositions into complete global orderings. Unfortunately, it appears unlikely that modular combination and reconciliation can always be done in a rational manner, as Doyle and Wellman (1991) reduce this problem to the problem of social choice, for which Arrow's theorem indicates no good method exists. See also (Doyle, 1991) for a discussion in terms of economically rational belief revision.

To sum up, practical belief revision must depart from the idealizations imposed by epistemic entrenchment. We do not yet know how to specify the necessary information in the most convenient fashion. But preliminary considerations suggest that reasons, not complete entrenchment orderings, offer the most convenient representation.

8 ASSESSING THE SUPERFLUITY CRITIQUE

The superfluity critique says that coherence approaches based on epistemic entrenchment already contains the information needed to identify reasons, obviating the main motivation for foundations approaches. In this section, we identify both some causes to doubt that epistemic entrenchment actually renders foundations approaches superfluous, and reasons to believe that foundations approaches can serve to represent information about epistemic entrenchment.

The program outlined by Gärdenfors for using epistemic entrenchment identify reasons for beliefs faces severe problems. Gärdenfors himself points out the first of these, namely that we do not now possess an adequate definition of reasons in terms of epistemic entrenchment, as the best current candidate does not always distinguish basic from derived beliefs. But this program faces other obstacles as well: an inability to treat multiple reasons for the same belief properly, and an inability to identify temporarily invalid reasons.

To understand the problem of multiple reasons, we consider whether a proposition α is a reason for $\alpha \vee \beta$. Suppose that α and β are epistemically independent propositions. Intuitively, α and β are independent reasons for $\alpha \vee \beta$, or for third propositions γ such that $\alpha \to \gamma$ and $\beta \to \gamma$ (so that $\alpha \vee \beta$ is a reason for γ). But neither α nor β need be a reason for $\alpha \vee \beta$ according to the (admittedly flawed) Spohn-Gärdenfors definition, which works only when one belief is the *only* reason for the other. If the two independent propositions are equally entrenched, then neither is a reason for the disjunction; contracting by either leaves the other unaffected, and so also the disjunction, so we have $\alpha \sim \beta < \alpha \vee \beta$, which means $\alpha \vee (\alpha \vee \beta) \not\leq \alpha$ and $\beta \vee (\alpha \vee \beta) \not\leq \beta$. While some better definition of reasons in terms of entrenchment might overcome this difficulty, the prospects seem dim for a definition that involves only the relative entrenchment of the two propositions and their logical combinations, since it appears that adding additional reasons for a belief can cause complex changes in the corresponding entrenchment ordering.

The problem of invalid reasons concerns whether $\alpha \rightarrow \beta$ is a reason for β. In the sense of "reason" formalized in RMS (according to which "reasons" are not themselves beliefs but instead are best viewed as inference rules, constitutive intentions, or constitutive preferences (Doyle, 1988; Doyle and Wellman, 1991)) , the answer is yes, since one may have a reason $(\{\alpha\}, \{\}, \beta)$ independent of whether either α or β is believed. In the sense of "reason" employed in the superfluity critique, the answer is no, since a proposition can have a reason only if both it and the reason are believed. The RMS sense would seem to be the more useful, particularly as a guide to hypothetical reasoning, but one would have to modify the notion of epistemic entrenchment, abandoning postulate ($\leq$4), in order to capture such distinctions.

Even if the superfluity critique is correct in supposing that reasons can be encoded in epistemic entrenchment orderings, the force of the critique is weak unless one also shows that reasons cannot in turn encode entrenchment orderings. But this seems false. We cannot offer a definitive answer here, however, and simply suggest a couple possible avenues towards encoding entrenchment relations in reasons.

The most obvious approach takes the Spohn-Gärdenfors definition at face value and assigns a set of reasons $R_\leq$ to each entrenchment ordering $\leq$ over beliefs K such that

$$R_\leq \stackrel{\text{def}}{=} \{(\{\alpha\}, \{\}, \beta) \mid \alpha, \beta \in K \;\wedge\; (\alpha \vee \beta \leq \alpha)\}.$$

While this approach might be made to work, doing so requires reconciling the different senses of the term "reason", as noted earlier.

Perhaps a better approach is to simply define the entrenchment ordering in terms of appropriate behaviors of RMS, just as (1) defines the ordering in terms of the results of contraction. For example, we might say that $\alpha \leq \beta$ holds in a RMS state (N, R) just in case removing all reasons for β also removes α, for formally, just in case $\alpha \notin N'$ for every legal state $(N', R \setminus \{(I, O, \beta) \mid I, O \subseteq \mathcal{N}\})$. For example, if

$$R = \left\{ \begin{array}{l} (\{\alpha\}, \{\}, \beta) \\ (\{\beta\}, \{\}, \alpha) \end{array} \right\}$$

then $\alpha \sim \beta$, while if

$$R = \left\{ \begin{array}{l} (\{\alpha\}, \{\}, \beta) \\ (\{\beta\}, \{\}, \alpha) \\ (\{\}, \{\}, \beta) \end{array} \right\}$$

then $\alpha < \beta$, and if

$$R = \left\{ \begin{array}{l} (\{\alpha\}, \{\}, \beta) \\ (\{\beta\}, \{\}, \alpha) \\ (\{\}, \{\}, \alpha) \\ (\{\}, \{\}, \beta) \end{array} \right\}$$

then $\alpha \sim \beta$ once again. If one also desires to capture the logical structure of epistemic entrenchment, one can also augment the set of nonlogical reasons with a set of monotonic reasons describing all logical dependencies among the propositions. That is, one expands the set of nodes to include new nodes representing all logical equivalence classes elements of the propositional algebra over the original nodes, and expands the set of reasons to include a reason $(I, \{\}, \alpha)$ whenever $I \vdash \alpha$ in the expanded set of nodes.

To sum up, a satisfactory reduction of reasons to entrenchment orderings remains to be provided, and this will support the superfluity critique only if one cannot similarly reduce entrenchment orderings to reasons.

9 CONCLUSION

Both coherence and foundations approaches to belief revision provide valuable perspectives. The AGM approach focuses on the ordering of beliefs according to epistemic entrenchment, while reason maintenance focuses on the reasons relating individual beliefs. Though reason maintenance has been criticized on grounds of cost, psychological accuracy, and logical necessity, a close examination of these criticisms reveals the situation to be much more complex than that portrayed by the criticisms. While a definitive conclusion about whether either of these approaches is better than the other awaits answers to questions about whether either one mathematically subsumes the other, we believe that reason maintenance incorporates the key elements of the coherence approach, while at the same time providing the most practical means of mechanizing coherence approaches.

Perhaps the most fruitful way of viewing the issue is to focus on the great and fundamental similarities of the approaches rather than on their apparently minor differences. At least as far as the specific AGM and RMS approaches are concerned, we see that:

- Both seek to recognize logical and inferential relations among beliefs, differing at most in how these relations are represented. Both must abandon most requirements of logical consistency and closure to be useful in practical mechanizations.

- Both make minimal changes of belief, differing at most in the set of possible alternatives entering into the minimization.

- Both allow flexibility in choosing whether to reflect reasons and other inferential relations in epistemic states, differing only in whether representations of reasons determine entrenchment orderings or representations of entrenchment orderings determine reasons. Both make no stipulations about what reasons or entrenchment orderings should be represented, other than to assume this information may change with each step of reasoning.

- Neither distinguishes in any fixed way between "fundamental" and "derived" beliefs. Instead, both allow one to ground beliefs only to the extent required by one's needs for explanations and updates, and to change the identification of basic beliefs along with the current purposes of reasoning.

Given these similarities, the important questions for artificial intelligence concern the relative computational efficiencies of different representational schemes: not just AGM coherence and traditional reason maintenance, but possibly mixed schemes as well. Getting a clearer theoretical picture of such schemes and their relative merits promises to yield many valuable practical returns.

Acknowledgments

I thank Peter Gärdenfors, David Makinson, Bernhard Nebel, Robert Stalnaker, Richmond Thomason, and Michael Wellman for valuable discussions of this topic. This work was supported by the USAF Rome Laboratory and DARPA under contract F30602-91-C-0018, and by the National Library of Medicine through National Institutes of Health Grant No. R01 LM04493.

References

Alchourrón, C.; Gärdenfors, P.; and Makinson, D. 1985. On the logic of theory change: Partial meet contraction functions and their associated revision functions. *Journal of Symbolic Logic* 50:510–530.

Doyle, Jon 1979. A truth maintenance system. *Artificial Intelligence* 12(2):231–272.

Doyle, Jon 1983a. The ins and outs of reason maintenance. In *Proceedings of the Eighth International Joint Conference on Artificial Intelligence*. 349–351.

Doyle, Jon 1983b. Some theories of reasoned assumptions: an essay in rational psychology. Technical Report 83-125, Department of Computer Science, Carnegie Mellon University, Pittsburgh, PA.

Doyle, Jon 1988. Artificial intelligence and rational self-government. Technical Report CS-88-124, Carnegie-Mellon University Computer Science Department.

Doyle, Jon 1991. Rational belief revision (preliminary report). In Fikes, Richard E. and Sandewall, Erik, editors, *Proceedings of the Second Conference on Principles of Knowledge Representation and Reasoning*, San Mateo, CA. Morgan Kaufmann. 163–174.

Doyle, Jon and Wellman, Michael P. 1990. Rational distributed reason maintenance for planning and replanning of large-scale activities. In Sycara, Katia, editor, *Proceedings of the DARPA Workshop on Planning and Scheduling*, San Mateo, CA. Morgan Kaufmann. 28–36.

Doyle, Jon and Wellman, Michael P. 1991. Impediments to universal preference-based default theories. *Artificial Intelligence* 49(1–3):97–128.

Gärdenfors, Peter 1988. *Knowledge in Flux: Modeling the Dynamics of Epistemic States*. MIT Press, Cambridge, MA.

Gärdenfors, Peter 1990. The dynamics of belief systems: Foundations vs. coherence theories. *Revue Internationale de Philosophie* 172:24–46.

Gärdenfors, Peter and Makinson, David 1988. Revisions of knowledge systems using epistemic entrenchment. In Vardi, Moshe Y., editor, *Proceedings of the Second Conference on Theoretical Aspects of Reasoning About Knowledge*, Los Altos, CA. Morgan Kaufmann. 83–95.

Harman, Gilbert 1986. *Change in View: Principles of Reasoning*. MIT Press, Cambridge, MA.

McAllester, David 1982. Reasoning Utility Package user's manual. Artificial Intelligence Memo 667, Artificial Intelligence Laboratory, Massachusetts Institute of Technology, Cambridge, MA.

McAllester, David 1990. Truth maintenance. In *Proceedings of the Eighth National Conference on Artificial Intelligence*, Menlo Park, CA. AAAI Press. 1109–1116.

McDermott, Drew and Doyle, Jon 1980. Non-monotonic logic—I. *Artificial Intelligence* 13:41–72.

Nebel, Bernhard 1989. A knowledge level analysis of belief revision. In Brachman, Ronald J.; Levesque, Hector J.; and Reiter, Raymond, editors, *Proceedings of the First International Conference on Principles of Knowledge Representation and Reasoning*, San Mateo, CA. Morgan Kaufmann. 301–311.

Nebel, Bernhard 1990. *Representation and Reasoning in Hybrid Representation Systems*. Number 422 in Lecture Notes in Artificial Intelligence. Springer-Verlag, Berlin.

Quine, Willard V. 1953. Two dogmas of empiricism. In *From a Logical Point of View: Logico-Philosophical Essays*. Harper and Row, New York, second edition. 20–46.

Quine, W. V. 1970. *Philosophy of Logic*. Prentice-Hall, Englewood Cliffs, NJ.

Quine, W. V. and Ullian, J. S. 1978. *The Web of Belief.* Random House, New York, second edition.

Spohn, W. 1983. Deterministic and probabilistic reasons and causes. *Erkenntnis* 19:371–396.

Syntax-Based Approaches to Belief Revision*

BERNHARD NEBEL

German Research Center for Artificial Intelligence (DFKI),
D-6600 Saarbrücken, Germany

1 INTRODUCTION

Belief revision is the process of incorporating new information into a knowledge base while preserving consistency. Recently, belief revision has received a lot of attention in AI,[1] which led to a number of different proposals for different applications (Ginsberg 1986; Ginsberg, Smith 1987; Dalal 1988; Gärdenfors, Makinson 1988; Winslett 1988; Myers, Smith 1988; Rao, Foo 1989; Nebel 1989; Winslett 1989; Katsuno, Mendelzon 1989; Katsuno, Mendelzon 1991; Doyle 1990). Most of this research has been considerably influenced by approaches in philosophical logic, in particular by Gärdenfors and his colleagues (Alchourrón, Gärdenfors, Makinson 1985; Gärdenfors 1988), who developed the *logic of theory change*, also called *theory of epistemic change*. This theory formalizes *epistemic states* as deductively closed theories and defines different change operations on such epistemic states.

Syntax-based approaches to belief revision to be introduced in Section 3 have been very popular because of their conceptual simplicity. However, there also has been criticisms since the outcome of a revision operation relies an arbitrary syntactic distinctions (see, e.g., (Dalal 1988; Winslett 1988; Katsuno, Mendelzon 1989))—and for this reason such operations cannot be analyzed on the *knowledge level*. In (Nebel 1989) we showed that syntax-based approaches can be interpreted as assigning higher relevance to explicitly represented sentences. Based on that view, one particular kind of syntax-based revision, called *base revision*, was shown to fit into the theory of epistemic change. In Section 4 we generalize this result to *prioritized bases*. It will be shown that the class of prioritized base revisions is identical with the class of belief revision operations generated by *epistemic relevance orderings* (Nebel 1990).

---

*This chapter is a revised and extended version of a paper with the title "Belief Revision and Default Reasoning: Syntax-Based Approaches" in J. A. Allen, R. Fikes, and E. Sandewall (eds.), *Principles of Knowledge Representation and Reasoning: Proceedings of the Second International Conference*, Morgan Kaufmann, San Mateo, CA, 1991, pp. 417–428.

[1]See also (Brachman 1990), in which "practical and well-founded theories of belief revision" are called for.

The belief revision operations generated by epistemic relevance orderings do not satisfy all *AGM postulates* belief revision operations should obey, however (see (Gärdenfors, this book)). In Section 5 some interesting special cases of epistemic relevance are analyzed that lead to the satisfaction of all AGM postulates. In particular, we show that *epistemic entrenchment* as introduced in (Gärdenfors, Makinson 1988) is a special case of *epistemic relevance*.

Makinson and Gärdenfors (1991) showed that there is a tight connection between belief revision and nonmonotonic logics. In Section 6 we will strengthen this result. First, we show that the form of *logical nonmonotonicity* observable when revising beliefs is a *necessary* consequence of *temporal nonmonotonicity* induced by belief revision. Second, we will prove that this similarity can be strengthened to equivalence of expressiveness for particular nonmonotonic logics and belief revision operations in the case of propositional logic. Poole's (1988) and Brewka's (1989; 1990) approaches are shown to be expressively equivalent to some forms of syntax-based belief revision approaches. An interesting consequence of this result is that the "absurd belief state" that is inconsistent turns out to be more important than assumed to be in the theory of epistemic change.

Additionally to the logical properties of belief revision and default reasoning, in Section 7 the computational properties are analyzed. As it turns out, the complexity of propositional syntax-based belief revision is located at the lower end of the polynomial hierarchy.

2 FORMAL PRELIMINARIES

Throughout this chapter, a propositional language $\mathcal{L}$ with the usual logical connectives ($\neg$, $\vee$, $\wedge$, $\rightarrow$ and $\leftrightarrow$) is assumed. The countable alphabet of propositional variables $p, q, r \ldots$ is denoted by Σ, propositional sentences by $\tau, \phi, \psi, \chi, \omega, \ldots$, constant truth by $\top$, its negation by $\bot$, and countable sets of propositional sentences by $K, L, M, \ldots$ and $A, B, C, \ldots$

The symbol $\vdash$ denotes derivability and Cn the corresponding closure operation, i.e.,

$$Cn(K) \overset{\text{def}}{=} \{\phi \in \mathcal{L} | K \vdash \phi\}. \tag{1}$$

Instead of $Cn(\{\phi\})$, we will also write $Cn(\phi)$. Deductively closed sets of propositional sentences, i.e., $K = Cn(K)$, are denoted by $K, L, M, \ldots$ and are called *belief sets*. Arbitrary sets of sentences are called *belief bases* and are denoted by the letters A, B, C. Systems of belief bases and belief sets are denoted by S. Finite belief bases C are often identified with the conjunction of all propositions $\bigwedge C$. If $S = \{A_1, \ldots, A_n\}$

is a finite family of finite belief bases, then $\bigvee S$ shall denote a proposition logically equivalent to $(\bigwedge A_1) \vee \ldots \vee (\bigwedge A_n)$. As usual, we set $\bigvee \emptyset = \bot$.

Sometimes, we will also talk about truth assignments and models of propositions and belief bases. A *truth assignment* is a function $\mathcal{I} \colon \Sigma \to \{\mathsf{T}, \mathsf{F}\}$. A *model* $\mathcal{I}$ of a proposition ϕ is a truth assignment that satisfies ϕ in the classical sense, written $\models_\mathcal{I} \phi$. A *model of a belief base* C is a truth assignment that satisfies all propositions in C, written $\models_\mathcal{I} C$.

As usual (see (Gärdenfors, this book)), $K + \phi$ is the *expansion* of K by ϕ, $K \dotplus \phi$ is the *revision* of the belief set K by ϕ, and $K \dotminus \phi$ is the *contraction* of K by ϕ. $(K \bot \phi)$ denotes the system of set-inclusion maximal subsets of K that do not imply ϕ, and γ denotes a *selection function* that selects a subset of $(K \bot \phi)$.

3   SYNTAX-BASED REVISION APPROACHES: BASE REVISIONS

The logic of theory change captures the *logical* portion of minimal change giving us a kind of yardstick to evaluate approaches to belief revision. However, it still leaves open the problem of how to specify additional restrictions so that a revision operation also satisfies a "pragmatic" measure of minimal change.

Two principal points of departure are conceivable. Starting with a *belief base* as the representation of a belief set, either the syntactic form of the belief base (Fagin, Ullman, Vardi 1983; Ginsberg 1986; Nebel 1989) or the possible states of the world described by the belief base—the models of the belief base—could be changed minimally (Dalal 1988; Winslett 1988; Katsuno, Mendelzon 1989; Katsuno, Mendelzon 1991). The former approach seems to be more reasonable if the belief base corresponds to a body of explicit beliefs that has some relevance, such as a code of norms or a scientific or naive theory which is almost correct. The latter view seems plausible if the application is oriented towards minimal change of the state of the world described by a belief set. In this paper, we adopt the former perspective. In order to distinguish operations on syntactic descriptions – on belief bases – from operations on belief sets, belief base changes are called *base revision* and *base contraction*.

The idea of *changing a belief base minimally* could be formalized by selecting maximal subsets of the belief base not implying a given sentence. If there is more than one such maximal subset, the intersection of the consequences of these subsets is used as the result. Thus, using $(C \bot \phi)$ as the set of maximal subsets of C not implying ϕ, *simple base revision*, written as $C \oplus \phi$, could be defined as follows (Fagin, Ullman, Vardi 1983;

Ginsberg 1986; Nebel 1989):

$$C \oplus \phi \stackrel{\text{def}}{=} \Big(\bigcap_{B \in (C \perp \neg \phi)} Cn(B) \Big) + \phi. \tag{2}$$

The operation $\oplus$ considers all sentences in a base as equally relevant. In most applications, however, we want to distinguish between the importance or relevance of different sentences. In (Fagin, Ullman, Vardi 1983) database priorities are assigned to propositions in order to reflect the distinction between facts and integrity rules. Ginsberg (1986) and Ginsberg and Smith (1987) make a distinction between facts that can change and those that are "protected."[2]

This idea of assigning different priorities to sentences can be formalized by employing a *complete preorder* with maximal elements, written $\phi \preceq \psi$, on the elements of a belief base C. In other words, we consider a *reflexive* and *transitive* relation such that for all $\phi, \psi \in C$ we have $\phi \preceq \psi$ or $\psi \preceq \phi$. For $\phi \preceq \psi$ and $\psi \not\preceq \phi$, we will also write $\phi \prec \psi$. Further, there exists at least one maximal element ϕ, i.e., for no element ψ: $\phi \prec \psi$. This relation will be called *epistemic relevance ordering*. It induces an equivalence relation, written $\phi \simeq \psi$, as follows:

$$\phi \simeq \psi \quad \text{iff} \quad (\phi \preceq \psi \text{ and } \psi \preceq \phi). \tag{3}$$

The corresponding equivalence classes are denoted by $\overline{\chi}$ and are called *degrees of epistemic relevance* of C. The set of equivalence classes $C/\simeq$ is denoted by $\overline{C}$. Since the preorder is complete, $\preceq$ is a linear order on $\overline{C}$. Further, there exists a maximal such degree because the preorder contains maximal elements.

A belief base together with an epistemic relevance ordering will be called *prioritized base*. If the belief base is finite, we will also use the notation $C_1, \ldots, C_n$ to denote the n degrees of epistemic relevance of C with the convention that C_1 has highest relevance.

Employing an epistemic relevance ordering, the *prioritized removal* of ϕ from C, written $C \Downarrow \phi$, will be defined as a system S of subsets of C. Each element $B \in S$ in turn is the union over a family consisting of subsets of all degrees of epistemic relevance, i.e.,

$$B = \bigcup \{B_{\overline{\chi}}\}_{\overline{\chi} \in \overline{C}} \text{ where } B_{\overline{\chi}} \subseteq \overline{\chi}. \tag{4}$$

---

[2]In particular, (Ginsberg, Smith 1987) makes clear, however, that usually more than one level of protected sentences is needed. For instance, the rule that an object can only occupy one place is, of course, an undeniable truth in our commonsense view of the world, while the rule that a room becomes stuffy when the ventilation is blocked may well be violated by an open window.

Formally, $B \in (C \Downarrow \phi)$ if, and only if,

1. $B = \bigcup_{\overline{\chi} \in \overline{C}} B_{\overline{\chi}}$,

2. for all $\overline{\chi} \in \overline{C}$, $B_{\overline{\chi}} \subseteq \overline{\chi}$, and

3. for all $\overline{\chi} \in \overline{C}$, $B_{\overline{\chi}}$ is set-inclusion maximal among the subsets of $\overline{\chi}$ such that $\bigcup_{\overline{\psi} \geq \overline{\chi}} B_{\overline{\psi}} \not\vdash \phi$.

Intuitively, the elements of $C \Downarrow \phi$ are constructed by selecting a maximal subset not implying ϕ from the greatest degree of epistemic relevance, then a maximal subset of the next important degree is added such that ϕ is not implied, and so on. Note, however, that this intuition about *constructing* the elements of $C \Downarrow \phi$ may fail in the general case. Since we did not place restrictions on the relevance ordering, it can happen that there are infinitely ascending chains of degrees of epistemic relevance. Nevertheless, also in this case the existence of elements of B's satisfying the above conditions is guaranteed by Zorn's lemma.

A prioritized removal operation selects by definition a subset of the maximal subsets of a base not implying a given proposition.

Proposition 1 *Given a base C and a relevance ordering $\preceq$, for all ϕ:*

$$(C \Downarrow \phi) \subseteq (C \perp \phi). \tag{5}$$

Thus, it makes sense to use $\Downarrow$ instead of $\perp$ in the definition (2). The resulting operation is called *prioritized base revision*, denoted by $\hat{\oplus}$. This operation is identical to simple base revision in case that there is only one degree of epistemic relevance.

In the interesting special case when we are dealing with finite belief bases—which corresponds to prioritized logical databases investigated in (Fagin, Ullman, Vardi 1983)—the result of a prioritized base revision can be finitely represented.

Proposition 2 *If C is a finite belief base then*

$$C \hat{\oplus} \phi = Cn\left((\bigvee(C \Downarrow \neg\phi)) \wedge \phi\right), \tag{6}$$

for every prioritized base revision $\hat{\oplus}$ on C.

Proof. Since C is finite, there can be only a finite number of finite degrees of epistemic relevance, hence, $C \Downarrow \neg\phi$ is a finite set of finite belief bases. In this case, the following equivalences hold

$$Cn(\bigwedge_{i=1}^{n} \phi_i) = Cn(\{\phi_1, \ldots, \phi_n\}) \tag{7}$$

$$Cn(\bigvee_{i=1}^{n} \phi_i) = \bigcap_{i=1}^{n} Cn(\phi_i), \tag{8}$$

and the proposition follows immediately. ∎

In order to demonstrate how base revision works, let us assume the following scenario. Assume that a suspect tells you that he went to the beach for swimming and assume that you have observed that the sun was shining. Further, you firmly believe that going to the beach for swimming when the sun is shining implies a sun tan. If you then discover that the suspect is not tanned, there is an inconsistency to resolve. Supposing the following propositions:

$$b = \text{"going to the beach for swimming"},$$
$$s = \text{"the sun is shining"},$$
$$t = \text{"sun tan"},$$

the situation can be modeled formally by a prioritized base C:

$$C_1 = \{((b \wedge s) \to t)\},$$
$$C_2 = \{s\},$$
$$C_3 = \{b\},$$
$$C = C_1 \cup C_2 \cup C_3.$$

From this belief base t can be derived. If we later observe that $\neg t$, the belief base has to be revised:

$$C \hat{\oplus} \neg t = \bigcap\left(Cn(C \Downarrow t)\right) + \neg t$$
$$= Cn\left(\bigvee\{\{((b \wedge s) \to t), s\}\}\right) + \neg t$$
$$= Cn(\{((b \wedge s) \to t), s, \neg t\}).$$

In particular, we would conclude that b was a lie.

A consequence of the definition of (simple and prioritized) base revision is that for two different belief bases A and B that have the same meaning, i.e., $Cn(A) = Cn(B)$, base revision can lead to different results, i.e., $Cn(A \hat{\oplus} \phi) \neq Cn(B \hat{\oplus} \phi)$. Base revision has a "morbid sensitivity to the syntax of the description of the world" (Winslett 1988), which is considered as an undesirable property. Dalal (1988) formulated the *principle of irrelevance of syntax* which states that a revision operation shall be independent of the syntactic form of the belief base representing a belief set and of the syntactic form of the sentence that has to be incorporated into the belief set (see also (Katsuno, Mendelzon 1989)), i.e., revision operations shall operate on the *knowledge level* (Newell 1982). In the theory of epistemic change this is accomplished by the requirements that the objects to be revised are belief sets and that the result of a revision does not depend on the syntactical form of the sentence to be added (AGM postulate (K$\dotplus$6)).

Obviously, base revision does not satisfy the principle of irrelevance of syntax—and is not a belief revision operation in the sense of the theory of epistemic change for this reason. Worse yet, abstracting from the syntactic representation of a belief base and considering the logical equivalent belief set leads nowhere. Simple base revision applied to belief sets is equivalent to full meet revision, thus, useless. For these reasons, it is argued in (Dalal 1988; Winslett 1988; Katsuno, Mendelzon 1989) that revision shall be performed on the *model-theoretic* level, i.e., by viewing a belief set as the set of models that satisfy a given belief base and by performing revision in a way that selects models that satisfy the new sentence and *differ minimally* from the models of the original belief base. In order to define what the term *minimal difference* means, we have to say something about how models are to be compared, though. In Dalal (1988), for instance, the "distance" between models is measured by the number of propositional variables that have different truth values. Katsuno and Mendelzon (1989) generalize this approach by considering complete preorders over models.

In any case, it is impossible to define a revision operation by referring only to logical properties. Some inherently extra-logical, pragmatic preferences are necessary to guide the revision process. This is actually one of the basic messages of the theory of epistemic change. We have to make up our minds about the importance of propositions or sets of propositions in order to select among the alternatives which are logically possible. If we consider all of them as equally important and combine them (by using full meet revision), we end up with nothing. Similarly, in case of a model-theoretic perspective, we cannot consider all models as equally possible candidates for a revision, since this would lead to a similar result.

As argued above, for some applications it does not seem to be a bad idea to derive preferences from the syntactic form of the representation of a belief set. Actually, from a more abstract point of view, it is not the particular syntactic form of a belief base we are interested in, but it is the fact that we believe that a particular set of sentences is more valuable or justified than another logically equivalent set, and we want to preserve as many of the "valuable" sentences as possible. Using this idea it is possible to reconstruct base revision in the framework of the theory of epistemic change by employing the notion of *epistemic relevance*.

4 BELIEF REVISION GENERATED BY EPISTEMIC RELEVANCE

The intention behind base revision is that all the sentences in a belief base A are considered as *relevant*—some perhaps more so than others. For this reason we want to give up as few sentences from A as possible, while with sentences that are only derivable we are more liberal. Formalizing this idea we employ as in the case of belief bases an *epistemic relevance ordering*, i.e. a complete pre-order with maximal elements on the entire *belief set*, with the intention of assigning the least degree of relevance to sentences that are only derivable. Based on these orderings, selection functions are constructed that select subsets that are maximally preferred with respect to epistemic relevance orderings.

We start by defining a *strict partial ordering* expressing preferences on subsets $A, B \in 2^K$, written as $A \ll B$, by

$$A \ll B \quad \text{iff} \quad \exists \bar{\tau} : \big((A \cap \bar{\tau} \subset B \cap \bar{\tau}) \text{ and } \forall \bar{\omega} \succ \bar{\tau} : (A \cap \bar{\omega} = B \cap \bar{\omega})\big), \tag{9}$$

which in turn can be used to define a function $\gamma_{\preceq}$ that selects all *maximally preferred* elements of $K \perp \phi$:

$$\gamma_{\preceq}(K \perp \phi) \overset{\text{def}}{=} \{L \in (K \perp \phi) | \forall M \in (K \perp \phi) : L \not\ll M\}. \tag{10}$$

Note that such maximally preferred sets always exist as can be easily inferred from the following lemma that relates maximally preferred sets to the elements of a prioritized removal.

Lemma 3 *Let K be a belief set with an epistemic relevance ordering $\preceq$. Then for any sentence ϕ:*

$$L \text{ is maximally preferred in } (K \perp \phi) \quad \text{iff} \quad L \in (K \Downarrow \phi). \tag{11}$$

Proof. Note that Proposition 1 applies also to belief sets because any belief set is also a belief base by definition. Hence, for all K and epistemic relevance orderings on K, for all ϕ:

$$(K \Downarrow \phi) \subseteq (K \perp \phi). \tag{12}$$

Assume that $B \in (K \Downarrow \phi)$. Assume for contradiction that there is a set $M \in (K \perp \phi)$ such that $B \ll M$. This means there exists a degree $\overline{\tau}$ such that $B_{\overline{\tau}} \subset M \cap \overline{\tau}$ while for all $\overline{\omega} \succ \overline{\tau}$ we have $B_{\overline{\omega}} = M \cap \overline{\omega}$. However, the set $B_{\overline{\tau}}$ is by definition of $\Downarrow$ a set-inclusion maximal subset of $\overline{\tau}$ such that $(\bigcup_{\overline{\omega} \succ \overline{\tau}} B_{\overline{\omega}}) \cup B_{\overline{\tau}}$ does not imply ϕ, hence, $M \cap \overline{\tau}$ cannot be a proper superset of $B_{\overline{\tau}}$.

For the other direction, assume L is maximal w.r.t. $\ll$ in $(K \perp \phi)$. Set $B = L$ and $B_{\overline{\chi}} = L \cap \overline{\chi}$. Obviously, the following conditions are satisfied:

1. $L = B = \bigcup_{\overline{\chi} \in \overline{K}} B_{\overline{\chi}}$,

2. $L \cap \overline{\chi} = B_{\overline{\chi}} \subseteq \overline{\chi}$, and

3. $L \cap \overline{\chi} = B_{\overline{\chi}}$ is set-inclusion maximal among the subsets of $\overline{\chi}$ such that $\bigcup_{\overline{\psi} \succeq \overline{\chi}} (L \cap \overline{\psi}) = \bigcup_{\overline{\psi} \succeq \overline{\chi}} B_{\overline{\psi}} \not\vdash \phi$.

Hence, $L \in (K \Downarrow \phi)$. ■

This means that $\gamma_{\preceq}$ selects a nonempty subset of $(K \perp \phi)$ provided $(K \perp \phi)$ is non-empty, i.e., $\gamma_{\preceq}$ is a *selection function* (see (Gärdenfors, this book)) that may be used to define a partial meet revision operation. Revisions defined in this way will be called *revisions generated by epistemic relevance*. Analyzing the properties of such revisions, we note that they satisfy most of the AGM postulates.

Theorem 4 *Revisions generated by epistemic relevance satisfy* $(K \dotplus 1)$–$(K \dotplus 7)$.

Proof. Since $\gamma_{\preceq}$ is a selection function, revisions generated by epistemic relevance satisfy $(K \dotplus 1)$–$(K \dotplus 6)$ by (Alchourrón, Gärdenfors, Makinson 1985, Observation 2.3).

Further, we have by definition of the selection function that there exists a relation $\sqsubseteq$, defined by putting

$$M \sqsubseteq L \quad \text{iff} \quad L \not\ll M, \tag{13}$$

such that for all ϕ,

$$\gamma(K \perp \phi) = \{L \in (K \perp \phi) | \forall M \in (K \perp \phi): M \sqsubseteq L\} \tag{14}$$

Thus, $\dotplus$ is a *relational* partial meet revision, which by (Alchourrón, Gärdenfors, Makinson 1985, Observations 3.1, 4.2 and 4.3) satisfies $(K \dotplus 7)$. ■

Note that the relation $\npreceq$ is not transitive and therefore revisions generated by epistemic relevance do not satisfy (K $\dot{+}$8) in general.[3] The interesting point about such revisions is that they coincide with prioritized base revision as defined in Section 3. That any revision generated by epistemic relevance can be conceived as a prioritized base revision follows already from Lemma 3. In order to show the other direction of the correspondence, the following Lemma (adapted from (Nebel 1989)) is helpful.

Lemma 5 *Let K be a belief set and ϕ be sentence such that $\neg\phi \in K$. Let C be any subset of K such that $C \nvdash \neg\phi$. Then*

$$\left(\bigcap\{M \in K \perp \neg\phi \mid C \subseteq M\}\right) + \phi = Cn(C) + \phi. \tag{15}$$

Proof. "$\supseteq$": Since by the assumption of the lemma $C \subseteq K$ and $C \nvdash \neg\phi$, $(\bigcap\{M \in K \perp \neg\phi \mid C \subseteq M\})$ contains C as a subset by definition. Further, since all elements of $(K \perp \phi)$ are belief sets and the intersection of belief sets is a belief set again, $(\bigcap\{M \in K \perp \neg\phi \mid C \subseteq M\})$ contains $Cn(C)$, hence, the right hand side is a subset of the left hand side.

"$\subseteq$": Assume the contrary, i.e., there is a sentence ψ that is an element of the left hand side of equation (15), but $\psi \notin Cn(C \cup \{\phi\})$. By the latter assumption $Cn(C \cup \{\neg\psi\} \cup \{\phi\})$ is consistent and $\neg\phi \notin Cn(C \cup \{\neg\psi\}) \supseteq Cn(C \cup \{\neg\psi \vee \neg\phi\})$. By the assumption of the lemma that $\neg\phi \in K$, we have $(\neg\phi \vee \neg\psi) \in K$. Since also $C \subseteq K$, there is at least one element in $(K \perp \neg\phi)$ that contains $C \cup \{\neg\psi \vee \neg\phi\}$. Call this set L.

From the first assumption that $\psi \in Cn((\bigcap\{M \in K \perp \neg\phi \mid C \subseteq M\}) \cup \{\phi\})$, we conclude $(\phi \rightarrow \psi) \in Cn(\bigcap\{M \in K \perp \neg\phi \mid C \subseteq M\})$. However, the set $L \in (K \perp \neg\phi)$ that contains C and $(\neg\psi \vee \neg\phi)$ cannot contain $(\phi \rightarrow \psi)$ because otherwise $L \vdash \neg\phi$.

By the fact that the intersection over a system of belief sets is already a belief set, we have $Cn(\bigcap\{M \in K \perp \neg\phi \mid C \subseteq M\}) = \bigcap\{M \in K \perp \neg\phi \mid C \subseteq M\}$.

Finally, because $L \in \{M \in K \perp \neg\phi \mid C \subseteq M\}$, it cannot be the case that $(\phi \rightarrow \psi) \in (\bigcap\{M \in K \perp \neg\phi \mid C \subseteq M\})$. Thus, we have a contradiction of our assumption. Hence, the left hand side must be a subset of the right hand side. ∎

It should be noted that if in the above lemma the set C is empty, the lemma describes the behavior of full meet revision. Another way to look at this lemma is that if the

---

[3] For a counter-example consult Section 6.

selection function selects elements of $K \perp \neg\phi$ by *focusing* on a particular set C, then the result of the revision is the set of consequences of the union of C and the new sentence. This result can be easily generalized to systems of *focusing sets*.

Lemma 6 *Let K be a belief set, and let ϕ be a sentence such that $\neg\phi \in K$. Let S be a system of subsets of K, where $C \not\vdash \neg\phi$ for all $C \in S$. Then*

$$\left(\bigcap\{M \in K \perp \neg\phi \mid \exists C \in S: C \subseteq M\}\right) + \phi \;=\; \left(\bigcap_{C \in S} Cn(C)\right) + \phi. \qquad (16)$$

Proof.

$$\left(\bigcap\{M \in K \perp \neg\phi \mid \exists C \in S: C \subseteq M\}\right) + \phi =$$

$$= Cn\left(\left(\bigcap\{M \in K \perp \neg\phi \mid \exists C \in S: C \subseteq M\}\right) \cup \{\phi\}\right) \qquad (17)$$

$$= Cn\left(\left(\bigcap(\bigcup_{C \in S}\{M \in K \perp \neg\phi \mid C \subseteq M\})\right) \cup \{\phi\}\right) \qquad (18)$$

$$= Cn\left(\left(\bigcap_{C \in S}(\bigcap\{M \in K \perp \neg\phi \mid C \subseteq M\})\right) \cup \{\phi\}\right) \qquad (19)$$

$$= Cn\left(\bigcap_{C \in S}\left((\bigcap\{M \in K \perp \neg\phi \mid C \subseteq M\}) \cup \{\phi\}\right)\right) \qquad (20)$$

$$= Cn\left(\bigcap_{C \in S} Cn\left((\bigcap\{M \in K \perp \neg\phi \mid C \subseteq M\}) \cup \{\phi\}\right)\right) \qquad (21)$$

$$= Cn\left(\bigcap_{C \in S} Cn\left(C \cup \{\phi\}\right)\right) \qquad (22)$$

$$= Cn\left(\bigcap_{C \in S} Cn\left(Cn(C) \cup \{\phi\}\right)\right) \qquad (23)$$

$$= Cn\left(\left(\bigcap_{C \in S} Cn(C)\right) \cup \{\phi\}\right) \qquad (24)$$

$$= \left(\bigcap_{C \in S} Cn(C)\right) + \phi. \qquad (25)$$

Equation 17 is the application of the definition of the expansion of a belief set. (18)–(20) follow by set theory. (21) follows because for any system of belief sets S the following equation holds:

$$Cn(\bigcap_{K \in S}(K \cup \{\phi\})) \;=\; Cn(\bigcap_{K \in S} Cn(K \cup \{\phi\})) \qquad (26)$$

The "$\subseteq$" direction is obvious. For the other direction assume a sentence ψ that is an element of the right hand side, i.e., such that for all $K \in S$ we have $\psi \in Cn(K \cup \{\phi\})$.

By the deduction theorem, $(\phi \rightarrow \psi) \in Cn(K)$ for all $K \in S$. Since $K = Cn(K)$, it holds that $(\phi \rightarrow \psi) \in (\bigcap_{K \in S} K)$, hence, $\psi \in Cn((\bigcap_{K \in S} K) \cup \{\phi\}) = Cn(\bigcap_{K \in S}(K \cap \{\phi\}))$.

(22) is an application of Lemma 5. (23) follows from properties of Cn, (24) is another application of equation (26), and, finally, (25) is another application of the definition of the expansion of a belief set. ∎

Using this lemma, the correspondence between revision generated by epistemic relevance and prioritized base revision can be easily shown.

Theorem 7 *For any revision operation $\dot{+}$ on a belief set K generated by epistemic relevance, there exists a corresponding prioritized base revision $\hat{\oplus}$ on some base C of K, and vice versa, such that for all ϕ:*

$$K \dot{+} \phi = C \hat{\oplus} \phi. \tag{27}$$

Proof. Assume a belief set K and an epistemic relevance ordering $\preceq$ on K. By definition, any belief set is also a belief base. Applying Lemma 3, it follows that

$$\gamma_{\preceq}(K \perp \neg\phi) = (K \Downarrow \neg\phi). \tag{28}$$

Hence, for a given revision on K generated by epistemic relevance, there is a prioritized base revision on some base C of K (namely, the base $C = K$)[4] such that for all ϕ:

$$K \dot{+} \phi = C \hat{\oplus} \phi. \tag{29}$$

For the other direction, assume a prioritized belief base C with degrees of epistemic relevance $\overline{C}$. Set $K = Cn(C)$ and set $\overline{K} = \overline{C} \cup \{\overline{0}\}$, where $\overline{0} = K - C$ and $\overline{0} \prec \overline{\chi}$ for all $\overline{\chi} \in \overline{C}$. Now we will show that

$$\gamma_{\preceq}(K \perp \neg\phi) = \{M \in (K \perp \neg\phi) | \exists A \in (C \Downarrow \neg\phi) : A \subseteq M\}. \tag{30}$$

"⊇": Let $A \in (C \Downarrow \neg\phi)$ and let $L \in (K \perp \neg\phi)$ such that $A \subseteq L$. Such a set L exists because $A \subseteq C \subseteq K$ and $A \nvdash \neg\phi$. Then L must be maximal w.r.t. $\ll$ in $(K \perp \neg\phi)$. Assuming otherwise would mean that there is a degree $\overline{\chi}$ and the selected subset

---

[4] Note, however, that a smaller base would be sufficient as can be seen from the proof of Proposition 8.

$A_{\overline{\chi}} \subseteq \overline{\chi}$ was not maximal w.r.t. to the conditions in the definition of the elements of a prioritized removal, or there is another set $N \in (K \perp \neg\phi)$ that is identical to L for all priority $\overline{\chi} \in \overline{C}$ but contains a larger subset of $\overline{0}$, which is impossible, however, because L is already a maximal subset of K.

"$\subseteq$": Assume that L is an element of the left hand side of equation (30), i.e., L is a maximal element w.r.t. $\ll$. Consider the set $A = L \cap C$. Assume for contradiction that $A \notin (C \Downarrow \neg\phi)$. Since $A \nvdash \neg\phi$, this means that there is set $B \in (C \Downarrow \neg\phi)$ such that $\bigcup_{\overline{\psi} \geq \overline{\chi}} (A \cap \overline{\psi}) \subset \bigcup_{\overline{\psi} \geq \overline{\chi}} B_{\overline{\psi}}$ for some degree $\overline{\chi} \in \overline{C}$. Now, since $B \nvdash \neg\phi$ and $B \subseteq K$, there must be a set $M \in (K \perp \neg\phi)$ that contains B. By definition of $\ll$, we would then have $L \ll M$. Hence, L cannot be a maximal element w.r.t. $\ll$ and we have a contradiction. Thus, the left hand side is a subset of the right hand side.

Applying Lemma 6 to equation (30) we get

$$\left(\bigcap \gamma_{\preceq}(K \perp \neg\phi) \right) + \phi \ = \ \left(\bigcap_{B \in (C \Downarrow \neg\phi)} Cn(B) \right) + \phi, \tag{31}$$

i.e., for any prioritized base revision on C there exists an equivalent revision on $Cn(C)$ generated by epistemic relevance. ∎

This means that prioritized base revision coincides with revision generated by epistemic relevance in the sense that the class of prioritized base revisions is identical with the class of revisions generated by epistemic relevance. This abstract view on syntax-based revision may also answer some of the questions raised by Myers and Smith (1988). They observed that sometimes base revision does not seem to be the appropriate operation because some derived information turns out to be more relevant than the syntactically represented sentences in a belief base, and we get the wrong results when using base revision. However, there is no magic involved here. Base revision leads to the right results only if the syntactic representation really reflects the epistemic relevance. For this reason, the notion of revision generated by epistemic relevance seems to be preferable over base revision because it avoids the confusion between surface-level syntactic representation and the intended relevance of propositions.

The question of whether the correspondence between belief revision generated by epistemic relevance and prioritized base revision can be exploited computationally cannot be answered positively in the general case. Although Theorem 7 states that it is possible to compute a revision on a belief set K generated by epistemic entrenchment by performing a prioritized base revision on some base of K, this does not help very much because in the proof we used K itself as the base. For the case of belief sets that are finite modulo logical equivalence, however, a revision operation generated by epistemic relevance can be performed by a prioritized base revision on a finite base.

Proposition 8 *Let K be a belief set finite modulo logical equivalence. If $\dot{+}$ is a revision on K generated by epistemic relevance, then there exists a finite prioritized base C, such that for all ϕ:*

$$K \dot{+} \phi \;=\; C \hat{\oplus} \phi. \tag{32}$$

Proof. Define C such that it contains one representative χ for each class of logically equivalent sentences $[\chi] = \{\phi \in K \mid \; \vdash \chi \leftrightarrow \phi\}$. These representatives are chosen to be maximal elements w.r.t. $\preceq$ in $[\chi]$. The relevance ordering on C is defined as the restriction of the epistemic relevance ordering on K.

Since K is finite modulo logical equivalence, C is finite. In order to show that (32) holds, it obviously suffices to prove the following condition:

$$A \in (C \Downarrow \neg\phi) \quad \text{iff} \quad Cn(A) \in \gamma_{\preceq}(K \perp \neg\phi). \tag{33}$$

"$\Rightarrow$": Assume $A \in (C \Downarrow \neg\phi)$. First, we verify that $Cn(A) \in (K \perp \neg\phi)$. By definition of $\Downarrow$ A does not imply $\neg\phi$. Furthermore, $Cn(A)$ is a maximal subset of K. Assuming otherwise, i.e., $Cn(A) \cup \psi \not\vdash \neg\phi$ for some $\psi \in K$, would mean that there is a sentence $\chi \in [\psi]$ such that $A \cup \chi \not\vdash \neg\phi$, which is impossible by the construction of C and the definition of $\Downarrow$.

Second, $Cn(A)$ must be maximal w.r.t. $\ll$ in $(K \perp \neg\phi)$. Let us assume the contrary, i.e., there is a set $L \in \gamma_{\preceq}(K \perp \neg\phi)$ and $Cn(A) \ll L$. This means for some degree $\overline{\tau}$: $Cn(A) \cap \overline{\tau} \subset L \cap \overline{\tau}$ while for all larger degrees the sets are identical. Chose a proposition $\psi \in (L \cap \overline{\tau}) - (Cn(A) \cap \overline{\tau})$. Let $\chi \in [\psi]$ be maximal w.r.t. $\preceq$. Note that $\chi \notin A$ and that $\tau \simeq \psi \preceq \chi$. By this we conclude that $L \supseteq (\bigcup_{\overline{\tau} \geq \overline{\chi}} A_{\overline{\tau}}) \cup \{\chi\} \vdash \neg\phi$. This means however, that there cannot be a set L that is larger than $Cn(A)$ w.r.t. $\ll$.

"$\Leftarrow$": Assume a set $L \in (K \perp \neg\phi)$ that is maximally preferred. Set $A = L \cap C$. Because of the construction of C, we have $Cn(A) = L$. Assume for contradiction that $A \notin (C \Downarrow \neg\phi)$. This means for some degree $\overline{\tau}$ there is a sentence $\chi \in \overline{\tau}$ such that $\chi \notin A$ but $(\bigcup_{\overline{\omega} \geq \overline{\tau}} A_{\overline{\omega}}) \cup \{\chi\} \not\vdash \neg\phi$. However, in this case there is also a set $M \in (K \perp \neg\phi)$ that contains $(\bigcup_{\overline{\omega} \geq \overline{\tau}} A_{\overline{\omega}}) \cup \{\chi\}$ and which is therefore more preferred than L. ∎

5 EPISTEMIC RELEVANCE AND EPISTEMIC ENTRENCHMENT

Although revisions generated by epistemic relevance do not satisfy all AGM postulates, there are special cases that do so. A trivial special case is a revision generated by only one degree of epistemic relevance, which is equivalent to full meet revision. There are more interesting cases, however.

Gärdenfors and Makinson claim that the notion of *epistemic entrenchment* introduced in (Gärdenfors, Makinson 1988) is closely related to the notion of *database priorities* as proposed in (Fagin, Ullman, Vardi 1983). Since the notion of database priorities is the finite special case of *epistemic relevance orderings* on belief bases as introduced in Section 3, which can in turn be used to generate belief revision operations, one would expect that epistemic entrenchment is closely related to epistemic relevance. Although the intuitions are clearly similar, the question is whether the different formalizations lead indeed to identical results.

Epistemic entrenchment orderings, written as $\phi \preceq_\epsilon \psi$, are defined over the entire set of sentences $\mathcal{L}$ and have to satisfy the following properties (see also (Gärdenfors, this book)):

(EE1) If $\phi \preceq_\epsilon \psi$ and $\psi \preceq_\epsilon \chi$, then $\phi \preceq_\epsilon \chi$.

(EE2) If $\phi \vdash \psi$, then $\phi \preceq_\epsilon \psi$.

(EE3) For any ϕ, ψ, $\phi \preceq_\epsilon (\phi \wedge \psi)$ or $\psi \preceq_\epsilon (\phi \wedge \psi)$.

(EE4) When $K \neq Cn(\bot)$, then $\phi \notin K$ iff $\phi \preceq_\epsilon \psi$ for all $\psi \in \mathcal{L}$.

(EE5) If $\psi \preceq_\epsilon \phi$ for all $\psi \in \mathcal{L}$, then $\vdash \phi$.

Using such a relation, Gärdenfors and Makinson define *belief contraction generated by epistemic entrenchment*, written $K \stackrel{\epsilon}{-} \phi$, by

$$\psi \in K \stackrel{\epsilon}{-} \phi \text{ iff } \psi \in K \text{ and } ((\phi \vee \psi) \npreceq_\epsilon \phi \text{ or } \vdash \phi) \tag{34}$$

and show that such a belief contraction operation satisfies all AGM postulates for contraction as well as the following condition (Gärdenfors, Makinson 1988, Theorem 4):

$$\phi \preceq_\epsilon \psi \quad \text{iff} \quad \phi \notin K \stackrel{\epsilon}{-} (\phi \wedge \psi) \text{ or } \vdash (\phi \wedge \psi). \tag{35}$$

Further, they show that any belief contraction operation satisfying all of the AGM postulates is generated by some epistemic entrenchment ordering (Gärdenfors, Makinson 1988, Theorem 5).

The question is now how to interpret these results in the framework of epistemic relevance orderings on belief sets. First of all, from (EE2), reflexivity follows. Second, from (EE2) and (EE3), it follows that either $\phi \preceq_\epsilon (\phi \wedge \psi) \preceq_\epsilon \psi$ or $\psi \preceq_\epsilon (\phi \wedge \psi) \preceq_\epsilon \phi$. This means, $\preceq_\epsilon$ is a complete preorder on $\mathcal{L}$. For the strict part of this ordering we will use the symbol $\prec_\epsilon$. Further, from (EE2) it follows that there are maximal elements, namely, all sentences logically equivalent to $\top$ (and perhaps some other sentences as well). Ignoring the minimal elements (the sentences that are not elements of the belief set (EE4)), the restriction of $\preceq_\epsilon$ to the sentences in a belief set can be considered as an epistemic relevance ordering as defined in the previous section. In this case, using interdefinability of revision and contraction, definition (34) coincides with a contraction operation that is defined by using the *Harper identity* and a revision operation generated by epistemic relevance.

Theorem 9 *Suppose a belief set K, an epistemic entrenchment ordering $\preceq_\epsilon$, and the contraction operation $\stackrel{\epsilon}{-}$ generated by $\preceq_\epsilon$. Let $\preceq$ be the epistemic relevance ordering that is the restriction of $\preceq_\epsilon$ to K, and let $\dot{+}$ be the revision generated by the epistemic relevance ordering $\preceq$. Then*

$$K \stackrel{\epsilon}{-} \phi = (K \dot{+} \neg\phi) \cap K. \tag{36}$$

Proof. For the limiting case $\vdash \phi$, we have $(K \dot{+} \neg\phi) = Cn(\bot)$, hence the right hand side equals K. By (34) we also get for the left hand side K.

For the case $\phi \notin K$, again $(K \cup \{\neg\phi\}) \cap K = K$. That the left hand side has the same value follows from (34) and the observation that by (EE4) $\phi \notin K$ and $\psi \in K$ implies $\phi \prec_\epsilon \psi$, which in turn implies by $\psi \vdash (\phi \vee \psi)$ and (EE2): $\phi \prec_\epsilon \psi \preceq_\epsilon (\phi \vee \psi)$.

For the principal case, $\phi \in K$ and $\not\vdash \phi$, we will show that

$$\psi \in \bigcap \gamma_{\preceq}(K \perp \phi) \quad \text{iff} \quad \psi \in K \text{ and } \phi \prec_\epsilon (\phi \vee \psi). \tag{37}$$

If this condition is satisfied, then equation (36) holds obviously for the principal case as well.

"$\Leftarrow$": Suppose $\psi \in K$ and $\phi \prec_\epsilon (\phi \vee \psi)$. Note that because of $((\phi \vee \psi) \wedge (\phi \vee \neg\psi)) \vdash \phi$ and (EE2) we have $((\phi \vee \psi) \wedge (\phi \vee \neg\psi)) \preceq_\epsilon \phi$, which leads by our assumption and (EE1) to $((\phi \vee \psi) \wedge (\phi \vee \neg\psi)) \prec_\epsilon (\phi \vee \psi)$. Because of (EE3), either $(\phi \vee \psi)$ or $(\phi \vee \neg\psi)$ is less entrenched than the conjunction of them. It cannot be the former since that is strictly more entrenched, hence

$$(\phi \vee \neg\psi) \preceq_\epsilon ((\phi \vee \psi) \wedge (\phi \vee \neg\psi)) \prec_\epsilon (\phi \vee \psi). \tag{38}$$

Consider an arbitrary set $L \in \gamma_{\preceq}(K \perp \phi)$. Assume that $(\phi \vee \psi) \in L$. Then $(\phi \vee \neg \psi) \notin L$, or, equivalently $L \cup \{\psi\} \not\vdash \phi$. Since L is a maximal subset of K not implying ϕ, we have $\psi \in L$. Thus, assume $(\phi \vee \psi) \notin L$. Consider $M = L \cap \{\chi \in K \mid (\phi \vee \psi) \preceq_\epsilon \chi\}$. Because L is a maximally preferred subset in $(K \perp \phi)$, we must have $M \cup \{(\phi \vee \psi)\} \vdash \phi$, or, using the deduction theorem $M \vdash ((\phi \vee \psi) \rightarrow \phi)$, hence $M \vdash (\neg \psi \vee \phi)$. By the compactness of propositional logic, there is a finite subset $N \subseteq M$ such that $\bigwedge N \vdash (\neg \psi \vee \phi)$, hence, by (EE2) $\bigwedge N \preceq_\epsilon (\neg \psi \vee \phi)$, which by (EE3) implies that there is a sentence $\tau \in N$ such that $\tau \preceq_\epsilon (\neg \psi \vee \phi)$. By (38) we get $\tau \prec_\epsilon (\psi \vee \phi)$ which is in contradiction to the construction of M, however. Thus, ψ is a member of every maximally preferred set in $(K \perp \phi)$.

"$\Rightarrow$": Assume $\psi \in \bigcap \gamma_{\preceq}(K \perp \phi)$. Assume for contradiction that we nevertheless have $(\phi \vee \psi) \preceq_\epsilon \phi$. By the fact that $\phi \vdash (\phi \vee \neg \psi)$, we conclude

$$(\phi \vee \psi) \preceq_\epsilon \phi \preceq_\epsilon (\phi \vee \neg \psi). \tag{39}$$

Since $\psi \in \bigcap \gamma_{\preceq}(K \perp \phi)$, every set $L \in \gamma_{\preceq}(K \perp \phi)$ must contain ψ and, hence, $(\phi \vee \psi)$, i.e., $(\phi \vee \neg \psi) \notin L$. Consider the set $M = L \cap \{\chi \in K \mid (\phi \vee \neg \psi) \prec_\epsilon \chi\}$. Since no element of $\gamma_{\preceq}(K \perp \phi)$ contains $(\phi \vee \neg \psi)$, all such sets M must already contain propositions that together with $(\phi \vee \neg \psi)$ leads to the derivation of ϕ, i.e., $M \cup \{(\phi \vee \neg \psi)\} \vdash \phi$, or, by the deduction theorem $M \vdash ((\phi \vee \neg \psi) \rightarrow \phi)$, hence $M \vdash (\phi \vee \psi)$. By compactness, (EE2), and (EE3) we conclude that there exists a proposition $\tau \in M$ such that $\tau \preceq_\epsilon (\phi \vee \psi)$, and by the construction of M: $(\phi \vee \neg \psi) \prec_\epsilon (\phi \vee \psi)$, contradicting (39). ∎

Thus, the notion of epistemic entrenchment can indeed be viewed as a special case of epistemic relevance orderings—and, in the finite case, as a special case of database priorities.

The next corollary makes explicit which of the conditions (EE1)–(EE5) are actually needed to lead to a fully rational revision operation generated by epistemic relevance.

Corollary 10 *Any revision generated by an epistemic relevance ordering $\preceq$ such that*

1. *if $\phi \vdash \psi$ then $\phi \preceq \psi$, and*

2. *for any ϕ, ψ: $\phi \preceq (\phi \wedge \psi)$ or $\psi \preceq (\phi \wedge \psi)$,*

satisfies all AGM postulates.

Proof. (EE1) is already entailed by the fact that $\preceq$ is a preorder. (EE4) concerns only elements that are not in the belief set, and are therefore not related by $\preceq$. Further, as can be seen from the proof of Theorem 9, (EE5) is not necessary at all. We can always add a maximal degree that contains all logically valid sentences and remove them from other degrees without changing the outcome of a revision. ∎

Epistemic entrenchment orderings lead to "fully rational" contraction and revision, and, moreover all such belief change operations are generated by some epistemic entrenchment ordering. It is not obvious, however, how to arrive at such epistemic entrenchment orderings. While epistemic relevance can be easily derived from a given prioritized belief base, it is not clear whether there are natural ways to generate epistemic entrenchment orderings. In (Gärdenfors, Makinson 1988) it is proposed to start with a complete ordering over the maximal disjunctions derivable from a belief base. Despite the fact that this does not sound very "natural", it also implies that a large amount of information has to be supplied, sometimes too much (see Proposition 17 in Section 7), in order to change a belief set.

Interestingly, there is another special case of epistemic relevance that leads to a belief revision operation that satisfies all AGM postulates. When all degrees of epistemic relevance of a prioritized belief base C are singletons, then the prioritized base revision (as well as the corresponding partial meet revision and the epistemic relevance ordering on $Cn(C)$) is called *unambiguous*.

Proposition 11 *Let C be a prioritized belief base such that all degrees of epistemic relevance are singletons. Then $(C \Downarrow \phi)$ is a singleton iff $\nvdash \phi$.*

Proof. Note that $(C \Downarrow \phi) \neq \emptyset$ if and only if $\nvdash \phi$.

If $C \nvdash \phi$ then trivially $(C \Downarrow \phi) = \{C\}$.

For the case $\nvdash \phi$ and $C \vdash \phi$, assume for contradiction that $A, A' \in (C \Downarrow \phi)$ and $A \neq A'$. By the definition of $\Downarrow$ there must be some degree $\overline{\chi}$ such that $A_{\overline{\chi}} \neq A'_{\overline{\chi}}$. Let $\overline{\chi}$ be the greatest such class. Now, since the degrees of epistemic relevance are singletons, we either have $(\bigcup_{\overline{\tau} \succ \overline{\chi}} A_{\overline{\tau}} \cup \overline{\chi}) = (\bigcup_{\overline{\tau} \succ \overline{\chi}} A'_{\overline{\tau}} \cup \overline{\chi}) \vdash \phi$ or not. In both cases, A and A' would agree on whether they contain $\overline{\chi}$. Hence, they cannot be different. ∎

Note that even when $(C \Downarrow \phi)$ is always a singleton (for $\nvdash \phi$), the corresponding selection function $\gamma_{\preceq}$ does not necessarily select singletons from $(Cn(C) \perp \phi)$, i.e., the corresponding belief revision operation is not a *maxi-choice revision*.

Clearly, the epistemic relevance ordering on the belief set $Cn(C)$ cannot always be extended to an epistemic entrenchment ordering. Nevertheless, belief revisions corresponding to unambiguous prioritized base revisions satisfy all AGM postulates.

Theorem 12 *Let $\preceq$ be an unambiguous epistemic relevance ordering on a belief set K. Then the revision generated by this ordering satisfies all AGM postulates.*

Proof. By Theorem 4, the revision operation satisfies $(K \dot{+} 1)$–$(K \dot{+} 7)$. Thus, we only have to verify $(K \dot{+} 8)$. By (Alchourrón, Gärdenfors, Makinson 1985, Corollary 4.5) it suffice to show that the revision operation is transitively relational, i.e., using definition (13), we have to show that $\not\ll$ is transitive.

Since $\preceq$ is an unambiguous epistemic relevance ordering on K, all degrees of epistemic relevance except for the least one are singletons. The least degree will be denoted by $\overline{0}$.

In order to show transitivity of $\not\ll$, we first show that incomparability of two sets $L, M \in (K \perp \neg\phi)$, written $L \| M$ and defined by

$$L \| M \quad \text{iff} \quad L \not\ll M \text{ and } M \not\ll L,$$

is an equivalence relation on $K \perp \neg\phi$. Symmetry and reflexivity of $\|$ are immediate consequences of the definition. For showing transitivity, suppose $L, M, N \in (K \perp \neg\phi)$ and $L \| M \| N$. If $L = M$ or $M = N$, then $L \| N$ follows immediately. Therefore assume $L \neq M \neq N$. If $L \| M$ and $L \neq M$, then there is a degree $\overline{\tau} \in \overline{K}$ such that

$$L \cap \overline{\tau} \not\subset \neq \not\supset M \cap \overline{\tau} \text{ and } \forall \overline{\omega} \succ \overline{\tau} : (L \cap \overline{\omega} = M \cap \overline{\omega}). \tag{40}$$

Since all degrees except $\overline{0}$ are singletons, it follows that $\overline{\tau} = \overline{0}$, i.e., $L \cap (K - \overline{0}) = M \cap (K - \overline{0})$. With the same argument, we conclude that $M \cap (K - \overline{0}) = N \cap (K - \overline{0})$, hence $L \cap (K - \overline{0}) = N \cap (K - \overline{0})$. Since L and N are maximal subsets of K, it cannot be the case that $L \cap \overline{0} \subset N \cap \overline{0}$ or $L \cap \overline{0} \supset N \cap \overline{0}$, hence $L \| N$.

From the fact that $\|$ is an equivalence relation, it follows straightforwardly that $L \| M$ and $M \ll N$ implies that $L \ll N$. For contradiction assume $L \not\ll N$. Then we must have $N \ll L$ because otherwise by transitivity of $\|$ we could conclude $M \| N$, which is a contradiction of the assumption. From $N \ll L$, the assumption that $M \ll N$ and the transitivity of $\ll$ it follows that $M \ll L$, which again contradicts the assumption. With the same argument, it follows that $L \ll M$ and $M \| N$ implies $L \ll N$.

Now assume $L \not\ll M \not\ll N$. By considering cases, transitivity of $\ll$ follows. (1) Assuming $L \| M$ and $M \| N$ leads to $L \| N$, hence, $L \not\ll N$. (2) Assuming $L \| M$ and

$N \ll M$ leads to $N \ll L$, hence $L \not\ll N$. (3) Assuming $M \ll L$ and $M \| N$ leads to $N \ll L$, hence $L \not\ll N$. (4) Assuming $M \ll L$ and $N \ll M$ leads to $N \ll L$, hence $L \not\ll N$. Thus, belief revisions generated by unambiguous epistemic relevance are transitively relational and satisfy for this reason (K$\dot{+}$8). ∎

Although an unambiguous relevance ordering is not necessarily an entrenchment ordering, it is possible to generate an epistemic entrenchment ordering using (35) that leads to an identical revision operation because unambiguous revisions are fully rational. Given an unambiguous prioritized base C, the epistemic entrenchment ordering can be derived as follows. For every pair of propositions $\phi, \psi \in Cn(C)$, determine $\{A\} = C \Downarrow \phi$ and $\{B\} = C \Downarrow \psi$, and set $\psi \prec_e \phi$ if and only if $A \ll B$. The verification that this is indeed the right epistemic entrenchment ordering is left as an exercise to the reader.

6 BELIEF REVISION AND DEFAULT REASONING

Doyle has remarked in (Doyle 1990, App. A) that "the adjective 'nonmonotonic' has suffered much careless usage recently in artificial intelligence, and the only thing common to many of its uses is the term 'nonmonotonic' itself." Doyle identified two principal ideas behind the use of this term, namely,

> [...] that attitudes are gained and lost over time, that reasoning is non-monotonic—this we call *temporal* nonmonotonicity—and that unsound assumptions can be the deliberate product of sound reasoning, incomplete information, and a "will to believe"—which we call *logical* nonmonotonicity.

Formally, the term *logical nonmonotonicity* refers to nonmonotonicity found in non-monotonic logics, i.e., given a deductive closure operation $C(\cdot)$ of a nonmonotonic logic,

$$A \subseteq B \quad \not\Rightarrow \quad C(A) \subseteq C(B). \tag{41}$$

The notion of *temporal nonmonotonicity* refers to the development of a set of beliefs over time, where K_t will be used to refer to K at time point t:

$$t_1 \leq t_2 \quad \not\Rightarrow \quad A_{t_1} \subseteq A_{t_2} \tag{42}$$

Although these two forms of nonmonotonicity should not be confused, sometimes they turn out to be intimately connected. In particular, the temporal nonmonotonicity induced by belief revision, i.e., the fact that in general we do not have $K \subseteq K \dotplus \phi$, is related to logical nonmonotonicity induced by some forms of default reasoning. Further, there exists also a connection between a form of contraction and default reasoning, as we will see below.

When reasoning with defaults in a setting as described in (Poole 1988; Brewka 1989), we are prepared to "drop" some of the defaults if they are inconsistent with the facts. This, however, is quite similar to what we are doing when revising beliefs in the theory of epistemic change. Propositions of a theory are given up when they are inconsistent with new facts. Since default reasoning leads to logical nonmonotonicity, one would expect that belief revision is nonmonotonic in the facts to be added, i.e., we would expect that $Cn(\phi) \subseteq Cn(\psi)$ does not imply $K \dotplus \phi \subseteq K \dotplus \psi$. Indeed, as is well known, requiring monotony in the second operand of a belief revision operation is impossible in the general case. Exploring the space of possible revision operations that imply monotony shows that the revision either violates one of the basic AGM postulates or it is a trivial revision on $Cn(\emptyset)$ or $Cn(\bot)$.

Proposition 13 *Let $\dotplus$ be a belief revision operation defined on a belief set K. If for all ϕ, ψ*

$$K \dotplus \phi \subseteq K \dotplus \psi \quad if \quad Cn(\phi) \subseteq Cn(\psi), \tag{43}$$

then

1. *The operation $\dotplus$ violates one of the basic AGM postulates (K$\dotplus$1)–(K$\dotplus$6), or*

2. *$K = Cn(\emptyset)$ and $K \dotplus \phi = Cn(\phi)$, or*

3. *$K = Cn(\bot)$ and $K \dotplus \phi = Cn(\phi)$.*

Proof. Assume $K \neq Cn(\bot)$ and a proposition ϕ with $\neg\phi \in K$ and $\nvdash \neg\phi$. By (43) we would have $K \dotplus \top \subseteq K \dotplus \phi$. Because of (K$\dotplus$3) and (K$\dotplus$4), $K \dotplus \top = K$. By assumption, we thus have $\neg\phi \in K \dotplus \top$. Now, by (K$\dotplus$2) $\phi \in K \dotplus \phi$. Because of (K$\dotplus$5) and the assumption $\nvdash \neg\phi$, $\neg\phi \notin K \dotplus \phi$. Thus, either the requirement $K \dotplus \top \subseteq K \dotplus \phi$ or one of the basic postulates is violated.

Let $\dotplus$ a belief revision operation on $Cn(\emptyset)$ and assume that all basic postulates are satisfied. Then by (K$\dotplus$1)–(K$\dotplus$3) it follows that $Cn(\phi) \subseteq Cn(\emptyset) \dotplus \phi \subseteq Cn(\emptyset \cup \{\phi\}) = Cn(\phi)$ and (43) is trivially satisfied.

Assume $K = Cn(\perp)$. If $\vdash \neg\phi$ then clearly $K \dotplus \phi = Cn(\perp) = Cn(\phi)$ by $(K\dotplus 1)$ and $(K\dotplus 2)$. Thus, assume $\nvdash \neg\phi$. By $(K\dotplus 1)$ and $(K\dotplus 2)$, we have $Cn(\phi) \subseteq K \dotplus \phi$. Now assume there is a proposition $\chi \in K \dotplus \phi$ such that $\chi \notin Cn(\phi)$. By (43) we would have $K \dotplus \phi \subseteq K \dotplus (\neg\chi \wedge \phi)$. However, this would violate $(K\dotplus 2)$ or $(K\dotplus 5)$. Thus, if the basic postulates and (43) are satisfied, $Cn(\perp) \dotplus \phi = Cn(\phi)$. ∎

Makinson and Gärdenfors (1991) use this similarity of logical nonmonotonicity and the nonmonotonicity of belief revision in the second operand as a starting point to investigate the relationship between nonmonotonic logics and belief revision on a very general level. They compare various general conditions on nonmonotonic provability relations with the AGM postulates.

For the approaches to belief revision described in the previous section there is an even stronger connection to some models of nonmonotonic reasoning. Prioritized base revision, and hence partial meet revision generated by epistemic relevance, is expressively equivalent to *skeptical* provability[5] in Poole's (1988) *theory formation* approach and Brewka's (1989) *level default theories* (LDT)—in the case of finitary propositional logic.

A common generalization of both approaches are *ranked default theories* (RDT). A RDT Δ is a pair $\Delta = (\mathcal{D}, \mathcal{F})$, where $\mathcal{D}$ is a finite sequence $\langle \mathcal{D}_1, \ldots, \mathcal{D}_n \rangle$ of finite sets of sentences (propositional, in our case) interpreted as ranked defaults and $\mathcal{F}$ is a finite set of sentences interpreted as hard facts.

An *extension* of Δ is a deductively closed set of propositions

$$E = Cn((\bigcup_{i=1}^{n} \mathcal{R}_i) \cup \mathcal{F}) \tag{44}$$

such that for all i with $1 \leq i \leq n$:

1. $\mathcal{R}_i \subseteq \mathcal{D}_i$,

2. $\mathcal{R}_i$ is set-inclusion maximal among the subsets of $\mathcal{D}_i$ such that $(\bigcup_{j=1}^{i} \mathcal{R}_j) \cup \mathcal{F}$ is consistent.[6]

---

[5]A correspondence to *credulous* derivability could be achieved if a notion of *nondeterministic* revision as proposed in (Doyle 1990) is adopted.

[6]Note that this definition, which is similar to the definition of an extension in (Poole 1988), excludes inconsistent extensions. Nevertheless, the definition of strong provability implies that $\perp$ can be derived iff $\mathcal{F}$ is inconsistent.

A sentence ϕ is *strongly provable* in Δ, written $\Delta\hspace{-1pt}\vdash\hspace{-6pt}\sim\hspace{-2pt}\phi$, iff for all extensions E of Δ: $\phi \in E$.

Poole's approach is a special case of RDT's where $\mathcal{D} = \langle\mathcal{D}_1\rangle$, and Brewka's LDT's are RDT's with $\mathcal{F} = \emptyset$. Note, however, that the expressive difference between RDT's and LDT's is actually very small and shows up only if $\mathcal{F}$ is inconsistent. In this case, RDT's allow the derivation of $\perp$ while this is impossible in LDT's.

Theorem 14 *Let $\Delta = (\langle\mathcal{D}_1,\ldots,\mathcal{D}_n\rangle, \mathcal{F})$ be a RDT. Let $C = \bigcup_{i=1}^{n}\mathcal{D}_i$ be a prioritized base with degrees of epistemic relevance $\mathcal{D}_1,\ldots,\mathcal{D}_n$. Then for all ϕ:*

$$\Delta\hspace{-1pt}\vdash\hspace{-6pt}\sim\hspace{-2pt}\phi \quad \textit{iff} \quad \phi \in (C\,\hat{\oplus}\,\mathcal{F}). \tag{45}$$

Proof. In the limiting case when $\mathcal{F} \vdash \perp$, $C\,\hat{\oplus}\,\mathcal{F} = Cn(\perp)$. Further, in this case there is no extension of Δ, hence $\Delta\hspace{-1pt}\vdash\hspace{-6pt}\sim\hspace{-2pt}\phi$ for all $\phi \in \mathcal{L}$ by the definition of strong provability.

When $\mathcal{F}$ is consistent, then $(C \Downarrow \neg(\bigwedge\mathcal{F}))$ is by definition a system S of subsets $B \subseteq C$ such that

1. $B = \bigcup_{i=1}^{n} B_i$,

2. $B_i \subseteq C_i$, for all $1 \leq i \leq n$, and

3. for all $1 \leq i \leq n$, B_i is set-inclusion maximal among the subsets of C_i such that $\bigcup_{j=1}^{i} B_j \not\vdash \neg(\bigwedge\mathcal{F})$.

Since the second condition of 3. is equivalent with the condition that $(\bigcup_{j=1}^{i} B_j) \cup \mathcal{F})$ is consistent, it follows that by definition for every extension E of Δ there exists a set $B \in (C \Downarrow \neg(\bigwedge\mathcal{F}))$ such that $E = Cn(B \cup \mathcal{F})$ and vice versa, hence

$$\bigcap_{\substack{E \text{ is an extension of } \Delta}} E = \bigcap_{\substack{B\in(C\Downarrow\neg(\bigwedge\mathcal{F}))}} Cn(B) + (\bigwedge\mathcal{F}), \tag{46}$$

which completes the proof. ∎

This means that ranked default theories have the same expressive power as finitary prioritized base revision operations, which coincide with finitary belief revisions generated by epistemic relevance.

It should be noted that in ranked default theories there is no requirement on the *internal* consistency of defaults. This means that the set $\bigcup_i \mathcal{D}_i$ may very well be inconsistent. In Theorem 14 that may lead to $\bot \in Cn(C)$, i.e., the belief set to be revised is inconsistent. Although this might sound unreasonable in the context of modeling (idealized) epistemic states—in fact, inconsistency is indeed explicitly excluded by requirement (2.2.1) in (Gärdenfors 1988)—it does not lead to technical problems in the theory of epistemic change. Additionally, it is possible to give a transformation between reasoning in RDT's and prioritized base revision using only consistent belief sets.

Corollary 15 *Let Δ be a RDT as above. Then there exists a consistent prioritized base C and a proposition ψ such that for all ϕ*

$$\Delta \mathrel{\vdash\hspace{-0.3em}\sim} \phi \quad iff \quad \phi \in \left(C \hat{\oplus} (\psi \wedge \mathcal{F})\right). \tag{47}$$

Proof. Define C as in Theorem 14. Transform every sentence in C into negation normal form (i.e., into a formula that contains only $\wedge$, $\vee$ and $\neg$, and all negation signs appear only in front of propositional variables). Assuming without loss of generality that the alphabet of propositional variables Σ is finite, extend Σ to Σ' by adding for every propositional variable p a fresh variable p'. Now replace any negative literal $\neg p$ in all sentences of C by p', call the new belief base C' and define

$$\psi \stackrel{\text{def}}{=} \bigwedge_{p \in \Sigma} (\neg p \leftrightarrow p'). \tag{48}$$

Since all sentences in C' contain only $\wedge$ and $\vee$ and no negation sign, C' is consistent.

Let ϕ any proposition over Σ, we will show that for any two belief bases B and B', where B' is a transformed belief base according to the above rules, the following relation holds:

$$B \vdash \phi \quad iff \quad B' \cup \{\psi\} \vdash \phi. \tag{49}$$

Assume $B \vdash \phi$ but $B' \cup \{\psi\} \not\vdash \phi$. This means $B' \cup \{\psi\} \cup \neg \phi$ is satisfiable. Restricting the truth assignment of this belief set to Σ, we get one that must satisfy $B \cup \{\neg \phi\}$ by construction of B'. This is impossible, however. Conversely, assuming satisfiability of $B \cup \{\neg \phi\}$, a truth assignment can be extended to Σ' such that it satisfies $B \cup \{\psi\} \cup \neg \phi$, hence also $B' \cup \{\psi\} \cup \neg \phi$.

That means that for any maximal subset $B \subseteq C$ that is consistent with a given proposition ϕ there exists a corresponding set $B' \subseteq C'$, that is consistent with ψ and

ϕ and maximal in C'. Further adding ψ to B' allows to derive the same propositions over Σ as can be derived from B. ∎

From the results above and the translation of (K$\dot{+}$8) to a condition on nonmonotonic derivability relations in (Makinson, Gärdenfors 1991), it follows that the derivability relation of RDT's w.r.t. the set of hard facts $\mathcal{F}$ does not satisfy *rational monotony* (see (Makinson, Gärdenfors 1991)).[7] This condition can be phrased as follows:

$$\text{If } \phi \mathrel{|\!\sim} \psi \text{ and } \phi \mathrel{|\!\not\sim} \neg\chi \text{ then } \phi \wedge \chi \mathrel{|\!\sim} \psi \tag{50}$$

In plain words, if a proposition ϕ permits the plausible conclusion ψ, this conclusion continues to hold for the stronger premise $\phi \wedge \chi$ provided there is no plausible reason to deny χ given the assumption ϕ. Applying this condition to RDT's we consider the nonmonotonic derivability relation as parameterized by the defaults $\mathcal{D}$, written $\mathcal{F} \mathrel{|\!\sim_{\mathcal{D}}} \phi$. For a counter-example to rational monotony, suppose a situation where two people of different sex meet the first time and try to get to know important facts about each other. Assume one person has the following background beliefs modeled as a set of defaults:

1. Being a parent implies being married ($p \rightarrow m$).

2. Living alone implies being a bachelor ($a \rightarrow b$).

3. Wearing a ring implies being a dandy or being married ($r \rightarrow (d \vee m)$).

All these defaults have the same priority. Further, suppose the postulate ($b \leftrightarrow \neg m$) and the facts p, a, and r. One extension, which contains m, is the consequential closure of the facts and rules 1 and 3. The other possible extension, which contains d, is the closure of the facts and rule 2. This means that ($m \vee d$) is a sceptical consequence:

$$(b \leftrightarrow \neg m) \wedge p \wedge a \wedge r \;\mathrel{|\!\sim_{\mathcal{D}}}\; (m \vee d). \tag{51}$$

If $\neg d$ is added to the facts the expected conclusion m does not follow, however. In this case one extension, which contains m and $\neg d$, is generated by the facts and rule 1 and 3. The other possible extension is generated by the facts and rule 2 and contains $\neg m$ and $\neg d$. Hence,

$$\neg d \wedge ((b \leftrightarrow \neg m) \wedge p \wedge a \wedge r) \;\mathrel{|\!\not\sim_{\mathcal{D}}}\; (m \vee d), \tag{52}$$

---

[7]Note that this result depends on the exact correspondence between RDT's and belief revision generated by epistemic relevance. In (Makinson, Gärdenfors 1991; Gärdenfors 1990) the correspondence between Poole's logic and belief revision was only approximate because the defaults were assumed to be deductively closed.

although

$$((b \leftrightarrow \neg m) \wedge p \wedge a \wedge r) \quad \not\vdash_{\mathcal{D}} \quad d. \tag{53}$$

Another interesting observation in this context is that the addition of *constraints* to RDT's is similar but not identical to a *belief contraction operation*. Poole (1988) introduced *constraints*—another set of sentences—as a means to restrict the applicability of defaults. A *ranked default theory with constraints* is a triple $\Delta = (\mathcal{D}, \mathcal{F}, \mathcal{C})$, where $\mathcal{D}$ and $\mathcal{F}$ are defined as above and $\mathcal{C}$ is a finite set of sentences interpreted as constraints. The notion of an extension is modified as follows. Instead of condition 2. it is required that

2. $\mathcal{R}_i$ is set-inclusion maximal among the subsets of $\mathcal{D}_i$ such that $(\bigcup_{i=1}^n \mathcal{R}_i) \cup \mathcal{F} \cup \mathcal{C}$ is consistent.

It should be obvious that the addition of constraints is a generalization of the basic framework, i.e., for all $\mathcal{F}, \mathcal{D}, \phi$:

$$(\mathcal{D}, \mathcal{F}, \emptyset) \vdash \phi \quad \text{iff} \quad (\mathcal{D}, \mathcal{F}) \vdash \phi. \tag{54}$$

Provided the set $\mathcal{F} \cup \mathcal{C}$ is consistent, which is the interesting case, skeptical derivability can be modeled as a form of contraction on *belief bases* (see (Nebel 1989)).

Theorem 16 *Let* $\Delta = (\langle \mathcal{D}_1, \ldots, \mathcal{D}_n \rangle, \mathcal{F}, \mathcal{C})$ *be an* RDT *with constraints such that* $\mathcal{F} \cup \mathcal{C}$ *is consistent. Let* $C = \mathcal{F} \cup \bigcup_{i=1}^n \mathcal{D}_i$ *be a prioritized base with* $\mathcal{F}, \mathcal{D}_1, \ldots, \mathcal{D}_n$ *the degrees of relevance of* C. *Then*

$$\Delta \vdash \phi \quad \text{iff} \quad \bigvee \left(C \Downarrow \neg(\wedge \mathcal{C}) \right) \vdash \phi \tag{55}$$

Proof. If $\mathcal{F} \cup \mathcal{C}$ is consistent, then every element $B \in (C \Downarrow \neg(\wedge \mathcal{C}))$ contains $\mathcal{F}$. Further, the subsets chosen from $\mathcal{D}_i$ are maximal subsets consistent with $\mathcal{F}$ and $\mathcal{C}$, hence, the extensions of Δ correspond to sets $B \in (C \Downarrow \neg(\wedge \mathcal{C}))$ and vice versa, such that $E = Cn(B)$. ∎

This goes some way to answering the question whether there is a counter-part to contraction in nonmonotonic logics, raised in (Makinson, Gärdenfors 1991). Default reasoning with constraints in Poole's theory formation approach can be modeled by using base contraction.

Trying to lift this result to belief sets, however, is impossible in the general case. Usually, ranked default theories with constraints do not allow the derivation of $\bigwedge C$, and this property is independent from consistency of the set of facts $\mathcal{F}$ with the set of defaults $\bigcup_i \mathcal{D}_i$. When contracting an inconsistent belief set, however, the contracted belief set contains the negation of the proposition used to contract the belief set. This property follows from the *Harper identity* when we set $K = Cn(\perp)$:

$$Cn(\perp) \dot{-} \chi = (Cn(\perp) \dot{+} \neg\chi) \cap Cn(\perp) = Cn(\perp) \dot{+} \neg\chi \supseteq Cn(\neg\chi) \qquad (56)$$

This means, provided we try to model derivability in such logics by belief contraction, in case when the defaults are inconsistent with the facts, a belief contraction would lead to the inclusion of the constraints—which may not be derivable in the corresponding default logic. Base contraction does not have this property because such operations remove more beliefs than belief contractions. In particular, while every contracted belief set $K \dot{-} \phi$ contains $Cn(K) \cap Cn(\neg\phi)$, a contracted base usually does not contain those beliefs (see also (Nebel 1989)).

7   COMPUTATIONAL COMPLEXITY

For the investigation of the computational complexity of belief revision, we consider the problem of determining membership of a sentence ψ in a belief set $K = Cn(C)$ revised by ϕ, i.e.,

$$\psi \in K \dot{+} \phi. \qquad (57)$$

As the input size we use the sum of the size $|C|$ of the belief base C that represents K and the sizes $|\phi|$ and $|\psi|$ of the sentences ϕ and ψ, respectively.

This assumption implies that the representation of the preference relation used to guide the revision process should be polynomially bounded by $|C|+|\phi|+|\psi|$. Although this sounds like a reasonable restriction, it is not met by all belief revision approaches. Belief revision generated by *epistemic entrenchment* orderings (Gärdenfors, Makinson 1988), for instance, requires more preference information in the general case. An epistemic entrenchment ordering over all elements of a belief set can be uniquely characterized by an *initial* complete order over the set of all derivable *maximal disjunctions* (over all literals) (Gärdenfors, Makinson 1988, Theorem 7). This set is logarithmic in the size of the set of formulas (modulo logical equivalence) in a *belief set*. However, the number of maximal disjunctions may still be very large.

Proposition 17 *The set of maximal disjunctions over all literals implied by a belief base has a worst-case size that is exponential in the size of the belief base.*

That does not mean that the concept of epistemic entrenchment is useless when it comes to computation. It just means that most probably we will not be able to realize every theoretically possible entrenchment ordering computationally. There may be large classes of such orderings that can be specified with less than exponential effort, though.

A similar statement could be made about revisions generated by epistemic relevance. It is, of course, possible to have a belief base C that represents K and an epistemic relevance ordering over K that is not representable in a polynomial way w.r.t. $|C|$. However, if we consider only complete preorders over C with the understanding that the degree of least relevant sentences is $Cn(C) - C$, then the ordering is represented in a way that is polynomially bounded by $|C|$ and $\dotplus$ can be computed by using the corresponding prioritized base revision. This means all "natural" epistemic relevance orderings are well-behaved.

Analyzing the computational complexity of the belief revision problems, the first thing one notes that deciding the trivial case $\psi \in Cn(\emptyset) \dotplus \phi$ is already co-NP-complete,[8] and we might give up immediately. However, finding a characterization of the complexity that is more fine grained than just saying it is NP-hard can help to understand the structure of the problem better. In particular, we may be able to compare the inherent complexity of different approaches and, most importantly, we may say something about feasible implementations, which most likely will make compromises along the line that the expressiveness of the logical language is restricted and/or incompleteness is tolerated at some point. For this purpose we have to know, however, what the sources of complexities are.

The belief revision problems considered in this paper fall into complexity classes located at the lower end of the *polynomial hierarchy*. Since this notion is not as common as the central complexity classes, it will be briefly sketched (Garey, Johnson 1979, Sect. 7.2). Let X be a class of decision problems. Then $\mathsf{P^X}$ denotes the class of decision problems $L \in \mathsf{P^X}$ such that there is a decision problem $L' \in \mathsf{X}$ and a polynomial Turing-reduction from L to L', i.e., all instances of L can be solved in polynomial time on a deterministic Turing machine that employs an oracle for L'. Similarly, $\mathsf{NP^X}$ denotes the class of decision problems $L \in \mathsf{NP^X}$ such that there is nondeterministic Turing-machine that solves all instances of L in polynomial time using an oracle for $L' \in \mathsf{X}$. Based on these notions, the sets Δ_k^p, Σ_k^p, and Π_k^p are

---

[8]We assume some familiarity with the basic notions of the theory of NP-completeness as presented in the first few chapters of (Garey, Johnson 1979). This means the terms *decision problem*, P, NP, co-NP, PSPACE, *polynomial transformation* (or *many-one reduction*), *polynomial Turing reduction*, *completeness* w.r.t. polynomial transformability or Turing reducibility should be familiar to the reader.

defined as follows:[9]

$$\Delta_0^p = \Sigma_0^p = \Pi_0^p = \mathsf{P}, \tag{58}$$

$$\Delta_{k+1}^p = \mathsf{P}^{\Sigma_k^p}, \tag{59}$$

$$\Sigma_{k+1}^p = \mathsf{NP}^{\Sigma_k^p}, \tag{60}$$

$$\Pi_{k+1}^p = \mathsf{co\text{-}}\Sigma_{k+1}^p. \tag{61}$$

Thus, $\Sigma_1^p = \mathsf{NP}$, $\Pi_1^p = \mathsf{co\text{-}NP}$, and Δ_2^p is the set of NP-easy problems. Further note that $\bigcup_{k \geq 0} \Delta_k^p = \bigcup_{k \geq 0} \Sigma_k^p = \bigcup_{k \geq 0} \Pi_k^p \subseteq \mathsf{PSPACE}$.

The role of the "canonical" complete problem (w.r.t. polynomial transformability), which is played by SAT for Σ_1^p, is played by k-QBF for Σ_k^p. k-QBF is the problem of deciding whether the following quantified boolean formula is true:

$$\underbrace{\exists \vec{p}\, \forall \vec{q} \ldots}_{k \text{ alternating quantifiers starting with } \exists} F(\vec{p}, \vec{q}, \ldots). \tag{62}$$

The complementary problem, denoted by $\overline{k\text{-QBF}}$, is complete for Π_k^p.

Turning now to the revision operations discussed in this paper, we first of all notice that the special belief revision problem of determining membership for a full meet revision, called FMR-problem, is comparably easy. With respect to Turing-reducibility, there is actually no difference to the complexity of ordinary propositional derivability, i.e., the FMR-problem is NP-equivalent.

Proposition 18 $\mathsf{FMR} \in \Delta_2^p - (\Sigma_1^p \cup \Pi_1^p)$ *provided* $\Sigma_1^p \neq \Pi_1^p$.

Proof. If $\dotdiv$ is a full meet revision, $\phi \in Cn(C) \dotdiv \psi$ can be solved by the following algorithm:

$$\text{if } C \nvdash \neg\phi$$
$$\quad \text{then } C \cup \{\phi\} \vdash \psi$$
$$\quad \text{else } \phi \vdash \psi$$

From this, membership in Δ_2^p follows.

Further, SAT can be polynomially transformed to FMR by solving $\phi \in Cn(\phi) \dotdiv \top$, and unsatisfiability ($\overline{\mathsf{SAT}}$) can be polynomially transformed to FMR by solving $\bot \in Cn(\emptyset) \dotdiv \phi$. Hence, assuming $\mathsf{FMR} \in \mathsf{NP} \cup \mathsf{co\text{-}NP}$ would lead to $\mathsf{NP} = \mathsf{co\text{-}NP}$. $\blacksquare$

---

[9]The superscript p is only used to distinguish these sets from the analogous sets in the Kleene hierarchy.

The membership problem for simple base revision will be called SBR-problem. This problem is obviously more complicated than the FMR-problem. However, the added complexity is not overwhelming—from a theoretical point of view.

Theorem 19 SBR *is* Π_2^p-*complete.*

Proof. We will prove that the complementary problem $C \oplus \phi \not\vdash \psi$, which is called $\overline{\text{SBR}}$, is Σ_2^p-complete. Hardness is shown by a polynomial transformation from 2-QBF to $\overline{\text{SBR}}$. Let $\vec{p} = p_1, \ldots, p_n$, let $\vec{q} = q_1, \ldots, q_m$, and let $\exists \vec{p} \forall \vec{q} \, F(\vec{p}, \vec{q})$ be an instance of 2-QBF. Set

$$C = \{p_1, \ldots, p_n, \neg p_1, \ldots, \neg p_n, \neg F(\vec{p}, \vec{q})\}. \tag{63}$$

Now we claim that

$$C \oplus \top \not\vdash \neg F(\vec{p}, \vec{q}) \quad \text{iff} \quad \exists \vec{p} \forall \vec{q} \, F(\vec{p}, \vec{q}) \text{ is true.} \tag{64}$$

$C \oplus \top \not\vdash \neg F(\vec{p}, \vec{q})$ if and only if there is an element $B \in (C \perp \top)$ such that $\neg F(\vec{p}, \vec{q}) \notin B$. Since every set of literals $\{l_1, \ldots l_n\}$ with $l_i = p_i$ or $l_i = \neg p_i$ is consistent, $\neg F(\vec{p}, \vec{q}) \notin B$ if and only if the set $\{l_1, \ldots, l_n\} \subseteq B$ is inconsistent with $\neg F(\vec{p}, \vec{q})$, i.e., $\{l_1, \ldots, l_n\} \vdash F(\vec{p}, \vec{q})$. This, in turn is equivalent with the fact that there is a truth assignment to $\vec{p}$ such that $F(\vec{p}, \vec{q})$ is true for all truth-assignments to $\vec{q}$. Thus, equivalence (64) holds.

Membership of $\overline{\text{SBR}}$ in Σ_2^p follows from the following algorithm that needs nondeterministic polynomial time using an oracle for SAT:

1. Guess a set $B \subseteq C$.

2. Verify that there is no $\chi \in C - B$ such that $B \cup \{\chi\} \not\vdash \neg\phi$.

3. Verify $B \cup \{\phi\} \not\vdash \psi$.

∎

This means that SBR is, on one hand, not much more difficult than FMR, and, on the other hand, apparently easier than derivability in most modal logics (e.g., K, T, and $S4$), which is a PSPACE-complete problem (Garey, Johnson 1979, p. 262). Asking for the computational significance of this result, the answer is somewhat unsatisfying.

All problems in the polynomial hierarchy have the same property as the NP-complete problems, namely, that they can be solved in polynomial time if and only if P = NP. Further, all problems in the polynomial hierarchy can be solved by an exhaustive search that takes exponential time. This means the worst-case behavior of any SBR algorithm is most probably not better or worse than the worst-case behavior of any propositional proof method. However, from the structure of the algorithm used in the proof one sees that even if we restrict ourselves to polynomial methods for computing propositional satisfiability—for instance, by restricting the expressiveness—there would still be the problem of determining the maximal consistent subsets B.

Having now a very precise idea of the complexity of the SBR-problem, we may ask what the computational costs of introducing priorities are. In other words whether the membership problem for prioritized base revision, called PBR-problem, is more difficult than SBR.

Theorem 20 PBR *is* Π_2^p-*complete.*

Proof. Π_2^p-hardness is immediate by Theorem 19. Membership of PBR in Π_2^p also follows easily. The maximality test (step 2 in the algorithm used in the proof of Theorem 19) has to be performed as often as there are priority classes, which is polynomially bounded by $|Z|$. ∎

This means that we do not have to pay for introducing priority classes. In the case of default logics, the generalization from Poole's logic to RDT's does not increase the computational costs. Note also, that the computational complexity of derivability for Brewka's LDT's is not easier because the reduction in the proof of Theorem 19 applies to the special case $\mathcal{F} = \emptyset$, as well.

The membership problem for unambiguous prioritized base revision, the UBR-problem, turns out to be easier than SBR and PBR.

Theorem 21 UBR $\in \Delta_2^p - (\Sigma_1^p \cup \Pi_1^p)$, *provided* $\Sigma_1^p \neq \Pi_1^p$.

Proof. In order to show that UBR $\in \Delta_2^p$, we specify an algorithm to compute $C \hat{\oplus} \phi \vdash \psi$, for $\hat{\oplus}$ based on singleton degrees of relevance:

   1. Initialize $A = \emptyset$ and $i = 1$.

2. Test $A \cup C_i \nvdash \neg\phi$. If so, set $A = A \cup C_i$.

3. Increment i.

4. If there are only $i - 1$ degrees return with the result $(A \cup \{\phi\} \vdash \psi)$.

5. Otherwise continue with step 2.

Using an oracle for SAT, this algorithms runs in polynomial time. Thus, we have $\mathsf{UBR} \in \Delta_2^p$.

Using the same arguments as in the proof of Proposition 18 leads to $\mathsf{FMR} \notin \mathsf{NP} \cup \mathsf{co\text{-}NP}$ provided $\mathsf{NP} \neq \mathsf{co\text{-}NP}$. ∎

From the proof, we can infer that if we can come up with a polynomial algorithm for satisfiability (by restricting the propositional language to Horn logic, for instance), then unambiguous base revision will be itself polynomial. This result gives a formal justification for the claim made in (Nebel 1989) that this form of revision is similar to the functionality the RUP system (McAllester 1982) offers—in an abstract sense, though.[10] The important point to note is that a feasible implementation of belief revision is possible if we restrict ourselves to polynomial methods for satisfiability by restricting the language or by tolerating incompleteness *and* by using a polynomial method for selecting among competing alternatives.

Finally, it may be interesting to compare syntax-based revision approaches with model-based approaches, such as the one proposed by Dalal (1988). In order to do so, we first need some definitions. Recall that a model $\mathcal{I}$ of a belief base C is a truth assignment that satisfies all propositions in C. $mod(C)$ denotes the set of all models of C. $\delta(\mathcal{I}, \mathcal{J})$ denotes the number of propositional variables such that $\mathcal{I}$ and $\mathcal{J}$ map them to different truth-values. Assuming that $\mathcal{M}$ denotes a set of truth assignments, $g^m(\mathcal{M})$ is the set of truth assignments $\mathcal{J}$ such that there is a truth-assignment $\mathcal{I} \in \mathcal{M}$ with $\delta(\mathcal{J}, \mathcal{I}) \leq m$. If C is a finite belief base, then $G^m(C)$ is some belief base such that $mod(G^m(C)) = g^m(mod(C))$. Although G^m is not a deterministic function, all possible results are obviously logically equivalent.

---

[10]The RUP system provides the possibility to put premises into different likelihood classes. However, it seems to be the case that in resolving inconsistencies it could select non-maximal sets w.r.t. $\ll$ [McAllester, 1990, personal communication].

Now, model-based revision, written $C \circ \phi$ is defined by:[11]

$$C \circ \phi \stackrel{def}{=} \begin{cases} G^m(C) \cup \{\phi\} & \text{for the least } m \text{ s.t.} \\ & G^m(C) \cup \{\phi\} \nvdash \bot \\ \{\phi\} & \text{if } C \vdash \bot \text{ or } \phi \vdash \bot. \end{cases} \tag{65}$$

Interestingly, the membership problem for model-based revision, called MBR-problem, has the same complexity as UBR and FMR. However, it is not obvious whether a restriction of the expressiveness of the logical language would lead to a polynomial algorithm in this case.

Theorem 22 MBR $\in \Delta_2^p - (\Sigma_1^p \cup \Pi_1^p)$, *provided* $\Sigma_1^p \neq \Pi_1^p$.

Proof. Note that for any fixed i, $G^i(C) \nvdash \phi$ is a problem that can be solved in non-deterministic polynomial time by guessing two truth assignment $\mathcal{I}, \mathcal{J}$ and verifying in polynomial time that

1. $\models_{\mathcal{I}} C$,

2. $\nvDash_{\mathcal{J}} \phi$, and

3. $\delta(\mathcal{I}, \mathcal{J}) \leq i$.

Note further that solving $G^i(C) \cup \{\phi\} \nvdash \psi$ can be reduced to solving $G^i(C) \nvdash (\phi \rightarrow \psi)$.

Let n be the number of different propositional variables in C. Then it is obvious that $g^k(C) = g^{k+1}(C)$ for all $k \geq n$.

Membership of MBR in Δ_2^p follows from the following algorithm:

1. Determine the least i, where $0 \leq i \leq n$ such that $G^i(C) \nvdash \neg\phi$.

   (a) If there is no such i, then return $\phi \vdash \psi$.

   (b) Otherwise, return $(G^i(C) \cup \{\phi\} \vdash \psi)$.

---

[11]This definition is a slight extension of the definition given in (Dalal 1988) that takes also care of the limiting cases when C or ϕ is inconsistent.

Since n is bounded polynomially by $|C|$, this algorithms runs in polynomial time using an oracle for the problem $G^i(C) \not\vdash \phi$.

MBR $\notin$ NP $\cup$ co-NP provided NP $\neq$ co-NP follows with the same argument as in the proof of Proposition 18. ∎

Reconsidering the complexity results, there appears to be an interesting pattern. Note that the best result for a belief revision problem we can hope for is membership in Δ_2^p because the problem involves consistency and inconsistency problems. While, the "fully rational" base revisions,[12] namely, FMR, UBR, and MBR (for the latter see (Dalal 1988)) turn out to be in this class, base revisions that are not "fully rational" cannot be shown to be in this class.

8 SUMMARY AND OUTLOOK

The class of *prioritized base revision* (a form of syntax-based approaches to belief revision) and the class of *belief revision operations generated by epistemic relevance* were shown to be identical, removing partially the restriction of the *theory of epistemic change* that states of beliefs have to be modeled as deductively closed sets of sentences.

Further, epistemic relevance orderings on belief sets were shown to be a generalization of *epistemic entrenchment orderings* confirming the intuition spelled out in (Gärdenfors, Makinson 1988) that epistemic entrenchment is related to the notion of *database priorities* as introduced in (Fagin, Ullman, Vardi 1983).

Complementing the results in (Makinson, Gärdenfors 1991), we showed that concrete models of nonmonotonic reasoning, namely, ranked default theories (RDT's)—a generalization of Poole's logic without constraints (Poole 1988) and Brewka's level default theories (Brewka 1989; Brewka 1990)—turn out to be expressively equivalent to prioritized base revision in the case of finitary propositional logic. In addition, some answer to the question raised in (Makinson, Gärdenfors 1991) whether contraction plays a role in nonmonotonic logics was given. The theory formation approach *with* constraints was shown to be equivalent—under some reasonable assumptions—to *base contraction*. It is not possible to lift this result to belief contraction, however.

Finally, the computational complexity of different base revision operations was investigated—where the results apply by the above mentioned correspondences to

---

[12]This means base revisions such that the corresponding belief revision operations satisfy all the AGM postulates.

reasoning in default logics, as well.

The results confirm the intuition that unambiguous prioritized base revision is not harder but apparently less complex than general prioritized base revision (Doyle 1990, Sect. 3.2), which in turn is not harder than simple base revision. An interesting point is that model-based revision as proposed by Dalal is still NP-easy.

One of the open questions is, whether the correspondence between belief revision and the analyzed default logics holds for the infinite case as well. However, for this purpose the theory of epistemic change has to be extended so that belief sets cannot only be revised by sentences but also by other belief sets. Another interesting question in this context is whether there are natural postulates for belief revision operations that characterizes syntax-based approaches completely.

Finally, the observation that all "fully rational" revision operations analyzed in this paper share the property of being NP-easy suggests analyzing that class of revision operations in more detail in order to detect interesting and tractable special cases.

ACKNOWLEDGEMENT
I would like to thank Gerd Brewka, Jon Doyle, Peter Gärdenfors, David Makinson, and David McAllester for discussions about the subject of this paper and Gerd Brewka and David Makinson for comments on an earlier draft. In particular, I am grateful to David Makinson for his extensive and helpful comments on the final draft. All remaining flaws are mine, of course.

This work was supported by the German Ministry for Research and Technology BMFT under contract ITW 8901 8 as part of the WIP project.

REFERENCES

Alchourrón, C. E., Gärdenfors, P., Makinson, D. (1985): On the Logic of Theory Change: Partial Meet Contraction and Revision Functions, in: *Journal of Symbolic Logic* 50(2), 510–530.

Brachman, R. J. (1990): The Future of Knowledge Representation, in: *Proceedings of the 8th National Conference of the American Association for Artificial Intelligence*, Boston, Mass., 1082–1092.

Brewka, G. (1989): Preferred Subtheories: An Extended Logical Framework for Default Reasoning, in: *Proceedings of the 11th International Joint Conference on Artificial Intelligence*, Detroit, Mich., 1043–1048.

Brewka, G. (1990): *Nonmonotonic Reasoning: Logical Foundations of Commonsense*, Cambridge University Press, Cambridge, England. To appear.

Dalal, M. (1988): Investigations Into a Theory of Knowledge Base Revision: Preliminary Report, in: *Proceedings of the 7th National Conference of the American Association for Artificial Intelligence*, Saint Paul, Minn., 475–479.

Doyle, J. (1990): Rational Belief Revision. Presented at the *Third International Workshop on Nonmonotonic Reasoning*, Stanford Sierra Camp, Cal.

Fagin, R., Ullman, J. D., Vardi, M. Y. (1983): On the Semantics of Updates in Databases, in: *2nd ACM SIGACT-SIGMOD Symposium on Principles of Database Systems*, Atlanta, Ga., 352–365.

Gärdenfors, P., Makinson, D. (1988): Revision of Knowledge Systems Using Epistemic Entrenchment, in: Vardi, M. (ed.): *Proceedings of the 2nd Workshop on Theoretical Aspects of Reasoning about Knowledge*, Morgan Kaufmann, Los Altos, Cal.

Gärdenfors, P. (1988): *Knowledge in Flux—Modeling the Dynamics of Epistemic States*, MIT Press, Cambridge, Mass.

Gärdenfors, P. (1990): Belief Revision and Nonmonotonic Logic: Two Sides of the Same Coin?, in: Aiello, L. C. (ed.): *Proceedings of the 9th European Conference on Artificial Intelligence*, Stockholm, Sweden, 768–773.

Garey, M. R., Johnson, D. S. (1979): *Computers and Intractability—A Guide to the Theory of NP-Completeness*, Freeman, San Francisco, Cal.

Ginsberg, M. L., Smith, D. E. (1987): Reasoning About Action I: A Possible Worlds Approach, in: Brown, F. M. (ed.): *The Frame Problem in Artificial Intelligence: Proceedings of the 1987 Workshop*, Morgan Kaufmann, Los Altos, Cal., 233–258.

Ginsberg, M. L. (1986): Counterfactuals, in: *Artificial Intelligence* 30(1), 35–79.

Katsuno, H., Mendelzon, A. O. (1989): A Unified View of Propositional Knowledge Base Updates, in: *Proceedings of the 11th International Joint Conference on Artificial Intelligence*, Detroit, Mich., 1413–1419.

Katsuno, H., Mendelzon, A. O. (1991): On the Difference Between Updating a Knowledge Base and Revising It, in: Allen, J. A., Fikes, R, Sandewall, E. (eds.), *Principles of Knowledge Representation and Reasoning: Proceedings of the 2nd International Conference*, Cambridge, MA, 387–394.

Makinson, D., Gärdenfors, P. (1991): Relations between the Logic of Theory Change and Nonmonotonic Logic, in: Fuhrmann, A., Morreau, M. (eds.): *The Logic of Theory Change*, volume 465 of Lecture Notes in Computer Science, Springer-Verlag, Berlin, Germany.

McAllester, D. A. (1982): Reasoning Utility Package User's Manual, AI Memo 667, AI Laboratory, Massachusetts Institute of Technology, Cambridge, Mass.

Myers, K. L., Smith, D. E. (1988): The Persistence of Derived Information, in: *Proceedings of the 7th National Conference of the American Association for Artificial Intelligence*, Saint Paul, Minn., 496–500.

Nebel, B. (1989): A Knowledge Level Analysis of Belief Revision, in: Brachman, R. J., Levesque, H. J., Reiter, R. (eds.): *Principles of Knowledge Representation and Reasoning: Proceedings of the 1st International Conference*, Toronto, Ont., 301–311.

Nebel, B. (1990): *Reasoning and Revision in Hybrid Representation Systems*, volume 422 of Lecture Notes in Computer Science, Springer-Verlag, Berlin, Germany.

Newell, A. (1982): The Knowledge Level, in: *Artificial Intelligence* 18(1), 87–127.

Poole, D. (1988): A Logical Framework for Default Reasoning, in: *Artificial Intelligence* 36, 27–47.

Rao, A. S., Foo, N. Y. (1989): Formal Theories of Belief Revision, in: Brachman, R. J., Levesque, H. J., Reiter, R. (eds.): *Principles of Knowledge Representation and Reasoning: Proceedings of the 1st International Conference*, Toronto, Ont., 369–380.

Winslett, M. S. (1988): Reasoning about Action Using a Possible Models Approach, in: *Proceedings of the 7th National Conference of the American Association for Artificial Intelligence*, Saint Paul, Minn., 89–93.

Winslett, M. S. (1989): Sometimes Updates are Circumscription, in: *Proceedings of the 11th International Joint Conference on Artificial Intelligence*, Detroit, Mich., 859–863.

A Dyadic Representation of Belief

SVEN OVE HANSSON

Department of Philosophy, Uppsala University

1. INTRODUCTION

Studies of the dynamics of (rational) belief have reached a new degree of sophistication through the formal models developed in particular by Levi (1980) and by Alchourrón, Gärdenfors, and Makinson (the AGM model, Alchourrón et al. 1985 and Gärdenfors 1988). In these models, an individual's beliefs are represented by a set that is closed under logical consequence. The AGM model and its underlying assumptions have had a profound influence on the study of belief base updating in computer science. Although states of belief are, for obvious reasons, represented in computer applications by *finite* sets of sentences, it is common to demand that "results from an update must be independent of the syntax of the original K[nowledge] B[ase]" (Katsuno and Mendelzon 1989). In other words, operations on finite sets are treated more or less as shadows of operations on the (infinite) logical closures of these sets.

In this paper, a different representation of beliefs will be introduced. A formalized belief state will consist of an ordered pair $<K,Cn>$. K, or the *belief base*, is a set of expressions that is n o t necessarily closed under logical consequence. It represents the basic facts on which an individual grounds her beliefs. Cn is a *consequence operator*, such that $Cn(K)$ represents her beliefs (namely both the elements of K and the conclusions she draws from them).

This model is based on the intuition that some of our beliefs have no independent standing but arise only as inferences from our more basic beliefs, on which they are entirely dependent. For instance, I believe that Paris is the capital of France (α). I also believe that there is milk in my fridge (β). As a consequence of this, I believe that Paris is the capital of France if and only if there is milk in my fridge ($\alpha \leftrightarrow \beta$). This is, however, a merely derivative belief. Its derivative character will be clearly seen when I find reasons to replace my belief in β with belief in ¬β ("not β"). I cannot then, on pain of inconsistency, retain both my belief in α and my belief in α↔β. To retain the derived belief α↔β and reject the basic belief α is not, however, a serious possibility. (Cf. Doyle 1991, section 3.)

In the AGM framework, all beliefs have an equal status. Thus, when I open my fridge and find no milk, I make a choice between retaining α and retaining α↔β. Presumably, my selection function (γ) will only select sets that contain α rather than α↔β.

In a model with an open belief base (i.e., a belief base not closed under logical consequence) a derived belief disappears automatically when the belief base is changed so that it can no longer be derived. Thus, in our example, the option of retaining α↔β will not even arise. In this way, the selection function (or corresponding mechanism) will be relieved of most of the tasks that it has in the original AGM framework. Its remaining task is to solve conflicts between non-derivative beliefs. These are, it seems, the type of conflicts in which actual subjects may experience making an epistemic choice.

Inferential belief changes can be accounted for in the dyadic model by operations involving changes of the second member of the pair *<K,Cn>*. Thus, a distinction can be made between such changes in belief that depend on the acceptance or rejection of facts and such changes that depend on new inferences from previously known facts.

The usefulness of open belief bases in studies of belief change has been pointed out by Alchourrón and Makinson (1982, p. 21), Makinson (1987), Hansson (1989, 1991a, 1991b), Fuhrmann (1991), Nebel (1991), and others. However, dyadic models with variable consequence operators have not to my knowledge been proposed previously.

2. THE DYADIC MODEL

Logical consequence will be represented by consequence operators:

> *Definition 1*: Let *L* (the language) be a set of expressions that is closed under truth-functional operations.
>
> A *consequence operation* on *L* is a function from ℘(*L*) to ℘(*L*) such that:

(i) $A \subseteq Cn(A)$ (inclusion)

(ii)   If $A \subseteq B$, then $Cn(A) \subseteq Cn(B)$ (monotony)

(iii) $Cn(A) = Cn(Cn(A))$ (iteration)

It will be assumed that all consequence operators include classical truth-functional logic. Furthermore, the properties of deduction and compactness will be assumed to hold.

> *Postulate 1*: All consequence operations will be assumed to satisfy the following three properties:
>
> (iv)   If α can be derived from A by classical truth-functional logic, then $\alpha \in Cn(A)$. (supraclassicality)
>
> (v)   If $\beta \in Cn(A \cup \{\alpha\})$, then $(\alpha \rightarrow \beta) \in Cn(A)$. (deduction)
>
> (vi)   If $\alpha \in Cn(A)$, then $\alpha \in Cn(A')$ for some finite subset A' of A. (compactness)

Consistency will be defined as follows:

> *Definition 2*: A subset A of L is *Cn-consistent* if and only if there is no expression α such that both $\alpha \in Cn(A)$ and $\neg\alpha \in Cn(A)$.
>
> A set A is *Cn-implied* by a set B if and only if $A \subseteq Cn(B)$. An expression α is *Cn*-implied by B if and only if $\{\alpha\}$ is *Cn*-implied by B.

We now have the logical tools necessary to introduce the dyadic belief representation:

> *Definition 3*: A pair $<K,Cn>$ is a *(dyadic) belief state* in L if and only if $K \subseteq L$ and Cn is a consequence operation on L.
>
> A belief state $<K,Cn>$ is *consistent* if and only if K is *Cn*-consistent.
>
> A belief state $<K,Cn>$ is *closed* if and only if $K = Cn(K)$.
>
> In a belief state $<K,Cn>$, K is the *belief base*, Cn is the *consequence operator* and $Cn(K)$ is the *set of beliefs*.
>
> $|<K,Cn>|$ is an alternative notation for $Cn(K)$.

3. OPERATIONS ON THE BELIEF BASE

In the AGM framework, there are three types of theory change: expansion, contraction, and revision. In an expansion, "a new proposition, hopefully consistent with a given theory A, is set-theoretically added to A, and this expanded set is then closed under logical consequence." In a contraction, "a proposition x, which was earlier in a theory A, is rejected." A revision is a procedure in which "a proposition x, inconsistent with a given theory A, is added to A under the condition that the revised theory be consistent and closed under logical consequence." (Alchourrón et al. 1985, p. 510) These definitions can be straightforwardly extended to cover expansions, contractions and revisions by sets of propositions rather than by single propositions (Arguments for changes by non-singleton sets have been given by Hansson 1989 and Niederée 1991.)

According to the AGM definitions of revisions and expansions, a revision by a proposition that is consistent with the original belief state yields the same result as an expansion by that same proposition. Therefore, (consistent) expansion may be treated as a special case of revision.

In this section, analogous contraction and revision operators on dyadic belief states will be introduced, starting with contraction.[1]

We need a generalization of the notation $A \perp B$ (the set of maximal subsets of A not implying any element of B) to allow for variable consequence operators:

> *Definition 4*: $A \perp_{Cn} B$ is the set of all subsets C of A such that $B \cap Cn(C) = \varnothing$ and that there is no set C' such that $C \subset C' \subseteq A$ and $B \cap Cn(C') = \varnothing$.

The same type of selection functions will be used as in the AGM framework:

> *Definition 5*: Let K be a belief base. Then a *selection function for K* is a function γ from and to $\wp(K)$ such that for all $A \subseteq \wp(K)$:
> (i)   If A is non-empty, then $\gamma(A)$ is a non-empty subset of A, and
> (ii)   If A is empty, then $\gamma(A) = \{K\}$.

---

[1] For further developments of some of the themes of this section, see Hansson 1991c.

The dynamics of belief in which operations based on selection functions are performed on dyadic belief states will be called *dyadic partial meet dynamics (DPM dynamics)*. Two variants of DPM dynamics will be considered. One is *closed DPM dynamics*, in which all belief states are required to be closed. The other is *open DPM dynamics*, in which no such requirement is made.

The contraction operator will be defined as follows:

> *Definition 6*: In both open and closed DPM dynamics, an operator of *partial meet contraction* for a belief state $<K,Cn>$ is an operator $\sim_{\gamma_K}$ such that for all $A \subseteq L$:
>
> $<K,Cn> \sim_{\gamma_K} A = <\cap \gamma_K (K \perp_{Cn} A),Cn>$,
>
> where γ_K is a selection function for K.

It follows directly from definitions 4-6 that if $<K,Cn>$ is closed, then so is $<K,Cn> \sim_{\gamma_K} A$. This is the reason why the same operator of partial meet contraction can be used for both closed and open DPM dynamics.

The following conditions will be used for an axiomatic characterization of partial meet contraction:

> *Definition 7*: The following are properties of a contraction operator $\doteq$ for $<K,Cn>$. A and B are subsets of L, and $<K,Cn> \doteq A = <K',Cn'>$:
>
> ($\doteq 1$) $K' \subseteq K$ (inclusion)
>
> ($\doteq 2$) $Cn = Cn'$ (inferential constancy)
>
> ($\doteq 3$) If $A \cap I<\varnothing,Cn>I = \varnothing$, then $A \cap I<K',Cn>I = \varnothing$. (success)
>
> ($\doteq 4$) If $\alpha \in K \backslash K'$, then there is some K'' such that $K' \subseteq K'' \subseteq K$ and that $A \cap I<K'',Cn>I = \varnothing$ and $A \cap I<K'' \cup \{\alpha\},Cn>I \neq \varnothing$. (relevance)
>
> ($\doteq 5$) If it holds for all subsets K'' of K that $A \cap I<K'',Cn>I = \varnothing$ if and only if $B \cap I<K'',Cn>I = \varnothing$, then:
>
> $<K,Cn> \doteq A = <K,Cn> \doteq B$. (uniformity)

Properties ($\doteq 1$) and ($\doteq 3$) directly correspond to two of Gärdenfors's (1982, 1988) conditions for the AGM dynamics. Property ($\doteq 2$) makes sure that inferential beliefs are not changed by a rejection of facts.

Property ($\doteq$4) corresponds to the condition "usefulness of exclusion" for the AGM framework (Hansson 1989, definition 3.13). ($\doteq$4) ensures that if an element α is excluded from K when A is rejected from $<K,Cn>$, then α plays some role for the fact that K but not the contracted belief base Cn-implies some element of A. Whereas ($\doteq$3) blocks the non-exclusion of elements that there are strong reasons to exclude, ($\doteq$4) blocks the exclusion of elements that there is no good reason to exclude. (In the AGM framework, this role is played by the postulate of recovery.)

Property ($\doteq$5) ensures that the result of contracting A from $<K,Cn>$ depends only on which subsets of K Cn-imply some element of A. In other words, if all subsets of K that Cn-imply some element of A also Cn-imply some element of B, and vice versa, then $<K,Cn>\doteq A = <K,Cn>\doteq B$. E.g., it follows from ($\doteq$5) that $<\{\alpha,\beta\},Cn>\doteq\{\alpha,\beta\} = <\{\alpha,\beta\},Cn>\doteq\{\alpha\vee\beta\}$.

The following theorem provides a characterization of a contraction operator for a belief state $<K,Cn>$:

> *Theorem 1*: Let $<K,Cn>$ be a belief state. Then the operator $\doteq$ satisfies ($\doteq$1)-($\doteq$5)
> if and only if there is a selection function γ for K such that for all $A \subseteq L$:
> $$<K,Cn>\doteq A = <K,Cn>\sim_\gamma A.$$

The proofs of this and the following theorems are given in the Appendix.

Here as in the AGM framework, a selection function is specific for a particular set of beliefs. By clause (ii) of definition 5, it is not even possible for a selection function for K to be at the same time a selection function for K', where K and K' are different belief bases.

In a more general account of belief dynamics, changes starting from different belief bases should be included in one and the same contraction operator. To achieve this, *superselectors* will be introduced. A superselector is a function that assigns a selection function to each belief base.

> *Definition 8*: A *superselector* is a function that assigns to each subset K of L a
> selection function γ_K for K.

A superselector f is *unified* if and only if for all subsets K and K' of L: if $f(K) = \gamma K$, $f(K') = \gamma K'$, and A is a non-empty set of subsets of K and also a non-empty set of subsets of K', then $\cap \gamma K(A) = \cap \gamma K'(A)$.

In other words, the selection functions assigned by a unified superselector coincide for all arguments such that this is possible according to definition 5. A *unified DPM dynamics* is based on a unified superselector. Unified partial meet contraction is defined as follows:

Definition 9: In both open and closed DPM dynamics, an operator of *unified partial meet contraction* is an operator $\dot{-}$ that is based on a superselector f in the following way: For all subsets K and A of L, and all consequence operators Cn:
$$\langle K,Cn\rangle \dot{-} A = \langle \cap \gamma K(K \perp_{Cn} A), Cn\rangle,$$
where $\gamma K = f(K)$.

The following theorem provides an axiomatic characterization of unified partial meet contraction:

Theorem 2: An operator $\dot{-}$ is an operator of unified partial meet contraction if and only if it satisfies conditions $(\dot{-}1)$-$(\dot{-}5)$ and in addition the following condition:
$(\dot{-}6)$ If $A \cap Cn(\emptyset) = \emptyset$, and each element of Z Cn-implies an element of A, then:
$$\langle K,Cn\rangle \dot{-} A = \langle K \cup Z,Cn\rangle \dot{-} A. \text{ (redundancy)}$$

Property $(\dot{-}6)$ states that the prior addition to K of one or several elements that each Cn-imply an element of A does not change the outcome of contracting $\langle K,Cn\rangle$ by A. In other words, if α Cn-implies an element of A, then the presence of α in a belief base K does not influence which of the other elements of K will be retained. As an example, $(\dot{-}6)$ requires that $\langle\{\alpha\vee\beta,\neg\alpha\vee\beta,\beta\wedge\delta\},Cn\rangle \dot{-} \{\beta\} = \langle\{\alpha\vee\beta,\neg\alpha\vee\beta\},Cn\rangle \dot{-} \{\beta\}$. From a computational point of view, $(\dot{-}6)$ allows that the obvious non-members of the base of $\langle K,Cn\rangle \dot{-} A$ are dropped from K before the selection mechanism is applied to K.

For convenience, the following notation will be used:

Definition 10: In dynamics based on a unified superselector, the index of the selection function will be omitted. Thus $\cap \gamma(K \perp A)$ is an abbreviation of $\cap \gamma K(K \perp A)$.

Since γ will only be used preceded by $\cap$, the suppressed index is of no consequence except for empty arguments. This notation is somewhat inappropriate. It has been chosen in order to deviate as little as possible from the well-established AGM notation.

In order to facilitate the introduction of the revision operator, two further symbols will be introduced:

> *Definition 11*: Let A be a subset of L. Then $n(A)$ is defined as follows:
> (1) $n(\emptyset) = \bot$, where $\bot$ is a contradiction.
> (2)   If $A = \{\alpha_1,...\alpha_m\}$ for some $m \geq 1$, then:
> $n(A) = \neg\alpha_1 \vee \neg\alpha_2 ... \vee \neg\alpha_m$.

The revision operators for open and closed DPM dynamics will be as follows:

> *Definition 12*: The operator $\dotplus$ of *partial meet revision* for *open* DPM dynamics is:
> $<K,Cn> \dotplus A = <(\cap\gamma(K \perp_{Cn}\{n(A)\})) \cup A, Cn>$
> The operator $\dotplus$ of partial meet revision for *closed* DPM dynamics is:
> $<K,Cn> \dotplus A = <Cn((\cap\gamma(K \perp_{Cn}\{n(A)\})) \cup A), Cn>$

It should be observed that these revision operators are only defined for revisions by finite sets. (One possible way to extend the definition to revisions by infinite sets is to replace $\{n(A)\}$ by the set of all expressions that are either negations of elements of A or (finite) disjunctions of such negations. This generalization will not be pursued here.)

To see why the set $K \perp_{Cn}\{n(A)\}$ appears in the definition, let $A = \{\alpha_1,...\alpha_n\}$. We are looking for subsets K' of K such that $K' \cup A$ is Cn-consistent and that K' is inclusion-maximal with this property. $K' \cup \{\alpha_1,...\alpha_n\}$ is Cn-consistent if and only if $K' \cup \{\alpha_1 \wedge ... \alpha_n\}$ is Cn-consistent, i.e., if and only if $\neg(\alpha_1 \wedge ... \alpha_n) \notin Cn(K')$, i.e., if and only if $n(A) \notin Cn(K')$. $K \perp_{Cn}\{n(A)\}$ is the set of inclusion-maximal sets with this property.

The revision operator for open dynamics does not preserve logical closure of the belief base. This is the reason why different revision operators are needed for open and closed dynamics.

The usefulness in some contexts of open DPM dynamics, as compared to models that operate on closed belief sets, can be seen from Tichy's (1976) well-known example of the man and the hat. Gärdenfors made use of this example to illustrate the limits of the conservativity principle in the AGM framework (namely the principle that when changing beliefs in response to new evidence, one should retain as many of one's old beliefs as possible).

"Suppose that I accept as known in my present state K that there is a man who always wears his hat when it rains, but when it does not rain, he wears his hat completely at random (about 50% of the days). I also know that it rained today and that he wore his hat. Let A be the proposition 'It rained today' and B 'The man wears his hat'. Thus both A and B are accepted in K. What can we say about the state K^*_{-A}? [The belief set resulting from revising K to include $-A$.] According to (Cons) [the conservativity principle], B should still be accepted in K^*_{-A} because the addition of $-A$ does not conflict with B. However, I no longer have any reason for believing B, so intuitively neither B nor $-B$ should be accepted in K^*_{-A}.

> This example shows that the structure of belief sets is not rich enough to describe our intuitions concerning the minimality of revisions of epistemic states." (Gärdenfors 1988, p. 67)

In open DPM dynamics, this example can readily be accounted for. B ('the man wears his hat') is obviously not part of the belief base. It is a derived belief, originating from A ('it rained today') and a belief C ('on days when it rains the man wears his hat') such that $B \in Cn(\{A,C\})$. A conservative revision of the belief base to include $\neg A$ will yield a belief base that contains C but does not imply B.

In addition to contraction and revision, there is a third type of belief change that can operate on a belief base:

Definition 13: By a *reorganization* of a belief state $<K,Cn>$ is meant a change from $<K,Cn>$ to some $<K',Cn>$ such that $|<K,Cn>| = |<K',Cn>|$.

In closed dynamics, from $|<K,Cn>| = |<K',Cn>|$ follows $K = K'$. Therefore, non-trivial reorganization is only possible in open dynamics.

Tichy's hat-and-rain example can serve to illustrate reorganization in open DPM dynamics. Suppose that my original belief base includes A and C but not B. Then I include B in the belief base. The set of beliefs has not changed by this, so that from a static point of view no change has taken place. However, the new belief state differs from the old one from a dynamic point of view. In particular, the result of revising the new belief state to include $\neg A$ is different from the result of the same revision on the previous belief state.

There are at least two important types of dynamic equivalence between belief states:

> *Definition 14*: A belief state $<K,Cn>$ is *contraction-equivalent* with a belief set $<K',Cn'>$ if and only if for all A: $|<K,Cn> \doteq A| = |<K',Cn'> \doteq A|$.
>
> Furthermore, $<K,Cn>$ is *revision-equivalent* with $<K',Cn'>$ if and only if for all A: $|<K,Cn> \dotplus A| = |<K',Cn'> \dotplus A|$.

Contraction-equivalence requires identity of the consequence operators:

> *Theorem 3*: (1) In closed DPM dynamics, if the two belief states $<K,Cn>$ and $<K',Cn'>$ are contraction-equivalent, then $<K,Cn> = <K',Cn'>$, i.e., $K = K'$ and $Cn = Cn'$.
>
> (2) In open DPM dynamics, if the two belief states $<K,Cn>$ and $<K',Cn'>$ are contraction-equivalent, then $Cn = Cn'$.

The following definitions and theorem provide equivalence classes of contraction- and revision-equivalent belief states in open dynamics:

> *Definition 15*: Two belief states with the same consequence operator, $<K,Cn>$ and $<K',Cn>$, are *conjunctive variants* if and only if (1) each element of K' is either an element of K, a conjunction of elements of K, or an element of $Cn(\emptyset)$, and (2) each element of K is either an element of K', a conjunction of elements of K', or an element of $Cn(\emptyset)$.

As an example, $<\{\alpha\vee\neg\alpha,\beta,\delta\},Cn>$ and $<\{\beta,\delta,\beta\wedge\delta\},Cn>$ are conjunctive variants.

Definition 16: Let Cn be a consequence operator. Then two subsets S and T of $\wp(L)$ are Cn-*equivalent* if and only if for each element A of S there is an element B of T such that $Cn(A) = Cn(B)$, and vice versa.

A superselector f is Cn-*normal* if and only if for all subsets V and W of L with $f(V) = \gamma_V$ and $f(W) = \gamma_W$: If $S \subseteq \wp(V)$, $T \subseteq \wp(W)$ and S and T are Cn-equivalent, then $\gamma_V(S)$ and $\gamma_W(T)$ are Cn-equivalent.

DPM dynamics that is based on a Cn-normal superselector is called Cn-normal DPM dynamics.

In other words, a superselector is Cn-normal if and only if it preserves Cn-equivalence.

Theorem 4: If $<K,Cn>$ and $<K',Cn>$ are conjunctive variants, then the following holds in open Cn-normal unified DPM dynamics:
(1) $<K,Cn>$ and $<K',Cn>$ are contraction-equivalent.
(2) $<K,Cn>$ and $<K',Cn>$ are revision-equivalent.
(3)   For all A, $<K,Cn>\dot{-}A$ and $<K',Cn>\dot{-}A$ are conjunctive variants.
(4)   For all A, $<K,Cn>\dot{+}A$ and $<K',Cn>\dot{+}A$ are conjunctive variants.

Conjunctive variants in Cn-normal DPM dynamics are "equivalent forever" (Fagin et al 1986), i.e., they generate the same set of beliefs and will continue to do so after any series of updates. From a computational point of view, theorem 4 indicates that if an element of a database is a conjunction of two or more other elements, then it can be deleted without any consequences for future contractions and revisions.

4. RECOVERY PROPERTIES

A central part in the AGM framework is played by the *recovery* property of the partial meet contraction operator, i.e., by the fact that $K \subseteq Cn((K \dot{-} \alpha) \cup \{\alpha\})$. (Cf. Makinson 1987 and Hansson 1991b.) The more general framework that was introduced in section 3 makes it possible to reformulate recovery in terms of revision instead of set-theoretical union (expansion). Furthermore, the property can be straightforwardly generalized to cover operations by finite sets of expressions, not only single expressions.

Definition 17: The contraction operator $\dot{-}$ and the revision operator $\dot{+}$ satisfy $\dot{-}\dot{+}$ *recovery* if and only if for all consistent belief states $<K,Cn>$ and all finite sets A such that $A \subseteq K$:

$$<K,Cn> = (<K,Cn> \doteq A) \dotplus A \quad \text{(strong version)}$$
$$|<K,Cn>| = |(<K,Cn> \doteq A) \dotplus A| \quad \text{(weak version)}$$

$\doteq$ and $\dotplus$ satisfy (strong or weak) $\doteq\dotplus$ *recovery of independent sets* if and only if they satisfy (strong or weak) $\doteq\dotplus$ recovery for all A such that $A \cap Cn(K \backslash A) = \emptyset$.

As should be expected from the relationship with AGM dynamics, full $\doteq\dotplus$ recovery holds in closed DPM dynamics. In open DPM dynamics, this is not the case, but $\doteq\dotplus$ recovery of independent sets is satisfied.

> *Theorem 5*: (1) In closed unified DPM dynamics, strong $\doteq\dotplus$ recovery holds.
>
> (2) In open unified DPM dynamics, strong $\doteq\dotplus$ recovery holds for independent sets.
>
> (3) In open unified DPM dynamics, weak $\doteq\dotplus$ recovery does not hold in general.

The lack of full $\doteq\dotplus$ recovery in open DPM dynamics is not necessarily regrettable. There are cases in which this property appears to be contrary to intuition. As an example, suppose that I have read in a book about Cleopatra that she had both a son and a daughter. My set of beliefs therefore contains both α and β, where α denotes that Cleopatra had a son and β that she had a daughter. I then learn from a knowledgeable friend that the book is in fact a historical novel, and that much of it does not correspond to what actually happened. I therefore retract $\alpha \vee \beta$ from my set of beliefs, i.e., I do not any longer believe that Cleopatra had a child. Soon after that, however, I learn from a reliable source that Cleopatra had a child. It seems perfectly reasonable for me to add $\alpha \vee \beta$ to my set of beliefs without also reintroducing either α or β.[2]

Corresponding recovery properties can be defined in which contraction and revision take place in the reverse order:

> *Definition 18*: The contraction operator $\doteq$ and the revision operator $\dotplus$ satisfy $\dotplus\doteq$ *recovery* if and only if for all consistent belief states $<K,Cn>$, if A is a Cn-consistent set such that $A \cap Cn(K) = \emptyset$:
> $$<K,Cn> = (<K,Cn> \dotplus A) \doteq A \quad \text{(strong version)}$$
> $$|<K,Cn>| = |(<K,Cn> \dotplus A) \doteq A| \quad \text{(weak version)}$$

---

[2] This example is also discussed in Hansson (1991b)

$\doteq$ and $+$ satisfy (strong or weak) $+\doteq$ *recovery of independent sets* if and only if they satisfy (strong or weak) $+\doteq$ recovery for all A such that $n(A) \notin Cn(K)$.

Theorem 6: (1) In closed unified DPM dynamics, weak $+\doteq$ recovery does not hold even for independent sets.

(2) In open unified DPM dynamics, strong $+\doteq$ recovery holds for independent sets.

(3) In open unified DPM dynamics, weak $+\doteq$ recovery does not hold in general.

To see the implausibility of full $+\doteq$ recovery, let α denote the state of affairs that the physical universe is of finite size. I have always, as long as I can remember, believed α to be false, i.e. $\neg\alpha$ to be true. Then I read my first book on cosmology. There I learn that α is true. I revise my beliefs to include α instead of $\neg\alpha$. Soon after this, however, I read my second book on the subject. There I learn what I consider to be a good argument against α. I may then very well contract α from my set of beliefs without reintroducing $\neg\alpha$.

On the other hand, the weaker property of $+\doteq$ recovery of independent beliefs seems to be intuitively valid. Let α denote a belief (e.g., that Einstein was left-handed) that is not inferentially connected to any of my previous beliefs. It is reasonable to expect my beliefs to be unchanged after first acquiring and then rejecting α. By theorem 6, this is what happens in open dynamics. In closed dynamics, however, $+\doteq$ recovery does not hold even for independent sets. The reason for this is that in closed dynamics, the rejected belief α cannot be completely eradicated. It leaves behind itself a multitude of *disjunctive residues*, i.e., expressions of the form $\alpha\vee\beta$, where β is not an element of the contracted belief set. ("Either Einstein was left-handed or Paris has more than 4 million inhabitants", "Either Einstein was left-handed or protons are heavier than antiprotons", etc.) These disjunctive residues provide the mechanism behind the full $\doteq+$ recovery in closed dynamics. However, at the same time they make $+\doteq$ recovery impossible, even for independent sets. A choice of open rather than closed dynamics means to buy full $\doteq+$ recovery at the price of losing the much more plausible property of $+\doteq$ recovery for independent sets.

5. OPERATORS OF CONCLUSION

The process of drawing a conclusion will be represented by an extension of the consequence operator. The formal properties of such an extension must be defined so that the extended operator satisfies definition 1 and postulate 1. To prepare for the formal statement, the properties of an extension Cn' of to a consequence operator Cn will first be discussed in an informal manner.

Cn' must be a function from $\wp(L)$ to $\wp(L)$. To satisfy compactness, if $\beta \in Cn'(G)$, then there must be a finite subset G' of G such that $\beta \in Cn'(G')$. Let α' be the conjunction of elements of G'. Then by deduction, $\beta \in Cn'(G')$ if and only if $(\alpha' \rightarrow \beta) \in Cn'(\varnothing)$.

It follows that Cn' will be uniquely determined by $Cn'(\varnothing)$. (Cf. the lemma for theorem 3 in the appendix.) The set to be added to $Cn(\varnothing)$ will be called an *inferential core*. Thus, to amend Cn to make β a logical conclusion from $\{\alpha_1,... \alpha_n\}$, we will add the inferential core $\alpha_1 \wedge ... \alpha_n \rightarrow \beta$ to $Cn(\varnothing)$. This "addition" to Cn must be done in a manner that preserves truth-functionality:

> *Definition 19*: Let Cn be a consequence operator and S a subset of L. Then $Cn\#S$,
> the *truth-functional composition* of Cn and S, is defined as follows:
>   For all G, $(Cn\#S)(G) = Cn(S \cup G)$.

> *Theorem 7*: Let Cn be a consequence operator that satisfies postulate 1.
> Furthermore, let S be a subset of L. Then $Cn\#S$ is a consequence operator that
> satisfies postulate 1.

A *conclusion* will be defined to be an operation on the belief state that extends the consequence operator. Some conclusions are belief-contravening. When I realize that two of my beliefs imply an inconsistency, I will have to give up at least one of them. Therefore, the operation of conclusion will, just like contraction and revision, involve minimal change of the belief base.

The following notation will be used to facilitate the introduction of the conclusion operator:

Definition 20: Let M be a subset of L and Cn a consequence operation on L. Then $X \in c(M,Cn)$ if and only if (1) $X \subseteq M$ and X is Cn-consistent, and (2) there is no X' such that $X \subset X' \subseteq M$ and X' is Cn-consistent. $c(M,Cn)$ is the set of *maximal Cn-consistent subsets* of M.

It should be noted that $c(M,Cn) = M \perp_{Cn} \{\perp\}$.

The operation of conclusion can now be introduced as follows:

Definition 21: An operator $\oplus$ of *partial meet conclusion* in *open* DPM dynamics is an operator such that:

$$<K,Cn>\oplus S = <\cap\gamma_K c(K,Cn\#S),Cn\#S>$$

Partial meet conclusion in *closed* DPM dynamics is defined as follows:

$$<K,Cn>\oplus S = <(Cn\#S)(\cap\gamma_K c(K,Cn\#S)),Cn\#S>$$

As will be seen from the definition, in the limiting case when $\varnothing$ is $(Cn\#S)$-inconsistent, then $|<K,Cn>\oplus S|$ is inconsistent.

S is *belief-contravening* with respect to $<K,Cn>$ if and only K is $(Cn\#S)$-inconsistent. S is *inconsistent* with respect to $<K,Cn>$ if and only if $\varnothing$ is $(Cn\#S)$-inconsistent.

Partial meet conclusion can be axiomatically characterized in open DPM dynamics as follows:

Definition 22: The following are properties of an operation such that $<K,Cn>\oplus S = <K',Cn'>$.

($\oplus$1) $K' \subseteq K$ (inclusion)

($\oplus$2)   If $|<\varnothing,Cn\#S>|$ is consistent, then so is $|<K',Cn'>|$. (consistency)

($\oplus$3) $Cn' = Cn\#S$ (success)

($\oplus$4)   If $\alpha \in K \backslash K'$, then there is some K'' such that $K' \subseteq K'' \subseteq K$ and that $|<K'',Cn\#S>|$ is consistent and $|<K''\cup\{\alpha\},Cn\#S>|$ is inconsistent. (relevance)

($\oplus$5)   If for all $M \subseteq K$, M is $Cn\#S$-consistent if and only if it is $Cn\#T$-consistent, then $<K,Cn>\oplus S$ and $<K,Cn>\oplus T$ have the same belief base. (uniformity)

Theorem 8: Let <*K,Cn*> be a belief set. Then, in open DPM dynamics, the operator ⊕ satisfies (⊕1)-(⊕5) if and only if there is a selection function γ for *K* such that for all *S* ⊆ *L*:

$$<K,Cn>⊕S = <∩γc(K,Cn\#S),Cn\#S>$$

It might be questioned whether or not the conclusion operator is necessary when we already have a revision operator. When one wishes to make β a conclusion from α why not add α→β to *K* instead of "adding" it to *Cn*? However, as will be seen from the following theorem, operators of revision and conclusion can be interchangeable only in a static, not in a dynamic sense:

Theorem 9: In both open and closed dynamics: If *S* is not a subset of *Cn*(∅), and I<*K,Cn*>⊕*S*I = I<*K,Cn*>∔*A*I, then there is a subset *B* of *L* such that I(<*K,Cn*>⊕*S*)∸*B*I ≠ I(<*K,Cn*>∔*A*)∸*B*I.

The following theorem confirms that it matters in which order belief-contravening conclusions are drawn:

Theorem 10: The following obtains in open unified DPM dynamics:
(1)   If both I<*K,Cn\#S*>I and I<*K,Cn\#T*>I are consistent, then (<*K,Cn*>⊕*S*)⊕*T* = (<*K,Cn*>⊕*T*)⊕*S*.
(2)   It does not hold in general that (<*K,Cn*>⊕*S*)⊕*T* = (<*K,Cn*>⊕*T*)⊕*S*.

The non-trivial cases of part (1) of the theorem are, of course, cases in which I<*K,(Cn\#S)\#T*)>I is inconsistent.

A possible further development of the dyadic framework (not to be pursued here) is to introduce operations of logical retraction, i.e., operations that replace *Cn* by *Cn*', where *Cn*'(∅) ⊂ *Cn*(∅).

6. DISAGREEMENTS

The distinction that is made in the dyadic model between the belief base and the total set of beliefs makes it possible to categorize different kinds of differences in beliefs.

If you believe that Zeus is married to Hera whereas I have no opinion in the matter, then we have a difference in belief. However, this is only a mild form of difference, since our beliefs are not contradictory. If, on the other hand, you believe that Zeus is married to Hera whereas I believe him to be unmarried, then we have a contradictory difference in belief, or in other words: a disagreement.

To decide whether or not there is a disagreement, one must decide whether or not there is a contradiction. There may very well be a contradiction according to one consequence operator but not according to another.

>*Definition 23*: Let i_1 and i_2 be two individuals whose beliefs are represented by the consistent belief states $<K_1,Cn_1>$ and $<K_2,Cn_2>$, respectively.
>
>i_1 and i_2 have an *(overall) difference in belief* if and only if $|<K_1,Cn_1>| \neq |<K_2,Cn_2>|$
>
>There is an *(overall) disagreement for i_1* between i_1 and i_2 if and only if $|<K_1,Cn_1>|\cup|<K_2,Cn_2>|$ is Cn_1-inconsistent.
>
>Similarly, there is an (overall) disagreement for i_2 between i_1 and i_2 if and only if $|<K_1,Cn_1>|\cup|<K_2,Cn_2>|$ is Cn_2-inconsistent.

This definition makes explicit how two individuals may, even with full knowledge of each other's beliefs, have different opinions on whether they disagree or not.

A difference in belief may depend on differences in the belief bases, or in the inferences made, or in both.

>*Definition 24*: Let i_1, i_2, $<K_1,Cn_1>$, and $<K_2,Cn_2>$ be as in definition 23.
>
>There is a *factual difference* for i_1 if and only if $Cn_1(K_1) \neq Cn_1(K_2)$.
>
>There is a *factual disagreement* for i_1 if and only if $K_1\cup K_2$ is Cn_1-inconsistent.
>
>There is an *inferential difference* for i_1 if and only if $Cn_1(K_2) \neq Cn_2(K_2)$.
>
>There is an *inferential disagreement* for i_1 if and only if $Cn_1(K_2)\cup Cn_2(K_2)$ is Cn_1-inconsistent.

Thus a factual disagreement for i_1 means that i_1 considers the basic beliefs that i_2 has to be in contradiction with the basic beliefs that i_1 herself has. An inferential disagreement for i_1 means that i_1 considers the inferences that i_2 makes from i_2's own basic beliefs to contradict the inferences that should be made from these basic beliefs.

Some relations between overall, factual, and inferential disagreements are provided in the following theorem:

> *Theorem 11*: (1) If there is factual disagreement for i_1, then there is overall disagreement for i_1.
>
> (2) If there is inferential disagreement for i_1, then there is overall disagreement for i_1.
>
> (3) There may be an overall disagreement for i_1 without any factual disagreement for i_1 or any inferential disagreement for i_1.

The plausibility of part 3 of the theorem can be seen from the following example: Let α signify that there are puffins in Britain and β that there are auks in Britain. I am convinced that auks are a species of arctic birds. Therefore, I believe β to be false. I know nothing about puffins. In particular, I know nothing about their relationship to auks or about where – if anywhere – puffins can be found. The relevant part of my belief base is $\{\neg\beta\}$.

My friend the ornithologist, on the other hand, has seen puffins in Britain and is therefore convinced that α is true. He also knows that puffins are by definition auks (*Alcidae*) and therefore he has the inferential belief that α implies β. The relevant part of his belief base is $\{\alpha\}$.

From my point of view there is no factual disagreement, since the union of the two belief bases, $\{\alpha,\neg\beta\}$ is consistent by my inferential standards. Furthermore, there is no inferential disagreement, since I do not disagree with the ornithologist about how he makes inferences from his belief base. Still there is overall disagreement, since the ornithologist believes that β, whereas I believe that $\neg\beta$.

Definitions 23 and 24 can be straightforwardly extended to cover disagreements and differences in belief in groups with more than two members. Pairwise disagreement (etc.) does not necessarily coincide with disagreement (etc.) in the group as a whole. As an example, let $Cn = Cn_0\#\{\neg(\alpha\wedge\beta\wedge\gamma\wedge\delta)\}$, where Cn_0 is purely truth-functional. Furthermore, let i_1, i_2 and i_3 be three individuals whose belief states are, respectively,

$<\{\alpha,\beta\},Cn>$, $<\{\beta,\gamma\},Cn>$, and $<\{\gamma,\delta\},Cn>$. Then there is no pairwise overall disagreement for any of the three individuals, but in the group as a whole there is overall disagreement for each of its members.

7. CONCLUDING REMARKS

For a model of belief change to be useful in computational applications, it must allow for repeated belief changes. Given an initial belief state, it should be possible to compute not only the result of a single contraction or revision, but also the results of chains of such operations such as: first contract by α, then revise by $\alpha\vee\beta$, then contract by β, etc. In DPM dynamics, such repeated belief changes can readily be accounted for by means of superselectors. (Cf. Hansson 1991a on the problems that the representation of repeated belief change gives rise to in the original AGM framework.) In addition, DPM dynamics allows for representations of how new conclusions are drawn from previously known facts and of such changes (reorganizations) of belief states that change their dynamic but not their static properties.

Acknowledgement: I would like to thank Peter Gärdenfors, Sten Lindström and Wlodzimierz Rabinowicz for valuable comments on an earlier version of this paper.

APPENDIX: PROOFS

Proof of theorem 1: We will first show that $<K,Cn>\sim_\gamma A$, i.e., $<\cap\gamma(K\perp_{Cn}A),Cn>$, satisfies ($\doteq$1)-($\doteq$5).

($\doteq$1) and ($\doteq$2) follow directly from definition 6.

($\doteq$3): Suppose that $A\cap|<\emptyset,Cn>| = \emptyset$. Then $K\perp_{Cn}A$ is non-empty, and $\gamma(K\perp_{Cn}A)$ is a set of subsets of K, none of which Cn-implies any element of A. It follows by the monotony property of Cn that $\cap\gamma(K\perp_{Cn}A)$ does not Cn-imply any element of A, or in others words that $A\cap|<K',Cn>| = \emptyset$.

($\doteq$4): We will first consider the case when $K\perp_{Cn}A = \emptyset$. Then it follows from definition 5 that $\gamma(K\perp_{Cn}A) = \{K\}$. Then $K' = K$ so that ($\doteq$4) holds vacuously.

In the other case, when $K \perp_{Cn} A \neq \varnothing$, $\gamma(K \perp_{Cn} A)$ is a non-empty set of elements of $K \perp_{Cn} A$. For each $\alpha \in K \backslash K'$ there is an element B of $\gamma(K \perp_{Cn} A)$ such that $\alpha \notin B$. By definition 4, $Cn(B) \cap A = \varnothing$ and (because of the maximality property) $Cn(B \cup \{\alpha\}) \cap A \neq \varnothing$. Since $K' \subseteq B \subseteq K$, it can be concluded that ($\dot{-}4$) holds.

($\dot{-}5$): Let γ be a selection function for K. Furthermore, let A and B be two subsets of L such that for all subsets K'' of K: $A \cap |<K'',Cn>| = \varnothing$ if and only if $B \cap |<K'',Cn>| = \varnothing$. Then $K \perp_{Cn} A = K \perp_{Cn} B$. It follows that $<K,Cn> \dot{-} A = <\cap \gamma(K \perp_{Cn} A),Cn> = <\cap \gamma(K \perp_{Cn} B),Cn> = <K,Cn> \dot{-} B$.

For the *other direction of the theorem*, let $\dot{-}$ be an operation that satisfies ($\dot{-}1$)-($\dot{-}5$). By ($\dot{-}2$), $Cn = Cn'$. Thus, to show that $\dot{-}$ is a partial meet contraction we need to find a selection function γ for K such that $K' = \cap \gamma(K \perp_{Cn} A)$.

Let γ be defined as follows: (1) If $E \neq \varnothing$, and there is a subset F of L such that $E = K \perp_{Cn} F$, then $\gamma(E) = \{B \in E \mid K/_{Cn} F \subseteq B\}$, where $K/_{Cn} F$ is the belief base of $<K,Cn> \dot{-} F$. (2) Otherwise, $\gamma(E) = E$ if E is non-empty and $\gamma(E) = \{K\}$ if $E = \varnothing$.

We now have to prove, first that γ is a selection function for K, and secondly that $K' = \gamma(K \perp_{Cn} A)$.

For γ to be a selection function, it must be a function. To see that it is a function, let $E = K \perp_{Cn} F_1 = K \perp_{Cn} F_2$. Then it follows by ($\dot{-}5$) that $K/_{Cn} F_1 = K/_{Cn} F_2$.

To prove that γ is a selection function it is now sufficient to show that in the case referred to in clause (1) of the definition, $\gamma(E)$ is non-empty. From $E \neq \varnothing$ follows that $K \perp_{Cn} F$ is non-empty, so that $F \cap Cn(\varnothing) = \varnothing$. By ($\dot{-}3$) (success), we have $F \cap Cn(K/_{Cn} F) = \varnothing$. By ($\dot{-}1$) (inclusion), $K/_{Cn} F \subseteq K$. Thus there is at least one $B \in K \perp_{Cn} F$ such that $K/_{Cn} F \subseteq B$. It follows that $\gamma(K \perp_{Cn} F)$ is a non-empty subset of $K \perp_{Cn} F$. We may conclude that γ is a selection function for K.

We now have to prove that, for all $A \subseteq L$, $K' = \cap \gamma(K \perp_{Cn} A)$. It will be seen from the definition of γ that $K' \subseteq \cap \gamma(K \perp_{Cn} A)$. It remains to be shown that $\cap \gamma(K \perp_{Cn} A) \subseteq K'$. The proof of this will be divided into two cases, according to whether or not $A \cap Cn(K) = \varnothing$.

In the first case, $A \cap Cn(K) = \varnothing$. Then it follows by relevance ($\dot{-}4$) that $K \backslash K'$ is empty, so that $K \subseteq K'$. By inclusion ($\dot{-}1$), $K = K'$.

It also follows from $A \cap Cn(K) = \varnothing$ that $\cap \gamma(K \perp_{Cn} A) = K$, so that $\cap \gamma(K \perp_{Cn} A) = K'$ can be concluded.

In the remaining case, when $A \cap Cn(K) \neq \varnothing$, we will proceed by showing that if $\alpha \notin K'$, then $\alpha \notin \cap \gamma(K \perp_{Cn} A)$. Since this holds trivially for $\alpha \notin K$, we may assume that $\alpha \in K$.

By ($\dot{-}4$) (relevance), from $\alpha \in K$ and $\alpha \notin K'$ follows that there is a set B such that $K' \subseteq B \subseteq K$, that $A \cap Cn(B) = \varnothing$ and $A \cap Cn(B \cup \{\alpha\}) \neq \varnothing$. Then there is an element B'' of $K \perp_{Cn} A$ such that $B \subseteq B''$ and $\alpha \notin B''$. Since $K' \subseteq B \subseteq B''$, it follows by the definition of γ that $B'' \in \gamma(K \perp_{Cn} A)$. Since $\alpha \notin B''$ we can draw the desired conclusion that $\alpha \notin \cap \gamma(K \perp_{Cn} A)$.

Proof of theorem 2: For one direction of the theorem, let f be a unified superselector and $\dot{-}$ a contraction operator based on f. It was shown in theorem 1 that ($\dot{-}1$)-($\dot{-}5$) hold. We are going to show that ($\dot{-}6$) holds.

Suppose that $A \cap Cn(\varnothing) = \varnothing$, and that each element of Z Cn-implies an element of A. Then $(K \cup Z) \perp_{Cn} A = K \perp_{Cn} A \neq \varnothing$. Let $f(K) = \gamma_K$ and $f(K \cup Z) = \gamma_{K \cup Z}$. It follows, since $\cap \gamma_{K \cup Z}$ and $\cap \gamma_K$ coincide for non-empty arguments, that $\cap \gamma_{K \cup Z}((K \cup Z) \perp_{Cn} A) = \cap \gamma_K (K \perp_{Cn} A)$, so that $<K \cup Z, Cn> \dot{-} A = <K, Cn> \dot{-} A$.

For the *other direction of the theorem*, suppose that ($\dot{-}1$)-($\dot{-}6$) hold for a contraction operator $\dot{-}$. By theorem 1 follows from ($\dot{-}1$)-($\dot{-}5$) that for each subset K of L there is a selection function γ_K for K such that for all A, $<K, Cn> \dot{-} A = <\cap \gamma_K (K \perp_{Cn} A), Cn>$. Let f be the superselector such that for all K, $f(K) = \gamma_K$. We have to show that f is unified. To do this, it is sufficient to show that if A, B, E, and F are subsets of L, and $(A \perp_{Cn} E) = (B \perp_{Cn} F) \neq \varnothing$, then $\cap \gamma_A (A \perp_{Cn} E) = \cap \gamma_B (B \perp_{Cn} F)$.

Let $\phi \in A \backslash B$. Since ϕ is not an element of any element of $B \perp_{Cn} F$, it is not an element of any element of $A \perp_{Cn} E$. It follows that ϕ Cn-implies an element of E.

Thus each element of $A\backslash B$ Cn-implies some element of E. Then no element of $A\backslash B$ can be an element of any element of $A\perp_{Cn}E$. It can be concluded that $A\perp_{Cn}E = (A\cap B)\perp_{Cn}E$. Similarly, $B\perp_{Cn}F = (A\cap B)\perp_{Cn}F$. It follows that $(A\cap B)\perp_{Cn}E = (A\cap B)\perp_{Cn}F$.

By ($\div 6$) it follows that $\cap\gamma_A(A\perp_{Cn}E) = \cap\gamma_{A\cap B}((A\cap B)\perp_{Cn}E)$. Similarly, $\cap\gamma_B(B\perp_{Cn}F) = \cap\gamma_{A\cap B}((A\cap B)\perp_{Cn}F)$. From $(A\cap B)\perp_{Cn}E = (A\cap B)\perp_{Cn}F$ follows that $\cap\gamma_{A\cap B}((A\cap B)\perp_{Cn}E) = \cap\gamma_{A\cap B}((A\cap B)\perp_{Cn}F)$, so that we can conclude $\cap\gamma_A(A\perp_{Cn}E) = \cap\gamma_B(B\perp_{Cn}F)$.

Lemma for theorem 3: Let Cn and Cn' be two consequence operators that satisfy postulate 1. Then $Cn = Cn'$ if and only if $Cn(\varnothing) = Cn'(\varnothing)$

Proof of the lemma for theorem 3: We are going to show that if $Cn(\varnothing) = Cn'(\varnothing)$ then for all $B \subseteq L$ and $\phi \in L$, $\phi \in Cn(B)$ if and only if $\phi \in Cn'(B)$.

Suppose that $Cn(\varnothing) = Cn'(\varnothing)$ and that $\phi \in Cn(B)$. By compactness, there is a finite subset B'' of B such that $\phi \in Cn(B'')$. Let β be the conjunction of the elements of B''. Then $\phi \in Cn(\{\beta\})$. By the deduction property of Cn, $(\beta\rightarrow\phi) \in Cn(\varnothing)$. By $Cn(\varnothing) = Cn'(\varnothing)$ follows that $(\beta\rightarrow\phi) \in Cn'(\varnothing)$. By deduction, $\phi \in Cn'(\{\beta\})$, thus $\phi \in Cn'(B'')$. By the monotony property of Cn', $\phi \in Cn'(B)$.

Since this holds for all $\phi \in Cn(B)$, it follows that $Cn(B) \subseteq Cn'(B)$. By a symmetrical proof, $Cn'(B) \subseteq Cn(B)$, so that $Cn'(B) = Cn(B)$ can be concluded.

Proof of theorem 3: Let $<K,Cn>$ and $<K',Cn'>$ be two contraction-equivalent belief states.

(i) We are first going to prove that $Cn = Cn'$. This part of the proof is valid for both open and closed DPM dynamics.

Let τ be any truth-functional tautology. Then from $|<K,Cn>\dot{-}\{\tau\}| = |<K',Cn'>\dot{-}\{\tau\}|$ follows that $Cn(K) = Cn'(K')$.

Suppose that $Cn \neq Cn'$. Then, by the lemma, $Cn(\varnothing) \neq Cn'(\varnothing)$. Without loss of generality we may assume that there is a ϕ such that $\phi \in Cn(\varnothing)\backslash Cn'(\varnothing)$. From $\phi \in Cn(\varnothing)$ follows that $\phi \in Cn(K)$. Since $Cn(K) = Cn'(K')$ we have $\phi \in Cn'(K')$.

From $\phi \in Cn(\emptyset)$ follows that $|<K,Cn>\dot{-}\{\phi\}| = Cn(K)$. Thus $\phi \in |<K,Cn>\dot{-}\{\phi\}|$.

Since $\phi \notin Cn'(\emptyset)$, $\phi \notin |<K',Cn'>\dot{-}\{\phi\}|$. It follows that $|<K,Cn>\dot{-}\{\phi\}| \neq |<K',Cn'>\dot{-}\{\phi\}|$. From this contradiction we may conclude that $Cn = Cn'$.

(ii) The second part of the proof consists in showing, for closed dynamics, that $K = K'$. It was shown in part (i) of the proof that $Cn(K) = Cn'(K')$. By the logical closure of the belief bases, $K = K'$.

> *Lemma for theorem 4*: If A and B are conjunctive variants, and B and C are conjunctive variants, then A and C are conjunctive variants.

Proof of the lemma for theorem 4: Suppose that A and B are conjunctive variants and that B and C are conjunctive variants. Let γ be an element of C. Then there are three cases:

    (1) $\gamma \in Cn(\emptyset)$.
    (2) $\gamma \notin Cn(\emptyset)$ and $\gamma \in B$.
    (3) $\gamma \notin Cn(\emptyset)$ and γ is a conjunction of some $\beta_1,... \beta_n \in B$.

In case (2), since $\gamma \in B$, γ is either an element of A or a conjunction of elements of A.

In case (3), we may assume that none of $\beta_1,... \beta_n$ is an element of $Cn(\emptyset)$. Then each of $\beta_1,... \beta_n$ is either an element of A or a conjunction of elements of A. It follows that $\beta_1\wedge...\beta_n$ is a conjunction of elements of A, i.e., that γ is such a conjunction.

Thus all elements of C are either elements of A, conjunctions of elements of A or elements of $Cn(\emptyset)$. The symmetrical property for elements of A follows by a symmetrical proof.

Proof of theorem 4: Let $K'' = K \cup K'$. Then $<K,Cn>$ and $<K'',Cn>$ are conjunctive variants. Since $K \subseteq K''$, there are sets S and T such that each element of S is a conjunction of elements of K, each element of T is an element of $Cn(\emptyset)$ and $K'' = K \cup S \cup T$.

Part 1. We are first going to show that $<K,Cn>$ and $<K'',Cn>$ are contraction-equivalent. Let A be any subset of L.

If $A \cap Cn(\varnothing) \neq \varnothing$, then $|<K,Cn> \doteq A| = Cn(K)$ and $|<K'',Cn> \doteq A| = Cn(K'')$. Since $Cn(K) = Cn(K'')$ it then follows that $|<K,Cn> \doteq A| = |<K'',Cn> \doteq A|$.

In the other case, when $A \cap Cn(\varnothing) = \varnothing$, we have $|<K,Cn> \doteq A| = |<\cap\gamma(K\perp_{Cn}A),Cn>| = Cn(\cap\gamma(K\perp_{Cn}A))$, and similarly $|<K'',Cn> \doteq A| = Cn(\cap\gamma(K''\perp_{Cn}A))$.

Each element of $K''\perp_{Cn}A$ contains all elements of T. Furthermore, it contains an element σ of S if and only if it contains a subset of K that Cn-implies σ. It follows that $K''\perp_{Cn}A$ and $K\perp_{Cn}A$ are Cn-equivalent. Since Cn-normal dynamics was postulated, it follows that $\gamma(K''\perp_{Cn}A)$ and $\gamma(K\perp_{Cn}A)$ are Cn-equivalent. It also follows that $\cap\gamma(K\perp_{Cn}A) \subseteq \cap\gamma(K''\perp_{Cn}A)$ and that each element of $\cap\gamma(K''\perp_{Cn}A)$ that is not an element of $\cap\gamma(K\perp_{Cn}A)$ is either an element of $Cn(\varnothing)$ or a conjunction of elements of $\cap\gamma(K\perp_{Cn}A)$. Thus $Cn(\cap\gamma(K''\perp_{Cn}A)) = Cn(\cap\gamma(K\perp_{Cn}A))$.

We have now shown that $|<K,Cn> \doteq A| = |<K'',Cn> \doteq A|$. By a symmetrical proof, $|<K',Cn> \doteq A| = |<K'',Cn> \doteq A|$. Thus $|<K,Cn> \doteq A| = |<K',Cn> \doteq A|$.

Part 2: We are first going to show that $<K,Cn>$ and $<K'',Cn>$ are revision-equivalent. Let A be any subset of L.

By definition 12, $|<K,Cn> \dotplus A| = Cn((\cap\gamma(K\perp_{Cn}\{n(A)\}))\cup A)$ and $|<K'',Cn> \dotplus A| = Cn((\cap\gamma(K''\perp_{Cn}\{n(A)\}))\cup A)$. In the same way as in part 1 of the proof, it follows that $\cap\gamma(K\perp_{Cn}\{n(A)\}) \subseteq \cap\gamma(K''\perp_{Cn}\{n(A)\})$ and that each element of $\cap\gamma(K''\perp_{Cn}\{n(A)\})$ that is not an element of $\cap\gamma(K\perp_{Cn}\{n(A)\})$ is either an element of $Cn(\varnothing)$ or a conjunction of elements of $\cap\gamma(K\perp_{Cn}\{n(A)\})$. It follows that $Cn((\cap\gamma(K\perp_{Cn}\{n(A)\}))\cup A) = Cn((\cap\gamma(K''\perp_{Cn}\{n(A)\}))\cup A)$, i.e. that $|<K,Cn> \dotplus A| = |<K'',Cn> \dotplus A|$.

By a symmetrical proof, $|<K',Cn> \dotplus A| = |<K'',Cn> \dotplus A|$, thus $|<K,Cn> \dotplus A| = |<K',Cn> \dotplus A|$.

Part 3: We are first going to show that $|<K,Cn>\dot{-}A|$ and $|<K'',Cn>\dot{-}A|$ are conjunctive variants.

If $A \cap Cn(\emptyset) \neq \emptyset$, then $<K,Cn>\dot{-}A = <K,Cn>$ and $<K'',Cn>\dot{-}A = <K'',Cn>$. As we already know, $<K,Cn>$ and $<K'',Cn>$ are conjunctive variants.

If $A \cap Cn(\emptyset) = \emptyset$, then $<K,Cn>\dot{-}A = <\cap\gamma(K\perp_{Cn}A),Cn>$ and $<K'',Cn>\dot{-}A = <\cap\gamma(K''\perp_{Cn}A),Cn>$. It was shown in part 1 of the proof that $\cap\gamma(K\perp_{Cn}A) \subseteq \cap\gamma(K''\perp_{Cn}A)$ and that each element of $\cap\gamma(K''\perp_{Cn}A)$ that is not an element of $\cap\gamma(K\perp_{Cn}A)$ is either an element of $Cn(\emptyset)$ or a conjunction of elements of $\cap\gamma(K\perp_{Cn}A)$. It follows that $<\cap\gamma(K''\perp_{Cn}A),Cn>$ and $<\cap\gamma(K\perp_{Cn}A),Cn>$ are conjunctive variants.

Thus $<K,Cn>\dot{-}A$ and $<K'',Cn>\dot{-}A$ are conjunctive variants. By a symmetrical proof, so are $<K',Cn>\dot{-}A$ and $<K'',Cn>\dot{-}A$. By the lemma, $<K,Cn>\dot{-}A$ and $<K',Cn>\dot{-}A$ are conjunctive variants.

Part 4: We are first going to show that $<K,Cn>\dot{+}A$ and $<K'',Cn>\dot{+}A$ are conjunctive variants.

By definition 12, $<K,Cn>\dot{+}A = <(\cap\gamma(K\perp_{Cn}\{n(A)\}))\cup A,Cn>$ and $<K'',Cn>\dot{+}A = <(\cap\gamma(K''\perp_{Cn}\{n(A)\}))\cup A,Cn>$. It follows as in part 2 of the proof that $\cap\gamma(K\perp_{Cn}\{n(A)\}) \subseteq \cap\gamma(K''\perp_{Cn}\{n(A)\})$, and that each element of $\cap\gamma(K''\perp_{Cn}\{n(A)\})$ that is not an element of $\cap\gamma(K\perp_{Cn}\{n(A)\})$ is either an element of $Cn(\emptyset)$ or a conjunction of elements of $\cap\gamma(K\perp_{Cn}\{n(A)\})$. It may be concluded that $(\cap\gamma(K\perp_{Cn}\{n(A)\}))\cup A \subseteq (\cap\gamma(K''\perp_{Cn}\{n(A)\}))\cup A$ and that each element of $(\cap\gamma(K''\perp_{Cn}\{n(A)\}))\cup A$ that is not an element of $(\cap\gamma(K\perp_{Cn}\{n(A)\}))\cup A$ is either an element of $Cn(\emptyset)$ or a conjunction of elements of $(\cap\gamma(K\perp_{Cn}\{n(A)\}))\cup A$. It follows that $<(\cap\gamma(K\perp_{Cn}\{n(A)\}))\cup A,Cn>$ and $<(\cap\gamma(K''\perp_{Cn}\{n(A)\}))\cup A,Cn>$ are conjunctive variants.

Thus $<K,Cn>\dot{+}A$ and $<K'',Cn>\dot{+}A$ are conjunctive variants. By a symmetrical proof, so are $<K',Cn>\dot{+}A$ and $<K'',Cn>\dot{+}A$. By the lemma, $<K,Cn>\dot{+}A$ and $<K',Cn>\dot{+}A$ are conjunctive variants.

Proof of theorem 5: *Part 1*: Suppose that $A \subseteq K$.

We will first consider the case when $A \cap Cn(\varnothing) \neq \varnothing$. Then $<K,Cn> \dotdiv A = <K,Cn>$. Thus $(<K,Cn> \dotdiv A) \dotplus A = <K,Cn> \dotplus A = <Cn((\cap\gamma(K \bot_{Cn}\{n(A)\})) \cup A),Cn>$. From $A \subseteq K$ and the Cn-consistency of K follows that $n(A) \notin K$. It may be concluded that $Cn((\cap\gamma(K \bot_{Cn}\{n(A)\})) \cup A) = Cn(K \cup A) = Cn(K) = K$. Thus $(<K,Cn> \dotdiv A) \dotplus A = <K,Cn>$.

Next, we will consider the case when $A \cap Cn(\varnothing) = \varnothing$. From $A \subseteq K$ and the Cn-consistency of K follows that $n(A) \notin K$, and thus $n(A) \notin \cap\gamma(K \bot_{Cn}A)$. Thus, $(<K,Cn> \dotdiv A) \dotplus A = <\cap\gamma(K \bot_{Cn}A),Cn> \dotplus A = <Cn((\cap\gamma(K \bot_{Cn}A) \cup A)),Cn>$.

Since $\cap\gamma(K \bot_{Cn}A)$ and A are both subsets of K, and $Cn(K) = K$, we have $Cn((\cap\gamma(K \bot_{Cn}A)) \cup A) \subseteq K$. It remains to be shown that $K \subseteq Cn((\cap\gamma(K \bot_{Cn}A)) \cup A)$.

Let $\&A$ be the conjunction of all elements of A. We are going to show that for all $X \in \gamma(K \bot_{Cn}A)$ and all $\phi \in K$, $(\&A \rightarrow \phi) \in X$.

By the logical closure of K, $(\&A \rightarrow \phi) \in K$. Suppose that $(\&A \rightarrow \phi) \notin X$. Then by $X \in \gamma(K \bot_{Cn}A)$ follows that there is some $\alpha \in A$ such that $\alpha \in Cn(X \cup \{\&A \rightarrow \phi\})$. By the deduction property of Cn we have that $((\&A \rightarrow \phi) \rightarrow \alpha) \in X$. Since $(\&A \rightarrow \alpha) \in Cn(\varnothing)$, $(\&A \rightarrow \alpha) \in Cn(X)$. Since $\alpha \in Cn(\{(\&A \rightarrow \phi) \rightarrow \alpha, \&A \rightarrow \alpha\})$, we have $\alpha \in Cn(X)$ and, by the Cn-closure of X, $\alpha \in X$, contrary to $X \in \gamma(K \bot_{Cn}A)$. Thus $(\&A \rightarrow \phi) \in X$.

Thus it holds for all $\phi \in K$ and all $X \in \gamma(K \bot_{Cn}A)$ that $(\&A \rightarrow \phi) \in X$. Thus $(\&A \rightarrow \phi) \in \cap\gamma(K \bot_{Cn}A)$. It follows that $\phi \in Cn((\cap\gamma(K \bot_{Cn}A)) \cup A)$. Since this holds for all $\phi \in K$, we have $K \subseteq Cn((\cap\gamma(K \bot_{Cn}A)) \cup A)$, concluding this part of the proof.

Part 2: Let A, K and Cn be such that $A \subseteq K$ and $A \cap Cn(K \backslash A) = \varnothing$.

We have $<K,Cn> \dotdiv A = <\cap\gamma(K \bot_{Cn}A),Cn>$. From $A \cap Cn(K \backslash A) = \varnothing$ it follows that $A \cap Cn(\varnothing) = \varnothing$, so that $\gamma(K \bot_{Cn}A)$ is a non-empty set of subsets of $K \bot_{Cn}A$. We are first going to show that $K \backslash A \subseteq \cap\gamma(K \bot_{Cn}A)$. Suppose that $\chi \in K \backslash A$ and $\chi \notin \cap\gamma(K \bot_{Cn}A)$. Then there is a set $M \in (K \bot_{Cn}A)$ such that $\chi \notin M$. It follows that there is an element $\alpha \in A$ such that $\alpha \in Cn(M \cup \{\chi\})$. Then, by the deduction property of Cn, $(\chi \rightarrow \alpha) \in Cn(M)$. Since $M \subseteq K\backslash A$, it follows that $(\chi \rightarrow \alpha) \in Cn(K\backslash A)$. Since, by the assumption, $\chi \in K\backslash A$, we may conclude that $\alpha \in Cn(K\backslash A)$, so that $A \cap Cn(K\backslash A) \neq \varnothing$, contrary to the conditions. It follows that $K\backslash A \subseteq \cap\gamma(K \perp Cn A)$. Since we also have $\cap\gamma(K \perp Cn A) \subseteq K$ and $A \cap (\cap\gamma(K \perp Cn A)) = \varnothing$ we may conclude that $\cap\gamma(K \perp Cn A) = K\backslash A$.

Thus $<K,Cn> \dot{-} A = <K\backslash A, Cn>$, so that $(<K,Cn> \dot{-} A) \dot{+} A = <K\backslash A, Cn> \dot{+} A = <(\cap\gamma((K\backslash A) \perp Cn\{n(A)\})) \cup A, Cn>$. Since K is Cn-consistent and $A \subseteq K$, we have $n(A) \notin Cn(K)$. By the monotony of Cn, $n(A) \notin Cn(K\backslash A)$. It follows that $\cap\gamma((K\backslash A) \perp Cn\{n(A)\}) = K\backslash A$, so that $(<K,Cn> \dot{-} A) \dot{+} A = <K,Cn>$, concluding this part of the proof.

Part 3: Let $K = \{\alpha, \beta, \alpha\vee\beta\}$ and $A = \{\alpha\vee\beta\}$, and let Cn be purely truth-functional. Then $<K,Cn> \dot{-} A = <\varnothing, Cn>$ and $(<K,Cn> \dot{-} A) \dot{+} A = <\{\alpha\vee\beta\}, Cn>$.

Proof of theorem 6: *Part 1*: Let α and β be logically independent. Let Cn be purely truth-functional, and let $K = Cn(\{\beta\})$ and $A = \{\alpha\}$. Let γ be any selection function for K such that if $B \in \gamma((Cn(\{\alpha,\beta\})) \perp Cn\{\alpha\})$, then $(\alpha\leftrightarrow\beta) \in B$. (The existence of such a selection function follows from $(\alpha\leftrightarrow\beta) \in Cn(\{\alpha,\beta\})$.)

Then $<K,Cn> \dot{+} A = <Cn(\{\alpha,\beta\}), Cn>$, and furthermore $(<K,Cn> \dot{+} A) \dot{-} A = <\cap\gamma((Cn(\{\alpha,\beta\})) \perp Cn\{\alpha\}), Cn>$. By the property of γ just specified, if $B \in \gamma((Cn(\{\alpha,\beta\})) \perp Cn\{\alpha\})$, then $(\alpha\leftrightarrow\beta) \in B$. Then, since $\alpha \notin Cn(B)$, $\beta \notin B$. It may then be concluded that $\beta \notin \cap\gamma((Cn(\{\alpha,\beta\})) \perp Cn\{\alpha\})$. Thus we have $\beta \notin |<\cap\gamma((Cn(\{\alpha,\beta\})) \perp Cn\{\alpha\}), Cn>|$, i.e., $\beta \notin |(<K,Cn> \dot{+} A) \dot{-} A|$. Since $\beta \in |<K,Cn>|$, $|<K,Cn>| \neq |(<K,Cn> \dot{+} A) \dot{-} A|$.

Part 2: Let A and K be such that A is Cn-consistent, that $A \cap Cn(K) = \varnothing$ and that $n(A) \notin Cn(K)$.

Since $n(A) \notin Cn(K)$, we have:

$$
\begin{aligned}
(<K,Cn> \dot{+} A) \dot{-} A &= <(\cap\gamma(K \perp Cn\{n(A)\})) \cup A, Cn> \dot{-} A \\
&= <K \cup A, Cn> \dot{-} A \\
&= <\cap\gamma((K \cup A) \perp Cn A), Cn>.
\end{aligned}
$$

We have to prove that $\cap\gamma((K\cup A)\perp_{Cn}A) = K$. From $A\cap Cn(K) = \emptyset$ it follows that $A\cap Cn(\emptyset) = \emptyset$, so that $\gamma((K\cup A)\perp_{Cn}A$ is a non-empty set of subsets of $K\cup A$. Let $M \in (K\cup A)\perp_{Cn}A$. Clearly, $M \subseteq K$.

Suppose that $\phi \in K$ and $\phi \notin M$. Then by the maximality property of M there is an $\alpha \in A$ such that $\alpha \in Cn(M\cup\{\phi\})$, i.e., by deduction, $(\phi\rightarrow\alpha) \in Cn(M)$. By the monotony property for Cn and $M \subseteq K$ it follows that $(\phi\rightarrow\alpha) \in Cn(K)$. From this and $\phi \in K$ follows that $\alpha \in Cn(K)$, contrary to the condition that $A\cap Cn(K) = \emptyset$. It follows that if $\phi \in K$ then $\phi \in M$.

Thus $M = K$. Since this holds for all $M \in (K\cup A)\perp_{Cn}A$, we may conclude that $\cap\gamma((K\cup A)\perp_{Cn}A) = K$, so that $(<K,Cn>\dotplus A)\dotminus A = <K,Cn>$.

Part 3: Let $K = \{\neg\alpha\}$ and $A = \{\alpha\}$. Let Cn be purely truth-functional. Then $(<K,Cn>\dotplus A)\dotminus A = <\{\alpha\},Cn>\dotminus A = <\emptyset,Cn>$. We then have $\neg\alpha \in |<K,Cn>|$ and $\neg\alpha \notin |(<K,Cn>)\dotplus A)\dotminus A|$.

Proof of theorem 7: Property (i), inclusion: By the inclusion and monotony properties of Cn, $G \subseteq Cn(G)$ and $Cn(G) \subseteq Cn(S\cup G)$. Thus $G \subseteq (Cn\#S)(G)$.

Property (ii), monotony: Suppose that $G \subseteq H$. Then $S\cup G \subseteq S\cup H$ and, by the monotony of Cn, $Cn(S\cup G) \subseteq Cn(S\cup H)$, from which follows $(Cn\#S)(G) \subseteq (Cn\#S)(H)$.

Property (iii), iteration: One direction of iteration follows directly from inclusion. For the other direction of this property, let us suppose that $\chi \in (Cn\#S)((Cn\#S)(A))$. Then $\chi \in Cn(S\cup(Cn(S\cup A)))$. Since $S\cup Cn(S\cup A) = Cn(S\cup A)$ we have $\chi \in Cn(Cn(S\cup A))$ and thus, by the iteration property of Cn, $\chi \in Cn(S\cup A)$, i.e. $\chi \in (Cn\#S)(A)$.

Property (iv), supraclassicality: Suppose that χ can be derived from A by truth-functional logic. Then χ can be derived from $S\cup A$ by truth-functional logic, so that, by the supraclassicality of Cn, $\chi \in Cn(S\cup A)$, i.e. $\chi \in (Cn\#S)(A)$.

Property (v), deduction: $\psi \in (Cn\#S)(A\cup\{\chi\})$ holds if and only if $\psi \in Cn(S\cup A\cup\{\chi\})$, thus (by deduction for Cn) if and only if $(\chi\rightarrow\psi) \in Cn(S\cup A)$, if and only if $(\chi\rightarrow\psi) \in (Cn\#S)(A)$.

Property (vi), compactness: Suppose that $\chi \in (Cn\#S)(A)$. Then $\chi \in Cn(S \cup A)$. By compactness for Cn, there are finite subsets S' of S and A' of A such that $\chi \in Cn(S' \cup A')$. By monotony, $\chi \in Cn(S \cup A')$, i.e. $\chi \in (Cn\#S)(A')$.

Proof of theorem 8: For one direction of the proof, we have to prove that partial meet conclusion satisfies $(\oplus 1)$-$(\oplus 5)$.

$(\oplus 1)$: This follows directly from the definitions of γ and of c.

$(\oplus 2)$: By the definitions, when $\varnothing$ is $Cn\#S$-consistent, then $\gamma Kc(K,Cn\#S)$ is a set of $Cn\#S$-consistent sets. It follows by the monotony property of $Cn\#S$ that $\cap\gamma Kc(K,Cn\#S)$ is $Cn\#S$-consistent.

$(\oplus 3)$ follows directly from the definition.

$(\oplus 4)$: Suppose that $\chi \in K \backslash K'$. Then by the definition there is an element K'' of $c(K,Cn\#S)$ such that $\chi \notin K''$ and $K' \subseteq K'' \subseteq K$. By $K'' \in c(K,Cn\#S)$ follows that K'' is $Cn\#S$-consistent and that $K'' \cup \{\chi\}$ is $Cn\#S$-inconsistent.

$(\oplus 5)$: Suppose that for all $M \subseteq K$, M is $Cn\#S$-consistent if and only if it is $Cn\#T$-consistent. Then $c(K,Cn\#S) = c(K,Cn\#T)$, so that $\cap\gamma c(K,Cn\#S) = \cap\gamma c(K,Cn\#T)$, i.e., the bases of $<K,Cn>\oplus S$ and $<K,Cn>\oplus T$ are the same.

For the *other direction of the proof*, let $\oplus$ be an operation that satisfies $(\oplus 1)$-$(\oplus 5)$. We need to find a selection function γ such that $<K',Cn'> = <\cap\gamma c(K,Cn\#S),Cn\#S>$. Let γ be defined so that for all sets A:

(1)   If A is non-empty and there is a set T such that $A = c(K,Cn\#T)$, then $\gamma(A) = \{B \in A \mid (K/_{Cn}T) \subseteq B\}$, where $K/_{Cn}T$ is the belief base of $<K,Cn>\oplus T$.

(2)   In all other cases, $\gamma(A) = A$ if A is non-empty and $\gamma(A) = \{K\}$ if $A = \varnothing$.

We need to show (I) that γ is a selection function for K, and (II) that $<K',Cn'> = <\cap\gamma c(K,Cn\#S),Cn\#S>$.

(I) For γ to be a selection function, it must be a function. To show that it is a function, it is sufficient to show that if $c(K,Cn\#T_1) = c(K,Cn\#T_2)$, then $K/C_nT_1 = K/C_nT_2$. Suppose that $c(K,Cn\#T_1) = c(K,Cn\#T_2)$. Then by monotony, all subsets of K are $Cn\#T_1$-consistent if and only if they are $Cn\#T_2$-consistent. It follows by ($\oplus5$) (uniformity) that $K/C_nT_1 = K/C_nT_2$.

To show that γ is a selection function for K it is now sufficient to show that when $c(K,Cn\#S)$ is non-empty, then $\gamma c(K,Cn\#S)$ is a non-empty subset of $c(K,Cn\#S)$. When $c(K,Cn\#S)$ is non-empty, it follows by the monotony property of $Cn\#S$ that $\varnothing$ is $Cn\#S$-consistent. Then, by ($\oplus2$) (consistency), $|<K',Cn'>|$ is consistent, i.e., by ($\oplus3$) (success), K' is $Cn\#S$-consistent. Furthermore, by ($\oplus1$) (inclusion), $K' \subseteq K$. Thus K' is a $Cn\#S$-consistent subset of K. It follows that there is some B such that $K' \subseteq B$ and $B \in c(K,Cn\#S)$. Then, by clause (1) of the definition of γ, $\gamma c(K,Cn\#S)$ is a non-empty subset of $c(K,Cn\#S)$. We have shown that γ is a selection function for K.

(II) We now have to show that $<K',Cn'> = <\cap\gamma c(K,Cn\#S),Cn\#S>$. It follows by ($\oplus3$) (success) that $Cn' = Cn\#S$. It remains to be shown that $K' = \cap\gamma c(K,Cn\#S)$.

When $c(K,Cn\#S)$ is empty, it follows from clause (2) of the definition of γ that $\cap\gamma c(K,Cn\#S) = K$. Furthermore, when $c(K,Cn\#S)$ is empty, it follows by the monotony property of $Cn\#S$ that $\varnothing$ is $Cn\#S$-inconsistent. From ($\oplus4$) (relevance) then follows that $K' = K$. Thus $K' = \cap\gamma c(K,Cn\#S)$.

When $c(K,Cn\#S)$ is non-empty, it follows from clause (1) of the definition of γ that $K' \subseteq \cap\gamma c(K,Cn\#S)$. It remains to be shown that $\cap\gamma c(K,Cn\#S) \subseteq K'$. We will do this by showing that for all ϕ, if $\phi \notin K'$, then $\phi \notin \cap\gamma c(K,Cn\#S)$. This is trivial for $\phi \notin K$, so we may assume that $\phi \in K$.

From $\phi \in K$ and $\phi \notin K'$ follows by ($\oplus4$) (relevance) that there is some set B such that $K' \subseteq B \subseteq K$, B is $Cn\#S$-consistent and $B\cup\{\phi\}$ is $Cn\#S$-inconsistent. It follows that there is some maximal B' with this property. Then $K' \subseteq B' \subseteq K$ and $B' \in c(K,Cn\#S)$. By clause (1) of the definition of γ, $B' \in \gamma c(K,Cn\#S)$. From this and $\phi \notin B'$ follows $\phi \notin \cap\gamma c(K,Cn\#S)$. This completes the proof.

Proof of theorem 9: Let $<K_S,Cn\#S> = <K,Cn>\oplus S$ and $<K_A,Cn> = <K,Cn>\dot{+}A$. Then the theorem follows from $Cn \neq Cn\#S$ and theorem 3.

Proof of theorem 10: Part 1: If both $|<K,Cn\#S>|$ and $|<K,Cn\#T>|$ are consistent, then by the definition of $\oplus$:

$$(<K,Cn>\oplus S)\oplus T \quad = <K,Cn\#S>\oplus T$$
$$= <\cap\gamma c(K,(Cn\#S)\#T),(Cn\#S)\#T>$$
$$= <\cap\gamma c(K,(Cn\#T)\#S),(Cn\#T)\#S>$$
$$= <K,Cn\#T>\oplus S$$
$$= (<K,Cn>\oplus T)\oplus S.$$

Part 2: Let $K = \{\phi,\chi,\psi\}$ and let Cn be purely truth-functional. Furthermore, let $S = \{\neg(\phi\wedge\chi)\}$ and let $T = \{\neg(\chi\wedge\psi)\}$. Let γ be based on a priority ordering of ϕ, χ and ψ such that ϕ is always retained when that is possible and that χ is retained rather than ψ whenever a choice between χ and ψ does not influence whether or not ϕ can be retained. Then:

$$<K,Cn>\oplus S = <\{\phi,\psi\},Cn\#S>$$
$$(<K,Cn>\oplus S)\oplus T = <\{\phi,\psi\},Cn\#S\#T>$$
$$<K,Cn>\oplus T = <\{\phi,\chi\},Cn\#T>$$
$$(<K,Cn>\oplus T)\oplus S = <\{\phi\},Cn\#S\#T>$$

Proof of theorem 11: Part 1: It follows by monotony that if $K_1\cup K_2$ is Cn_1-inconsistent, then so is $Cn_1(K_1)\cup Cn_2(K_2)$.

Part 2: It follows by monotony that if $Cn_1(K_2)\cup Cn_2(K_2)$ is Cn_1-inconsistent, then so is $Cn_1(K_1)\cup Cn_2(K_2)$.

Part 3: Let α and β be logically independent, and let $K_1 = \{\neg\beta\}$ and $K_2 = \{\alpha\}$. Let Cn_1 be purely truth-functional, and let $Cn_2 = Cn_1\#\{\alpha\rightarrow\beta\}$.

Since $\{\neg\beta,\alpha,\alpha\rightarrow\beta\} \subseteq Cn_1(K_1)\cup Cn_2(K_2)$, $Cn_1(K_1)\cup Cn_2(K_2)$ is Cn_1-inconsistent, so that there is overall disagreement for i_1.

Since $K_1\cup K_2 = \{\alpha,\neg\beta\}$ is Cn_1-consistent, there is no factual disagreement for i_1.

$Cn_1(K_2) \cup Cn_2(K_2) = Cn_1(\{\alpha\}) \cup Cn_2(\{\alpha\}) = Cn_1(\{\alpha\}) \cup Cn_1(\{\alpha, \alpha \rightarrow \beta\})$ is a Cn_1-consistent set. It follows that there is no inferential disagreement for i_1.

REFERENCES

Alchourrón, CE and D Makinson (1982) "The logic of theory change: Contraction functions and their associated revision functions", *Theoria* 48:14-37.

Alchourrón, CE, P Gärdenfors and D Makinson (1985) "On the logic of theory change: Partial meet functions for contraction and revision", *Journal of Symbolic Logic* 50:510-530.

Doyle, J (1991) "Reason Maintenance and Belief Revision. Foundations vs. Coherence Theories", *this volume*.

Fagin, R, GM Kuper, JD Ullman, and MY Vardi (1986) "Updating logical databases", *Advances in Computing Research* 3:1-18.

Fuhrmann, A (1991) "Theory contraction through base contraction", *Journal of Philosophical Logic*, 20:175-203.

Gärdenfors, P (1982) "Rules for rational changes of belief", pp. 88-101 in T Pauli (ed) *<320311> Philosophical Essays dedicated to Lennart Åqvist on his fiftieth birthday*, Philosophical Studies no. 34, Uppsala.

Gärdenfors, P (1984) "Epistemic importance and minimal changes of belief", *Australasian Journal of Philosophy* 62:136-157.

Gärdenfors, P (1988) *Knowledge in Flux*.

Hansson, SO (1989) "New operators for theory change", *Theoria*, 55:114-132.

Hansson, SO (1991a) "In defense of base contraction", *Synthese*, in print.

Hansson, SO (1991b) "Belief contraction without recovery", *Studia Logica*, in print.

Hansson, SO (1991c) "Reversing the Levi Identity", *manuscript*.

Katsuno, H and AO Mendelzon (1989) "A Unified View of Propositional Knowledge Base Updates", *11th International Joint Conference on Artificial Intelligence*, Detroit.

Levi, I (1980) *The Enterprise of Knowledge*.

Makinson, D (1985) "How to give it up: A survey of some formal aspects of the logic of theory change", *Synthese* 62:347-363.

Makinson, D (1987) "On the status of the postulate of recovery in the logic of theory change", *Journal of Philosophical Logic* 16:383-394.

Nebel, B (1991) "Syntax-Based Approaches to Belief Revision", *this volume*.

Niederée, R (1991) "Multiple contraction. A further case against Gärdenfors' principle of recovery", pp. 322-334 in A Fuhrmann and M Mourreau, eds., *The Logic of Theory Change*, Lecture Notes in Artificial Intelligence 465, Springer Verlag, Berlin.

Tichy, P (1976) "A counterexample to the Stalnaker-Lewis analysis of counterfactuals", *Philosophical Studies* 29:271-273.

On the Logic of Theory Change:
More Maps Between Different Kinds of Contraction Function

HANS ROTT

Department of Philosophy, University of Konstanz,
P.O. Box 5560, D–7750 Konstanz, Germany

1 INTRODUCTION

There are many ways to change a theory. The tasks of adding a sentence to a theory and of retracting a sentence from a theory are non-trivial because they are usually constrained by at least three requirements. The result of a revision or contraction of a theory should again be a theory, i.e., closed under logical consequence, it should be consistent whenever possible, and it should not change the original theory beyond necessity. In the course of the Alchourrón-Gärdenfors-Makinson research programme, at least three different methods for constructing contractions of theories have been proposed. Among these the "safe contraction functions" of Alchourrón and Makinson (1985, 1986) have played as it were the role of an outsider. Gärdenfors and Makinson (1988, p. 88) for instance state that 'another, *quite different*, way of doing this [contracting and revising theories] was described by Alchourrón and Makinson (1985).' (Italics mine.) The aim of the present paper is to show that this is a miscasting.

In any case, it seems that the intuitions behind *safe contractions* are fundamentally different from those behind its rivals, the *partial meet contractions* of Alchourrón, Gärdenfors and Makinson (1985) and the *epistemic entrenchment contractions* of Gärdenfors and Makinson (1988). Whereas the latter notions are tailored especially to handling *theories* (as opposed to sets of sentences which are not closed under a given consequence operation), safe contraction by its very idea focusses on *minimal sets of premises* sufficient to derive a certain sentence. Thus safe contraction has a certain "foundationalist" appearance, in contrast to the "coherentist" guise of its competitors. (The distinction between foundationalist and coherentist approaches to belief revision is due to Harman 1986 and elaborated in Gärdenfors 1990. Also see Doyle 1992.)

Safe contractions appear to possess some definite epistemological advantages over both partial meet and epistemic entrenchment contractions. Like epistemic entrenchment contractions, they are based on some kind of relation between *sentences* and not on a relation between *sets of sentences*, as it is the case with partial meet contractions. This constitutes an intuitive disadvantage of the latter. In addition, safe contractions rest on relatively weak requirements for the relation involved, which seem to give them the intuitive priority over epistemic entrenchment contractions.

This neat picture of a clear separability of different concepts of theory contraction, however, contrasts with some results on the intertranslatability of the different contraction functions. On the one hand, Alchourrón and Makinson (1986) revealed a far-reaching parallel between safe contractions and partial meet contractions of various strength for the finite case, while Rott (1991a) investigated close connections between partial meet contractions and epistemic entrenchment contractions. On the other hand, Alchourrón and Makinson (1985) showed that a distinguished kind of safe contraction conforms to the so-called *Gärdenfors postulates* for theory contraction, while Gärdenfors and Makinson (1988) proved that every such contraction is representable as an epistemic entrenchment contraction. (The situation is depicted in figure 1.) So it is clear that safe contractions can *somehow* be linked with epistemic entrenchment contractions. But for a serious epistemological comparison of safe contractions and epistemic entrenchment contractions it will not do just to graft one complicated construction found in the literature onto another. What we need is a natural, transparent and direct connection between safe contractions and epistemic entrenchment contractions, one of which we can gain an easy intuitive grasp. In particular, it would be nice to find an explicit map between the relations on which the respective contraction operations are built on. This is what I shall try to supply in this paper. The interest of the following constructions does not lie in the bare demonstration that safe contractions and epistemic entrenchment contractions *can* be related but in the fact that the relevant transitions are plain and that the relations involved can be linked directly to each other even in the infinite case.

We presuppose a language with the usual n-ary propositional operators $\perp$ and $\top$ ($n = 0$), $\neg$ ($n=1$), $\vee$, $\wedge$ and $\rightarrow$ ($n=2$), and a logic (consequence operation) Cn which includes classical propositional logic, is compact and satisfies the deduction theorem. By L, we denote the set of sentences of the language at hand, and we usually write $M \vdash \phi$ for $\phi \in Cn(M)$, for every set of sentences M and every sentence ϕ. By K, we denote an arbitrary theory, i.e., a subset of L that is closed under Cn.

2 HIERARCHIES AND SAFE CONTRACTION FUNCTIONS

Some ten years ago, Peter Gärdenfors put up a set of eight postulates for theory contraction that have become widely known as the *Gärdenfors postulates*. We repeat

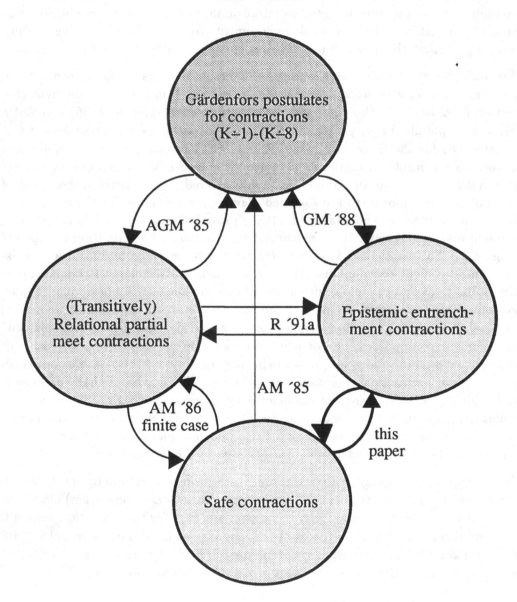

Figure 1: Three methods of explicit construction of Gärdenfors contractions

them in order to make this paper self-contained. $K \dot{-} \phi$ is to be read as 'the theory K contracted with respect to the sentence ϕ'.

(K$\dot{-}$1) $\quad K \dot{-} \phi$ is a theory

(K$\dot{-}$2) $\quad K \dot{-} \phi \subseteq K$

(K$\dot{-}$3) $\quad$ if $\phi \notin K$ then $K \dot{-} \phi = K$

(K$\dot{-}$4) $\quad$ if $\not\vdash \phi$, then $\phi \notin K \dot{-} \phi$

(K$\dot{-}$5) $\quad K \subseteq Cn((K \dot{-} \phi) \cup \{\phi\})$

(K$\dot{-}$6) $\quad$ if $\vdash \phi \leftrightarrow \psi$ then $K \dot{-} \phi = K \dot{-} \psi$

(K$\dot{-}$7) $\quad K \dot{-} \phi \cap K \dot{-} \psi \subseteq K \dot{-} \phi \wedge \psi$

(K$\dot{-}$8) $\quad$ if $\phi \notin K \dot{-} \phi \wedge \psi$ then $K \dot{-} \phi \wedge \psi \subseteq K \dot{-} \phi$

A brief account of the motivation of these postulates is given in Gärdenfors's (1992) introduction to this volume. Contraction functions $\dot{-}$ satisfying (K$\dot{-}$1) – (K$\dot{-}$8) are called *Gärdenfors contractions* in what follows. In this paper we are mainly interested in contractions that meet exactly the Gärdenfors postulates.

We take over the appropriate set of conditions for the hierarchies used in safe contractions from Alchourrón and Makinson (1985):

Definition 1. Let K be a set of sentences and $<_H$ be a relation over K. We call $<_H$ a *hierarchy over* K iff $<_H$ is *acyclic* over K, in the sense that for every $\phi_1, \ldots, \phi_n$ in K,

(H1) $\quad$ if $\phi_1 <_H \ldots <_H \phi_n$ then not $\phi_n <_H \phi_1$

A hierarchy $<_H$ is said to *continue up* $\vdash$ over K, or *continue down* $\vdash$ over K, iff for every ϕ, ψ, χ in K,

(H2$^\uparrow$) $\quad$ if $\phi <_H \psi$ and $\psi \vdash \chi$ then $\phi <_H \chi$, $\quad$ or respectively,

(H2$^\downarrow$) $\quad$ if $\phi <_H \psi$ and $\chi \vdash \phi$ then $\chi <_H \psi$

A hierarchy $<_H$ is said to be *regular* over K iff it continues up and down $\vdash$ over K. Finally, a hierarchy $<_H$ is said to be *virtually connected* over K iff for every ϕ, ψ, χ in K,

(H3) $\quad$ if $\phi <_H \psi$ then $\phi <_H \chi$ or $\chi <_H \psi$.

In the presence of (H1) and (H3), conditions (H2$^\downarrow$) and (H2$^\uparrow$) are equivalent. Virtual connectivity of $<_H$, which is sometimes called *negative transitivity* (the name derives from a contrapositive reading of (H3)), guarantees that the symmetric complement $\sim_H$ of a hierarchy $<_H$, defined by $\phi \sim_H \psi$ iff neither $\phi <_H \psi$ nor $\psi <_H \phi$, is an equivalence relation. According to Alchourrón and Makinson (1985, p. 411), the relation $\phi <_H \psi$ is to reflect the idea that ϕ is less "secure or reliable or plausible", or more "exposed" or "vulnerable" than ψ. The authors go on and define:

Definition 2. If K is a theory and $<_H$ is a hierarchy over K then the associated *safe contraction function* $\dot{-} = C(<_H)$ is given by $K \dot{-} \phi = Cn(K/\phi)$, where K/ϕ is the set of sentences in K that are $<_H$-*safe with respect to* ϕ in the sense that they are not $<_H$-minimal in any $\subseteq$-minimal subset M of K such that $M \vdash \phi$ (i.e., if a sentence ψ which is $<_H$-safe with respect to ϕ is in such an M, then there is a χ in M such that $\chi <_H \psi$).

To facilitate the notation below, we generalize hierarchies to relations between sets of sentences.

Definition 3. Let K be a set of sentences and $<_H$ be a hierarchy over K. Then the associated *generalized hierarchy* $<_{GH} = GH(<_H)$ *over* 2^L is given by

$$M <_{GH} N \quad \text{iff} \quad M \neq \emptyset \text{ and for every } \psi \text{ in } N \text{ there is}$$
$$\text{a } \phi \text{ in } M \text{ such that } \phi <_H \psi.$$

That is, a set of sentences N is safer (in terms of $<_{GH}$) than a set of sentences M if and only if M is non-empty and for every element ψ in N there is an element ϕ in M which is less safe (in terms of $<_H$) than ψ. Obviously, $\phi <_H \psi$ iff $\{\phi\} <_{GH} \{\psi\}$, for every ϕ and ψ in K. The relation $<_{GH}$ is not particularly well-behaved. It is not even irreflexive in general, as we may have $M <_{GH} M$ for an infinite set M. We can take down, however, some nice properties which will be useful later.

Lemma 1. Let K be a set of sentences and $<_H$ be a hierarchy over K. Then the generalized hierarchy $<_{GH} = GH(<_H)$ over 2^L satisfies

(GH1) if $M <_{GH} N$, $M \subseteq M'$ and $N' \subseteq N$, then $M' <_{GH} N'$

(GH2) if $M <_{GH} N_i$ for every i in an index set I, then $M <_{GH} \bigcup\{N_i : i \in I\}$

(GH3) if $M_1, \ldots, M_n$ are finite and $M_1 <_{GH} M_2$, $M_2 <_{GH} M_3$, $\ldots$, $M_{n-1} <_{GH} M_n$, then $M_n \not<_{GH} M_1$

(GH4) if M and N are finite, $M \cup N \neq \emptyset$ and $M \cup N <_{GH} M$, then $M \cup N \not<_{GH} N$

(GH5) $N <_{GH} M$ for every $N \neq \emptyset$ iff $M = \emptyset$.

If $<_H$ is transitive then $<_{GH}$ satisfies

(GH6) if $M <_{GH} N$ and $N <_{GH} P$ then $M <_{GH} P$

(GH7) if M is finite and $M \cup N <_{GH} M$ then $N <_{GH} M$

If $<_H$ is virtually connected then $<_{GH}$ satisfies

(GH8) if $M <_{GH} N$ then $M <_{GH} P$ or $P <_{GH} N$.

Proof. (GH1) and (GH2) are immediate from the definition of $<_{GH}$. — For (GH3), suppose for reductio that $M_1, \ldots, M_n$ are all finite and that $M_1 <_{GH} M_2 <_{GH} \cdots <_{GH} M_n <_{GH} M_1$. Letting $+$ denote addition modulo n, we have by definition for any $i = 1, \ldots, n$: $M_i \neq \emptyset$, and for every $\phi \in M_{i+1}$ there is a $\psi \in M_i$ such that $\psi <_H \phi$. Now take any $\phi \in M_1$. Then we find a $\psi \in M_n$ such that $\psi <_H \phi$. Again, we find a $\chi \in M_{n-1}$ such that $\chi <_H \psi$, and a $\rho \in M_{n-2}$ such that $\rho <_H \chi$, and so on, and so on. Since the M_i's form a cycle under $<_{GH}$, we can continue this process infinitely many times. But $\bigcup\{M_i : i = 1, \ldots, n\}$ is finite. So at least one element of $\bigcup\{M_i\}$ must be mentioned twice in the infinite descending chain $\ldots <_H \rho <_H \chi <_H \psi <_H \phi$, which therefore must contain a cycle. This contradicts (H1). — For (GH4), let M and N be finite, $M \cup N \neq \emptyset$ and suppose that $M \cup N <_{GH} M$ and $M \cup N <_{GH} N$. By definition, this means that for every ϕ in M and every ψ in N there is a χ in $M \cup N$ such that $\chi <_H \phi$ or $\chi <_H \psi$ respectively. This again generates an infinite descending $<_H$-chain in the finite set $M \cup N$, which is ruled out by (H1). — The direction from right to left in (GH5) is obvious. From left to right, suppose that $M \neq \emptyset$. Take some finite non-empty subset $M_0 \subseteq M$. By (GH3), $M_0 \not<_{GH} M_0$. Hence, by (GH1), $M_0 \not<_{GH} M$, so there is a non-empty set N such that $N \not<_{GH} M$. — Now let $<_H$ be transitive. Then (GH6), the transitivity of $<_{GH}$, is immediate by the definition of $<_{GH}$. — For (GH7), let M be finite and $M \cup N <_{GH} M$. By definition, this means that for every ϕ in M there is a ψ in $M \cup N$ such that $\psi <_H \phi$. Now take any $\phi \in M$. We have to show that there is a ψ in N such that $\psi <_H \phi$. By hypothesis, we know that there is such a ψ in $M \cup N$. If ψ is in N, we are ready. If ψ is in M then we know that there is a $\chi \in M \cup N$ such that $\chi <_H \psi$. We are ready, if $\chi \in N$, because, by the transitivity of $<_H$, $\chi <_H \phi$, as desired. If $\chi \in M$, then there is a $\rho \in M \cup N$ such that $\rho <_H \chi$, and so on, and so on. This process must lead us to some sentence in N, because there can be no infinite descending chain $\ldots <_H \rho <_H \chi <_H \psi <_H \phi$ in M, since M is finite and $<_H$ is acyclic. Using the transitivity of $<_H$, we conclude that this sentence in N is indeed smaller under $<_H$ than ϕ, as desired. — Now let $<_H$ be virtually connected. Suppose for reductio that, first, $M <_{GH} N$, secondly $M \not<_{GH} P$, and thirdly $P \not<_{GH} N$. That is, first, $M \neq \emptyset$ and for every $\phi \in N$ there is a $\psi \in M$ such that $\psi <_H \phi$. By $M \neq \emptyset$, the second supposition yields that there is a $\chi_1 \in P$ such that $\rho_1 \not<_H \chi_1$ for every $\rho_1 \in M$. Hence $P \neq \emptyset$. So the third supposition yields that there is a $\chi_2 \in N$ such that $\rho_2 \not<_H \chi_2$ for every $\rho_2 \in P$. Combining these two facts with the help of (H3), we get that there is a $\chi_2 \in N$ such that $\rho_1 \not<_H \chi_2$ for every $\rho_1 \in M$. But this just means that $M \not<_{GH} N$, contradicting the first supposition. $\square$

Corollary. (GH9) If M is finite, then $M \nless_{GH} M$

(GH10) if M and N are finite and $M <_{GH} N$, then $N \nless_{GH} M$

(GH11) if M is finite and $N \subseteq M$, then $N \nless_{GH} M$

(GH12) $M \neq \emptyset$ iff $M <_{GH} \emptyset$.

We see that $<_{GH}$ is well-behaved as long as we restrict our attention to finite sets of sentences. It should be noted that the proofs of lemma 1 and its corollary do not use the regularity conditions (H2$^\uparrow$) and (H2$^\downarrow$).

3 RELATIONS OF EPISTEMIC ENTRENCHMENT AND THEIR ASSOCIATED CONTRACTION FUNCTIONS

Relations of *epistemic entrenchment*, or simply *E-relations*, were introduced by Gärdenfors in 1984, but applied systematically only in Gärdenfors (1988) and Gärdenfors and Makinson (1988).

Definition 4. Let K be a theory and $\leq_E$ be a relation over L. We call $\leq_E$ an *E-relation with respect to K* iff for all sentences ϕ, ψ, χ,

(E1)   if $\phi \leq_E \psi$ and $\psi \leq_E \chi$ then $\phi \leq_E \chi$

(E2)   if $\phi \vdash \psi$ then $\phi \leq_E \psi$

(E3) $\phi \leq_E \phi \wedge \psi$ or $\psi \leq_E \phi \wedge \psi$

(E4)   if $\perp \notin K$, then $\phi \leq_E \rho$ for every ρ iff $\phi \notin K$

(E5)   if $\rho \leq_E \phi$ for every ρ then $\vdash \phi$.

A brief account of the motivation of these postulates is given in Gärdenfors's (1992) introduction to this volume. The correct interpretation of E-relations is very similar to that of hierarchies. I think that a good paraphrase of $\phi \leq_E \psi$ is 'Giving up ψ is not easier than giving up ϕ'.

E-relations are employed in the construction of contraction functions as follows (Gärdenfors and Makinson 1988):

Definition 5. If K is a theory and $\leq_E$ is an E-relation with respect to K then the associated *epistemic entrenchment contraction function* $\dot{-} = C(\leq_E)$ is given by $K \dot{-} \phi = K \cap \{\psi : \phi <_E \phi \vee \psi\}$ for sentences ϕ such that $\nvdash \phi$, and $K \dot{-} \phi = K$ for sentences ϕ such that $\vdash \phi$.

Notice that this definition makes reference to the asymmetric part $<_E\; =\; \leq_E -(\leq_E)^{-1}$ of an E-relation $\leq_E$. Conditions (E1) – (E3) imply the connectivity of $\leq_E$, i.e. that for every pair of sentences ϕ and ψ either $\phi \leq_E \psi$ or $\psi \leq_E \phi$. Hence we may identify $<_E$ with the converse complement of $\leq_E$: $\phi <_E \psi$ iff $\psi \not\leq_E \phi$. As we wish to work with strict relations later on, we restate, in a 1-1-fashion, the conditions (E1) – (E5) as conditions for the converse complement $<_E$ of $\leq_E$:

Definition 6. Let K be a theory and $<_E$ be a binary relation over L. We call $<_E$ a *(strict) E-relation with respect to K* iff for all sentences ϕ, ψ, χ,

(E1)   if $\phi <_E \psi$ then $\phi <_E \chi$ or $\chi <_E \psi$

(E2)   if $\psi \vdash \phi$ then $\phi \not<_E \psi$

(E3)   if $\phi \wedge \psi <_E \phi$ then $\phi \wedge \psi \not<_E \psi$

(E4)   if $\bot \notin K$, then $\rho <_E \phi$ for some ρ iff $\phi \in K$

(E5)   if $\not\vdash \phi$ then $\phi <_E \rho$ for some ρ.

A suitable reading of $\phi <_E \psi$ is 'Giving up ψ is harder than giving up ϕ'. For the rest of this paper, we will always refer to the strict versions when we speak of "E-relations" and when we mention (E1) – (E5).

Two further conditions of considerable interest are

(E3$^\uparrow$)   if $\phi <_E \psi$ and $\phi <_E \chi$ then $\phi <_E \psi \wedge \chi$

(E3$^\downarrow$)   if $\phi \wedge \psi <_E \psi$ then $\phi <_E \psi$

Like (E3), (E3$^\uparrow$) and (E3$^\downarrow$) are conditions concerning conjunctions — conjunctions which appear in (E3$^\uparrow$) on the right-hand side of $<_E$ and in (E3$^\downarrow$) on the left-hand side of $<_E$. It is easy to show that (E1) and (E3) jointly imply (E3$^\uparrow$) and (E3$^\downarrow$). On the other hand, (E3$^\uparrow$) implies (E3), provided that $<_E$ is irreflexive (which follows from (E2)). And (E3$^\downarrow$) implies (E3), provided that $<_E$ is asymmetric and we may substitute logical equivalents on the left of $<_E$. (E3$^\uparrow$) and (E3$^\downarrow$) are useful if one wants to get along without virtual connectivity, (E1). A generalized concept of epistemic entrenchment can be axiomatized by (H1), (H2$^\uparrow$), (H2$^\downarrow$), (E3$^\uparrow$) and (E3$^\downarrow$) (see Rott 1991c, where in fact (H1) is replaced by the weaker axiom $\top \not< \top$).

4 CONNECTING SAFE AND EPISTEMIC ENTRENCHMENT CONTRACTIONS

Clearly, constructing contractions with the help of relations of epistemic entrenchment is easier than with the help of hierarchies (contrast definition 2 with definition 5).

On the other hand, we shall presently verify that the requirements for hierarchies are weaker than those for E-relations. It would therefore be desirable to combine the "cheap" method of definition 5 with "cheap" relations of definition 1. However, it turns out that contractions thus constructed fail to satisfy the most basic rationality postulates (K$\dot{-}$1) and (K$\dot{-}$4), even if $<_H$ is regular and virtually connected:

Example 1. Consider the propositional language L with two atoms p and q, let Cn be classical propositional logic and $K = Cn(\{p\})$. Let $<_H$ be the regular and virtually connected hierarchy over K which is characterized by $p <_H p \lor q \sim_H p \lor \neg q <_H \top$ (where $\phi \sim_H \psi$ iff neither $\phi <_H \psi$ nor $\psi <_H \phi$). See figure 2. As every element

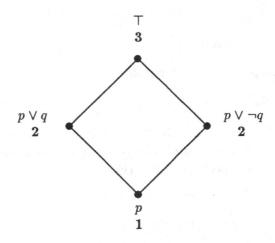

Figure 2: Example 1

of K is equivalent under Cn with one of the sentences mentioned, our information clearly determines a unique regular and virtually connected hierarchy $<_H$ over K. Applying definition 5, we get that $K\dot{-}p$ contains exactly those sentences in K which are equivalent to $p \lor q$, $p \lor \neg q$ or $\top$. But this means that $K\dot{-}p$ is not closed under Cn: it contains $p \lor q$ and $p \lor \neg q$ but does not contain p. And of course, closing under Cn would only make bad things worse, because we would then have p in $K\dot{-}p$ which is to say that the alleged contraction of K with respect to p does not remove p from K at all. (End of example.)

The rest of this paper is devoted to the demonstration that the concepts of safe contraction and epistemic entrenchment contraction are nevertheless equivalent in a very strong sense. Given an arbitrary hierarchy $<_H$ over K, the main problem is how to "conjure up" the conjunctiveness condition (E3) without disturbing anything else. The following definition will turn out appropriate.

Definition 7. Let K be a theory.

(i) If $<_E$ is an E-relation with respect to K, then the associated (regular and virtually connected) hierarchy $<_H = H(<_E)$ is just $<_E$ restricted to K.

(ii) If $<_H$ is a hierarchy over K and $<_{GH} = GH(<_H)$, then the associated E-relation $<_E = E(<_H)$ is given by

$$\phi <_E \psi \quad \text{iff} \quad \text{there is an } M \subseteq K \text{ such that } M \vdash \psi \text{ and}$$
$$\text{for every } N \subseteq K \text{ such that } N \vdash \phi, \, N <_{GH} M.$$

Part (i) of definition 7 is trivial. Part (ii) says that ψ is epistemically more firmly entrenched than ϕ iff there is a "proof set" M for ψ in K which is safer (in terms of $<_{GH}$) than every "proof set" N for ϕ in K. This is, I think, a very perspicuous way of extracting a notion of epistemic entrenchment from a given hierarchy.

Lemma 2. If $<_E = E(<_H)$, then $\phi <_E \psi$ iff there is a finite $M \subseteq K$ such that $M \vdash \psi$ and for every finite $N \subseteq K$ such that $N \vdash \phi$, $N <_{GH} M$.

Proof. From left to right: Assume that there is an $M \subseteq K$ such that $M \vdash \psi$ and $N <_{GH} M$ for every $N \subseteq K$ such that $N \vdash \phi$. By compactness, there is some finite $M_0 \subseteq M$ with $M_0 \vdash \psi$, and by (GH1), $N <_{GH} M_0$ for every $N \subseteq K$ such that $N \vdash \phi$, so in particular for every finite such N.
From right to left: Assume that there is a finite $M_0 \subseteq K$ such that $M_0 \vdash \psi$ and $N_0 <_{GH} M_0$ for every finite $N_0 \subseteq K$ such that $N_0 \vdash \phi$. Let $N \subseteq K$ be such that $N \vdash \phi$. By compactness, there is some finite subset $N_0 \subseteq N$ such that $N_0 \vdash \phi$. So $N_0 <_{GH} M_0$, so by (GH1) $N <_{GH} M_0$. $\square$

This lemma brings out the fact that we can restrict our attention to the finite subsets of K. The next lemma justifies part (i) of definition 7, and part (ii) for virtually connected hierarchies $<_H$. If $<_H$ is only transitive then definition 7(ii) leads to the generalized concept of epistemic entrenchment of Rott (1991c), and if $<_H$ is not even transitive then it involves a slight abuse of the term 'E-relation' which should not cause, however, any confusion.

Lemma 3. Let K be a theory, $<_H$ a hierarchy over K and $<_E$ an E-relation with respect to K. Then

(i) $H(<_E)$ is a regular and virtually connected hierarchy over K.

(ii) $E(<_H)$ is a regular hierarchy over K, and it satisfies (E2) – (E5) and (E3$^\uparrow$); if $<_H$ is transitive then $E(<_H)$ satisfies (E3$^\downarrow$); if $<_H$ is virtually connected then $E(<_H)$ satisfies (E1).

(iii) $E(H(<_E)) = \; <_E$.

Proof. (i) We write $<'_H$ for $H(<_E)$. For (H1), first observe that (E1) – (E3) give us asymmetry over K: If $\phi <'_H \psi$, then by (E1) either $\phi <'_H \phi \wedge \psi$ or $\phi \wedge \psi <'_H \psi$. But as the former is excluded by (E2), the latter must hold. Hence, by (E3), $\phi \wedge \psi \not<'_H \phi$. Moreover, by (E2), $\psi \not<'_H \phi \wedge \psi$, so by (E1) $\psi \not<'_H \phi$. Asymmetry and virtual connectivity, (E1), imply transitivity and acyclicity. — For (H2$^\downarrow$), let $\phi \vdash \psi$ and $\psi <'_H \chi$. From the former and (E2), we get $\psi \not<'_H \phi$, so by (E1) $\phi <'_H \chi$. — (H2$^\uparrow$) is proven similarly. — (H3) is (E1) restricted to K.

(ii) We write $<'_E$ for $E(<_H)$. For (H1), suppose that $\phi_1 <'_E \phi_2 <'_E \ldots <'_E \phi_n <'_E \phi_1$. Letting $+$ denote addition modulo n and applying lemma 2, we have for every $i = 1, \ldots, n$: there is a finite $M_{i+1} \subseteq K$ such that $M_{i+1} \vdash \phi_{i+1}$ and $N_i <_{GH} M_{i+1}$ for every finite $N_i \subseteq K$ such that $N_i \vdash \phi_i$. In particular, we have $M_1 <_{GH} M_2 <_{GH} \ldots <_{GH} M_n <_{GH} M_1$ for these finite M_i's, contradicting (GH3).

(H2$^\uparrow$) and (H2$^\downarrow$) follow immediately from the definition of $<'_E$.

For (E2), let $\psi \vdash \phi$ and suppose that $\phi <'_E \psi$. That is, by lemma 2, there exists a finite $M \subseteq K$ such that $M \vdash \psi$ and $N <_{GH} M$ for every finite $N \subseteq K$ such that $N \vdash \phi$. $M \not<_{GH} M$, by (GH9). But $M \vdash \phi$, contradicting our supposition.

For (E3), suppose for reductio that both $\phi \wedge \psi <'_E \phi$ and $\phi \wedge \psi <'_E \psi$. That is, by lemma 2, there is a finite $M \subseteq K$ such that $M \vdash \phi$ and $P <_{GH} M$ for every finite $P \subseteq K$ such that $P \vdash \phi \wedge \psi$, and there is a finite $N \subseteq K$ such that $N \vdash \psi$ and $P <_{GH} N$ for every finite $P \subseteq K$ such that $P \vdash \phi \wedge \psi$. By (GH4), $P <_{GH} M \cup N$ for every finite $P \subseteq K$ such that $P \vdash \phi \wedge \psi$. But $M \cup N$ is finite and $M \cup N \vdash \phi \wedge \psi$, so $M \cup N <_{GH} M \cup N$, contradicting (GH9).

For (E4), let $K \neq L$. First assume that there is a ψ such that $\psi <'_E \phi$. We need to show that $\phi \in K$. But $\psi <'_E \phi$ means in particular that there is a $M \subseteq K$ such that $M \vdash \phi$, so $\phi \in K$, because K is a theory. For the converse, assume that $\phi \in K$. Take any $\psi \notin K$. Such a ψ exists, since $K \neq L$, and $K \not\vdash \psi$, since K is a theory. We have $K \vdash \phi$, and trivially $N <_{GH} K$ for every $N \subseteq K$ such that $N \vdash \psi$, because there is no such N. So $\psi <'_E \phi$ by definition.

For (E5), let $\not\vdash \phi$. Then every N such that $N \vdash \phi$ is non-empty and, by (GH12), $N <_{GH} \emptyset$. Taking $\psi = \top$ and $M = \emptyset$, and we find that $\phi <'_E \top$ by definition.

For (E3$^\uparrow$), let $\phi <'_E \psi$ and $\phi <'_E \chi$. This means, by definition, that there is an $M \subseteq K$ and an $N \subseteq K$ such that $M \vdash \psi$, $N \vdash \chi$, and $P <_{GH} M$ and $P <_{GH} N$ for every $P \subseteq K$ such that $P \vdash \phi$. Thus $M \cup N \vdash \psi \wedge \chi$ and, by (GH2), $P <_{GH} M \cup N$ for every $P \subseteq K$ such that $P \vdash \phi$, so $\phi <'_E \psi \wedge \chi$ by definition.

Now let $<_H$ be transitive. Suppose that $\phi \wedge \psi <'_E \psi$. For (E3$^\downarrow$), we have to show that $\phi <'_E \psi$. By lemma 2, our supposition means that there is a finite $M \subseteq K$ such that $M \vdash \psi$ and $N <_{GH} M$ for every finite $N \subseteq K$ such that $N \vdash \phi \wedge \psi$. Now take this M. By lemma 2 again, we are ready if we can show that $P <_{GH} M$ for every finite $P \subseteq K$ such that $P \vdash \phi$. Take any such P. Clearly, $M \cup P \vdash \phi \wedge \psi$. So by supposition $M \cup P <_{GH} M$. Since M is finite, we get by (GH7) that $P <_{GH} M$, as desired.

Now let $<_H$ be virtually connected. Suppose that $\phi \not<'_E \chi$ and $\chi \not<'_E \psi$. For (E1), we have to show that $\phi \not<'_E \psi$. Our suppositions mean that, first, for every $M_1 \subseteq K$ such that $M_1 \vdash \chi$ there is an $N_1 \subseteq K$ such that $N_1 \vdash \phi$ and $N_1 \not<_{GH} M_1$, and, secondly, that for every $M_2 \subseteq K$ such that $M_2 \vdash \psi$ there is an $N_2 \subseteq K$ such that $N_2 \vdash \chi$ and $N_2 \not<_{GH} M_2$. Applying (GH8), we get that for every $M_2 \subseteq K$ such that $M_2 \vdash \psi$ there is an $N_1 \subseteq K$ such that $N_1 \vdash \phi$ and $N_1 \not<_{GH} M_2$. That is, by definition, $\phi \not<'_E \psi$.

(iii) Writing $<'_E$ for $E(H(<_E))$, we have to show that $\phi <'_E \psi$ iff $\phi <_E \psi$. By the definition of an E-relation and by parts (i) and (ii) of this lemma, both $<_E$ and $<'_E$ satisfy (E4) and (E5), so it suffices to consider the principal case where ϕ and ψ are from $K - Cn(\emptyset)$.

First suppose that $\phi <'_E \psi$. By definition, then, there is an $M \subseteq K$ such that $M \vdash \psi$ and for every $N \subseteq K$ such that $N \vdash \phi$ it holds that for every $\chi \in M$ there is a $\rho \in N$ such that $\rho <_E \chi$. Since $\phi \in K$, we can in particular take $N = \{\phi\}$. So there is an $M \subseteq K$ such that $M \vdash \psi$ and $\phi <_E \chi$ for every $\chi \in M$. By compactness, M can be chosen finite, so there are $\chi_1, \ldots, \chi_n$ such that $\chi_1 \wedge \ldots \wedge \chi_n \vdash \psi$ and $\phi <_E \chi_i$ for every $i = 1, \ldots, n$. By repeated application of (E3†), we get $\phi <_E \chi_1 \wedge \ldots \wedge \chi_n$, so $\phi <_E \psi$ by continuing up, as desired.

To show the converse, suppose that $\phi <_E \psi$. By continuing down, then, $\rho_1 \wedge \ldots \wedge \rho_m <_E \psi$ for all $\rho_1, \ldots, \rho_m$ such that $\rho_1 \wedge \ldots \wedge \rho_m \vdash \phi$. (Since $\not\vdash \phi$ by hypothesis, $m \geq 1$.) Hence $\rho_j <_E \psi$ for some $j = 1, \ldots, m$. For otherwise, if $\rho_j \not<_E \psi$ for every j, we would get, since either $\rho_1 \wedge \rho_2 \not<_E \rho_1$ or $\rho_1 \wedge \rho_2 \not<_E \rho_2$ by (E3), $\rho_1 \wedge \rho_2 \not<_E \psi$, by (E1), and by repeated application of (E3) and (E1) again, $\rho_1 \wedge \ldots \wedge \rho_m \not<_E \psi$, contradicting the above. By compactness, we then get that for every $N \subseteq K$ such that $N \vdash \phi$, it holds that $N \neq \emptyset$ and there is a $\rho \in N$ such that $\rho <_E \psi$. Now $\psi \in K$. So taking $M = \{\psi\}$, we find that there is an $M \subseteq K$ such that $M \vdash \psi$ and for every $N \subseteq K$ such that $N \vdash \phi$ it holds that $N \neq \emptyset$ and for every $\chi \in M$ there is a $\rho \in N$ such that $\rho <_E \chi$. That is, by definition, $\phi <'_E \psi$. $\square$

Part (i) of lemma 3 demonstrates that Alchourrón and Makinson's concept of a hierarchy is a weakening of the concept of a (strict) E-relation, even if the hierarchy is supposed to be regular and virtually connected. A similar weakening for non-strict relations of epistemic entrenchment is proposed in Schlechta (1991). Alternative weakenings which are closer to the spirit of the original ideas of Gärdenfors are discussed in Lindström and Rabinowicz (1991) and Rott (1991c). The "cheap" method of contraction construction as described in definition 5 cannot sensibly be based on

Schlechta's preference relations (as example 1 makes clear), nor — as far as I can see — on Lindström and Rabinowicz's epistemic entrenchment orderings, but it can be based on the generalized epistemic entrenchment relations introduced by myself.

Of course, we do not in general have $<_H \subseteq H(E(<_H))$, because $H(E(<_H))$ satisfies the conjunctiveness condition (E3) (within K) which is not required for $<_H$. More interestingly, we do not even get $H(E(<_H)) \subseteq <_H$, i.e., $E(<_H)$ restricted to K is not just the result of cancelling certain pairs from $<_H$ until it satisfies (E3). All this is true even when $<_H$ is regular and virtually connected:

Example 2. Consider the propositional language L with two atoms p and q, let Cn be classical propositional logic and $K = Cn(\{p, q\})$. Let $<_H$ be the regular and virtually connected hierarchy over K which is characterized by $p \wedge q \sim_H p <_H q \sim_H p \leftrightarrow q \sim_H \neg p \vee q <_H p \vee q \sim_H p \vee \neg q <_H \top$. See figure 3. As every element of K

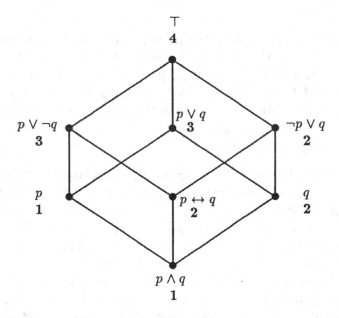

Figure 3: Example 2

is equivalent under Cn with one of the sentences mentioned, it is easy to check that our information in fact determines a unique regular and virtually connected hierarchy over K. We find that $M = \{p \vee q, p \vee \neg q\} \vdash p$ and that every N such that $N \vdash q$ includes a sentence ϕ with $\phi <_H p \vee q$ and $\phi <_H p \vee \neg q$, so that $N <_{GH} M$ for every proof set N of q in K. But this just means that $q <_E p$, although $p <_H q$ and thus $q \not<_H p$. Note that the only E-relation $<_E$ with $<_E \subseteq <_H$ is the trivial one which has $\phi \sim_E \psi$ for every ϕ and ψ in $K - Cn(\emptyset)$: by the definition of $<_H$, $\phi \not<_H p$, and, by (E3), either $p \sim_E (p \vee q) \wedge (p \vee \neg q) \not<_E p \vee q$ or $p \sim_E (p \vee q) \wedge (p \vee \neg q) \not<_E p \vee \neg q$, and again by the definition of $<_H$, $p \vee q \not<_H \psi$ and $p \vee \neg q \not<_H \psi$, so by repeated application of (E1), $\phi \not<_E \psi$. The proof of $\psi \not<_E \phi$ is analogous. This seems to indicate that there are interesting hierarchies $<_H$ which cannot be narrowed down to interesting E-relations by just cancelling pairs from $<_H$. (A method of this kind is employed in Schlechta (1991).) (End of example.)

What we do get, however, is that the safe contraction based on a hierarchy $<_H$ which continues down $\vdash$ over K and the epistemic entrenchment contraction based on an E-relation $<_E$ are equivalent, if $<_H$ and $<_E$ are related by either part (i) or part (ii) of definition 7. In fact, this is the main result of the present paper.

Theorem 4. Let K be a theory, $<_H$ a hierarchy which continues down $\vdash$ over K, and let $<_E$ an E-relation with respect to K. Then

(i) $\quad C(E(<_H)) = C(<_H)$.

(ii) $\quad C(H(<_E)) = C(<_E)$.

Proof. Let $<_{GH} = GH(<_H)$.

(i) If $\vdash \phi$, then both $C(E(<_H))$ and $C(<_H)$ yield $K \dot- \phi = K$. So let $\not\vdash \phi$. According to the contraction function $C(E(<_H))$, then, a sentence ψ is in $K \dot- \phi$ iff ψ is in K and there is an $M \subseteq K$ such that $M \vdash \phi \vee \psi$ and for every $N \subseteq K$ such that $N \vdash \phi$, $N <_{GH} M$. According to the contraction function $C(<_H)$, on the other hand, a sentence ψ from K is in $K \dot- \phi$ iff it is implied by a set M' of sentences which are $<_H$-safe with respect to ϕ. That is, iff there is an $M' \subseteq K$ such that $M' \vdash \psi$ and for any minimal set $N' \subseteq K$ such that $N' \vdash \phi$, it holds that $N' <_{GH} M' \cap N'$. What we have to show is that for every ψ in K the following two conditions are equivalent:

(∗) $\quad$ there is an $M \subseteq K$ such that $M \vdash \phi \vee \psi$ and for every $N \subseteq K$ such that $N \vdash \phi$, $N <_{GH} M$,

and

(∗∗) $\quad$ there is an $M' \subseteq K$ such that $M' \vdash \psi$ and for every $\subseteq$-minimal $N' \subseteq K$ such that $N' \vdash \phi$, $N' <_{GH} M' \cap N'$.

To show that (∗) implies (∗∗), take an M from (∗) and set $M' = M \cup \{\neg \phi \vee \psi\}$. Since K is a theory containing ψ, $M' \subseteq K$ and since $M \vdash \phi \vee \psi$, $M' \vdash \psi$. If $N' \subseteq K$ is a $\subseteq$-minimal set such that $N' \vdash \phi$, N' does not contain $\neg \phi \vee \psi$. For otherwise the deduction theorem for Cn tells us that $N' - \{\neg \phi \vee \psi\} \vdash (\neg \phi \vee \psi) \rightarrow \phi$, thus $N' - \{\neg \phi \vee \psi\} \vdash \phi$, contradicting the minimality of N'. Hence $N' \cap M' = N' \cap M$. It remains to show that $N' <_{GH} N' \cap M$. But (∗) tells us that $N' <_{GH} M$, so by (GH1) $N' <_{GH} N' \cap M$, as desired.

Conversely, to show that (∗∗) implies (∗), we take an M' from (∗∗). Obviously,

$M' \vdash \phi \vee \psi$. Take a subset M of M' such that M minimally implies $\phi \vee \psi$. Since Cn is assumed to be compact, M is finite. If $M = \emptyset$, then $(*)$ follows from the hypothesis $\nvdash \phi$ and (GH12). So let M be non-empty. Now take an $N \subseteq K$ such that $N \vdash \phi$. For $(*)$, we have to show that for every $\chi \in M$ there is a $\rho \in N$ such that $\rho <_H \chi$. Suppose for reductio that there is some $\chi \in M$ with $\rho \not<_H \chi$ for every $\rho \in N$.

We first note that $\neg\chi \nvdash \phi \vee \psi$. For $\neg\chi \vdash \phi \vee \psi$, taken together with $M \vdash \phi \vee \psi$, i.e. $(M - \{\chi\}) \cup \{\chi\} \vdash \phi \vee \psi$, would give us $M - \{\chi\} \vdash \phi \vee \psi$, by our assumption that Cn satisfies disjunction in the antecedent. But the latter condition contradicts the hypothesis that M minimally implies $\phi \vee \psi$. (The point of this paragraph is proven as lemma 3.1 in Alchourrón and Makinson 1985.)

Now consider the set $\neg\chi \vee N =_{df} \{\neg\chi \vee \rho : \rho \in N\}$. Since $N \subseteq K$ and K is a theory, $\neg\chi \vee N \subseteq K$. Since $N \vdash \phi$, clearly $\{\chi\} \cup (\neg\chi \vee N) \vdash \phi$. Now take some $N' \subseteq \{\chi\} \cup (\neg\chi \vee N) \subseteq K$ such that N' minimally implies ϕ. We find that $\chi \in N'$. For suppose for reductio that $\chi \notin N'$. Then $N' \subseteq \neg\chi \vee N$, and as $N' \vdash \phi$, we get that $\neg\chi \vee N \vdash \phi$. Thus $\neg\chi \vdash \phi$, contradicting the above observation that $\neg\chi \nvdash \phi \vee \psi$.

Considering the fact that N' minimally implies ϕ and that $\chi \in M' \cap N'$, we can apply $(**)$ in order to see that there is a $\sigma \in N'$ such that $\sigma <_H \chi$.

By the irreflexivity of $<_H$, which follows from the acyclicity condition (H1), $\sigma \neq \chi$. So σ is of the form $\neg\chi \vee \rho$ for some $\rho \in N$. Now $\rho \vdash \sigma$, so, by (H2$^{\downarrow}$), $\rho <_H \chi$, contradicting our supposition.

(ii) By lemma 3(i), $H(<_E)$ is a regular hierarchy over K, hence, by part (i) of this theorem, $C(H(<_E)) = C(E(H(<_E)))$. But as $<_E$ is an E-relation with respect to K, lemma 3(iii) gives us that $E(H(<_E)) =<_E$, so $C(E(H(<_E))) = C(<_E)$. In sum, we get $C(H(<_E)) = C(<_E)$. $\square$

It is remarkable that part (i) of the theorem uses only the fact that $<_H$ is irreflexive and continues down $\vdash$. Granted that safe contractions make sense in this case, it shows that "the cheap method" of contracting theories according to definition 5 is applicable even if $<_E =_{df} E(<_H)$ is no full E-relation. For in general, when $<_H$ is not virtually connected, $E(<_H)$ does not satisfy (E1). It is shown in Rott (1991c) that relations of "generalized epistemic entrenchment" are fit to be used for contractions constructed according to definition 5. However, $E(<_H)$ need not even satisfy the milder requirements of generalized epistemic entrenchment, unless $<_H$ is transitive.

As a consequence of theorem 4, we get the following *representation theorem* that generalizes a result implicit in Alchourrón and Makinson (1986) to the infinite case:

Corollary. Every contraction function $\dot{-}$ over K satisfying the Gärdenfors postulates (K$\dot{-}$1) – (K$\dot{-}$8) can be represented as a safe contraction function generated by a regular and virtually connected hierarchy $<_H$ over K, i.e., there is such a $<_H$ with

$\dot{-} = C(<_H)$.

Proof. Let $\dot{-}$ over K satisfy (K$\dot{-}$1) – (K$\dot{-}$8), and define $<_E$ by putting

$$\phi <_E \psi \text{ iff } \psi \in K \dot{-} \phi \wedge \psi \text{ and } \not\vdash \phi \wedge \psi.$$

It is shown in Gärdenfors and Makinson (1988, theorem 5 and corollary 6) that $<_E$ is an E-relation with respect to K and that $C(<_E) = \dot{-}$. Hence, by theorem 4(ii), $C(H(<_E)) = \dot{-}$, so the restriction $H(<_E)$ of $<_E$ to K is a suitable hierarchy. By Lemma 3(i), $H(<_E)$ is regular and virtually connected. $\square$

As another corollary, we get that safe contractions based on regular and transitive hierarchies satisfy a weaker form of (K$\dot{-}$8) which plays a central role in Rott (1991c).

Corollary. If $<_H$ is a regular and transitive hierarchy over K then $C(<_H)$ satisfies

(K$\dot{-}$8c) if $\psi \in K \dot{-} \phi \wedge \psi$ then $K \dot{-} \phi \wedge \psi \subseteq K \dot{-} \phi$.

Proof. Immediate from theorem 4(i) and lemma 3(ii) above and theorem 2(i) of Rott (1991c). $\square$

It is interesting to have a closer look at the finite case. A set of sentences K is *finite* (modulo Cn) iff the consequence relation Cn partitions it into finitely many equivalence classes. If K is a finite theory then it can be viewed as a finite Boolean algebra. Of special interest are the *top elements* or *co-atoms* of K, that is, the elements ϕ of K such that $\not\vdash \phi$ and for every $\psi \in Cn(\phi) \cap K$ either $\vdash \psi$ or $\vdash \phi \leftrightarrow \psi$. Let T_K be the set of all top elements of K and $T_K(\phi)$ be the set of all top elements of K that "cover" ϕ, i.e., $T_K(\phi) = T_K \cap Cn(\phi)$. When K is a finite theory, we can simplify the principal case in the construction of an E-relation out of a hierarchy (definition 7(ii)):

Lemma 5. Let K be a finite theory and $<_H$ be a regular hierarchy over K. Then the following two conditions are equivalent for any ϕ and ψ in $K - Cn(\emptyset)$:

(i) there is an $M \subseteq K$ such that $M \vdash \psi$ and for every $N \subseteq K$ such that $N \vdash \phi$, $N <_{GH} M$

(ii) $T_K(\phi) <_{GH} T_K(\psi)$.

Proof. Clearly, $T_K(\phi) \subseteq K$ and, by Boolean algebra, $T_K(\phi) \vdash \phi$, and likewise for ψ. — To show that (i) implies (ii), we note that (i) implies that there is an $M \subseteq K$ such that $M \vdash \psi$ and $T_K(\phi) <_{GH} M$. Now take an arbitrary $\chi \in T_K(\psi)$. We have to show that there is a $\rho \in T_K(\phi)$ such that $\rho <_H \chi$. Since $M \vdash \psi$ and χ is a top element of K implied by ψ, there must be a $\sigma \in M$ such that $\sigma \vdash \chi$. But by $T_K(\phi) <_{GH} M$, there is a $\rho \in T_K(\phi)$ such that $\rho <_H \sigma$, so by (H2$^\uparrow$), $\rho <_H \chi$, as desired. — To show that (ii) implies (i), we show that for every $N \subseteq K$ such that $N \vdash \phi$ it holds that

$N <_{GH} T_K(\psi)$. Let $N \subseteq K$ be such that $N \vdash \phi$ and let $\chi \in T_K(\psi)$. We have to show that there is a $\rho \in N$ such that $\rho <_H \chi$. By $T_K(\phi) <_{GH} T_K(\psi)$, there is a $\sigma \in T_K(\phi)$ such that $\sigma <_H \chi$. Since $N \vdash \phi$ and σ is a top element of K implied by ϕ, there is a $\rho \in N$ such that $\rho \vdash \sigma$. So by (H2$^\downarrow$), $\rho <_H \chi$, as desired. $\Box$

The results connecting hierarchies with E-relations enable us to derive some properties of safe contractions quite easily. Here is an example.

Corollary. Let K be a finite theory and $<_H$ and $<'_H$ be two regular hierarchies over K. Then $C(<_H) = C(<'_H)$ if and only if $<_H$ and $<'_H$ agree within T_K.

Proof. If $<_H$ and $<'_H$ agree within T_K then $GH(<_H)$ and $GH(<'_H)$ agree within the power set of T_K. But then, by definition 7(ii) and lemma 5, $E(<_H) = E(<'_H)$. Therefore, by theorem 4(i), $C(<_H) = C(E(<_H)) = C(E(<'_H)) = C(<'_H)$. — Conversely, suppose that $C(<_H) = C(<'_H)$. Hence, by theorem 4(i), $C(E(<_H)) = C(E(<'_H))$, and also, by corollary 6 of Gärdenfors and Makinson (1988), $E(<_H) = E(C(E(<_H))) = E(C(E(<'_H))) = E(<'_H)$. In particular, $E(<_H)$ and $E(<'_H)$ agree within T_K. But as for any ϕ and ψ in T_K, $T_K(\phi) = \{\phi\}$ and $T_K(\psi) = \{\psi\}$, we can see from definition 7(ii) and lemma 5 that within T_K, $<_H$ agrees with $E(<_H)$ and $<'_H$ agrees with $E(<'_H)$. Hence $<_H$ and $<'_H$ agree within T_K. $\Box$

As David Makinson (personal communication) has pointed out, this corollary is also an immediate consequence of a lemma of Alchourrón and Makinson (1986, p. 192).

5 CONCLUSION

The foregoing arguments show, I believe, that safe contractions and epistemic entrenchment contractions are equivalent in a very strict sense. We can transform every virtually connected hierarchy $<_H$ into an E-relation by a very perspicuous construction, and conversely we already have a (regular and virtually connected) hierarchy if we have an E-relation $<_E$. The contraction functions that ensue are identical, if $<_H$ continues down $\vdash$ over K. It may also be worthwhile to remark that the interpretations of hierarchies and E-relations are similar. The notion of 'epistemic entrenchment', formerly called 'epistemic importance', must not be taken for a relation reflecting some kind of 'informational content' or 'inferential fruitfulness'.

Given a theory K and a contraction function $\dot{-}$ over K which satisfies the Gärdenfors postulates, there are in general many (regular and virtually connected) hierarchies $<_H$ over K that lead to this contraction function in the sense that $\dot{-} = C(<_H)$. But there is only one E-relation $<_E$ suitable for $\dot{-}$, and $<_E$ can be read off directly from the contraction behaviour: $\phi <_E \psi$ if and only if $\psi \in K \dot{-} \phi \wedge \psi$ and $\phi \notin K \dot{-} \phi \wedge \psi$ (cf. Gärdenfors and Makinson 1988, Rott 1991c). It is plausible to consider $H(<_E)$

as the canonical hierarchy for a given Gärdenfors contraction function $\dot{-}$, namely the hierarchy $<_H$ for which either $\phi \wedge \psi \not<_H \phi$ or $\phi \wedge \psi \not<_H \psi$, for all sentences ϕ and ψ. There is no reason to object to postulating epistemic entrenchment relations that satisfy the conjunctiveness condition (E3), because all the regular and virtually connected hierarchies $<_H$ for which $\dot{-} = C(<_H)$ give rise to one and the same E-relation $<_E = E(<_H) = E(C(<_H))$.

In the finite case, the only information needed is, both for safe and epistemic entrenchment contractions, the ordering over the set T_K of top elements of K. And again, given such an ordering, we can in general find many hierarchies but only one single E-relation conforming to this ordering. That E-relation is, so to speak, the most well-behaved hierarchy one can think of, and as such it might be called the canonical hierarchy corresponding to a prefixed ordering of T_K.

It should be noted that the gain from the results of this paper is philosophical rather than computational. Philosophically, people applying epistemic entrenchment are freed from the need of justifying (E3) (and (E4) and (E5)). But in order to perform theory contractions, the "cheap" method of definition 5 does not save us any work if all we are given is a hierarchy. This is because establishing an appropriate E-relation via definition 7(ii) requires at least as much computational effort as the contraction construction used in definition 2. In the case where K is finite and we have information about the relationships in T_K, both methods, safe contraction and epistemic entrenchment contraction, are equally simple.

Summing up: If we are interested in Gärdenfors contraction functions, there is no reason why contraction functions based on relations of epistemic entrenchment should be epistemologically more questionable than safe contraction functions based on hierarchies. Up to now, it is not entirely clear how to weaken or strengthen (E1) – (E5) in such a way that certain interesting properties of contraction functions get lost or added. First steps in this direction are taken in Rott (1991c). Furthermore, it would be desirable to describe the application of E-relations to sets of sentences that are not closed under logical consequence. About that nothing is known as yet. But *if* we are concerned with theory change along the Gärdenfors lines, then postulating the existence of epistemic entrenchment relations appears to be just as safe as postulating hierarchies. Everybody who is willing to accept safe contractions should be willing to accept epistemic entrenchment contractions as well. In my opinion, the maps proposed in this paper remove some of the more fundamental reservations against any undertaking which is, like e.g. Rott (1991b), based on relations of epistemic entrenchment.

ACKNOWLEDGEMENT

This contribution is a substantially revised version of a paper with the same title distributed as technical report AIMS No. 03-90 of the Institut für Maschinelle Sprachverarbeitung at the University of Stuttgart. I would like to thank David Makinson for stimulating me to write the paper and for useful comments on an earlier version of it.

REFERENCES

Alchourrón, C., P. Gärdenfors and D. Makinson (1985): "On the Logic of Theory Change: Partial Meet Contraction and Revision Functions", *Journal of Symbolic Logic* **50**, 510–530.

Alchourrón, C., and D. Makinson (1985): "On the Logic of Theory Change: Safe Contraction", *Studia Logica* **44**, 405–422.

Alchourrón, C., and D. Makinson (1986): "Maps Between Some Different Kinds of Contraction Function: The Finite Case", *Studia Logica* **45**, 187–198.

Doyle, J. (1992): "Reason Maintenance and Belief Revision: Foundations vs. Coherence Theories", *this volume*.

Gärdenfors, P. (1988): *Knowledge in Flux: Modeling the Dynamics of Epistemic States*, Bradford Books, MIT Press, Cambrige, Mass.

Gärdenfors, P. (1990): "The Dynamics of Belief Systems: Foundations vs. Coherence Theories", *Revue Internationale de Philosophie* **44**, 24–46.

Gärdenfors, P. (1992): "Belief Revision: An Introduction", *this volume*.

Gärdenfors, P., and D. Makinson (1988): "Revisions of Knowledge Systems Using Epistemic Entrenchment", in M.V. Vardi (ed.), *Theoretical Aspects of Reasoning about Knowledge*, Morgan Kaufmann, Los Altos, 83–95.

Harman, G. (1986): *Change in View*, Bradford Books, MIT Press, Cambrige, Mass.

Lindström, S., and W. Rabinowicz (1991): "Epistemic Entrenchment with Incomparabilities and Relational Belief Revision", in A. Fuhrmann and M. Morreau (eds.), *The Logic of Theory Change*, Springer LNCS 465, Berlin etc., 93-126.

Rott, H. (1991a): "Two Methods of Constructing Contractions and Revisions of Knowledge Systems", *Journal of Philosophical Logic* **20**, 149–173.

Rott, H. (1991b): "A Nonmonotonic Conditional Logic for Belief Revision I", in A.

Fuhrmann and M. Morreau (eds.), *The Logic of Theory Change*, Springer LNCS 465, Berlin etc., 135–181.

Rott, H. (1991c): "Preferential Belief Change Using Generalized Epistemic Entrenchment", *Journal of Logic, Language and Information*, to appear.

Schlechta, K. (1991): "Some Results on Theory Revision", in A. Fuhrmann and M. Morreau (eds.), *The Logic of Theory Change*, Springer LNCS 465, Berlin etc., 72–92.

Belief Change and Possibility Theory

Didier DUBOIS and Henri PRADE

Institut de Recherche en Informatique de Toulouse (I.R.I.T.), Université Paul Sabatier, 118 route de Narbonne, 31062 Toulouse Cedex, France

INTRODUCTION

In the last five years, there has been much concern in Artificial Intelligence about the problem of belief revision. A rather exciting feature of the on-going debate is that it has led to an interaction between fields which usually ignore each other, such as logic, probability theory, fuzzy set and possibility theory, and their epistemological underpinnings. In his book, Gärdenfors (1988) emphasizes in a convincing way that notions of epistemic state can be defined in the framework of logic as well as in the one of probability theory and that similar postulates can be put forward in the two settings, for the purpose of devising rational updating operations that take place upon the arrival of new pieces of information. On the other hand Spohn (1988), in trying to refine the logical notion of epistemic state, viewed as a consistent and deductively closed set of propositions, comes close to Shackle's (1961) notions of degrees of potential surprise, as well as Zadeh's (1978) possibility theory. However he proposes revision rules that are in some way in accordance with probability theory where probabilities only take infinitesimal values (Spohn, 1990). Besides, one of the main outcomes of Gärdenfors' logical theory of belief change is that any revision process underlies an ordering of propositions that form the epistemic state; the rationality postulates force this ordering to satisfy specific properties, and the only numerical set-functions that can account for these properties are the so-called necessity measures that play a basic role in possibility theory (Dubois and Prade, 1988).

Given this state of affairs, it becomes interesting to investigate the potential of possibility theory as such for describing belief updating processes in accordance to the framework devised by Gärdenfors. The aim of this paper is first to try to extend the rationality postulates of revision, expansion and contraction over to ordered sets of propositions where the ordering is induced by a necessity measure. While the notion of epistemic entrenchment appears in Gärdenfors (1988) as a consequence of the revision postulates, and is implicitly at work in a given rational revision procedure, here we assume that the epistemic entrenchment ordering is taken for granted as primitive data, and belief change is based on the ordering. It is shown that an ordering on a finite set of propositions determines an ordering of possible worlds that can be described by means of a possibility distribution; it is very close to what Spohn (1988) names "well ordered partitions" and relates to Shoham's (1988) preference logic. Notions of expansion, revision and contraction of possibility distributions are defined in accordance with Gärdenfors' postulates. It is shown that these updating rules are faithful representations of these postulates that account for a principle of minimal change. In some sense it overcomes some of Spohn's objections to the representation of epistemic states by means of well-ordered partitions. The revision rule is obtained under the form of a conditional possibility distribution that is similar to conditional probability. It is closely related to the conditioning of degrees of potential surprise of Shackle (1961) as well as to the so-called "might-counterfactual" of David Lewis' (1973) conditional logic systems. Again, this paper is an answer to Spohn's questions about the motivations behind Shackle's ordinal view of conditioning.

Another point addressed in this paper is to lay bare the links between the rational updating of possibility distributions and the handling of inconsistencies in possibilistic logic (Dubois, Lang and Prade, 1989), a logic whose syntax contains first order logic formulas weighted by a lower bound of a degree of necessity, and whose basic inference rule is a weighted extension of the resolution principle (Dubois and Prade, 1987a). It is indicated that syntactic revision rules may be more expressive and more respectful of the a priori knowledge than the revision rules based on semantic representations of a set of weighted formulas.

A third issue considered in this paper is an analysis of Spohn's theory of ordinal conditional functions and their relationships with possibility theory. It is shown that Spohn's disbelief functions, once mapped back to the unit interval, do correspond to a special class of possibility distributions. However the basic revision rule in possibility theory, as studied in this paper is different from the basic belief change rule of Spohn's theory. The latter rather fits Dempster rule of conditioning, currently used in Shafer's (1976) theory of evidence, and particularized to consonant belief functions. The comparison with Spohn's theory led us into considering belief change operations on the basis of uncertain evidence. An extension of the possibilistic expansion and revision rules to the case when the input information itself takes the form of a possibility distribution is devised. Gärdenfors' postulates of expansion and revision are generalized to such a situation, and it is proved that the possibilistic expansion rule does satisfy the postulates. The revision rules only satisfies six out of the eight postulates, and it is suggested why this might be natural. Again the revision rule differs from Spohn's rule of λ-conditionalization. The effects of both belief change rules are carefully analyzed and the differences pointed out.

The paper is organized in four parts: the first part deals with qualitative necessity and possibility relations, and their numerical representations; it highlights the close links with Gärdenfors' epistemic entrenchment concept. Part 2 extends the belief change postulates to epistemic states described in terms of possibility distributions and supplies rules for expansion, revision and contraction. The major role played by the specificity ordering of epistemic states is laid bare: expansion results in increasing the specificity while contraction results in decreasing the specificity of an epistemic state. Part 3 is devoted to the applications to possibilistic logic. Part 4 considers the case when the input information itself is uncertain.

1 EPISTEMIC STATES IN POSSIBILITY THEORY

In this paper, knowledge is supposed to be expressed by means of (not necessarily closed) sets K of sentences denoted ϕ, ψ, χ... that belong to a finite Boolean algebra $\mathcal{B}$ of sentences. Hence negation $\neg\phi$, conjunction $\phi \wedge \psi$ and disjunction $\phi \vee \psi$ belong to $\mathcal{B}$ as well. $\top$ and $\bot$ are the top and the bottom elements of $\mathcal{B}$ and denote the tautology and the contradiction respectively. The ordering relation in $\mathcal{B}$ is denoted $\vdash$ (syntactic entailment) and defined as usual by $\phi \vdash \psi$ if and only if $\phi \rightarrow \psi = \neg\phi \vee \psi = \top$.

1.1 Epistemic States as Qualitative Necessity Relations

An epistemic state will be described by an ordering relation on $\mathcal{B}$, denoted $\geq_c$ that compares sentences in terms of their levels of certainty. $\phi \geq_c \psi$ thus means that ϕ is considered as at least as certain as ψ. Denote $\phi >_c \psi$ when $\phi \geq_c \psi$ but not ($\psi \geq_c \phi$). The relation $\geq_c$ is supposed to satisfy the axioms of a so-called "qualitative necessity relation" (Dubois, 1986), namely

(A0)	$\top >_c \bot$	(non-triviality)
(A1)	$\phi \geq_c \psi$ or $\psi \geq_c \phi$	(completeness)
(A2)	$\phi \geq_c \psi$ and $\psi \geq_c \chi$ imply $\phi \geq_c \chi$	(transitivity)
(A3)	$\phi \geq_c \bot$	
(C)	if $\phi \geq_c \psi$ then $\forall\chi, \phi \wedge \chi \geq_c \psi \wedge \chi$	

(A0) is natural so far as tautologies can be held as sure statements while contradictions are never accepted by a rational mind. (A1) and (A2) are normative axioms that enable levels of certainty to be ordered on a linear scale. It is especially meaningful in the scope of using certainty valuations on the unit interval, as it is the case with degrees of probability. Interestingly indeed axioms (A0)-(A3) have been suggested by De Finetti (1937) in the first attempt to model the relation "at least as probable as" on a set of events. Axiom (C) is the basic axiom for our notion of certainty. Its rationale corresponds to the following idea: if a set of sentences K is considered as accepted beliefs, and if, in order to augment K with some new piece of knowledge, we can choose between ϕ and ψ where ϕ is considered as at least as certain as ψ then $K \cup \{\phi\}$ is preferred to $K \cup \{\psi\}$, i.e. one would rather trust $K \cup \{\phi\}$ rather than $K \cup \{\psi\}$. Here a set of accepted sentences K is viewed as equivalent to the conjunction of these sentences. Interestingly, De Finetti (1937) did not propose (C) as an axiom for qualitative probability relation $\geq p$ but rather suggested,

$$(P) \qquad \text{if } \chi \wedge (\phi \vee \psi) = \bot \text{ then } (\phi \geq p \ \psi \text{ is equivalent to } \phi \vee \chi \geq p \ \psi \vee \chi)$$

This is called the qualitative additivity axiom. Indeed starting with a probability measure P as a function $\mathcal{B} \rightarrow [0,1]$ such that $P(\phi \vee \psi) = P(\phi) + P(\psi)$ when $\phi \wedge \psi = \bot$, the relation $\phi \geq p \ \psi$ defined from $P(\phi) \geq P(\psi)$ satisfies (P) but generally violates (C) (except if P is deterministic). In fact axiom (C) neither entails nor is a consequence of (P).

The following properties of qualitative necessity relations have been established (Dubois, 1986):

<u>Proposition 1</u>: Axiom (C) is equivalent, under (A0)-(A3) to the following axiom

$$(C') \qquad \text{if } \phi \geq_c \psi \text{ then } \phi \wedge \psi \sim_c \psi$$

where $\phi \sim_c \psi$ means $\phi \geq_c \psi$ and $\psi \geq_c \phi$.

<u>Proposition 2</u>: if $\phi \vdash \psi$ then $\psi \geq_c \phi$. Particularly $T \geq_c \phi, \forall \phi$ holds and is equivalent to $\phi \geq_c \bot, \forall \phi$ when (C) holds.

<u>Proposition 3</u>: Either $\phi \sim_c \bot$ or $\neg \phi \sim_c \bot$ or both.

<u>Proposition 4</u>: Any numerical function N: $\mathcal{B} \rightarrow [0,1]$, such that $\phi \geq_c \psi$ if and only if $N(\phi) \geq N(\psi)$, satisfies the following characteristic property

$$N(\phi \wedge \psi) = \min(N(\phi), N(\psi)), \forall \phi, \psi \in \mathcal{B} \qquad (1)$$

Conversely all functions N satisfying (1) induce a qualitative necessity relation.

Proposition 1 reflects the idea that our level of trust in a set of sentences is dictated by the sentence with the lowest level of certainty. Proposition 2 is a natural coherence requirement between entailment and certainty. Proposition 3 claims that it would be contradictory to consider both ϕ and its contrary $\neg\phi$ as somewhat certain. Especially, $\phi \sim_c \perp$ means that ϕ is not certain; if $\phi \sim_c \neg\phi$ then it is a state of ignorance about ϕ. Proposition 4 claims that the only numerical counterparts of certainty orderings that belong to our framework, are "necessity measures" of possibility theory (Zadeh, 1978; Dubois and Prade, 1988). By convention necessity measures are such that $N(\perp) = 0$, $N(T) = 1$.

This comment leads us to consider qualitative counterparts of Zadeh's (1978) possibility measures, i.e. functions $\Pi: \mathcal{B} \to [0,1]$ such that

$$\Pi(\phi \vee \psi) = \max(\Pi(\phi), \Pi(\psi)) \tag{2}$$

This study of qualitative possibility relations $\phi \geq_\Pi \psi$ where $\geq_\Pi$ models the notions of "at least as possible as" has also been carried out in Dubois (1986). Indeed, possibility measures are related to necessity measures through the duality relationship $N(\phi) = 1 - \Pi(\neg\phi)$ which is reminding of the duality between the modalities "possible" and "necessary" in modal logics. The counterpart of this duality in the setting of qualitative possibility and necessity relations is simply

$$\phi \geq_\Pi \psi \text{ if and only if } \neg\psi \geq_c \neg\phi \tag{3}$$

i.e. ϕ is considered as more possible than ψ whenever $\neg\psi$ is considered as more certain than $\neg\phi$. Possibility orderings range from complete possibility to impossibility. It is easy to show that qualitative possibility relations satisfy (A0)-(A3) and properties that are dual to qualitative necessity relations, that is, denoting $>_\Pi$ the strict ordering associated to $\geq_\Pi$, and $\sim_\Pi$ the corresponding equivalence relation:

- (Π) if $\phi \geq_\Pi \psi$ then $\phi \vee \chi \geq_\Pi \psi \vee \chi$
- (Π') if $\phi \geq_\Pi \psi$ then $\phi \vee \psi \sim_\Pi \phi$
- if $\phi \vdash \psi$ then $\psi \geq_\Pi \phi$
- either $\phi \sim_\Pi T$ or $\neg\phi \sim_\Pi T$ or both
- any function $\Pi: \mathcal{B} \to [0,1]$ such that $\Pi(\phi) \geq \Pi(\psi)$ if and only if $\phi \geq_\Pi \psi$, satisfies the characteristic axiom (2) and conversely.

1.2 Relationships with Other Works

It has been recently pointed out (Dubois and Prade, 1991a) that a qualitative necessity relation is very close to an epistemic entrenchment relation after Gärdenfors (1988), except that in the epistemic entrenchment framework, the condition $T >_c \phi$ is requested instead of (A0), i.e. non-tautological statements are always strictly less certain than tautologies. This is natural in the framework of Gärdenfors' belief sets, where any non-tautological sentence can disappear upon a revision process. On the other hand it is easy to imagine situations where some non-tautological sentences must be protected, i.e. it is forbidden to question them. Hence $T \geq_c \phi$ looks less drastic in that context and leaves room for $\phi \neq T$ such that $\phi \sim_c T$. Gärdenfors (1991) also considers so-called "plausibility valuations" or "expectation functions" that are basically like necessity measures, i.e. satisfy (1). However $N(\phi)$, in Gärdenfors paper, is valued on a linearly ordered unbounded set S for $\phi \neq \perp, T$. The name "plausibility valuation" looks rather unfortunate however, since in Shafer's terminology, plausibility functions generalize possibility measures Π but not necessity measures.

More recently, it has been discovered that qualitative possibility relations had been introduced in a logical setting by Lewis (1973). Namely he proposes a logic called V including a connective '$\leq$' such that $\phi \leq \psi$ means ϕ is at least as possible as ψ, i.e. his notation is the converse as ours. As fundamental axioms, he requires transitivity (A2) and completeness (A1) as well as axiom

$$(V) \qquad \phi \geq_\Pi \phi \vee \psi \text{ or } \psi \geq_\Pi \phi \vee \psi$$

It is easy to check that in the framework of (A0)-(A3), (V) is equivalent to any of (Π) or (Π'). More results on the links between qualitative necessity relations and Lewis' logic of counterfactuals appear in Fariñas del Cerro and Herzig (1991). Roth (1991b) also puts together epistemic entrenchment and conditional logics after Lewis.

1.3 Ordered Belief Sets

According to Gärdenfors a subset K of sentences is called a belief set if and only if $\perp$ is not a consequence of K, and K is closed under the consequence relation $\vdash$. K can thus be viewed as a proper subset of the Boolean algebra $\mathcal{B}$ such that $\exists \phi \in \mathcal{B}, \phi \neq \perp, K = \{\psi \mid \phi \vdash \psi\}$. If $K = \{\phi_1, \phi_2, ..., \phi_n\}$ is not closed under the consequence relation then its closure Cn(K) is $\{\psi \mid \phi_1 \wedge \phi_2 \wedge ... \wedge \phi_n \vdash \psi\}$, provided that $\phi_1 \wedge \phi_2 \wedge ... \wedge \phi_n \neq \perp$. Otherwise K is inconsistent and Cn(K) = $\mathcal{B}$ itself, which is then interpreted as the absurd belief set. Given a qualitative necessity relation $\geq_c$ over $\mathcal{B}$, it is possible to prove

Proposition 5: $K = \{\phi \mid \phi >_c \bot\}$ is a belief set.

Proof: From Proposition 3, it is not possible to have $\phi, \psi \in K$, such that $\phi \wedge \psi = \bot$ and $\phi >_c \bot, \psi >_c \bot$. Hence $\bot \notin K$. From Proposition 2, if $\phi \in K$, and $\phi \vdash \psi$, then $\psi \geq_c \phi >_c \bot$, hence $\psi >_c \bot$, and $\psi \in K$. Lastly if $\phi \in K$ and $\psi \in K$ then assume $\phi \geq_c \psi$ without loss of generality. Then $\phi \wedge \psi \sim_c \psi > \bot$ hence $\phi \wedge \psi \in K$.   Q.E.D.

This result independently proved in Dubois and Prade (1991a) and Roth (1991a) indicates that the epistemic states described by qualitative necessity relations generalize the notion of belief sets after Gärdenfors by ordering the sentences in a belief set. When $\exists \phi, \psi \in K$, $\phi >_c \psi$, K is called an ordered belief set. By duality it is meaningful to introduce "plausibility sets", defined as $L = \{\phi \mid \phi >_\Pi \bot\}$ using the associated qualitative possibility relation. A plausibility set is such that $\bot \notin L$ and $\forall \phi \in L$, $\phi \vdash \psi$ implies $\psi \in L$. Note that L is not a belief set since we do not have $\phi > \bot, \psi > \bot$ imply $\phi \wedge \psi > \bot$. L contains not only sentences that are somewhat certain, but also those which are not definitely rejected. Especially we have $L = \mathcal{B} - \{\neg \phi \mid \phi \sim_c \top\}$ since $\phi \sim_\Pi \bot$ is equivalent to $\neg \phi \sim_c \top$. When $\geq_c$ is a regular epistemic entrenchment relation, however, $L = \mathcal{B} - \{\bot\}$ since only tautologies are totally certain in Gärdenfors approach. In other words this notion is of limited interest for epistemic entrenchment relations. When $\exists \phi, \psi \in L$, $\phi >_\Pi \psi$, L is called an ordered plausibility set. Clearly, the ordered belief set associated to $\geq_c$ is contained in the associated ordered plausibility set.

Before any revision operation is specified, Gärdenfors' belief sets are such that $\forall \phi$, $\psi \in K, \phi \sim_c \psi$. More generally an ordered belief set K may be partitioned by means of the equivalence relation $\sim_c$. Equivalence classes of equal certainty are linearly ordered by means of $>_c$. Moreover, the set of sentences at least as certain as a sentence $\psi \in K$ is itself a (possibly ordered) belief set (Roth, 1991a). Hence an ordered belief set is a nested family of belief sets of decreasing levels of certainty as one goes from the core to the periphery.

1.4 Models Based on Possible Worlds

As in Gärdenfors (1988) we shall assume that the content of sentences can be described by sets of possible worlds $w \in \Omega$. Namely, $\forall \phi \in \mathcal{B}$, $A = [\phi]$ is a subset of worlds w in which ϕ is true. We shall adopt usual definitions such as $[\phi \wedge \psi] = [\phi] \cap [\psi]$, $[\neg \phi] = \overline{[\phi]}$, $[\top] = \Omega$, $[\bot] = \emptyset$ (the empty set) etc. An epistemic state can then be viewed as a subset A of possible worlds such that $A = [K]$ where K is a set of sentences in $\mathcal{B}$ and $[K]$ is the set of possible worlds in which all sentences in K are simultaneously true. [K] is viewed by Gärdenfors as "the largest set of possible worlds that is compatible with the individual's convictions" (as modelled by K). Adopting the vocabulary of possibility theory, the characteristic function $\mu_{[K]}$ of [K] is viewed as a possibility distribution, denoted π; namely when $w \in [K]$, $\pi(w) = 1$, and w is considered as a possible world; when $w \notin [K]$, $\pi(w) = 0$, w is an impossible world for the individual who accepts the sentences in K. Clearly if $K = \{\phi_1, \phi_2, ..., \phi_n\}$ we have

$$\forall\ w \in \Omega,\ \pi(w) = \min_{i=1,n} \mu_{[\phi_i]}(w) \tag{4}$$

induced by the constraints $\pi \leq \mu_{[\phi_i]}$. In (4) we have computed the greatest possibility distribution over Ω, compatible with the constraints "ϕ_i is accepted" for $\phi_i \in K$. This is called the "principle of minimum specificity" in possibility theory (Yager, 1983; Dubois and Prade, 1987b).

Let us study what happens when considering ordered belief sets. The qualitative necessity relation $\geq_c$ over $\mathcal{B}$ will induce an ordering of Ω, in terms of possibility levels. To see it, let us borrow again from (Dubois, 1986). Let $\mathcal{A}$ be the set of atoms of the finite Boolean algebra $\mathcal{B}$, i.e. $\mathcal{A} = \{\alpha \in \mathcal{B}, \alpha \neq \bot, \nexists\ \phi \neq \bot, \phi \neq \alpha, \text{ and } \phi \vdash \alpha\}$. The set $\{[\alpha], \alpha \in \mathcal{A}\}$ forms a partition of Ω, and it is the finest one induced by $\mathcal{B}$. Namely w, w' $\in [\alpha]$ for $\alpha \in \mathcal{A}$ cannot be distinguished using the language that generates $\mathcal{B}$.

Let us consider the restriction to $\mathcal{A}$ of the qualitative possibility relation $\geq_\Pi$ over $\mathcal{B}$ obtained from (3), and define an ordering $\geq_\pi$ over Ω as follows:

$$\forall w, w',\ w \geq_\pi w' \text{ if and only if } \alpha \geq_\Pi \beta \text{ where } \alpha, \beta \in \mathcal{A}, w \in [\alpha], w' \in [\beta] \tag{5}$$

Clearly this implies that $\forall\ \alpha \in \mathcal{A}$, $w \in [\alpha]$, w' $\in [\alpha]$ implies $w \sim_\pi w'$. The relation $\geq_\pi$ on Ω determines which worlds are more possible than others according to the epistemic state defined on $\mathcal{B}$ by $\geq_c$ (or its equivalent ordered belief set). Now if $\phi \neq \bot$, let $\phi^* = \vee\{\alpha \in \mathcal{A}, \alpha \vdash \phi \text{ and } \alpha \sim_\Pi \phi\}$. ϕ^* is the set of preferred interpretations of ϕ and $[\phi^*]$ contains the most possible worlds in which ϕ is true. The following proposition holds.

<u>Proposition 6</u>: When $\phi, \psi \neq \bot$, $\psi \geq_\Pi \phi$ is equivalent to $\forall\ w \in [\phi^*]$, $\forall\ w' \in [\psi^*]$, w' $\geq_\pi$ w.

<u>Proof</u>: Clearly $\psi \sim_\Pi \psi^*$ and $\phi \sim_\Pi \phi^*$. Moreover $\forall w, w' \in [\psi^*]$, $w \sim_\pi w'$, and similarly for $[\phi^*]$. Hence the result.   Q.E.D.

The ordering $\geq_\pi$ on Ω is complete and transitive, and completely determines the qualitative possibility relation on $\mathcal{B}$, hence the relation $\geq_c$ as well. Namely if we start from $\geq_\pi$ on Ω as defined by (5), we can extend it to any atoms α, β in $\mathcal{A}$ as follows

$$\alpha \geq_{\Pi'} \beta \text{ if and only if } \exists\, w' \in [\beta], \exists\, w \in [\alpha], w \geq_\pi w'$$

Indeed, by construction, all possible worlds in $[\beta]$ are equivalent with respect to $\geq_\pi$ and the same in $[\alpha]$. Hence $\geq_\Pi$ and $\geq_{\Pi'}$ are the same on $\mathcal{A}$. $\geq_{\Pi'}$ can then be extended over to all $\mathcal{B}$, letting

$$\phi \geq_{\Pi'} \psi \text{ if and only if } \forall\, \beta \in \mathcal{A} \text{ such that } \beta \vdash \psi, \exists\, \alpha \in \mathcal{A}, \alpha \vdash \phi \text{ and } \alpha \geq_{\Pi'} \beta$$

The fact that $\geq_{\Pi'}$ is equivalent to $\geq_\Pi$ is rather obvious.

The set of atoms $\mathcal{A}$ of $\mathcal{B}$ can be partitioned according to $\sim_\Pi$, and the equivalence classes E_i linearly ordered using $>_\Pi$. Assume the number of equivalence classes is $n + 1$. Clearly $n \geq 1$ since $\top >_\Pi \bot$. Consider a linear ordering $V = \{a_0, a_1, ..., a_n\}$. For instance we can choose $a_0 = 0 < a_1 < a_2 < ... < a_n = 1$ in the unit interval. Then it is possible to define a possibility measure as a surjective mapping $\Pi: \mathcal{B} \to V$ such that $\phi \sim_\Pi \psi$ if and only if $\Pi(\phi) = \Pi(\psi) = a_i$ for some $a_i \in V$. Namely, $\Pi(\bot) = a_0$, $\Pi(\top) = a_n$ and

$$\text{if } \alpha \in \mathcal{A}, \alpha \in E_i \text{ then } \Pi(\alpha) = a_i$$

Then $\forall\, \phi \in \mathcal{B}$, $\Pi(\phi) = \max\{\Pi(\alpha) \mid \alpha \in \mathcal{A}, \alpha \vdash \phi\}$, in accordance with axiom (Π'). $\Pi(\phi)$ is the level of possibility of ϕ, with $a_0 =$ impossible, and $a_n =$ totally possible. And then it is easy to check that $\phi \geq_\Pi \psi \Leftrightarrow \Pi(\phi) \geq \Pi(\psi)$. Degrees of certainty can be obtained by reversing the plausibility scale since by definition $\phi \geq_c \psi \Leftrightarrow \Pi(\neg\psi) \geq \Pi(\neg\phi)$. Define $N(\psi) = a_i$ if and only if $\Pi(\psi) = a_{n-i}$. Then when $N(\psi)$ ranges from a_0 to a_n, the belief about ψ goes from uncertainty to total certainty, since at the same time $\Pi(\neg\psi)$ goes from a_n to a_0. On the unit interval, the usual convention $N(\phi) = 1 - \Pi(\neg\phi)$ is retrieved if we let $a_{n-i} = 1 - a_i$, $a_0 = 0$, $a_n = 1$.

If $\mathcal{B}$ is not finite, then axiom (2) is not sufficient to ensure the existence of a possibility distribution π on Ω that enables the possibility measure to be reconstructed. As with probability theory, axiom (1) must be extended to infinite families of subsets. But starting more basically from a complete and transitive relation $\geq$ on Ω, it is possible to induce a qualitative possibility relation $\geq_\Pi$ among subsets of Ω as follows

$$A \geq_\Pi B \text{ if and only if } \forall\, w \in B, \exists\, w' \in A, w' \geq w$$

This relation does verify all properties of a qualitative possibility relation. Given a partitioning on Ω inducing a finite Boolean algebra $\mathcal{B}$, a qualitative possibility relation and a qualitative necessity relation on $\mathcal{B}$ are thus obtained. Going backwards from $\mathcal{B}$ to Ω, only an approximation of the ordering on Ω is retrieved due to the impossibility to rank-order worlds w and w' which correspond to the same atom in $\mathcal{B}$.

1.5 More Relationships with Other Works

These remarks stress the similarity between Spohn's (1988) proposal for modeling epistemic states and possibility theory. The linearly ordered sets E_i of atoms of $\mathcal{B}$ introduced in Dubois (1986) correspond to what Spohn (1988) calls well-ordered partitions. Spohn then suggests to describe a ranking of sentences of a Boolean algebra by means of a function $\kappa: \mathcal{B} \to V$ such that $\kappa(\phi) \leq \kappa(\psi)$ means that ϕ is less disbelieved than ψ (the convention is opposite ours). However the set V is allowed to be infinite (a set of ordinals), and not bounded from above. Moreover $\kappa(\phi) = \min\{\kappa(\alpha) \mid \alpha \in \mathcal{A}, \alpha \vdash \phi\}$ is defined from a ranking of atoms, such that $\kappa(\alpha) = a_0$ for some $\alpha \in \mathcal{A}$. For Spohn, a_0 denotes complete possibility, and a_i a certain level of impossibility (that grows with i), but only the contradiction is completely impossible (as is the case with Gärdenfors framework). In our ordinal setting $\kappa(\phi)$ can be assimilated to $N(\neg\phi)$, since $N(\neg\phi) = \max V$ means that ϕ is indeed impossible (V is then bounded).

There is also a strong similarity between the setting of possibility theory and Shoham's (1988) idea of a preference relation over possible worlds (e.g. Dubois and Prade, 1991b). As clear from above, an ordered belief set on $\mathcal{B}$ generates a preference relation $\geq_\Pi$ over the atoms of $\mathcal{B}$, which in turn generates an ordering relation $\geq_\pi$ over the set of possible worlds. The strict part $>_\pi$ of $\geq_\pi$ does verify Shoham's requirements. Here preference is expressed in terms of possibility.

Shackle (1961) has considered so-called "degrees of potential surprise" $s(\phi)$ valued on [0,1], which satisfy $s(\phi \vee \psi) = \min(s(\phi), s(\psi))$ just as Spohn's disbelief functions. Clearly, $N(\neg\phi) = s(\phi)$ is equivalent to Shackle's degrees of surprise.

Lastly, there is a deep agreement between the possible world semantics of belief sets and Zadeh's (1979) approximate reasoning framework. Indeed, mapping $\mathcal{B}$ over the finite linear order V leads to represent an ordered belief set in terms of a possibility distribution π over possible worlds namely:

$$\pi(w) = a_i \text{ such that } w \in [\alpha], \alpha \in \mathcal{A}, \Pi(\alpha) = a_i$$

Here a_0 denotes complete impossibility, a_n complete possibility. For Zadeh any set of sentences in natural language induces a possibility distribution acting as a flexible constraint, a fuzzy restriction on the values of underlying parameters. This is perfectly coherent with Gärdenfors' framework for possible worlds semantics of belief sets. Strangely enough many scholars in logic, who have criticized fuzzy sets and what Zadeh calls "fuzzy logic", have apparently misunderstood his work (e.g. Morgan and Pelletier, 1977; Haack, 1979). They have viewed Zadeh's approximate reasoning approach as a deviant kind of truth-functional multiple-valued logic, without grasping the idea that it is an attempt to reason with incomplete knowledge including preference orderings (which Zadeh names "flexible constraints").

It makes sense to build possibility distributions on a set of possible worlds right away, as Zadeh does, from sentences involving fuzzy predicates. For instance the fuzziness of "tall" in the classical example "John is tall" translates into a possibility distribution $\pi = \mu_{tall}$ on the set Ω of possible sizes where the value size(John) may lie. Clearly the fuzziness means for instance that if the sentence "John is tall" is the available information, 1.80 meters is preferred to 1.70 as a guess for John's size. Membership functions of fuzzy sets are, at an elementary level, ordering relations (see Levchenkov, 1987). Especially, in the considered situation, "John is tall" does not mean that the degree of membership of size(John) in the fuzzy set "tall" is maximal. Indeed, this degree of membership is out of reach (since the size of John is unknown). What is only available is the preference ordering on sizes induced by the sentence, conveniently expressed by a possibility distribution that matches the membership function of "tall". Zadeh's fuzzy logic basically handles possibility distributions, instead of truth-valued sentences like "John is tall is true to degree .3" whose semantics is far from obvious as often pointed out.

2 BELIEF DYNAMICS IN POSSIBILITY THEORY

So far, we have given a formal framework by which an ordered set of accepted beliefs is equivalent to a possibility distribution on a set of possible worlds. Now we are going to discuss basic operations in the dynamics of belief, such as expansion, contraction and revision in terms of changes of a possibility distribution. In the following, we assume that the involved possibility distributions π and subsets $A \subseteq \Omega$ are such that the maximum of π

over A is attained in A. This is true when Ω is finite, when π derives from a finite Boolean algebra on Ω as mentioned above, when π is continuous and A is closed, etc.... Then $\Pi(A) = \pi(w)$ for some $w \in A$. This assumption enables tedious technicalities to be obviated.

2.1 Specificity Ordering between Epistemic States

A possibility distribution π is viewed as a mapping from Ω to a totally ordered set V containing a greatest element (denoted 1) and a least element (denoted 0). For instance V = [0,1]. However any finite or infinite and bounded chain will do as well. A consistent epistemic state π is such that $\pi(w) = 1$ for some w, i.e. at least one of the worlds is considered as completely possible in Ω. Let π and π' be two possibility distributions on Ω describing epistemic states. When $\pi \leq \pi'$, π is said to be more specific than π' (Yager, 1983), i.e. the epistemic state described by π is more complete, contains more information than the epistemic state described by π'. Especially if there is a world $w_0 \in \Omega$ such that $\pi(w_0) = 1$, and $\pi(w) = 0$ if $w \neq w_0$, π is said to be maximally specific and corresponds to an *ideally complete* epistemic state. Note that if epistemic states are described by means of sentences which form a finite Boolean algebra $\mathcal{B}$, ideally complete epistemic states are out of reach because atoms of the Boolean algebra generally correspond to more than one world in Ω. Only complete epistemic states (with respect to $\mathcal{B}$) are expressible, i.e. such that $\Pi(\alpha) = 1$ for $\alpha \in \mathcal{A}$ (atoms of $\mathcal{B}$) and $\Pi(\beta) = 0$ for $\beta \in \mathcal{A}$, $\beta \neq \alpha$; then $\pi(w) = 1$, $\forall w \in [\alpha]$ and $\pi(w) = 0$ otherwise, by virtue of the principle of minimum specificity. Ideal completeness can only be expressed in languages in which all worlds of Ω are discernible. Conversely the vacuous epistemic state is expressed by the least specific possibility distribution on Ω, i.e. $\pi_T(w) = 1$, $\forall w$. It corresponds to the state of total ignorance. Lastly the absurd epistemic state, where nothing is possible is $\pi_\perp$ such that $\pi_\perp(w) = 0$, $\forall w \in \Omega$. In the following, by epistemic state we mean either a consistent epistemic state or the absurd one.

Interpreted in this framework, the three basic forms of belief dynamics described by Gärdenfors (1988) can easily be depicted. The result of an expansion, that stems from receiving new information consistent with a previously available epistemic state described by π, is another possibility distribution π' that is more specific than π. Note that π', by definition, is also such that $\pi'(w) = 1$. Hence if we let $C(\pi) = \{w \mid \pi(w) = 1\}$ be the core of π (i.e. the set of preferred worlds in a given epistemic state), we have $C(\pi') \neq \emptyset$ and $C(\pi') \subseteq C(\pi)$. A contraction, i.e. the result of forgetting some piece of information among those that form an epistemic state, will be expressed by going from π to a less specific possibility distribution $\pi' \geq \pi$. The term revision will be interpreted as any other belief change which is neither a contraction nor an expansion. Namely, it is when from π, we reach π' where neither $\pi \geq \pi'$ nor $\pi' \leq \pi$ hold. More specifically we shall encounter a special kind of revision that will be termed "strict", such that $C(\pi) \cap C(\pi') = \varnothing$. This type of revision will be met when updating an epistemic state upon receiving a piece of information under the form of a sentence taken as absolutely true. However expansions, contractions and strict revisions do not exhaust the set of possible belief changes in the possibilistic setting; as for the setting of Spohn's ordinal conditional functions, more refined changes may take place such as slightly increasing the possibility of one world while decreasing the possibility of another world without altering $C(\pi)$ nor the support $S(\pi) = \{w \mid \pi(w) > 0\}$ containing the worlds considered as somewhat possible.

2.2 Expansion in Possibility Theory Due to a Sure Piece of Information

Let π be the possibility distribution representing a nonabsurd (consistent) epistemic state, and let ϕ be a newly received piece of information taken as certain. Let $A = [\phi]$ be the set of models of ϕ. The expansion of π by A, denoted by $\pi^+{}_A$ is defined as follows:

$$\text{if } \exists w \in A, \pi(w) = 1 \quad \text{then} \quad \pi^+{}_A(w) = \pi(w) \text{ if } w \in A$$
$$= 0 \text{ otherwise}$$
$$\text{else} \quad \pi^+{}_A(w) = 0, \forall w.$$

When $C(\pi) \cap A \neq \varnothing$ (or equivalently $\Pi(A) = 1$), i.e. ϕ does not contradict the preferred worlds, we have

$$\pi^+{}_A = \min(\mu_A, \pi) \tag{6}$$

where μA is the characteristic function of A. Otherwise, $\min(\mu_A, \pi) < 1$ and $\pi^+{}_A$ given by (6) is no longer the description of a consistent epistemic state. In that case expansion results in the absurd belief state by convention ($\pi^+{}_A = \pi_\perp$). Note that this definition, which is in the spirit of Gärdenfors theory can be questioned in the last case. Indeed when the new information contradicts the old epistemic state, it might look as reasonable to reach a vacuous epistemic state $\pi_\top$ as to reach an absurd epistemic state, since conflicting information may result in the awareness of ignorance (see (Yager, 1985) for this type of conflict resolution). However the above definition is natural in the scope of successive expansions that result in more and more specific possibility distributions ($\pi^+{}_A \leq \pi$), and can never decrease specificity.

Let us check that this definition of expansions of possibility distributions verifies the 6 Gärdenfors' postulates of expansion, that we express in terms of possibility distributions.

(Π+1) π^+_A is a possibility distribution describing an epistemic state (stability)

It is enough to verify that $\pi^+_A(w) = 1$ for some w, and to admit the absurd possibility distribution $\pi_\perp$ as representing a special epistemic state as Gärdenfors does with the absurd belief set.

(Π+2) $N^+_A(A) = 1$ (priority to the new information)

It claims that in the new epistemic state, the sentence ϕ such that A = [ϕ] is considered as sure, N^+_A being the necessity measure based on π^+_A. This is equivalent to require that only worlds in A are not impossible, i.e. $S(\pi^+_A) \leq A$. This is clearly true when $\pi^+_A = \min(\pi,\mu_A) \leq \mu_A$. When $\pi = \pi_\perp$, we have $\Pi_\perp(B) = 0$, $\forall B$ and thus $N_\perp(B) = 1$, $\forall B$. Particularly $N^+_A(A) = 1$.

(Π+3) π^+_A is not less specific than π (improvement of knowledge)

When A is consistent with π (i.e. A $\cap$ C(π) $\neq$ $\emptyset$), it comes down to verify that $\pi^+_A \leq \pi$, that is, learning A results in a more informative epistemic state, i.e. a more specific possibility distribution. The result is obvious. When $\pi^+_A = \pi_\perp$ the property trivially holds as well.

(Π+4) if N(A) = 1, then $\pi^+_A = \pi$ (invariance under redundancy)

This is true since N(A) = 1 (where N is based on π) is equivalent to $S(\pi) \subseteq A$. The condition N(A) = 1 excludes the case when $\pi^+_A = \pi_\perp$. Expansion is ineffective when we already know what we learn.

(Π+5) if π is more specific than π' then π^+_A is more specific than π'^+_A (monotonicity)

In other words $\pi \leq \pi'$ implies $\pi^+_A \leq \pi'^+_A$. This is obvious.

(Π+6) for any π and A, π^+_A is the least specific possibility distribution that satisfies (Π+1)-(Π+5) (principle of minimal specificity)

<u>Proof:</u> (Π+2) implies that $\pi^+_A(w) = 0$ whenever $\mu_A(w) = 0$. (Π+3) implies that $\forall w, \pi^+_A(w) \leq \pi(w)$. ($\Pi$+2) and ($\Pi$+3) force us to look for $\pi^+_A \leq \min(\pi,\mu_A)$. When A $\cap$ C(π) $\neq$ $\emptyset$, the least specific possibility distribution satisfying these two conditions is $\pi^+_A = \min(\pi,\mu_A)$; when C($\pi$) $\cap$ A = $\emptyset$, no possibility distribution $\pi^+_A \leq \min(\pi,\mu_A)$ describes an epistemic state except $\pi^+_A = \pi_\perp$. (Π+4) and (Π+5) are satisfied of course.

Hence we obtain for expansions the same result as Gärdenfors, in the possibilistic setting. It is easy to check that if π is a non-fuzzy possibility distribution, i.e. the set of models of a belief set K (as in equation (4)), then $(\Pi+1)$-$(\Pi+6)$ specialize in exactly Gärdenfors' expansion axioms.

2.3 Revision in Possibility Theory

Revision in possibility theory will be accomplished by means of a conditioning device similar to the one in probability theory. The notion of conditional possibility measure goes back to Hisdal (1978) who introduces the set function $\Pi(\cdot \mid A)$ through the equality

$$\forall B, B \cap A \neq \emptyset, \Pi(A \cap B) = \min(\Pi(B \mid A), \Pi(A)) \tag{7}$$

Equation (7) already appears in Shackle's (1961) book under a different guise, namely, using $s(A) = N(\bar{A})$ instead of $\Pi(A)$, and is criticized by Spohn (1988) as being ill motivated. However since this equation may have more than one solution in terms of $\Pi(B \mid A)$, Dubois and Prade (1986) have proposed to select as the most reasonable solution the least specific solution of (7), that is, when $\Pi(A) > 0$,

$$
\begin{aligned}
\Pi(B \mid A) &= 1 \text{ if } \Pi(A \cap B) = \Pi(A) > 0 \\
&= \Pi(A \cap B) \text{ otherwise} \\
&= 0 \text{ if } A \cap B = \emptyset.
\end{aligned} \tag{8}
$$

The conditional necessity function is defined by $N(B \mid A) = 1 - \Pi(\bar{B} \mid A)$, by duality. The possibility distribution π underlying the conditional possibility measure $\Pi(\cdot \mid A)$ is defined by $\pi(\cdot \mid A)$

$$
\begin{aligned}
\pi(w \mid A) &= 1 \text{ if } \pi(w) = \Pi(A), w \in A \\
&= \pi(w) \text{ if } \pi(w) < \Pi(A), w \in A \\
&= 0 \text{ if } w \notin A.
\end{aligned} \tag{9}
$$

To see it, one just has to let $B = \{w\}$ in (7) and to choose maximal values for $\Pi(\{w\} \mid A)$. Note that if $\Pi(A) = 0$ then $\pi(\cdot \mid A)$ is still a solution to (7) and is equal to μ_A. In this case, μ_A is simply substituted to π. This includes the case when $A = \emptyset$, which results in $\pi = \pi_\perp$.

Our aim here is to show that if π^+_A denotes a possibility distribution obtained by revising π with input A, it makes sense to let $\pi^+_A = \pi(\cdot \mid A)$ and then $\Pi^+_A(\cdot) = \Pi(\cdot \mid A)$. Let us translate the axioms of belief revision into the possibilistic setting, showing that in each case, $\pi(\cdot \mid A)$ fits.

(Π+1) for any subset $A \subseteq \Omega$, π^+_A represents an epistemic state (stability)

Indeed $\pi(w \mid A) = 1$ for some w, unless $\pi(\cdot \mid A) = \pi_\perp$, which occurs if $A = \emptyset$

(Π+2) $N^+_A(A) = 1$ (priority to the new information)

Again this is equivalent to require that $S(\pi^+_A) \subseteq A$; this is true of course, since $N(A \mid A) = 1$.

(Π+3) π^+_A is not less specific than π^+_A

We must check that $\pi(\cdot \mid A) \geq \pi^+_A$, and this is again quite clear.

(Π+4) if $\Pi(A) = 1$ then $\pi^+_A \leq \pi^+_A$

In fact (Π+4) holds in the sense that $\pi(\cdot \mid A) = \pi^+_A = \min(\pi, \mu_A)$ as soon as A is fully consistent with π, i.e. $C(\pi) \cap A \neq \emptyset$. Otherwise $\pi(\cdot \mid A) > \pi^+_A = \pi_\perp$. We find again, like Gärdenfors (1988) that revision substitutes to expansion when the latter yields absurd results; expansion and revision coincide otherwise.

(Π+5) $\pi^+_A = \pi_\perp$ if and only if $A = \emptyset$

This is clearly true by definition, for conditional possibilities.

(Π+6) equivalent pieces of information lead to equivalent revisions

This is obvious since we work on the possible worlds.

(Π+7) $\pi^+_{A \cap B} \geq (\pi^+_A)^+_B$

If $A \cap B = \emptyset$ then $\Pi(B \mid A) = 0$ so that $(\pi^+_A)^+_B = \pi(\cdot \mid A)^+_B = \pi_\perp$ and the property holds. If $A \cap B \neq \emptyset$ then let $w \in A \cap B$. If $\pi(w) = \Pi(A \cap B)$, $\pi^+_{A \cap B}(w) = \pi(w \mid A \cap B) = 1$ and the property holds. If $\pi(w) < \Pi(A \cap B)$ then $\pi(w) < \Pi(A)$ as well, and $\pi^+_{A \cap B}(w) = \pi(w \mid A \cap B) = \pi(w) \geq \pi^+_B$. Lastly assume $w \notin A \cap B$. Then letting again $\pi^+_A = \pi(\cdot \mid A)$: if $w \notin A$, $\pi^+_A(w) = 0 = (\pi^+_A)^+_B(w)$; if $w \in A - B$ then obviously $(\pi^+_A)^+_B(w) = 0$, due to $w \notin B$. Q.E.D.

(Π+8) if $\Pi^+_A(B) = 1$ then $\pi^+_{A \cap B} \leq (\pi^+_A)^+_B$

$\Pi(B \mid A) = 1$ means $\Pi(A \cap B) = \Pi(A)$ and $A \cap B \neq \emptyset$. Let us assume $\Pi(A) > 0$; then it means that some of the most possible worlds in A belong to B as well. Hence $\exists w \in B$, $\pi(w \mid A) = 1$. Hence $(\pi^+_A)^+_B = \min(\pi^+_A, \mu_B)$, where $\pi^+_A = \pi(\cdot \mid A)$. Now if $w \in A \cap B$ and $\Pi(A \cap B) = \Pi(A) = \pi(w)$, $\pi^+_{A \cap B}(w) = 1 = \pi^+_A(w) =$

$\min(\pi^+{}_A(w),\mu_B(w))$; if $w \in A \cap B$ and $\Pi(A \cap B) = \Pi(A) > \pi(w)$ then $\pi^+{}_{A\cap B}(w) = \pi(w) = \pi^+{}_A(w) = \min(\pi^+{}_A,\mu_B)$ otherwise $\pi^+{}_{A\cap B}(w) = 0$ and either $\pi^+{}_A(w) = 0$ or $\mu_B(w) = 0$. If $\Pi(A \cap B) = \Pi(A) = 0$ then $\pi(w) = 0$, $\forall\ w \in A \cap B$ and $\pi^+{}_{A\cap B} = \mu_{A\cap B} = \min(\mu_A,\mu_B)$, but $\pi^+{}_A = \mu_A$, and $(\mu_A)^+{}_B = \min(\mu_A,\mu_B)$.   Q.E.D.

In fact, $(\Pi+7)$ and $(\Pi+8)$ correspond to the fact that if B is consistent with the revised epistemic state accepting A, then $\pi^+{}_{A\cap B} = \min(\pi^+{}_A,\mu_B)$. $\pi^+{}_A = \pi(\cdot \mid A)$ as defined by (9) is not the unique possibility distribution that satisfies $(\Pi+1)$-$(\Pi+8)$. However it embodies a principle of minimal change. If π and π' define two real-valued possibility distributions on a finite Ω then the Hamming distance between π and π' (Kaufmann, 1975) is defined by $H(\pi,\pi') = \sum_{w \in \Omega} |\pi(w) - \pi'(w)|$. Then we have the following result:

Proposition 7: Given A and π, $\pi^+{}_A$, chosen as $\pi(\cdot \mid A)$ is the possibility distribution closest from π that complies with $(\Pi+1)$-$(\Pi+8)$, as long as there is a single world w_A where $\pi(w_A) = \Pi(A)$.

Proof: From $(\Pi+2)$, $\pi^+{}_A \le \mu_A$, thus $\pi^+{}_A(w) = 0$ for $w \notin A$. Hence $H(\pi,\pi^+{}_A) \ge \sum_{w \notin A} \pi(w)$. From $(\Pi+3)$, we have $\pi^+{}_A \ge \pi^+{}_A$. If $\Pi(A) = 1$ we must choose $\pi^+{}_A = \pi$ on A so that $H(\pi^+{}_A,\pi) = \sum_{w \notin A} \pi(w)$ exactly, in order to satisfy the minimal change principle. If $\Pi(A) \ne 1$, the equality $\pi^+{}_A = \pi$ can no longer hold because we must have $\pi^+{}_A(w) = 1 > \pi(w)$ for some $w \in A$. Let w_A such that $\pi(w_A) = \Pi(A)$. It is such that $\pi(w_A) > \pi(w)$, $\forall\ w \in A$ since it is unique. It is then enough to let $\pi^+{}_A(w_A) = 1$, $\pi^+{}_A(w) = \pi(w)$, $\forall\ w \notin A$, $w \ne w_A$ so as to minimize $H(\pi,\pi')$. Hence $= \pi^+{}_A = \pi(\cdot \mid A)$.
                    Q.E.D.

Remarks:
– When there are several w such that $\pi(w) = \Pi(A)$ the minimal change solution becomes ambiguous since letting $\pi^+{}_A(w) = 1$ for any such w gives an optimal solution. It corresponds to the idea of conditional possibility distribution proposed by Ramer (1989). Here we advocate the use of the minimal specificity principle and define $\pi^+{}_A$ as the upper envelope of minimal change solutions in that case.

– The above proposition is meaningful for π valued on finite chains $\{a_0, ..., a_n\}$ as well, just defining $|a_i - a_j| = |i - j|$.

- When $\Pi(A) = 0$, the solution $\pi^+_A = \pi(\cdot \mid A)$ corresponds to the choice of throwing away all of π, and keeping A as such; in other words it is what Gärdenfors (1988) calls a revision constructed from a fullmeet contraction.

- When $\Pi(A) = 0$ the least specific solution to (7) is given by $\Pi'(B \mid A) = 1$, $\forall$ B $\neq \emptyset$, and $\Pi'(\emptyset \mid A) = 0$. It corresponds to $\pi'(\cdot \mid A) = \pi_T$ and not μ_A. Particularly if A = $\emptyset$ then $\pi'(\cdot \mid \emptyset) = \pi_T$ again. This definition of conditional possibility (adopted in Dubois and Prade, 1991b) would violate axioms $(\Pi+2)$ and $(\Pi+5)$, but would obey the following ones instead

$(\Pi'+2)$ $N^+_A(A) = 1$ *if and only if* $\Pi(A) > 0$

$(\Pi'+5)$ *If* $\Pi(A) = 0$ *then* $\pi^+_A = \pi_T$

With $(\Pi+2)$ and $(\Pi+5)$ an absolute priority is given to the input information even when it was considered as impossible a priori. And receiving a self contradictory information A = $\emptyset$ leads us to an absurd belief state ($\pi_\perp$). On the contrary, with $(\Pi'+2)$, receiving an input that totally contradicts what was believed before results in a state of ignorance. What looks like a significant gap between the two approaches should not be regarded as such. Indeed in Gärdenfors theory, $(\Pi+2)$ is natural because in his model, nothing is a priori impossible except the contradiction. It comes down to assume $\Pi(A) > 0$, $\forall$ A $\neq \emptyset$ in our model. On the contrary, possibility theory is capable of expressing that a non-contradictory proposition should be considered as impossible, and $(\Pi'+2)$ expresses that the priority to the input information is less natural when the latter is a priori impossible. $(\Pi'+5)$ is consistent with $(\Pi'+2)$ in the limit. Now the choice between $(\Pi'+2)$ and $(\Pi+2)$ is rather a matter of taste. Receiving a contradictory input leaves us in an absurd belief state as much as in a state of ignorance.

Some worth noticing corollaries of the framework presented here are the counterparts of properties noticed by Gärdenfors, namely:

- $\pi^+_A = [\max(\pi, \pi^+_A)]^+_A$
- $\pi^+_A = \pi^+_B$ if and only if $\pi^+_B \leq \mu_A$ and $\pi^+_A \leq \mu_B$ (each is equivalent to $S(\pi) \cap A = S(\pi) \cap B$).

2.4 Relationship with Other Works

In the previous section, we have proved that the revision of possibility distributions is closely related to a notion of conditional possibility as depicted in equation (7). This equation is clearly very close to the one that founds conditional probability, in the case of uncertainty degrees taking values in [0,1]. In that case, looking at (7) leads to the problem of finding functions f such that $\Pi(A \cap B)$ is of the form $f(\Pi(B \mid A), \Pi(A))$, thus defining $\Pi(B \mid A)$. This problem has been first solved by Cox (1946) who noticed that f must be an associative function when A, B belong to a Boolean algebra.

When f is strictly increasing in both places, results in the theory of functional equations (Aczel, 1966) forces f to be a product up to an isomorphism. Cox' (1946) aim was to justify conditional probability. In the case of possibility theory, it leads to

$$\forall B, B \cap A \neq \emptyset, \Pi(B \mid A) = \frac{\Pi(A \cap B)}{\Pi(A)} \qquad (10)$$

provided that $\Pi(A) \neq \emptyset$. This is Dempster rule of conditioning, specialized to possibility measures, i.e. consonant plausibility measures of Shafer (1976). The corresponding revised possibility distribution is

$$\pi'_A(w) = \frac{\pi(w)}{\Pi(A)}, \forall w \in A$$
$$= 0 \text{ otherwise} \qquad (11)$$

This revision rule is the one that is obtained when mapping integer-valued disbelief functions of Spohn (1988) back into unit interval, applying the mapping to Spohn's notion of conditioning (see Dubois and Prade, 1990d, 1991a). Namely if κ is an ordinal conditional function from the set $\mathcal{A}$ of atoms of $\mathcal{B}$ to $\mathbb{N}$, then if $A = [\phi]$ for some $\phi \in \mathcal{B}$,

$$\kappa(w \mid A) = -\kappa(A) + \kappa(w) \text{ where } \kappa(w) = \kappa(\alpha) \text{ for } w \in [\alpha], \alpha \in \mathcal{A}.$$

Then letting $\pi(w) = e^{-\kappa(w)}$, $\kappa(w \mid A)$ leads to (11). It points out a discrepancy between our approach and Spohn's. π'_A is undefined for $\Pi(A) = 0$ and thus violates ($\Pi+1$) strictly speaking. However if we use (7) (where min is changed into product) instead of (10), $\pi'_A = \mu_A$ is still a solution when $\Pi(A) = 0$. Up to this slight modification, π'_A satisfies all postulates ($\Pi+1$)-($\Pi+8$) as well, but is not a minimal change update since all $\pi(w) > 0$ for $w \in A$ are modified. However (11) makes sense if Ω is a continuous universe, if π is continuous and revision is required to preserve continuity. Note that the similarity between Spohn's rule of conditioning, Dempster rule of conditioning, and conditional probability questions Gärdenfors' (1988) interpretation of conditional probability as an expansion. It may be argued that it is a revision process as well.

Our notion of conditional possibility is the result of solving Cox's equation by allowing f to be only isotonic, i.e. $f(x,y)$ increases when *both* x and y increase; see (Dubois and

Prade, 1990c). While (11) looks as a more natural counterpart of probabilistic conditioning, π^+_A is more closely akin to the concept of "would counterfactual" following Lewis, and denoted A □→ B, which is intended to mean "if it were the case that A, then it would be the case that B". Lewis proposes to consider A □→ B as true in world w_i if and only if some accessible world in A ∩ B is closer to w_i than any world in A ∩ $\bar{B}$, if there are worlds in A. Let us interpret "closer to world w_i" as "preferred" in the sense of possibility degrees (w_i thus denote the "ideal world"). And let us notice that we do have when $\Pi(A) > 0$ (as pointed out in Dubois and Prade (1991b)),

$$\forall B, B \cap A \neq \emptyset, N(B \mid A) > 0 \text{ if and only if } \Pi(B \cap A) > \Pi(\bar{B} \cap A) \quad (12)$$

where $\bar{B}$ is the complement of B and $N(\cdot \mid A)$ is based on π^+_A. The latter inequality means that there is a world in B ∩ A which is more possible than any world in $\bar{B}$ ∩ A, and this works if $\Pi(A) > 0$. Hence $N(B \mid A) > 0$ agrees with the truth of A □→ B. The counterpart of Lewis' "might conditional" A ◊→ B is of course $\Pi(B \mid A)$ in the sense of (7).

We have pointed out the proximity between the possibilistic approach and Spohn's well-ordered partitions (WOP). It is easy to check that given a WOP, $E_0, E_1, E_2, ..., E_n$ which partitions Ω, and assuming $\forall w \in E_i$, $\pi(w) = a_i$ with a_0 = impossible and a_n = completely possible, our approach to revision is to consider, as a result, a WOP on A, namely $\{E_i \cap A, i = 0,n\}$ where we must delete empty terms. Spohn objected to this kind of definition because in the revised state all worlds in $\bar{A}$ are completely disbelieved, and because the revision is not reversible. However belief changes are commutative. Moreover the input information A is taken as absolute truth in this section, and reversibility makes no sense in such a context. The case when A is no longer taken as absolute truth is considered in Section 4, in accordance with a purely ordinal setting.

2.5 Contraction in Possibility Theory

Contraction of a possibility distribution with respect to A ⊆ Ω corresponds to forgetting whether A is true or not. In other words, the result π^-_A of the contraction must lead to a possibility measure Π^-_A such that $\Pi^-_A(A) = \Pi^-_A(\bar{A}) = 1$, i.e. complete ignorance about A. Intuitively if $\Pi(A) = \Pi(\bar{A}) = 1$ already, then we should have $\pi^-_A = \pi$. Besides if $\Pi(A) = 1 > \Pi(\bar{A})$ then we should have $\pi^-_A(w) = 1$ for some w in $\bar{A}$, and especially for those w such that $\Pi(\bar{A}) = \pi(w)$. It leads to the following proposal

$$\pi^{+}_{A}(w) \ = 1 \text{ if } \pi(w) = \prod(\bar{A}), \, w \notin A$$
$$= \pi(w) \text{ otherwise.} \tag{13}$$

Again let us translate Gärdenfors' postulates for contraction into the possibilistic setting

(*$\prod^{+}1$*) *for any subset $A \subsetneq \Omega$, π^{+}_{A} represents an epistemic state*

Clearly, $\forall A$, $\pi^{+}_{A}(w) = 1$ for some w, with definition (13), if $\pi \neq \pi_{\perp}$.

(*$\prod^{+}2$*) *$\pi^{+}_{A} \geq \pi$*

After retracting A, there is less information than before, so that π^{+}_{A} is not more specific than π.

(*$\prod^{+}3$*) *if $N(A) = 0$ then $\pi^{+}_{A} = \pi$*

In other words if A is not held for somewhat certain, it is useless to retract it. $N(A) = 0$ means $\prod(\bar{A}) = 1$, hence π is not modified on $\bar{A}$, if definition (13) is adopted.

(*$\prod^{+}4$*) *$N^{+}_{A}(A) = 0$ unless $A = \Omega$*

Indeed, with (13), if $A \neq \Omega$, $\prod^{+}_{A}(\bar{A}) = 1 = 1 - N^{+}_{A}(A)$.

(*$\prod^{+}5$*) *if $N(A) > 0$ then $\pi \geq min(\pi^{+}_{A}, \mu_{A})$*

Indeed $N(A) > 0$ means that $\prod(A) > \prod(\bar{A})$. Hence $\pi^{+}_{A} = \pi$ on A, after definition (13).

(*$\prod^{+}6$*) *equivalent pieces of information lead to equivalent contractions.*

(*$\prod^{+}7$*) *$max(\pi^{+}_{A}, \pi^{+}_{B}) \geq \pi^{+}_{A \cap B}$*

$\forall w \in \bar{A} \cup \bar{B}$, if $\prod(\bar{A} \cup \bar{B}) = \pi(w)$, we have $\pi^{+}_{A \cap B}(w) = 1$. Then since $\prod(\bar{A} \cup \bar{B}) = max(\prod(\bar{A}), \prod(\bar{B}))$, either $\pi^{+}_{A}(w) = 1$ (if $w \in \bar{A}$) or $\pi^{+}_{B}(w) = 1$ (if $w \in \bar{B}$). Otherwise $\pi^{+}_{A \cap B} = \pi$, and the inequality holds as well due to ($\prod^{+}2$). ($\prod^{+}7$) means that retracting $A \cap B$ leads to loosing less information than when retracting A or retracting B, since when retracting $A \cap B$ it is enough to retract any of A and B.

(*$\prod^{+}8$*) *if $N^{+}_{A \cap B}(A) = 0$ then $\pi^{+}_{A \cap B} \geq \pi^{+}_{A}$*

$N^{+}_{A \cap B}(A) = 0$ means that $\prod^{+}_{A \cap B}(\bar{A}) = 1$. If $\exists w \in \bar{A}$, $\pi(w) = 1$ then $\pi^{+}_{A \cap B} = \pi^{+}_{A} = \pi$. If $\pi(w) < 1$, $\forall w \in \bar{A}$, then $\exists w \in \bar{A}$, $\prod(\bar{A} \cup \bar{B}) = \pi(w)$, since $\exists w \in \bar{A}$,

$\pi^{+}_{A \cap B}(w) = 1$. Hence $\pi(w) = \prod(\bar{A}) \geq \prod(\bar{B})$ and $\pi^{+}_{A}(w) = 1 = \pi^{+}_{A \cap B}(w)$. Now, the following inclusion holds

$$\{w \in \bar{A} \cup \bar{B}, \pi(w) = \prod(\bar{A} \cup \bar{B})\} \supseteq \{w \in \bar{A}, \pi(w) = \prod(\bar{A})\}$$

$\pi^{+}_{A \cap B}$ and π^{+}_{A} are respectively equal to 1 on these sets and are equal to π otherwise. Hence $\pi^{+}_{A \cap B} \geq \pi^{+}_{A}$. ($\prod$·8) means that if by retracting $A \cap B$, A is no longer certain any more, then we do not loose more information by retracting A directly.

By construction, when defined by (13), π^{+}_{A} again corresponds to the idea of minimally changing π so as to forget A, when there is a unique $w \in \bar{A}$ such that $1 > \prod(\bar{A}) = \pi(w)$. When there are several elements in $\{w \notin A, \pi(w) = \prod(\bar{A})\}$, minimal change contractions correspond to letting $\pi'(w) = 1$ for any such world, and π^{+}_{A} corresponds to consider the envelope of the minimal change solutions. If $\prod(\bar{A}) = 0$, what is obtained is the fullmeet contraction (Gärdenfors, 1988).

As in the classical case Levi and Harper's identities remain valid, namely

<u>Proposition 8</u>: $\pi^{+}_{A} = (\pi^{+}_{\bar{A}})^{+}_{A}$; $\pi^{+}_{A} = \max(\pi, \pi^{+}_{\bar{A}})$

<u>Proof</u>: Let us compute $(\pi^{+}_{\bar{A}})^{+}_{A}(w)$. Note that $\exists\, w \in A$ such that $\pi^{+}_{\bar{A}}(w) = 1$. Hence,

$$\begin{aligned}
(\pi^{+}_{\bar{A}})^{+}_{A}(w) &= \min(\mu_A(w), \pi^{+}_{\bar{A}}(w)) \\
&= 1 \text{ for } w \in A, \pi(w) = \prod(A) \\
&= \pi(w) \text{ for } w \in A, \pi(w) < \prod(A) \\
&= 0 \text{ otherwise}
\end{aligned}$$

hence Levi's identity holds. As for Harper's identity

$$\begin{aligned}
\max(\pi, \pi^{+}_{\bar{A}}) &= \pi(w) \text{ if } w \in A \\
&= 1 \text{ if } w \in \bar{A}, \pi(w) = \prod(\bar{A}) \\
&= \pi(w) \text{ otherwise.} \qquad \text{Q.E.D.}
\end{aligned}$$

3 BELIEF CHANGE IN POSSIBILISTIC LOGIC

Possibilistic logic is a logic of incomplete evidence. Its syntax consists of sentences in the first order calculus to which are attached lower bounds on the degree of necessity or of possibility of these sentences (Dubois and Prade, 1987, 1990a). Here we consider only the fragment of possibilistic logic with propositional sentences to which lower bounds of degrees of necessity are attached. If $\phi \in \mathcal{B}$ is a propositional sentence, $(\phi\ a)$ is a short notation for $N(\phi) \geq a$. When a goes from 0 to 1, ϕ goes from uncertainty to certainty, $(\phi\ 1)$ standing for the sure assertion of ϕ. In order to express that ϕ is unknown, one must assert $(\phi\ 0)$ and $(\neg\phi\ 0)$. However, only $(\phi\ a)$ such that $a > 0$ is explicitly used in the language. Reasoning in possibilistic logic is done by means of an extension of the resolution principle to weighted clauses:

$$(\gamma\ a)\ ;\ (\gamma'\ b) \vdash (Res(\gamma,\gamma')\ min(a,b))$$

where γ and γ' are propositional clauses, and $Res(\gamma,\gamma')$ is their resolvent. For instance $(\neg\phi \vee \psi\ a)\ ;\ (\phi \vee \chi\ b) \vdash (\psi \vee \chi\ min(a,b))$. This inference rule presupposes that when in a possibilistic formula $(\phi\ a)$ ϕ is not in a clausal form, it can be turned into a set $\{(\gamma_i,a), i=1,n\}$ of weighted clauses such that ϕ is equivalent to $\gamma_1 \wedge \gamma_2 \ldots \wedge \gamma_n$. This is justified by the semantics of propositional logic, and by the fact that $N(\phi) \geq a$ is equivalent to $N(\gamma_i) \geq a, i=1,n$.

The set of possible worlds in which a possibilistic logic sentence $(\phi\ a)$ is true is a fuzzy set on Ω defined by

$$\mu_{[\phi\ a]}(w)\ = 1\ \text{if}\ w \in [\phi]$$
$$= 1 - a\ \text{otherwise}$$

$\mu_{[\phi\ a]}$ is the least specific possibility distribution π such that $N([\phi]) = \inf_{w \notin [\phi]} 1 - \pi(w) \geq a$. The fuzzy set of worlds which satisfy a possibilistic knowledge base $K = \{(\phi_i,a_i), i=1,m\}$ is defined in terms of a possibility distribution π such that

$$\forall\ w \in \Omega,\ \pi(w) = min_{i=1,m}\ max(\mu_{[\phi_i]}(w), 1 - a_i) \tag{14}$$

which extends (4) from a set of sentences to a set of weighted sentences. Semantic entailment is defined in terms of specificity ordering $(\pi \leq \pi')$. Namely $K \models (\phi\ a)$ if and only if $\pi \leq max(\mu_{[\phi]}, 1 - a)$. This notion of semantic entailment is exactly the one of Zadeh (1979). These definitions make sense for consistent possibilistic knowledge bases, i.e. these such that $\pi(w) = 1$ for some $w \in \Omega$. Consistency of K is equivalent to the consistency of the classical knowledge base K* obtained by removing the weights (see Dubois and Prade, 1987). When $max_{w \in \Omega}\ \pi(w) = c < 1$, K is said to be partially inconsistent, c being the degree of consistency of K. When $c = 0$, K is completely inconsistent. At the syntactic level the consistency of K can be checked by means of repeated uses of the resolution principle until the empty clause is attained, with some weight. This is denoted $K \vdash (\perp a)$. By definition, $K \vdash (\phi\ a)$ means that $K \cup \{(\neg\phi\ 1)\} \vdash (\perp a)$ (refutation method). The degree of inconsistency inc(K) is then defined by max$\{a \mid K \vdash (\perp a)\}$. Possibilistic logic is sound and complete with respect to refutation based on resolution (Dubois et al., 1989). Namely it can be checked that

$$\text{inc}(K) = 1 - c = 1 - \max_{w \in \Omega} \pi(w)$$

$$K \vdash (\phi\ a) \text{ if and only if } K \vDash (\phi\ a) \text{ whenever K is consistent.}$$

When K is partially inconsistent, i.e. inc(K) > 0, non-trivial deductions can still be made from K, namely all $(\phi\ a)$ such that $K \vdash (\phi\ a)$, such that $a > $ inc(K). Indeed $(\phi\ a)$ is then the consequence of a consistent subpart of K. In that case $\max_{w \in \Omega} \pi(w) = 1 - $ inc(K) < 1 and $\forall\phi$, $\min(N(\phi),N(\neg\phi)) = $ inc(K). Let $\tilde{\pi}$ be a possibility distribution on Ω defined by

$$\tilde{\pi}(w) = \pi(w) \text{ if } \pi(w) < 1 - \text{inc}(K)$$
$$= 1 \text{ otherwise}$$

then it is easy to verify that the necessity measures N and Ñ based on π and $\tilde{\pi}$ respectively are related by the following relation

$$N(\phi) > N(\neg\phi) \Rightarrow \tilde{N}(\phi) = N(\phi) > N(\neg\phi) = \text{inc}(K) > \tilde{N}(\neg\phi) = 0$$

In fact, we have that

$$\tilde{\pi}(w) = \min_{i:a_i > \text{inc}(K)} \max(\mu_{[\phi_i]}(w), 1 - a_i).$$

Belief updating in possibilistic logic can then be envisaged as the syntactic counterpart of updating possibility distributions. As in Gärdenfors (1988), we can use closed ordered belief sets. The closure of K is the set of weighted sentences cn(K) = $\{(\phi\ a) \mid K \vdash (\phi\ a)\}$. A set K of weighted sentences is closed as soon as $(\perp a) \notin K$, $\forall\ a > 0$, and $(\phi\ a) \in K$ whenever $K \vdash (\phi\ a)$.

Let K be a consistent set of possibilistic formulae. Expansion of K by ϕ consists of forming $K \cup \{(\phi\ 1)\}$, and when inc(K $\cup \{(\phi\ 1)\}$) = 0, computing cn(K $\cup \{(\phi\ 1)\}$). Clearly the possibility distribution π' that restricts the fuzzy set of worlds that satisfy $K \cup \{(\phi\ 1)\}$ is

$$\pi' = \min(\pi, \mu_{[\phi]}) = \pi^+{}_{[\phi]}$$

When K is no longer consistent but inc(K) < 1, cn(K) is made of two parts, namely:

$$cn(K) = \{(\phi \ inc(K)), \phi \in \mathcal{B}\} \cup cn\{(\phi_i \ a_i) \in K, a_i > inc(K)\}$$

i.e. an absurd belief set containing sentences weighted by inc(K), and sentences with weights higher than inc(K) forming a consistent, ordered belief set. The union sign in the above expression includes the following subsumption: $\{(\phi \ a)\} \cup \{(\phi \ b)\} = \{(\phi \ \max(a,b))\}$.

Let us consider the case when K is consistent but $K' = K \cup \{(\phi \ 1)\}$ is not, and let a = inc(K $\cup$ {(ϕ 1)}) > 0. The following identity is easy to prove (Dubois and Prade, 1991b):

$$K \cup \{(\phi \ 1)\} \vdash (\psi \ b) \text{ with } b > a \text{ if and only if } N(\psi \mid \phi) > 0$$

where $N(\psi \mid \phi)$ is the necessity measure induced from $\pi^+{}_{[\phi]}$ the possibility distribution expressing the content of K, revised with respect to the set of models of ϕ. Indeed let π' be the possibility distribution on Ω induced by K' then

$$\pi' = \min(\pi, \mu_{[\phi]})$$
$$0 < \max_{w \in \Omega} \pi'(w) = 1 - a < 1$$

and the possibility distribution $\tilde{\pi}'$ induced from the consistent part of K' made of sentences whose weights is higher than a, is defined as

$$\tilde{\pi}'(w) = \pi(w) \text{ if } w \in [\phi] \text{ and } \pi'(w) < 1 - a$$
$$= 1 \text{ if } w \in [\phi] \text{ and } \pi(w) = 1 - a$$
$$= \pi'(w) = 0 \text{ otherwise.}$$

Hence $\tilde{\pi}' = \pi^+{}_{[\phi]}$, the result of revising π by $[\phi]$. The corresponding revision is rather drastic since all sentences $(\phi_i \ a_i)$ with weights $a_i \leq a$ are thrown away, and replaced by (ϕ 1). Note that when $\Pi(\phi) > 0$, $N(\psi \mid \phi) > 0$ is equivalent to $N(\neg\phi \vee \psi) > N(\neg\phi \vee \neg\psi)$, i.e., in terms of epistemic entrenchment, $\neg\phi \vee \psi >_c \neg\phi \vee \neg\psi$, and corresponds to a characteristic condition for having ψ in the (ordered) belief set obtained by revising cn(K) with respect to ϕ, in Gärdenfors (1988). Besides it is shown in Dubois and Prade (1991b) that when $\Pi(\phi) > 0$ the relation $\phi \vdash \psi$ if and only if $N(\psi \mid \phi) > 0$ possesses all properties of a well-behaved non-monotonic entailment. Hence revision and non-monotonic reasoning are nicely related in the setting of possibility theory.

When $inc(K \cup \{(\phi \ 1)) = 1$, $\tilde{\pi}'$ is no longer equal to $\pi^+_{[\phi]}$, since $\pi^+_{[\phi]} = \pi_\perp$ while $\tilde{\pi}' = \pi_\top$. We again find the problem of choosing between ignorance and absurdity when the input information totally contradicts the background one. In terms of non-monotonic reasoning, $\tilde{\pi}'$ corresponds to a slightly different definition of the preferential entailment $\vdash\!\!\!\sim$ which is not supraclassical (see Dubois and Prade, 1991b) ; especially, contradiction then preferentially entails nothing (rather than anything). $\tilde{\pi}'$ is exactly in agreement with the alternative definition of conditional necessity in Section 2.3.

A more conversative revision process is outlined in (Dubois and Prade, 1991a) and studied from the syntactic point of view in (Dubois et al., 1990). Namely if $K \cup \{(\phi \ 1)\}$ is partially inconsistent, we look for all the minimal inconsistent subsets of $K^* \cup \{\phi\}$ and the least certain sentence in each subset is deleted. It corresponds to a contraction process since the reason why $K \cup \{(\phi \ 1)\}$ is inconsistent is that $K \vdash (\neg\phi \ a)$ for a > 0. After deletion of the least certain sentences of all minimal inconsistent subsets of $K \cup \{(\phi \ 1)\}$, K is changed into a subset K^- of it, such that $K^- \vdash (\neg\phi \ a)$ is no longer possible for a > 0, nor $K^- \vdash (\phi \ a)$ since $K \vdash (\phi \ a)$ was not true either. Revision is then achieved by considering the expansion $K^- \cup \{(\phi \ 1)\}$. K^- is generally a superset of $\{(\phi_i \ a_i) \in K \mid a_i > inc(K \cup \{(\phi \ 1)\})\}$ since it may contain sentences with weights a_i smaller than a which are not responsible for any inconsistency related to $(\phi \ 1)$. Such a parsimony in the revision process is clearly due to the ordering on sentences as supplied by the weights, and the most parsimonious effect is achieved when logically independent sentences in K bear distinct weights (see Dubois and Prade, 1991a).

This revision process cannot be expressed at the semantic level, where all sentences in the knowledge base $K \cup \{(\phi \ 1)\}$ have been combined. Especially if $(\psi \ b) \in K$ and $b < inc(K \cup \{(\phi \ 1)\})$ then

$$\min(\pi, \mu_{[\phi]}) \leq \max(\mu_{[\psi]}, 1 - b)$$

i.e. all happens as if $(\psi \ b)$ had never been in K. The above described revision rule, by breaking the minimal inconsistent subsets of $K \cup \{(\phi \ 1)\}$ in a parsimonious way, enables pieces of evidence like $(\psi \ b)$ to be spared when they are not involved in the inconsistency of $K \cup \{(\phi \ 1)\}$.

Example: Consider the elementary knowledge base K = {(¬φ a), (ψ b)} with b < a.

Then $\pi(w) = \min(\max(1 - \mu_{[\phi]}(w), 1 - a), \max(\mu_{[\psi]}(w), 1 - b))$

$= 1$ if $w \in [\neg\phi \wedge \psi]$

$= 1 - a$ if $w \in [\phi]$

$= 1 - b$ if $w \in [\neg\phi \wedge \neg\psi]$

Hence $\pi'(w) = 1 - a$ if $w \in [\phi]$

$= 0$ otherwise

and the effect of the revision is K' = {(φ 1)}. Acting at the syntactic level, the only minimal inconsistent subset of K is {(φ 1), (¬φ a)} which is most parsimoniously broken by removing (¬φ a) only and the result of the revision is {(φ 1), (ψ b)}.

4 BELIEF CHANGE WITH UNCERTAIN PIECES OF EVIDENCE

In this section we consider the following question: given some epistemic state described by means of a possibility distribution, and some partially unreliable piece of evidence, how to modify the epistemic state on the basis of this piece of evidence while accounting for its level of uncertainty.

4.1 Numerical Rules for Belief Change

This kind of problem has not been so often considered in the literature. In the Bayesian setting, where an epistemic state is described by means of a probability measure P, an uncertain piece of evidence corresponds to an event $A \subseteq \Omega$ along with a probability a that this event did happen. The updated probability measure P(B | (A,a)) can be computed using Jeffrey's (1965) rule as

$$P(B \mid (A,a)) = aP(B \mid A) + (1 - a)P(B \mid \bar{A}) \qquad (15)$$

where P(B | A) and P(B | Ā) are obtained by regular conditioning. This formula has been extended to the case where the set of possible observations, one of which is the true one, forms a partition {A_1, A_2, ..., A_n} of Ω, and the probability that A_i is the actual observation is a_i, into

$$P(B \mid \{(A_i,a_i)\}_{i=1,n}) = \Sigma_{i=1,n} \, a_i P(B \mid A_i) \qquad (16)$$

In a strict Bayesian view of (15) and (16), a_i is interpreted as a conditional probability $P(A_i \mid E)$ where E denotes the (sure) event underlying the uncertain information. Then (16) assumes that $P(B \mid A_i) = P(B \mid A_i \cap E)$, i.e. that for all A_i, E is independent of B in the context A_i (e.g. Pearl, 1988).

(16) can be justified at the formal level by the fact that the only way of combining the conditional probabilities $P(B \mid A_i)$ in an eventwise manner (i.e. using the same combination law for all events B) is to use a linear weighted combination such as (16) (Lehrer and Wagner, 1981; McConway, 1981). Hence the weights a_i are absolutely needed in order to modify a probability measure upon receiving an uncertain piece of evidence. Lastly it is obvious that pushing (16) to the limit, by assuming $\Omega = \{w_1, ..., w_n\}$ and $A_i = \{w_i\}$, i.e. choosing the finest partition in Ω, then letting $a_i = P_2(\{w_i\})$ for a probability measure P_2, Jeffrey's rule (16) comes down to a simple substitution of P_1 by P_2. In other words, the new piece of evidence totally destroys the epistemic state. It emphasizes the dissymmetry of the belief change process; priority is given to the new information.

Spohn (1988) has carried out the same program in the language of his ordinal disbelief functions. Let κ be a disbelief function on Ω and A be an uncertain piece of evidence expressed by a weight n which is interpreted as the degree of disbelief in the observation A. Then the (A,n) conditioning of κ is

$$\kappa(w \mid (A,n)) = \kappa(w \mid A) \text{ if } w \in A$$
$$= n + \kappa(w \mid \bar{A}) \text{ if } w \notin A \qquad (17)$$

where $\kappa(w \mid A) = \kappa(w) - \kappa(A)$, as already introduced in Section 2.4. This notion is extended over to an ordinal conditional function λ defined on the partition $\{A_1, ..., A_n\}$ and that acts as uncertain evidence. Then (17) generalizes into

$$\kappa(w \mid \lambda) = \lambda(A_i) + \kappa(w \mid A_i), \forall w \in A_i, i = 1,n \qquad (18)$$

If we use Spohn's (1990) probabilistic interpretation of ordinal disbelief functions, namely $\kappa(w) = n$ means $P(w) = \varepsilon^{-n}$ where ε is an infinitely small number, then, noticing that if $w \in A_i$, $P(w \mid \{(A_i,a_i)\}_{i=1,n}) = a_i P(w \mid A_i)$ (with $a_i = e^{-\lambda(A_i)}$), it is obvious that (18) is an infinitesimal view of Jeffrey's rule.

In the opposite way, (17) and (18) can be expressed in the setting of possibility theory, letting $\pi(w) = e^{-\kappa(w)}$ for all $w \in \Omega$, as done in a previous paper (Dubois and Prade, 1990d). Then denoting $\bar{a} = e^{-n}$, $a_i = e^{-\lambda(A_i)}$, we obtain

$$\pi(w \mid (A,a)) \ = \frac{\pi(w)}{\prod(A)} \quad w \in A$$

$$= \frac{\bar{a}\pi(w)}{\prod(\bar{A})} \quad w \notin A \tag{19}$$

$$\pi(w \mid \{(A_i,a_i), i = 1,n\}) = \frac{a_i \pi(w)}{\prod(A_i)} \quad w \in A_i \tag{20}$$

Note that due to Spohn's assumption that $\kappa(w)$ is finite when $\mathbb{N}$-valued, $\prod(A_i) > 0$, $\forall i$. Gärdenfors (1988) points out that the (A,n) conditionalization is able to account for revision, contraction and expansion. Let us show it from (19). To do it, let us denote a and $\bar{a}$ the possibility that A and $\bar{A}$ are the input propositions respectively. Moreover we shall assume that $\prod(A) = 1 > \prod(\bar{A})$ in the epistemic state. Of course we have $\max(a,\bar{a}) = 1$. When $a < 1$, the input information tends to reject A; when $\bar{a} < 1$, the input information tends to assert A.

Proposition 9: Given a possibility distribution π with $\prod(A) = 1 > \prod(\bar{A})$, the updated possibility distribution π' that accounts for the information $\{(A,a), (\bar{A}\ \bar{a})\}$ is

– a contraction of π with respect to A if and only if $a = \bar{a} = 1$
– more specific than π if and only if $a = 1$, $\bar{a} < \prod(\bar{A})$ (expansion)
– a strict revision of π if and only if $a < 1$.

Proof:
i)   contraction: we must have $\pi' \geq \pi$ and $\prod'(\bar{A}) = \prod'(A) = 1$. Hence, for $w \in A$, $a\pi(w) \geq \pi(w)$ which forces $a = 1$, and for $w \in \bar{A}$, $\bar{a}\pi(w)/\prod(\bar{A}) \geq \pi(w)$ which forces $\bar{a} \geq \prod(\bar{A})$. More precisely $\exists w \in \bar{A}$, $\bar{a}\pi(w)/\prod(\bar{A}) = 1$ (since $\prod'(\bar{A}) = 1$), and we must have $\bar{a} = 1$. It is easy to see that the result is indeed a contraction:

$$\pi'(w) \ = \pi(w) \text{ if } w \in A$$

$$= \frac{\pi(w)}{\prod(\bar{A})} \text{ otherwise}$$

and its satisfies $(\prod^{\pm}1)$-$(\prod^{\pm}8)$.

ii) <u>expansion</u>: we must have $\pi \geq \pi'$. More specifically for $w \in A$, $a\pi(w) \leq \pi(w)$, but $a\pi(w) = 1$ for some $w \in A$. Hence $a = 1$. Moreover $\forall\, w \in \bar{A}$, $\bar{a}\pi(w)/\prod(\bar{A}) \leq \pi(w)$ which forces $\bar{a} < \prod(\bar{A})$. In other words A must be rejected more strongly by the input information than it is by the epistemic state. Note that if $\bar{a} > \prod(\bar{A})$ the result is a weak contraction, in the sense that $\pi' \geq \pi$ but $\prod'(\bar{A}) < 1$ (if $\bar{a} < 1$).

iii) <u>revision</u>: we now require $\prod'(A) < \prod'(\bar{A}) = 1$. Hence $a\pi(w) < \pi(w)$ on A, which leads to $a < 1$, and forces $\bar{a} = 1$. Now we do have $\forall\, w \in \bar{A}$, $\pi(w)/\prod(\bar{A}) > \pi(w)$. Hence, it requires that the input information rejects A. The obtained result is indeed a revision since $\exists\, w \in \bar{A}$, $\pi'(w) = 1$, while $\forall\, w \in A$, $\pi'(w) < 1$. Moreover $\pi > \pi'$ on A and $\pi \leq \pi'$ on $\bar{A}$.
Q.E.D.

It is possible to check Gärdenfors' postulates by comparing the belief sets $K' = \{\phi, N'(\phi) > 0\}$ and $K = \{\phi, N(\phi) > 0\}$, as done by Gärdenfors (1988) himself in the language of Spohn's disbelief functions. Another way is to extend the postulates themselves to the case of uncertain input information; this will be done later on.

Note that as for Jeffrey's rule, Spohn's rule leads to a mere substitution of the epistemic state by the input information, when the partition $\{A_1, ..., A_n\}$ is fine enough. Indeed if $A_i = \{w\}$ on a finite set Ω, (20) leads to let $\pi'(w_i) = a_i$ as the result of the belief change. In some sense, this is not satisfactory. It means that if π is revised on the light of a fuzzy piece of evidence F corresponding to a possibility distribution μ_F, where $\forall\, w \in \Omega$, $\pi(w) > 0$, and $\mu_F(w) > 0$, π is simply changed into μ_F. Yet, it is easy to imagine situations where we would like to preserve some trace of the prior epistemic state in the revised belief state. This is typically the case when μ_F does not contradict π, in the sense that their cores intersect. Then we should allow μ_F to refine π rather than to replace it. Yet, the result π' of Spohn's rule is an expansion of π ($\pi' \leq \pi$) only if $\mu_F \leq \pi$. This is not coherent with Gärdenfors' (1988) notion of expansion by which an input ϕ leads to an expansion of a belief set K as soon as ϕ is consistent with K.

4.2 A New Ordinal Rule for Belief Change

In order to work out a possibilistic belief change rule that obviates this problem, let us look at the uncertain piece of information described by the possibility distribution μ_F in another way. Namely, instead of considering $\{(w_i, a_i), w_i \in \Omega\}$ where $a_i = \mu_F(w_i)$, we may represent μ_F in terms of the level-cuts of F, namely $F_a = \{w \mid \mu_F(w) \geq a\}$ for $1 \geq a > 0$. Indeed, we have the following representation theorem (Zadeh, 1971)

$$\mu_F(w) = \sup_{a \in (0,1]} \min(a, \mu_{F_a}(w)) \tag{21}$$

where μ_{F_a} is the characterisitic function of F_a. F_a is similar to a confidence interval, and a evaluates to what extent all worlds $w \in F_a$ are relevant to F. A natural belief change rule can thus be derived from (21), changing $\mu_{F_a}(w)$ into the conditional possibility $\pi(w \mid F_a)$ as defined by (9) in section 2.3. In other words we are all the more willing to update on F_a as F_a contains only plausible worlds in the sense of the input information. It gives

$$\pi(w \mid F) = \sup_{a \in (0,1]} \min(a, \pi(w \mid F_a)) \tag{22}$$

where a acts as a weight bearing on $\pi(w \mid F_a)$ and the supremum acts as an aggregation operation. Besides (22) can be expressed in terms of possibility measures namely

$$\forall B, \; \Pi(B \mid F) = \sup_{a \in (0,1]} \min(a, \Pi(B \mid F_a)) \tag{23}$$

where $\Pi(B \mid F_a)$ is given by (8). The unicity of the supremum as an aggregation operation between possibility measures has been established in Dubois and Prade (1990b). It is the counterpart of the unicity of the mixture operations in (16) for probability measures.

The structural similarity of (23) and Jeffrey's rule (16) is striking, changing sup into sum, min into product; while Jeffrey's rule updates with a partition, the possibilistic rule updates on the basis of a family of nested sets (a "system of spheres" in the terminology mentioned by Gärdenfors (1988)). This similarity in the structure of the rule, and the contrast between disjointness and nestedness of sets between Jeffrey's rule and (23) are very common features when comparing probability and possibility theory. Despite their structural similarity, (23) and (16) behave quite differently.

Let us calculate $\pi(w \mid F)$ as defined by (22) more explicitly. The following properties are noticeable

i) $\qquad\qquad\qquad \pi(w \mid F) \leq \mu_F(w), \; \forall w \tag{24}$

<u>Proof</u>: $\forall w$, if $w \notin F_a$, then $\pi(w \mid F_a) = 0$, hence $\pi(w \mid F_a) \leq \mu_{F_a}(w)$, and

$$\pi(w \mid F) = \sup_{a:w \in F_a} \min(a, \pi(w \mid F_a)) \leq \sup_a \min(a, \mu_{F_a}(w)) = \mu_F(w)$$

$$\text{Q.E.D.}$$

ii) If the cores $C(\pi)$ and $C(F)$ of π and μ_F intersect then $\pi(w \mid F) = \min(\mu_F(w), \pi(w))$.

<u>Proof</u>: In this circumstance, $C(\pi) \cap F_a \neq \emptyset$, $\forall a$; hence $\forall a$, $\pi(w \mid F_a) = \min(\mu_{F_a}(w), \pi(w))$ (see axiom $\Pi+4$). Hence $\pi(w \mid F) = \sup_a \min(a, \mu_{F_a}(w), \pi(w)) = \min(\mu_F(w), \pi(w))$. Q.E.D.

iii) $\forall F \neq \emptyset$, $\exists w \in C(F)$, such that $\pi(w \mid F) = 1$.

<u>Proof</u>: Let $w \in C(F)$ such that $\Pi(C(F)) = \pi(w)$ then applying (22) with $a = 1$, we get $\pi(w \mid F) \geq \min(1, \pi(w \mid C(F)) = 1$ since $\pi(w \mid C(F)) = 1$. Q.E.D.

More generally we have the following result.

<u>Proposition 10</u>: $\forall w$, if $\exists a > 0$ such that $\Pi(F_a) = \pi(w)$ then $\pi(w \mid F) = \mu_F(w)$; otherwise $\pi(w \mid F) = \min(\mu_F(w), \pi(w))$.

<u>Proof</u>: Let $w \in \Omega$ and $a > 0$ such that $\Pi(F_a) = \pi(w)$. Clearly $w \in F_a$, and $\pi(w \mid F_a) = 1$. Assume $\mu_F(w) > a$ and let $\mu_F(w) \geq b > a$. Then since $w \in F_b$, $\pi(w) \leq \Pi(F_b) \leq \Pi(F_a)$. Hence $\Pi(F_b) = \pi(w)$ as well. Hence it is always possible to choose $a = \mu_F(w)$, and respect $\Pi(F_a) = \pi(w)$. In that case, $\sup_a \min(a, \pi(w \mid F_a))$ is attained for $a = \mu_F(w)$ and $\pi(w \mid F) = \min(\mu_F(w), 1) = \mu_F(w)$. If w is such that $\forall a > 0$, $\Pi(F_a) \neq \pi(w)$, then $\pi(w \mid F_a) = \pi(w)$ (if $w \in F_a$) or 0 (if $w \notin F_a$). Hence $\pi(w \mid F) = \sup_{a:w \in F_a} \min(a, \pi(w)) = \min(\mu_F(w), \pi(w))$. Q.E.D.

This result leads us to a more compact expression of $\pi(w \mid F)$ as:

$$\pi(w \mid F) = \min(\mu_F(w), \pi(w \mid F_{\mu_F(w)})) \tag{25}$$

since Proposition 10 points out that the supremum in (22) is attained from $a = \mu_F(w)$, $\forall w$. This expression makes sense for continuous sets of possible worlds, provided that μ_F is upper semi-continuous, so that F_a is closed $\forall a \in (0,1]$. In order to compare (25) with Spohn's rule, let us assume that there is a partition $\{A_1, ..., A_n\}$ with $\mu_F(w) = a_i$, $\forall w \in A_i$, and $a_1 = 1 \geq a_2 ... \geq a_n$. Then

$$\forall w \in A_i, \pi(w \mid F) = \min(a_i, \pi(w \mid F_{a_i}))$$
$$= \min(a_i, \pi(w \mid \bigcup_{j=1,i} A_j))$$

Hence

$$\pi(w \mid F) = \begin{cases} a_i \text{ if } \pi(w) = \max_{j=1,i} \Pi(A_j) \\ \min(a_i, \pi(w)) \text{ otherwise} \end{cases} \tag{26}$$

The differences between Spohn's updating rule (20) and (25) are now clear

a) The possibilistic rule always tries to refine the a priori epistemic state and operates a revision otherwise. If is never a contraction, since we never have $\pi(\cdot \mid F) > \pi$. Contrastedly Spohn's rule may lead to a decrease in specificity of π, even when the a priori epistemic state is consistent with the input information

b) The possibilistic rule is of a truly ordinal nature, while Spohn's rule, once mapped into the unit interval, requires an additive-like structure on the unit interval. It is possible to make Spohn's rule completely based on ordering by turning (20) into

$$\pi(w \mid \{(A_i, a_i), i = 1, n\}) = \min(a_i, \pi(w \mid A_i)), \forall w \in A_i \tag{27}$$

where $\pi(w \mid A_i)$ is the possibilistic min-based conditioning. It can be checked that this rule has exactly the same properties as Spohn's rule (20) with regards to contraction, revision and expansion, i.e. it obeys Proposition 9 as well. (27) could be useful to define an updating rule for well-ordered partitions that avoids all worlds in $\overline{A}$ to be equally disbelieved, hence coping with defects of purely ordinal proposals made by Spohn (1988) himself (see his discussion on pp. 113-114).

Let us compare rules (20) and (25) in a more precise way so as to formally express the first difference.

<u>Proposition 11</u>: Assume that the epistemic state is described by π such that $\Pi(A) = 1 > \Pi(\overline{A}) = \overline{b}$. Let the input information be of the form $N(A) = 1 - \overline{a}$, such that $\overline{a} > \overline{b}$. Then the updated epistemic state π' is such that $N'(A) = 1 - \overline{a}$ if Spohn's rule (20) (or its ordinal counterpart (27)) is used, and such that $\pi' = \pi$ if the possibilistic revision rule (25) is used.

<u>Proof</u>: The input information is μ_F such that $\mu_F(w) = 1$ if $w \in A$, and $\mu_F(w) = \overline{a}$ otherwise. Hence using (19) we get $\Pi(A \mid (A, \overline{a})) = \Pi(A) = 1$ and $\Pi(\overline{A} \mid (A, \overline{a})) = \overline{a}$. Hence the degree of certainty of A decreases and becomes $1 - \overline{a}$; the same phenomenon occurs with (27). Now using the possibilistic revision rule we get, since $C(F) = A$

$$\pi(w \mid F)) = \min(\pi(w), \mu_F(w)) = \pi(w) \text{ if } w \in A$$
$$= \min(\pi(w), \bar{a}) = \pi(w) \text{ if } w \notin A \text{ since } \sup_{w \notin A} \pi(w) = \bar{b} < \bar{a}$$

Hence the input information is simply rejected by the epistemic state.   Q.E.D.

In other words, Spohn's updating rule leads to become more uncertain about A, when the input information is that A is less certain that what is implied by the a priori epistemic state. On the contrary, the possibilistic revision rule rejects pieces of information that do not contradict what is held for plausible by the epistemic state, but that are considered as not informative enough.

4.3 Postulates for Belief Change with Uncertain Evidence

It is now interesting to consider extensions of Gärdenfors' postulates to the case when the input information itself comes under the form of a possibility distribution μ_F. Let us first consider expansions, and denote π^+_F the result of expanding π using μ_F. (Π+1), (Π+3), (Π+5) and (Π+6) can be reconducted as such for π^+_F. For (Π+2) and (Π+4) conditions of the form N(A) = 1 must be modified since N(F) is undefined when F is a fuzzy set (in fact see (Dubois and Prade, 1990a) for the definition of the certainty of a fuzzy event). Here we shall use the semantic entailment of Zadeh's (1979) approximate reasoning theory and possibilistic logic. Let us postulate that F is entailed by the updated epistemic state, i.e.

(Π+2) $\pi^+_F \leq \mu_F$

The other postulate claims that no updating takes place if F is already entailed by the epistemic state:

(Π+4) if $\pi \leq \mu_F$ then $\pi^+_F = \pi$

Let us now define the expansion π^+_F in accordance with the possibilistic revision rule (25), as

$$\pi^+_F(w) = \min(\pi(w), \mu_F(w)) \text{ if } \exists w', \pi(w') = \mu_F(w') = 1$$
$$= 0, \forall w \text{ otherwise (absurd belief state)}$$

Now by (Π+2) and (Π+3), we do have $\pi^+_F \leq \min(\pi, \mu_F)$, and it is obvious that the above expansion rule is the only one that satisfies (Π+1)-(Π+6). Note that Spohn's updating rule violates (Π+4) and (Π+3) since we may get $\pi' = \mu_F$ as the result of an update even if $\pi \leq \mu_F$. Revision postulates (Π+1) to (Π+6) can be reconducted similarly; especially

(Π+2): $\pi^+_F \leq \mu_F$

(Π+4): if $\exists w$, $\mu_F(w) = \pi(w) = 1$ then $\pi^+_F \leq \pi^+_F$, interpreting $\Pi(F) = 1$ as $\sup_w \min(\mu_F(w), \pi(w)) = 1$ (Zadeh's (1978) possibility of a fuzzy event)

(Π+5): if $\nexists w$, $\mu_F(w) = 1$ then $\pi = \pi_\perp$

To make any sense out of (Π+7) and (Π+8) we need to define intersections of fuzzy sets viewed as possibility distributions. Especially, the conjunction of two epistemic states μ_F and μ_G must be an epistemic state again. Zadeh's intersection of fuzzy sets reads:

$$\mu_{F \cap G}(w) = \min(\mu_F(w), \mu_G(w)).$$

When $\forall w$, $\mu_F(w) < 1$ or $\mu_G(w) < 1$, $\pi^+_{F \cap G} = \pi_\perp$ from axiom (Π+5). Then (Π+7) and (Π+8) can be extended right away.

Let us consider the possibilistic revision rule in order to check the postulates: (Π+1) is obvious, (Π+2) is (24), (Π+3) is obvious from (25), (Π+4) is true since $\pi(w \mid F) = \min(\mu_F, \pi)$ when cores intersect, i.e. coincide with the expansion (Π+5) is partly a matter of convention since $\pi(\cdot \mid F)$ is defined only when μ_F is normalized and $\pi(\cdot \mid \emptyset) = \pi_\perp$. It is permitted to let $\pi(\cdot \mid F) = \pi_\perp$ also when $\mu_F(w) < 1$, $\forall\, w \in \Omega$. (Π+6) is rather obvious.

The two other axioms translate into:

(Π+7): $\pi^+_{F \cap G} \geq (\pi^+_F)^+_G$

(Π+8): if the cores of π^+_F and G intersect then $\pi^+_{F \cap G} \leq (\pi^+_F)^+_G$

These two axioms are not satisfied by $\pi^+_F = \pi(\cdot \mid F)$. To see it, first note that if the cores of π^+_F and G do not intersect, then $(\pi^+_F)^+_G = \pi_\perp$ and (Π+7) trivially holds. If they intersect then

$$(\pi^+_F)^+_G = \min(\mu_G(w), \pi(w \mid F))$$

Let $a = \mu_F(w)$, $b = \mu_G(w)$. The expressions for $\pi^+_{F \cap G}$ and $(\pi^+_F)^+_G$ write:

$$\pi^+_{F \cap G}(w) = \min(a, b, \pi(w \mid (F \cap G)_{\min(a,b)}))$$
$$(\pi^+_F)^+_G(w) = \min(a, b, \pi(w \mid F_a))$$

Let us assume that $b < a$. $(\pi^+{}_F)^+{}_G(w) > \pi^+{}_{F \cap G}(w)$ holds when $\pi(w \mid F_a) = 1$ and $\pi(w \mid (F \cap G)_b) < b$. It means that $\pi(w) = \Pi(F_a) < \Pi(F_b \cap G_b)$ and $\pi(w) < b$. This situation occurs if $F_b \cap G_b \not\subset F_a$ (it makes sense since $F_a \subseteq F_b$), and for some $w' \in (F_b \cap G_b) - F_a$ we have $\pi(w) < \pi(w') < b$. Hence (Π+7) can be violated. This situation never occurs when F is not fuzzy since then $a = 1$ or 0.

Similarly, (Π+8) is violated if for some w, $(\pi^+{}_F)^+{}_G(w) < \pi^+{}_{F \cap G}(w)$. It may occur if $\pi(w \mid F_a) < \min(a,b)$ and $\pi(w \mid (F \cap G)_{\min(a,b)}) = 1$. It means that $\pi(w) = \Pi((F \cap G)_{\min(a,b)}) < \Pi(F_a)$ and $\pi(w) < \min(a,b)$. Assume $b > a$ then we need $\pi(w) = \Pi(F_a \cap G_a) < \Pi(F_a)$. This situation occurs whenever $\exists\, w' \in F_a - G_a$, $\pi(w) < \min(\pi(w'), a)$. When F and G are not fuzzy, this situation never occurs since $C(F) = F$, $C(G) = G$ and for $w \in C(F \cap G)$, $\pi^+{}_F$ coincides with $\pi(\cdot \mid C(F))$. $(\pi^+{}_F)^+{}_G$ coincides with $(\pi^+{}_{C(F)})^+{}_{C(G)}$, and from Section 2.3, (Π+8) does hold in the classical case.

The failure of (Π+7) and (Π+8) for the possibilistic revision rules means that one must distinguish two successive updating steps by means of uncertain pieces of evidence, from the case when these pieces of evidence correspond to two parallel sources of information and are merged prior to updating. Note that Spohn's rule does not satisfy (Π+4) since it involves contraction-like effects.

The question of how to define a genuine contraction rule with uncertain evidence in the possibilistic setting is left for further research. Indeed, one must first try to realize what it means to "forget an uncertain piece of information". Insofar as it means "to raise its level of uncertainty", the possibilistic counterpart of Spohn's rule (equation (27)) may be enough. On the other hand one may think of extrapolating the identity $K \dot{-} \phi = K \cap (K \dot{+} \neg\phi)$ over to possibilistic evidence, using $\mu_{\bar{F}} = 1 - \mu_F$ to define the negation. Then we get

$$\pi^{\dot{-}}{}_F(w) = \max(\pi, \pi(w \mid \bar{F}))$$

The study of the contraction axioms and the meaningfulness of this rule is left for further research.

CONCLUSION

The main thrust of this paper is that the setting of possibility theory offers a convenient tool for discussing the problem of belief revision. The numbers in the unit interval may look as the most questionable part of the model. In a finite setting resorting to numbers is superfluous; however, if it is remembered that necessity measures are special cases of belief functions (Shafer, 1976), themselves being special cases, mathematically speaking, of upper and lower probabilities (Walley, 1991), getting rid of numbers is also getting rid of an important connexion to probability theory, that clearly differs from the type of connexion Spohn (1990) proposed in order to link his disbelief functions to probability measures.

The study of updating under uncertain information has pointed out the ambiguity of the basic revision principle saying that the epistemic input should be accepted in the resulting epistemic state, when the epistemic input is uncertain. The dilemma is whether the level of uncertainty should be viewed as a degree of reliability of the epistemic input, or whether it should be viewed as an integral part of this input so that accepting the input means to accept the uncertainty as well. In the first case, the receiver always tries to improve its knowledge by refining it (expansion), modifying it (revision), or possibly rejecting the input information when it is likely to turn certainties into uncertainties. This is the case of the possibilistic expansion and revision rules by which the input information is accepted insofar as it is not less specific as the a priori epistemic state; otherwise it is rejected as being redundant. This updating attitude is obtained when adopting an "horizontal view" of the input information, as a system of nested spheres (the level cuts of the input possibility distribution).

In the second case, the receiver takes the input information for granted; if the input information is very uncertain then the receiver forgets previous certainties by acknowledging that he has lost them. Especially, it is easy to see that if the input information is the complete ignorance, ($\mu_F(w) = 1$, $\forall w$) then Spohn's rule (as well as its ordinal counterpart (27)) erases the contents of the knowledge base that model the epistemic state. Hence updating may result in a contraction, contrary to the possibilistic rule. Spohn's rule shares this feature with Jeffrey's rule of updating in probability theory, and views the input information as an ordered partition of the set of possible worlds. Curiously, the result of Spohn's rule heavily depends upon the granularity of this partition. Especially, there are a lot of ways of representing the total ignorance input ($\mu_F(w) = 1$, $\forall w$) by means of a partition of equally weighted subsets of Ω; each representation gives a different updated epistemic state. Especially, if the partition contains only one element ($\{\Omega\}$), Spohn's rule rejects the input, while if the partition is the finest one, the input information destroys the epistemic state. It corresponds to two ways of representing ignorance: $\Pi(\Omega) = 1$ and $\mu_F(w) = 1$, $\forall\, w \in \Omega$. The two are equivalent if we accept the principle of minimum specificity otherwise one may consider that $\Pi(\Omega) = 1$ is weaker than $\mu_F(w) = 1$, $\forall w$; the latter expresses a certainty of ignorance that is forced upon the epistemic state by Spohn's rule, while $\Pi(\Omega) = 1$ is viewed as the absence of information. These remarks may explain the sensitivity of Spohn's updating scheme to the granularity of the input information. This situation also occurs with Jeffrey's rule where updating upon the absence of knowledge $(P(\Omega) = 1)$ is ineffective while updating upon a uniform distribution on Ω $(P(\{w_i\}) = 1/|\Omega|$ for finite universes, leads again to destroying the prior epistemic state. Such a distinction is not made by the possibilistic rule.

The two attitudes towards updating in the face of uncertain information are equally interesting and do not address the same kind of problems, as pictured in the two following imaginary dialogues.

possibilistic revision rule:

> input: A seems to be true but I'm not so sure
>
> receiver: I am already pretty sure that A is true, so you do not help me very much. I know more than you.

Spohn's-λ conditioning:

> input: I am sure that A is almost unknown; you cannot claim that it is true
>
> receiver: I thought A was true, but since you are sure I should not be so affirmative, I am ready to retract it.

A last point is the existence of several unequally structured settings for updating under uncertain information. Scanning from propositional logic to probability theory, one goes through a completely ordinal model, i.e. possibility theory where everything, including the most refined updating rules, relies on total orderings. Spohn's model is one step further towards an additive structure since, while the representation of epistemic states remain ordinal, the updating rules use the addition of natural integers; especially the conditioning rules are infinitesimal counterparts of Bayes and Jeffrey's rules of updating in probability theory. What is not clear so far is how much structure do we need, how much is enough, to address the belief revision problem not only at the theoretical level, but also at the level of implemented devices. In this respect, possibilistic logic seems to offer a computationally promising tool.

REFERENCES

Aczel J. (1966): *Lectures on Functional Equations and their Applications*, New York: Academic Press.

Cox R.T. (1946): "Probability, frequency and reasonable expectation", *American Journal of Physics 14*, 1-13.

De Finetti B. (1937): "Foresight: its logical laws, its subjective sources", *Annales de l'Institut H. Poincaré 7*. Reprinted in *Studies in Subjective Probability*, ed. by H.E. Kyburg, Jr., H.E. Smokler, New York: Wiley & Sons, 1964, 93-158.

Dubois D. (1986): "Belief structures, possibility theory and decomposable confidence measures on finite sets", *Computers and Artificial Intelligence (Bratislava) 5(5)*, 403-416.

Dubois D., Lang J., and Prade H. (1989): "Automated reasoning using possibilistic logic: semantics, belief revision, variable certainty weights", *Proceedings of the 5th Workshop on Uncertainty in Artificial Intelligence*, Windsor, Ontario, Aug. 18-20, pp. 81-87.

Dubois D., Lang J., and Prade H. (1990): "Inconsistency of possibilistic knowledge bases – To live or not live with it", in Tech. Report IRIT/90-54/R, IRIT, Univ. P. Sabatier, Toulouse, France. To appear in *Fuzzy Logic for the Management of Uncertainty*, ed. by L.A. Zadeh, and J. Kacprzyk, New York: Wiley.

Dubois D., and Prade H. (1986): "Possibilistic inference under matrix form", in *Fuzzy Logic in Knowledge Engineering*, ed. by H. Prade, and C.V. Negoita, Köln: Verlag TÜV Rheinland, 112-126.

Dubois D., and Prade H. (1987a): "Necessity measures and the resolution principle", *IEEE Trans. on Systems, Man and Cybernetics 17*, 474-478.

Dubois D., and Prade H. (1987b): "The principle of minimum specificity as a basis for evidential reasoning", in *Uncertainty in Knowledge-Based Systems*, ed. by B. Bouchon, and R.R. Yager (Inter. Conf. on Information Processing and Management of Uncertainty in Knowledge-Based Systems (IPMU'86), Paris, France, June 30/July 4 1986), Berlin: Springer Verlag, 75-84.

Dubois D., and Prade H. (with the collaboration of Farreny H., Martin-Clouaire R., and Testemale C.) (1988): *Possibility Theory: An Approach to Computerized Processing of Uncertainty*, New York: Plenum Press. (Masson, Paris, 1985 and 1987 for the French editions).

Dubois D., and Prade H. (1990a): "Resolution principles in possibilistic logic", *Int. J. on Approximate Reasoning 4(1)*, 1-21.

Dubois D., and Prade H. (1990b): "Aggregation of possibility measures", in *Multiperson Decision Making using Fuzzy Sets and Possibility Theory*, ed. by J. Kacprzyk, and M. Fedrizzi, Kluwer Acad. Publ., 55-63.

Dubois D., and Prade H. (1990c): "The logical view of conditioning and its application to possibility and evidence theories", *Int. J. of Approximate Reasoning 4*, 23-46.

Dubois D., and Prade H. (1990d): "Updating with belief functions, ordinal conditional functions and possibility measures", *Preprints of the 6th Conf. on Uncertainty in Artificial Intelligence*, Cambridge, Mass., July 27-29, pp. 307-315. To appear in

Uncertainty in Artificial Intelligence 6, ed. by P.P. Bonissone, M. Henrion, L.N. Kanal, and J.F. Lemmer, Amsterdam: North-Holland.

Dubois D., and Prade H. (1991a): "Epistemic entrenchment and possibilistic logic", *Artificial Intelligence 50*, 223-239.

Dubois D., and Prade H. (1991b): "Possibilistic logic, preferential models, non-monotonicity and related issues", *Proceedings of the 12th Inter. Joint Conf. on Artificial Intelligence (IJCAI-91)*, Sydney, Australia, Aug. 24-30, pp. 419-424.

Fariñas del Cerro L., and Herzig A. (1991): "A modal analysis of possibility theory", in *Fundamentals of Artificial Intelligence Research*, ed. by Ph. Jorrand, and J. Kelemen, Proceedings of the Inter. Workshop FAIR'91, Smolenice Castle, Czechoslovakia, Sept. 8-12, Springer Verlag, pp. 11-18.

Gärdenfors P. (1988): *Knowledge in Flux – Modeling the Dynamics of Epistemic States*, Cambridge, Mass.: The MIT Press.

Gärdenfors P. (1991): "Nonmonotonic inferences based on expectations: a preliminary report", *Proceedings of the 2nd Inter. Conf. on Principle of Knowledge Representation and Reasoning*, Cambridge, Mass., 1991, ed. by J. Allen et al., Morgan & Kaufmann, pp. 585-590.

Haack S. (1979): "Do we need "fuzzy logic" ?", *Int. J. of Man-Machine Studies 11*, 437-445.

Hisdal E. (1978): "Conditional possibilities – Independence and non-interactivity", *Fuzzy Sets and Systems 1*, 283-297.

Jeffrey R. (1965): *The Logic of Decision*, New York: McGraw-Hill.

Kaufmann A. (1975): *Introduction to the Theory of Fuzzy Subsets*, New York: Academic Press.

Lehrer K., and Wagner C.G. (1981): *Rational Consensus in Science and Society*, Boston: D. Reidel Publ. Co..

Levchenkov V.S. (1987): "The fuzzy set interpretation based on choice theory: collective estimate of fuzzy propositions", (In Russian) *Coll. Papers of the Institute for Systems Studies 14*, Moscow, USSR, 74-82.

Lewis D. (1973): "Counterfactuals and comparative possibility", *J. Philosophical Logic 2*. Also in *Ifs – Conditionals, Belief, Decision, Chance, and Time*, ed. by W.L. Harper, R. Stalnaker, and G. Pearce, Dordrecht: D. Reidel, 1981, 57-85.

McConway (1981): "Marginalization and linear opinion pools", *J. of the American Statistical Association 76*, 410-414.

Morgan C.G., and Pelletier F.J. (1977): "Some notes concerning fuzzy logics", *Linguistics and Philosophy 1(1)*, 79-97.

Pearl J. (1988): *Probabilistic Reasoning in Intelligent Systems: Networks of Plausible Inference*, San Mateo, Ca.: Morgan Kaufmann.

Ramer A. (1989): "Conditional possibility measures", *Cybernetics and Systems: An Int. J. 20*, 233-247.

Rott H. (1991a): "Two methods of constructing contractions and revisions of knowledge systems", *J. of Philosophical Logic 20*, 149-173.

Rott H. (1991b): "A nonmonotonic conditional logic for belief revision", in *The Logic of Theory Change*, ed. by A. Fuhrmann, and M. Morreau, Proc. of Workshop, Konstanz, Germany, Oct. 1989, Berlin: Springer Verlag, 135-181.

Shackle G.L.S. (1961): *Decision, Order and Time in Human Affairs*, (2nd edition) Cambridge, Mass.: Cambridge University Press.

Shafer G. (1976): *A Mathematical Theory of Evidence*, Princeton: Princeton University Press.

Shoham Y. (1988): *Reasoning About Change – Time and Causation from the Standpoint of Artificial Intelligence*, Cambridge, Mass.: The MIT Press.

Spohn W. (1988): "Ordinal conditional functions: a dynamic theory of epistemic states", in *Causation in Decision, Belief Change and Statistics*, ed. by W. Harper, and B. Skyrms, 105-134.

Spohn W. (1990): "A general non-probabilistic theory of inductive reasoning", in *Uncertainty in Artificial Intelligence 4*, ed. by R.D. Shachter, T.S. Levitt, L.N. Kanal, and J.F. Lemmer, Amsterdam: North-Holland, 149-158.

Walley P. (1991): *Statistical Reasoning with Imprecise Probabilities*, Chapman and Hall.

Yager R.R. (1983): "An introduction to applications of possibility theory", *Human Systems Management 3*, 246-269.

Yager R.R. (1985): "On the relationships of methods of aggregation evidence in expert systems", *Cybernetics and Systems 16*, 1-21.

Zadeh L.A. (1971): "Similarity relations and fuzzy orderings", *Information Sciences 3*, 177-200.

Zadeh L.A. (1978): "Fuzzy sets as a basis for a theory of possibility", *Fuzzy Sets and Systems 1*, 3-28.

Zadeh L.A. (1979): "A theory of approximate reasoning", in *Machine Intelligence 9*, ed. by J.E. Hayes, D. Michie, and L.I. Mikulich, New York: Elsevier, 149-194.

On the Difference between Updating a Knowledge Base and Revising it[1]

HIROFUMI KATSUNO

NTT Basic Research Laboratories
Musashino-shi, Tokyo 180, Japan

ALBERTO O. MENDELZON

Computer Systems Research Institute
University of Toronto
Toronto, Canada M5S 1A4

1. INTRODUCTION

Consider a knowledge base represented by a theory ψ of some logic, say propositional logic. We want to incorporate into ψ a new fact, represented by a sentence μ of the same language. What should the resulting theory be? A growing body of work (Dalal 1988, Katsuno and Mendelzon 1989, Nebel 1989, Rao and Foo 1989) takes as a departure point the *rationality postulates* proposed by Alchourrón, Gärdenfors and Makinson (1985). These are rules that every adequate revision operator should be expected to satisfy. For example: the new fact μ must be a consequence of the revised knowledge base.

In this paper, we argue that no such set of postulates will be adequate for every application. In particular, we make a fundamental distinction between two kinds of modifications to a knowledge base. The first one, *update*, consists of bringing the knowledge base up to date when the world described by it changes. For example, most database updates are of this variety, e.g. "increase Joe's salary by 5%". Another example is the incorporation into the knowledge base of changes caused in the world by the actions of a robot (Ginsberg and Smith 1987, Winslett 1988, Winslett 1990). We show that the AGM postulates must be drastically modified to describe update.

The second type of modification, *revision*, is used when we are obtaining new information about a static world. For example, we may be trying to diagnose a faulty circuit and want to incorporate into the knowledge base the results of successive tests, where newer results may contradict old ones. We claim the AGM postulates describe only revision.

---

[1]A preliminary version of this paper was presented at the Second International Conference on Principles of Knowledge Representation and Reasoning, Cambridge, Mass., 1991.

The distinction between update and revision was made by Keller and Winslett (1985) in the context of extended relational databases. They distinguished *change-recording updates* (which we call updates) and *knowledge-adding updates* (which we call revisions). Our work extends theirs in several ways. We formalize the distinction, which they made informally. We provide an axiomatization for update obtained from the AGM. Keller and Winslett's work does not treat inconsistent knowledge-bases or addition of inconsistent knowledge, while ours does. And we treat arbitrary propositional knowledge-bases, while their setting is relational databases extended with null values and disjunction.

Gärdenfors (1988) considers two types of revision functions in the context of probabilistic reasoning: *imaging* and *conditionalization*. We can regard imaging as a probabilistic version of update, and conditionalization as a probabilistic version of revision.

Morreau in this volume also recognizes the distinction between update and revision, and shows how to use update in planning.

Rao and Foo (1989) extend the AGM postulates in order to apply them to reasoning about action. They introduce the notion of time and consider a modal logic. However, they do not identify the difference between revision and update. In this paper we clarify exactly why the postulates apply to revision but not to update. We give a new set of postulates that apply to update operators, and characterize the set of operators that satisfy the postulates in terms of a set of partial orders defined among possible worlds.

The difference between the postulates for revision and for update can be explained intuitively as follows. Suppose knowledge base ψ is to be revised with sentence μ. Revision methods that satisfy the AGM postulates are exactly those that select from the models of μ those that are "closest" to models of ψ, where the notion of closeness is defined by an ordering relationship among models that satisfies certain conditions (Katsuno and Mendelzon, 1989). The models selected determine the new theory, which we denote by $\psi \circ \mu$. On the other hand, update methods select, for each model M of the knowledge base ψ, the set of models of μ that are closest to M. The new theory describes the union of all such models. Suppose that ψ has exactly two models, I and J; that is, there are two possible worlds described by the knowledge base. Suppose that μ describes exactly two worlds, K and L, and that K is "closer" to I than L is, and K is also closer to I than L is to J. Then K is selected for the new knowledge base, but L is not. Note the knowledge base has effectively forgotten that J used to be a possible world; the new fact μ has been used as evidence for the retroactive impossibility of J. That is, not only do we refuse to have J as a model of the new knowledge base, but we also conclude that J should not have been in the old knowledge base to begin with.

If we are doing revisions, this behaviour is rational. Since the real world has not changed, and μ has to be true in all the new possible worlds, we can forget about some of the old possible worlds on the grounds that they are too different from what we now know to be the case. On the other hand, suppose we are doing updates. The models of ψ are possible worlds; we think one of them is the real world, but we do not know which one. Now the real world has changed; we examine each of the old possible worlds and find the minimal way of changing each one of them so that it becomes a model of μ. The fact that the real world has changed gives us no grounds to conclude that some of the old worlds were actually not possible.

To illustrate this distinction between update and revision, let us consider two examples which are formally identical to the one above but have different intuitively desirable results. First, in the spirit of Ginsberg and Smith (1987) and Winslett (1988), suppose our knowledge base describes five objects A,B,C,D,E inside a room. There is a table in the room, and objects may be on or off the table. The sentence a means "object A is on the table," and similarly for sentences b,c,d, and e. The knowledge base ψ is the sentence

$$(a \wedge \neg b \wedge \neg c \wedge \neg d \wedge \neg e) \vee (\neg a \wedge \neg b \wedge c \wedge d \wedge e).$$

That is, either object A is on the table by itself, or objects C,D and E are. This knowledge base has exactly two models I and J. We send a robot into the room, instructing it to achieve a situation in which all or none of the objects are on the table. This change can be modelled by incorporating the following sentence μ:

$$(a \wedge b \wedge c \wedge d \wedge e) \vee (\neg a \wedge \neg b \wedge \neg c \wedge \neg d \wedge \neg e).$$

Let us take Dalal's notion of "closeness" and the revision operator that results Dalal (1988). According to this measure, the distance between two models is simply the number of propositional letters on which they differ. The models selected for the new KB will be those models of μ which are at minimal distance from models of ψ. Now K, the model where nothing is on the table, is at distance 1 from I (the model where A is on the table) and at distance 3 from J (the model where C,D and E are). On the other hand L, the model where every object is on the table, is at distance 4 from I and 2 from J. Dalal's revision operator will therefore select K as the only model of the new knowledge base. But intuitively, it seems clear that this is incorrect. After the robot is done, all we know is that either all objects are on the table or all are off; there is no reason to conclude that they are all off, which is what revision does.

Consider now an example that is formally identical, but where the desired result is given by revision, not by update. Suppose the knowledge base describes the state of a five bit register which we read through noisy communication lines. Each of the propositional letters a,b,c,d,e now represents one bit. The state of the register is unchanging. Two different readings have been obtained: 10000 and 00111. By an independent analysis of the circuits that control the register, we learn that all bits must have the same value. That is, only 11111 and 00000 are possible patterns.

Dalal's revision method tells us to keep 00000 as the new knowledge base; that is, we conclude that 00111 is relatively too far from the possible patterns to be an acceptable result. It might be argued that it is better to forget the two readings in the KB and just keep both 00000 and 11111 as possible worlds. However, consider an example in which the register is thousands of bits long, the two readings agree on every bit except the first five, and the new fact only says that the first five bits must be all 0's or all 1's. It is clearly a waste of information now to discard the old KB and just keep the new fact.

With this motivation, let us postulate that an update method should give each of the old possible worlds equal consideration. One way of capturing this condition syntactically is to require that the result of updating $\psi \lor \phi$ with μ be equivalent to the disjunction of ψ updated with μ and ϕ updated with μ. Let us call this the *disjunction rule*. This rule turns out to have far-reaching consequences. In particular, consider the case where μ is consistent with ψ, that is, no conflict exists. The AGM postulates require the result of the revision to be simply the conjunction of ψ and μ. As we will see, this apparently obvious requirement is inconsistent with the disjunction rule.

The outline of the paper is as follows. In Section 2 we give preliminaries. We review the AGM postulates and our characterization from Katsuno and Mendelzon (1989) of all revision methods that satisfy the postulates in terms of a pre-order among models. In Section 3 we define the update operation and give a set of rationality postulates for it. We show that these postulates characterize all update operators that select for each model I of ψ those models of μ that are "closest" to I in a certain sense. In Section 4, we discuss briefly how update and revision could be combined for reasoning about action. In Section 5, we propose a new operation called *erasure*. Erasure is the analogue of contraction (Alchourrón, Gärdenfors and Makinson 1985, Makinson 1985) for update operators. We show that Winslett's *Forget* operator is a special case of *symmetric erasure*, an operator defined in terms of erasure. Finally, in Section 6 we sketch a way to unify update and revision by using a single theory change operator parameterized by time.

2. PRELIMINARIES

Throughout this paper, we consider a finitary propositional language L, and we denote the finite set consisting of all the propositional letters in L by Ξ. We represent a knowledge base by a propositional formula ψ, since we need a finite fixed representation of a KB to store it in a computer. An *interpretation* of L is a function from Ξ to $\{T, F\}$. A *model* of a propositional formula ψ is an interpretation that makes ψ true in the usual sense. $Mod(\psi)$ denotes the set of all the models of ψ. The knowledge base ψ may be *inconsistent*, in which case $Mod(\psi) = \emptyset$. A propositional formula ϕ is *complete* if for any propositional formula, μ, ϕ implies μ or ϕ implies $\neg\mu$.

2.1. Revision and the AGM Postulates

Given a knowledge base ψ and a sentence μ, $\psi \circ \mu$ denotes the *revision* of ψ by μ; that is, the new knowledge base obtained by adding new knowledge μ to the old knowledge base ψ. Note that other papers in this volume use the symbol $\dot{+}$ to denote revision. We, however, use $\circ$ instead of $\dot{+}$ to clarify that we represent a KB by a propositional formula ψ, while other papers use a (possibly infinite) set K of formulas.

Alchourrón, Gärdenfors and Makinson propose eight postulates, (G*1)∼(G*8), which they argue must be satisfied by any reasonable revision function. By specializing to the case of propositional logic and rephrasing them in terms of finite covers for infinite "knowledge sets," the postulates become the six rules below. See (Katsuno and Mendelzon 1989, 1990) for a discussion of the intuitive meaning and formal properties of these rules.

(R1) $\psi \circ \mu$ implies μ.

(R2) If $\psi \wedge \mu$ is satisfiable then $\psi \circ \mu \leftrightarrow \psi \wedge \mu$.

(R3) If μ is satisfiable then $\psi \circ \mu$ is also satisfiable.

(R4) If $\psi_1 \leftrightarrow \psi_2$ and $\mu_1 \leftrightarrow \mu_2$ then $\psi_1 \circ \mu_1 \leftrightarrow \psi_2 \circ \mu_2$.

(R5) $(\psi \circ \mu) \wedge \phi$ implies $\psi \circ (\mu \wedge \phi)$.

(R6) If $(\psi \circ \mu) \wedge \phi$ is satisfiable then $\psi \circ (\mu \wedge \phi)$ implies $(\psi \circ \mu) \wedge \phi$.

2.2. Orders between Interpretations

The postulates (R5) and (R6) represent the condition that revision be accomplished with minimal change. In Katsuno and Mendelzon (1989), we gave a model theoretic characterization of minimal change.

Let $\mathcal{I}$ be the set of all the interpretations of L. A *pre-order* $\leq$ over $\mathcal{I}$ is a reflexive and transitive relation on $\mathcal{I}$. We define $<$ as $I < I'$ if and only if $I \leq I'$ and $I' \not\leq I$. A pre-order is *total* if for every $I, J \in \mathcal{I}$, either $I \leq J$ or $J \leq I$. Consider a function that assigns to each propositional formula ψ a pre-order $\leq_\psi$ over $\mathcal{I}$. We say this assignment is *faithful*[2] if the following three conditions hold:

1. If $I, I' \in Mod(\psi)$ then $I <_\psi I'$ does not hold.

2. If $I \in Mod(\psi)$ and $I' \notin Mod(\psi)$ then $I <_\psi I'$ holds.

---

[2] The term *persistent* was used instead of "faithful" in Katsuno and Mendelzon (1989).

3. If $\psi \leftrightarrow \phi$, then $\leq_\psi = \leq_\phi$.

That is, a model of ψ cannot be strictly less than any other model of ψ and must be strictly less than any non-model of ψ.

Let $\mathcal{M}$ be a subset of $\mathcal{I}$. An interpretation I is minimal in $\mathcal{M}$ with respect to $\leq_\psi$ if $I \in \mathcal{M}$ and there is no $I' \in \mathcal{M}$ such that $I' <_\psi I$. Let $Min(\mathcal{M}, \leq_\psi)$ be the set of all $I \in \mathcal{M}$ such that I is minimal in $\mathcal{M}$ with respect to $\leq_\psi$. The following characterization of all revision operators that satisfy the postulates was established in Katsuno and Mendelzon (1989).

Theorem 2.1 *Revision operator $\circ$ satisfies Conditions (R1)$\sim$(R6) if and only if there exists a faithful assignment that maps each KB ψ to a total pre-order $\leq_\psi$ such that $Mod(\psi \circ \mu) = Min(Mod(\mu), \leq_\psi)$.*

3.   UPDATE

In this section we axiomatize all update operators that can be defined by partial orders or partial pre-orders over interpretations. The class of operators defined generalizes Winslett's *Possible Models Approach* (PMA) (Winslett 1988, 1989). Winslett argues that the PMA is suitable for reasoning about action in certain applications. According to our classification, the PMA is an update operator, because it changes each possible world independently. For background, we review this approach first.

3.1.   Possible Models Approach

Let ψ be a KB and μ a new sentence. We denote the PMA operator by $\diamond_{pma}$. For each model I of ψ, the PMA selects from the models of μ those which are "closest" to I. The models of the new KB ($\psi \diamond_{pma} \mu$) are the union of these selected models. Formally, the PMA is defined by

$$Mod(\psi \diamond_{pma} \mu) = \bigcup_{I \in Mod(\psi)} Incorporate(Mod(\mu), I),$$

where $Incorporate(Mod(\mu), I)$ is the set of models that are "closest" to I in $Mod(\mu)$.

The closeness between two interpretations, I and J is measured by the set $Diff(I, J)$ of propositional letters that have different truth values under I and J. For two interpretations, J_1 and J_2, J_1 is closer to I than J_2 (denoted by $J_1 \leq_{I,pma} J_2$) if and only if $Diff(I, J_1)$ is a subset of $Diff(I, J_2)$. Then, $Incorporate(Mod(\mu), I)$ is the set of all the minimal elements with respect to $\leq_{I,pma}$ in the set $Mod(\mu)$, that is, $Min(Mod(\mu), \leq_{I,pma})$.

Example 3.1 Let L have only two propositional letters, b and m. Let $\psi \leftrightarrow (b \wedge \neg m) \vee (\neg b \wedge m)$ and $\mu \leftrightarrow b$. Then, $I = \langle F, T \rangle$ is a model of ψ. $J_1 = \langle T, T \rangle$ and $J_2 = \langle T, F \rangle$ are two models of μ. $J_1 \leq_{I,pma} J_2$ follows from the fact $Diff(I, J_1) = \{b\}$ is a subset of $Diff(I, J_2) = \{b, m\}$. Similarly, by considering the case where J_2 is a model of ψ, we obtain $\psi \diamond_{pma} \mu \leftrightarrow b$.

To interpret this example in the context of (Winslett 1988, 1989), let us go back to a room with two objects in it, a book and a magazine. Suppose b means the book is on the floor, and m means the magazine is on the floor. Then, ψ states that either the book is on the floor or the magazine is, but not both. Now, we order a robot to put the book on the floor. The result of this action should be represented by the update of ψ with b. After the robot puts the book on the floor, all we know is b, and this is in fact the result of appying the PMA. Note that ψ is consistent with μ. According to revision postulate (R2), the result of $\psi \circ \mu$ should therefore be $\psi \wedge \mu$, that is, $b \wedge \neg m$. But why should we conclude that the magazine is not on the floor?

3.2. Postulates for Update

The PMA is defined in terms of a certain partial order over interpretations. This subsection generalizes the PMA by axiomatizing all update operators that can be defined by partial orders or partial pre-orders over interpretations.

We use $\psi \diamond \mu$ to denote the result of updating KB ψ with sentence μ. Our postulates for update are:

(U1) $\psi \diamond \mu$ implies μ.

(U2) If ψ implies μ then $\psi \diamond \mu$ is equivalent to ψ.

(U3) If both ψ and μ are satisfiable then $\psi \diamond \mu$ is also satisfiable.

(U4) If $\psi_1 \leftrightarrow \psi_2$ and $\mu_1 \leftrightarrow \mu_2$ then $\psi_1 \diamond \mu_1 \leftrightarrow \psi_2 \diamond \mu_2$.

(U5) $(\psi \diamond \mu) \wedge \phi$ implies $\psi \diamond (\mu \wedge \phi)$.

(U6) If $\psi \diamond \mu_1$ implies μ_2 and $\psi \diamond \mu_2$ implies μ_1 then $\psi \diamond \mu_1 \leftrightarrow \psi \diamond \mu_2$.

(U7) If ψ is complete then $(\psi \diamond \mu_1) \wedge (\psi \diamond \mu_2)$ implies $\psi \diamond (\mu_1 \vee \mu_2)$.

(U8) $(\psi_1 \vee \psi_2) \diamond \mu \leftrightarrow (\psi_1 \diamond \mu) \vee (\psi_2 \diamond \mu)$.

Postulates (U1)~(U5) correspond directly to the the corresponding postulates for revision given in Section 2. Note that postulate (U2) says that if a new sentence μ is derivable from KB ψ, then updating by μ does not influence the KB. In the case where ψ is consistent, postulate (U2) is strictly weaker than (R2). An immediate consequence of (U2) is the following.

Lemma 3.1 *If an update operator $\diamond$ satisfies (U2), and ψ is inconsistent, then $\psi \diamond \mu$ is inconsistent for any μ.*

The property above might appear undesirable: once an inconsistency is introduced in the knowledge base, there is no way to eliminate it. However, all we are saying is there is no way to eliminate it *by using update*. For example, revision does not have this behaviour; in fact, (R3) guarantees that the result of a revision is consistent provided that the new sentence introduced is itself consistent. This is another manifestation of the difference between update and revision. An inconsistent knowledge base is the result of an inadequate theory, and can be remedied with revision (or contraction) by adding new knowledge that supersedes the inconsistency (or removing contradictory knowledge using contraction). We can never repair an inconsistent theory using update, because update specifies a change in the world. If there is no set of worlds that fits our current description, we have no way of recording the change in the real world.

We drop rule (R6), and add instead three new postulates, (U6)~(U8). (U6) says that if updating a knowledge base with μ_1 guarantees μ_2, and updating the same knowledge base with μ_2 guarantees μ_1, then the two updates have the same effect. This is similar to condition (C7) in Gardenfors's analysis of minimal changes of belief Gärdenfors (1978) and to conditional logic axiom *CSO* in Nute (1984). (U7) applies only to complete KB's, in which there is no uncertainty over what are the possible worlds. If some possible world results from updating a complete KB with μ_1 and it also results from updating it with μ_2, then this possible world must also result from updating the KB with $\mu_1 \vee \mu_2$. Finally, (U8) is what we called the "disjunction rule" in the Introduction. It guarantees that each possible world of the KB is given independent consideration. (U8) can be regarded as a nonprobabilistic version of the *homomorphic* condition about probabilistic revision functions in Gärdenfors (1988).

The following lemma shows that we can obtain one direction of (R2) by using (U2) and (U8)

Lemma 3.2 *If an update operator $\diamond$ satisfies (U2) and (U8), then $\psi \wedge \mu$ implies $\psi \diamond \mu$.*

Proof. Since ψ is equivalent to $(\psi \wedge \mu) \vee (\psi \wedge \neg\mu)$, it follows from (U8) that $\psi \diamond \mu$ is equivalent to $((\psi \wedge \mu) \diamond \mu) \vee ((\psi \wedge \neg\mu) \diamond \mu)$. By (U2), $(\psi \wedge \mu) \diamond \mu$ is equivalent to $\psi \wedge \mu$. Hence, $\psi \wedge \mu$ implies $\psi \diamond \mu$.

However, as Example 3.1 showed, update operators do not necessarily satisfy that $\psi \diamond \mu$ implies $\psi \wedge \mu$ when ψ is consistent with μ.

An interesting consequence of the postulates is *monotonicity*.

Lemma 3.3 *If an update operator $\diamond$ satisfies (U8), and ϕ implies ψ, then $\phi \diamond \mu$ implies $\psi \diamond \mu$.*

Monotonicity has been deemed undesirable by the philosophers of theory revision. The reason is a result called "Gärdenfors's impossibility theorem" (Arló Costa 1989, Gärdenfors 1988, Makinson 1989), which shows that monotonicity is incompatible with postulates (R1)~(R4). More precisely, Theorem 7.10 of Gärdenfors (1988) implies that there is no non-trivial revision operator that satisfies monotonicity and (R1)–(R4). Since update operators do not satisfy (R2), this result does not apply to update.

Gärdenfors's motivation in studying this problem is to use theory revision to define the conditional connective used in counterfactual reasoning. The idea is to use the *Ramsey Test*: interpret the conditional statement "given the state of the world described by ψ, if μ were true, then η would also be true" as $\psi \circ \mu$ implies η. Intuitively, it would seem that this kind of statement is better modelled by using update instead of revision in the Ramsey Test. This intuition, together with the immunity of updates to Gärdenfors's result, suggest further study of the connection between updates and conditional reasoning may be fruitful. Preliminary results are reported by Katsuno and Saoth (1991) and Grahne (1991).

We can now formalize a notion of closeness between models that generalizes the particular measure used in the PMA. Instead of associating each KB with an ordering, let us consider a function that maps each interpretation I to a partial pre-order $\leq_I$. We say that this assignment is *faithful* if the following condition holds:

- For any $J \in \mathcal{I}$, if $I \neq J$ then $I <_I J$.

The following theorem shows that the postulates exactly capture all update operators defined by a partial pre-order. It turns out that the classes of operators defined by partial orders and partial pre-orders are the same.

Theorem 3.4 *Let $\diamond$ be an update operator. The following conditions are equivalent:*

1. *The update operator $\diamond$ satisfies Conditions (U1)~(U8).*

2. *There exists a faithful assignment that maps each interpretation I to a partial pre-order $\leq_I$ such that*

$$Mod(\psi \diamond \mu) = \bigcup_{I \in Mod(\psi)} Min(Mod(\mu), \leq_I).$$

3. *There exists a persistent assignment that maps each interpretation I to a partial order $\leq_I$ such that*

$$Mod(\psi \diamond \mu) = \bigcup_{I \in Mod(\psi)} Min(Mod(\mu), \leq_I).$$

We give a proof sketch here. A detailed proof can be found in the Appendix.

Proof Sketch. $(1 \Rightarrow 2)$ We assign to each interpretation I a relation $\leq_I$ defined as follows. For any interpretations J and J', $J \leq_I J'$ if and only if either $J = I$ or $Mod(form(I) \diamond form(J, J')) = \{J\}$. We verify that Conditions (U1)~(U8) imply that this mapping is a faithful assignment such that

$$Mod(\psi \diamond \mu) = \bigcup_{I \in Mod(\psi)} Min(Mod(\mu), \leq_I).$$

$(2 \Rightarrow 3)$ For a pre-order $\leq_I$, we define a relation $\leq'_I$ as $J \leq'_I J'$ if and only if $J = J'$ or $J <_I J'$. It is easy to show that $\leq'_I$ is a partial order and that $J <_I J'$ if and only if $J <'_I J'$. Hence, Statement 3 follows from Statement 2 by changing $\leq_I$ to $\leq'_I$.

$(3 \Rightarrow 1)$ Assume that there is a faithful assignment mapping each interpretation I to a partial order $\leq_I$. We define an update operator $\diamond$ by

$$Mod(\psi \diamond \mu) = \bigcup_{I \in Mod(\psi)} Min(Mod(\mu), \leq_I).$$

We show that the update operator $\diamond$ satisfies (U1)~(U8).

Comparing this result with Theorem 2.1, we see two differences between revision and update from a model-theoretic point of view. First, Theorem 3.1 refers to *partial* preorders while Theorem 2.1 uses *total* preorders. It turns out that a version of the revision postulates that accommodates partial preorders can be given, and we show this in Katsuno and Mendelzon (1990). It is also possible to design a class of update operators based on total pre-orders. If we replace (U6) and (U7) by postulate (U9) below, then we can prove the total pre-order analogue of Theorem 3.1. The proof is similar to that of Theorem 3.1, by defining, for any two interpretations J and J', $J \leq_I J'$ if and only if either $J = I$ or $J \in Mod(form(I) \diamond form(J, J'))$.

(U9) If ψ is complete and $(\psi \diamond \mu) \wedge \phi$ is satisfiable then $\psi \diamond (\mu \wedge \phi)$ implies $(\psi \diamond \mu) \wedge \phi$.

It is worth pointing out that a total preorder associated with interpretation I is what Lewis (1973) calls *a system of spheres centered at I*. Systems of spheres play a central role in the semantics of Lewis's conditional logic; this brings up again the suggested connection between updates and conditional logic, which is explored further by Grahne (1991).

The second and more important difference between revision and update is that, in the case of update, a different ordering is induced by each model of ψ, while for revision, only one ordering is induced by the whole of ψ. This "local" behaviour of update, contrasted with the "global" behaviour of revision, is essential to the difference between the two operators.

4. REASONING ABOUT ACTION

For the purposes of reasoning about action, the usual approach is to represent a particular action as a pair of a precondition and a postcondition. The precondition for the action encodes what the world must be like in order for the action to be executable. The postcondition describes the immediate consequences resulting from the action. Any update operator that satisfies our postulates can be used for reasoning about action by regarding postconditions for an action as new knowledge and by assuming that preconditions for the action are satisfied by the current KB. That is, the effect on KB ψ of performing action with precondition α and postcondition β will be ψ if ψ does not imply α, and $\psi \diamond \beta$ otherwise. Winslett (1989) discusses how the frame, qualification and ramification problems are handled by this approach.[3]

Let us extend this idea by examining more closely what happens when ψ does not satisfy the precondition α. Presumably, the robot will return and report one of two outcomes: either α was true, and the action was carried out, or α failed and the action was not carried out. If we want a more elaborate model, we can also allow other outcomes, such as: α was true but the action could not be carried out for other reasons, or α could not be either verified or falsified. In each case, we can take advantage of the distinction between revision and update to incorporate into ψ all the information gained by the robot. For example, if the action was carried out, we can change the KB to $(\psi \circ \alpha) \diamond \beta$. If the precondition was found false, we use $\psi \circ \neg \alpha$. If the truth value of the precondition could not be determined, we use $\psi \bullet \alpha$ (contraction is discussed in the next section).

5. CONTRACTION AND ERASURE

Contraction is a change of belief or knowledge state induced by the loss of confidence in some sentence. For example, if we believed that a paper was written by Turing, but new evidence has cast doubt on this belief, we contract the corresponding sentence from our knowledge base.

Alchourrón *et al.* (1985) proposed rationality postulates for contraction. We denote by $\psi \bullet \mu$ a new knowledge base obtained from an old knowledge base ψ by contracting μ. The postulates for contraction, rephrased in our terms, are as follows.

(C1) ψ implies $\psi \bullet \mu$.

(C2) If ψ does not imply μ then $\psi \bullet \mu$ is equivalent to ψ.

(C3) If μ is not a tautology then $\psi \bullet \mu$ does not imply μ.

---

[3]Actually, Winslett uses for this purpose a variant of the PMA that orders interpretations in a way similar to the partial pre-order used in prioritized circumscription. Such variants are included in our class of update operators.

(C4) If $\psi_1 \leftrightarrow \psi_2$ and $\mu_1 \leftrightarrow \mu_2$ then $\psi_1 \bullet \mu_1 \leftrightarrow \psi_2 \bullet \mu_2$.

(C5) $(\psi \bullet \mu) \wedge \mu$ implies ψ.

Alchourrón *et al.* (1985) showed that contraction and revision are closely related: they proved that, given a revision operator o that satisfies (R1)~(R4), if we define a contraction operator $\bullet$ by

$$\psi \bullet \mu \leftrightarrow \psi \vee (\psi \circ \neg\mu)$$

then the operator $\bullet$ satisfies (C1)~(C5). Conversely, given a contraction operator $\bullet$ that satisfies (C1)~(C4), if we define a revision operator o by

$$\psi \circ \mu \leftrightarrow (\psi \bullet \neg\mu) \wedge \mu$$

then the operator o satisfies (R1)~(R4).

We propose a new operator, *erasure*, which is to contraction as update is to revision. Erasing sentence μ from ψ means adding models to ψ; for each model I, we add all those models closest to I in which μ is false. Intuitively, erasing μ means the world may have changed in such a way that μ is not true. In contrast, contracting μ means our description of the set of possible worlds must be adjusted to the possibility of μ being false.

The erasure operator $\blacklozenge$ for a given update operator $\diamond$ is defined by

$$\psi \blacklozenge \mu \leftrightarrow \psi \vee (\psi \diamond \neg\mu) \qquad\qquad (U \to E).$$

This erasure operator satisfies the following postulates (E1)~(E5) and (E8) if the update operator satisfies (U1)~(U4) and (U8).

(E1) ψ implies $\psi \blacklozenge \mu$.

(E2) If ψ implies $\neg\mu$ then $\psi \blacklozenge \mu$ is equivalent to ψ.

(E3) If ψ is satisfiable and μ is not a tautology then $\psi \blacklozenge \mu$ does not imply μ.

(E4) If $\psi_1 \leftrightarrow \psi_2$ and $\mu_1 \leftrightarrow \mu_2$ then $\psi_1 \blacklozenge \mu_1 \leftrightarrow \psi_2 \blacklozenge \mu_2$.

(E5) $(\psi \blacklozenge \mu) \wedge \mu$ implies ψ.

(E8) $(\psi_1 \vee \psi_2) \blacklozenge \mu$ is equivalent to $(\psi_1 \blacklozenge \mu) \vee (\psi_2 \blacklozenge \mu)$.

There are two differences between contraction and erasure in terms of postulates. One is that (E2) is weaker than (C2); since contraction of a sentence μ does not influence a KB ψ if ψ does not imply μ, but erasure of μ might modify ψ if ψ does not imply $\neg\mu$. The other one is that erasure needs the disjunctive rule (E8), but contraction does not.

Example 5.1 Consider Example 3.1 again. Recall we have a room with two objects in it, a book and a magazine, b means the book is on the floor, and m means the magazine is on the floor. The knowledge base ψ states that either the book is on the floor or the magazine is, but not both. Suppose that a contraction operator $\bullet$ satisfies (C2). If we contract ψ by b then $\psi \bullet b$ is equivalent to ψ, since ψ does not imply b. This means that since the sentence that the book is on the floor is already questionable under ψ, contraction does not change ψ.

On the other hand, let an erasure operator $\blacklozenge$ be defined based on the PMA $\diamond_{pma}$. If we erase b from ψ then $\psi \blacklozenge b$ is equivalent to $(b \wedge \neg m) \vee \neg b$. This can be interpreted as follows. ψ represents two possible worlds, M_1 and M_2. In world M_1, the book is on the floor but the magazine is not. Since b holds in M_1, M_1 is altered to two worlds, M_1 itself and the world M_3 represented by $\neg b \wedge \neg m$, that is, neither the book nor the magazine is on the floor. In world M_2, the magazine is on the floor but the book is not. Since b does not hold in M_2, M_2 is retained as itself. Hence, $\psi \blacklozenge \mu$ represents the three worlds, M_1, M_2 and M_3.

The intuitive difference between contraction and erasure can be explained in this example as follows. Contracting b means nothing has changed in the room, but if the KB believes that the book is on the floor, make sure this belief is retracted. Since the KB has no such belief, the contraction has no effect. Erasing b means the state of the room has changed in such a way that, if the book was on the floor before, it has now been moved in an unpredictable way. This affects only those possible worlds in which the book was on the floor. The result is that we can no longer deduce anything about the location of the magazine from the fact that the book is not on the floor.

There is another operation which appears perhaps more natural than erasure. Suppose the state of the room has changed in such a way that the location of the book is now unpredictable, and we want to reflect this change in the knowledge base. We formalize this operation, called *symmetric erasure*, after the Theorem below.

The following theorem, proved in the Appendix, gives a correspondence between update and erasure similar to the correspondence between revision and contraction.

Theorem 5.1

1. *If an update operator $\diamond$ satisfies (U1)$\sim$(U4) and (U8), then the erasure operator $\blacklozenge$ defined by $(U \to E)$ satisfies (E1)$\sim$(E5) and (E8).*

2. *If an erasure operator $\blacklozenge$ satisfies (E1)$\sim$(E4) and (E8), then the update operator $\diamond$ defined by*

$$\psi \diamond \mu \leftrightarrow (\psi \blacklozenge \neg \mu) \wedge \mu \qquad\qquad (E \to U)$$

satisfies (U1)$\sim$(U4) and (U8).

3. *Suppose that an update operator $\diamond$ satisfies (U1)~(U4) and (U8). Then, we can define an erasure operator by $(U \rightarrow E)$. The update operator obtained from the erasure operator by $(E \rightarrow U)$ is equal to the original update operator $\diamond$.*

4. *Suppose that an erasure operator $\diamond$ satisfies (E1)~(E5) and (E8). Then, we can define an update operator by $(E \rightarrow U)$. The erasure operator obtained from the update operator by $(U \rightarrow E)$ is equal to the original erasure operator $\blacklozenge$.*

Winslett (1989) discusses an operator called *Forget*, which she compares with contraction. It turns out that *Forget*, given an update operator $\diamond$, is equivalent to

$$(\psi \diamond \mu) \vee (\psi \diamond \neg\mu).$$

We call this operator *symmetric erasure* because μ and its negation play the same role in its definition. The main difference between erasure and symmetric erasure is that erasure does not affect the possible worlds in which $\neg\mu$ holds, but symmetric erasure does. Going back to Example 5.1, the symmetric erasure of b from ψ reflects the fact that someone has picked up the book and unpredictably decided to place it on the floor or on the table. The result of this symmetric erasure is the knowledge base with no information, since there is nothing we can say about either the book or the magazine after this change.

We can show similar postulates for symmetric erasure to those for erasure, and prove a similar theorem to Theorem 5.1. A natural definition of *symmetric contraction* follows from the above discussions, and similar results can be shown for it. Gärdenfors (1981) defines an operator similar to symmetric contraction, which he calls *complete contraction*, and proposes to use it to model "even if" conditionals.

6. TIME, REVISION AND UPDATE

So far in this paper we have devoted our efforts to distinguishing update from revision. We would like now to suggest how they can be unified. The essential difference between revision and update is a temporal one: revision is a change to our description of a world that has not itself changed, while update is the incorporation into our world description of the fact that the world has changed. Suppose now that we make this hidden temporal parameter explicit in the knowledge base. That is, instead of just a theory, a knowledge base is now a pair $\langle \psi, t \rangle$ where ψ is a theory and t denotes a time instant. This is in the spirit of the situation calculus MaCarthy and Hayes (1969) and other temporal formalisms. It is not important for our purposes what exactly is the ontology of time, whether it is discrete or continuous, etc. For example, returning to our familiar book and magazine example, the knowledge base that says exactly one of them is on the table at 10am is $\langle (b \wedge \neg m) \vee (\neg b \wedge m), 10am \rangle$.

Instead of two distinct change operations, update and revision, let us introduce a single one called $\text{Tell}(\mu, t)$ where μ is the new formula to be incorporated and t is a time instant. The effect of applying Tell(μ, t) to a knowledge base is to *replace* the knowledge base with a new one that incorporates the sentence μ and has time parameter t, unless t is earlier than the KB's time. More precisely, we define the result of applying Tell(μ, t') to $\langle \psi, t \rangle$ as $\langle \psi \circ \mu, t \rangle$ if $t = t'$, and $\langle \psi \diamond \mu, t' \rangle$ if $t' > t$. For now, the result will be left undefined when $t' < t$. So, when we send the robot into the room to put the book on the table, and the robot returns at 10:05 reporting mission accomplished, we apply Tell($b, 10{:}05am$) to the KB. This behaves as an update, yielding $\langle b, 10{:}05am \rangle$ as a result. On the other hand, suppose the reason we knew there was exactly one object on the table was because of an aerial photograph taken at 10am from a high altitude. Further analysis of the photograph reveals that the object on the table was actually the book. We then apply the change Tell($b, 10am$), which behaves as revision, and obtain $\langle b \wedge \neg m, 10am \rangle$. Intuitively, it is now correct to conclude that the magazine is not on the table at time 10am.

This proposal relieves the user from the burden of deciding whether each change is a revision or an update, which become special cases of a more general operator parameterized by time. It also raises interesting questions that we cannot answer in this paper, but leave as topics for further research. For example, we did not define the meaning of Tell(μ, t') when t' is earlier than the KB time. An obvious generalization is to have not one pair of theory and instant, but a whole sequence of theories, one for each instant, and to allow changes to any past, present, or future KB. The next step would be to introduce *persistence*: if we know something is true at time t, and have no reason to believe it has changed, we assume it is still true at time $t + 1$. We can then distinguish at each instant t between knowledge, that is, those sentences we have been told are true at time t, and defeasible knowledge, those that have been inferred by persistence from the past (or from the future). An appealing way of doing this is to define the set of worlds described by the KB at time $t + 1$ as the result of *updating* all knowledge, defeasible or not, about instant t, with the non-defeasible knowledge at $t + 1$. A symmetric construction can be used for supporting persistence from the future into the past. This approach will be elaborated in the future.

7. CONCLUSION

The distinction between update and revision is an important one, and it has been overlooked in the literature since it was pointed out by Keller and Winslett (1985). We have formalized this distinction and given a model-theoretic characterization of updates in terms of orderings among interpretations. We have defined and characterized *erasure*, which is to update as contraction is to revision.

Many problems remain to explore. The connection between updates and conditional logic is one being pursued by several researchers (Katsuno and Satoh 1991, Grahne 1991). Another is computational tractability of updates and erasures. For example, Grahne and Mendelzon (1991) show that by restricting the form of the knowledge base, PMA updates can be computed in time polynomial in the size of the knowledge base. A third is the combined use of different theory change operators–revision, contraction, update, erasure– in specific applications, as suggested in Section 4. A temporal framework that unifies these operators, as sketched in Section 5, may be the best way to do this.

Acknowledgements

We thank Ken Satoh for suggesting rule (U6). The second author thanks the Natural Sciences and Engineering Research Council of Canada and the Institute for Robotics and Intelligent Systems for their support. A preliminary version of this paper appeared in Katsuno and Mendelzon (1991)

Appendix

Theorem 3.1 *Let $\diamond$ be an update operator. The following conditions are equivalent:*

1. *The update operator $\diamond$ satisfies Conditions (U1)$\sim$(U8).*

2. *There exists a faithful assignment that maps each interpretation I to a partial pre-order $\leq_I$ such that*

$$Mod(\psi \diamond \mu) = \bigcup_{I \in Mod(\psi)} Min(Mod(\mu), \leq_I).$$

3. *There exists a faithful assignment that maps each interpretation I to a partial order $\leq_I$ such that*

$$Mod(\psi \diamond \mu) = \bigcup_{I \in Mod(\psi)} Min(Mod(\mu), \leq_I).$$

Proof. ($1 \Rightarrow 2$) For any interpretations J and J' ($J = J'$ is permitted), we define a relation $\leq_I$ as $J \leq_I J'$ if and only if either $J = I$ or $Mod(form(I) \diamond form(J, J')) = \{J\}$.

We first show that $\leq_I$ is a pre-order. In order to show that $\leq_I$ is reflexive, we show $Mod(form(I) \diamond form(J)) = \{J\}$. It is obvious that the equation follows from (U1) and (U3).

We show that $\leq_I$ is transitive. Assume $J_1 \leq_I J_2$ and $J_2 \leq_I J_3$. Then, we obtain that $form(I) \diamond form(J_1, J_2) \leftrightarrow form(J_1)$ and $form(I) \diamond form(J_2, J_3) \leftrightarrow form(J_2)$. Let $\mu \leftrightarrow form(J_1, J_2, J_3)$. By (U5), $(form(I) \diamond \mu) \wedge form(J_2, J_3)$ implies $form(I) \diamond form(J_2, J_3)$. Since $form(I) \diamond form(J_2, J_3) \leftrightarrow form(J_2)$, J_3 is not a model of $form(I) \diamond \mu$. We can also obtain that J_2 is not a model of $form(I) \diamond \mu$ in a similar way by using (U5) and $form(I) \diamond form(J_1, J_2) \leftrightarrow form(J_1)$. Therefore, it follows from (U3) that $form(I) \diamond \mu$ is logically equivalent to $form(J_1)$. Thus, $form(I) \diamond \mu$ implies $form(J_1, J_3)$. On the other hand, it follows from (U1) that $form(I) \diamond form(J_1, J_3)$ implies μ. By (U6), we obtain that $form(I) \diamond \mu$ is logically equivalent to $form(I) \diamond form(J_1, J_3)$. Thus, $form(I) \diamond form(J_1, J_3)$ is logically equivalent to $form(J_1)$. Therefore, $I_1 \leq_I I_3$ holds.

It follows from (U2) that the assignment mapping each interpretation I to $\leq_I$ is faithful.

We show $Mod(form(I) \diamond \mu) = Min(Mod(\mu), \leq_I)$. If μ is inconsistent then $Mod(\mu)$ is empty and it also follows from (U1) that $Mod(form(I) \diamond \mu)$ is empty. Hence, the equation holds. So, we assume in the following that μ is consistent. Suppose that J is a model of $form(I) \diamond \mu$ and J is not minimal in $Mod(\mu)$ with respect to $\leq_I$. There is a model J' of $Mod(\mu)$ such that $J' <_I J$. By (U5), $(form(I) \diamond \mu) \wedge form(J, J')$ implies $form(I) \diamond form(J, J')$. Since $J' <_I J$, $form(I) \diamond form(J, J')$ is equivalent to $form(J')$. Hence, J is not a model of $(form(I) \diamond \mu) \wedge form(J, J')$. This contradicts the assumption that J is a model of $form(I) \diamond \mu$. Therefore, $Mod(form(I) \diamond \mu) \subset Min(Mod(\mu), \leq_I)$ holds.

We show the converse inclusion. Assume that J is minimal in $Mod(\mu)$ with respect to $\leq_I$. Let $Mod(\mu) = \{J_1, \ldots, J_k\}$. Note that μ is logically equivalent to

$$form(J, J_1) \vee form(J, J_2) \vee \ldots \vee form(J, J_k).$$

Also, since there is no $J_j \in Mod(\mu)$ such that $J_j <_I J$, it follows that

$$J \in Mod(form(I) \diamond form(J, J_j))$$

for every $J_j \in Mod(\mu)$. Hence, J is a model of

$$(form(I) \diamond form(J, J_1)) \wedge \ldots \wedge (form(I) \diamond form(J, J_k)).$$

By repeated applications of (U7), this implies J is a model of

$$form(I) \diamond (form(J, J_1) \vee \ldots \vee form(J, J_k)),$$

that is, $J \in Mod(form(I) \diamond \mu)$.

If ψ is consistent then it follows from (U8) that

$$Mod(\psi \diamond \mu) = \bigcup_{I \in Mod(\psi)} Min(Mod(\mu), \leq_I).$$

If ψ is inconsistent then both sides of the above equation are empty, that is, the equation holds.

($2 \Rightarrow 3$) The proof of this part is shown in the main text.

($3 \Rightarrow 1$) Assume that there is a faithful assignment mapping each interpretation I to a partial order $\leq_I$. We define an update operator $\diamond$ by

$$Mod(\psi \diamond \mu) = \bigcup_{I \in Mod(\psi)} Min(Mod(\mu), \leq_I).$$

We show that the update operator $\diamond$ satisfies (U1)$\sim$(U8). (U1), (U3), (U4) and (U8) are obvious. If ψ is inconsistent then (U2), (U5), (U6) and (U7) trivially hold. We assume in the following that ψ is consistent.

We show (U2). It follows from the definition of faithfulness that if I is a model of μ then $form(I) \diamond \mu$ is equivalent to $form(I)$. Hence, we obtain (U2) by using (U8).

We show (U5). If $(\psi \diamond \mu) \wedge \phi$ is inconsistent then (U5) holds trivially. Let J be a model of $(\psi \diamond \mu) \wedge \phi$. There is some model I of ψ such that J is minimal in $Mod(\mu)$ with respect to $\leq_I$. Since $Mod(\mu \wedge \phi)$ is a subset of $Mod(\mu)$ and J is a model of ϕ, J is minimal in $Mod(\psi \diamond (\mu \wedge \phi))$ with respect to $\leq_I$. Hence, $(\psi \diamond \mu) \wedge \phi$ implies $\psi \diamond (\mu \wedge \phi)$.

We show (U6). Suppose that $\psi \diamond \mu_1$ implies μ_2 and that $\psi \diamond \mu_2$ implies μ_1. Assume that J is a model of $\psi \diamond \mu_1$, but J is not a model of $\psi \diamond \mu_2$. Since $\psi \diamond \mu_1$ implies μ_2, J is a model of μ_2. Since we assume that J is not a model of $\psi \diamond \mu_2$, for each model I of ψ, there exists a model J_I of μ_2 such that $J_I <_I J$ and J_I is minimal in $Mod(\mu_2)$ with respect to $\leq_I$. Then, each J_I is a model of $\psi \diamond \mu_2$. Since $\psi \diamond \mu_2$ implies μ_1, J_I is also a model of μ_1. Hence, for any model I of ψ, J is not minimal in $Mod(\mu_1)$ with respect to $\leq_I$. This contradicts that J is a model of $\psi \diamond \mu_1$. Therefore, $\psi \diamond \mu_1$ implies $\psi \diamond \mu_2$. Similarly, we can obtain $\psi \diamond \mu_2$ implies $\psi \diamond \mu_1$.

We show (U7). Let ψ be complete. Then, there exists a model I of ψ such that ψ is equivalent to $form(I)$. Let J be a model of $(\psi \diamond \mu_1) \wedge (\psi \diamond \mu_2)$. Assume that J is not a model of $\psi \diamond (\mu_1 \vee \mu_2)$. Then, there is a model J' of $\psi \diamond (\mu_1 \vee \mu_2)$ such that $J' <_I J$. If J' is a model of μ_1, this contradicts the minimality of J in $Mod(\mu_1)$ with respect to $\leq_I$. If J' is a model of μ_2, this also contradicts the minimality of J in $Mod(\mu_2)$ with respect to $\leq_I$.

Theorem 5.1

1. *If an update operator $\diamond$ satisfies (U1)$\sim$(U4) and (U8), then the erasure operator $\blacklozenge$ defined by $(U \rightarrow E)$ satisfies (E1)$\sim$(E5) and (E8).*

2. *If an erasure operator $\blacklozenge$ satisfies (E1)$\sim$(E4) and (E8), then the update operator $\diamond$ defined by*

$$\psi \diamond \mu \leftrightarrow (\psi \blacklozenge \neg \mu) \wedge \mu \qquad (E \rightarrow U)$$

   satisfies (U1)$\sim$(U4) and (U8).

3. *Suppose that an update operator $\diamond$ satisfies (U1)$\sim$(U4) and (U8). Then, we can define an erasure operator by $(U \rightarrow E)$. The update operator obtained from the erasure operator by $(E \rightarrow U)$ is equal to the original update operator $\diamond$.*

4. *Suppose that an erasure operator $\diamond$ satisfies (E1)$\sim$(E5) and (E8). Then, we can define an update operator by $(E \rightarrow U)$. The erasure operator obtained from the update operator by $(U \rightarrow E)$ is equal to the original erasure operator $\blacklozenge$.*

Proof. 1. Assume that an update operator $\diamond$ satisfies (U1)~(U4) and (U8), and an erasure operator $\blacklozenge$ is defined by $(U \to E)$. (E1) follows from $(U \to E)$. We show (E2) If ψ implies $\neg\mu$ then it follows from (U2) that $\psi \diamond \neg\mu$ is equivalent to ψ. Therefore, $\psi \blacklozenge \mu$ is equivalent to ψ. (E3), (E4) and (E8) easily follow from (U3), (U4) and (U8), respectively. We show (E5). By (U1), $(\psi \diamond \neg\mu) \wedge \mu$ is inconsistent. Hence, $(\psi \blacklozenge \mu) \wedge \mu$ is equivalent to $\psi \wedge \mu$. Therefore, $(\psi \blacklozenge \mu) \wedge \mu$ implies ψ.

2. Assume that an erasure operator $\blacklozenge$ satisfies (E1)~(E4) and (E8), and an update operator $\diamond$ is defined by $(E \to U)$. Then, (U1) follows from $(E \to U)$. We show (U2). If ψ implies μ then it follows from (E2) that $\psi \blacklozenge \neg\mu$ is equivalent to ψ. Hence, we obtain (U2). (U3), (U4) and (U8) easily follow from (E3), (E4), and (E8).

3. Assume that an update operator $\diamond$ satisfies (U1)~(U4) and (U8). We show that $(\psi \vee (\psi \diamond \mu)) \wedge \mu$ is equivalent to $\psi \diamond \mu$. By (U1), $(\psi \diamond \mu) \wedge \mu$ is equivalent to $\psi \diamond \mu$. By Lemma 3.2, $\psi \wedge \mu$ implies $\psi \diamond \mu$. Hence, $(\psi \vee (\psi \diamond \mu)) \wedge \mu$ is equivalent to $\psi \diamond \mu$.

4. Assume that an erasure operator $\blacklozenge$ satisfies (E1)~(E5) and (E8). Let $\psi \blacklozenge\!\!\!\!/ \mu$ be $\psi \vee ((\psi \blacklozenge \mu) \wedge \neg\mu)$. We show that $\psi \blacklozenge\!\!\!\!/ \mu$ is equivalent to $\psi \blacklozenge \mu$. First, we show that $(\psi \blacklozenge\!\!\!\!/ \mu) \wedge \mu$ is equivalent to $(\psi \blacklozenge \mu) \wedge \mu$. We know $(\psi \blacklozenge\!\!\!\!/ \mu) \wedge \mu$ is equivalent to $\psi \wedge \mu$. By (E5), $(\psi \blacklozenge \mu) \wedge \mu$ implies $\psi \wedge \mu$. By (E1), $\psi \wedge \mu$ implies $(\psi \blacklozenge \mu) \wedge \mu$. Hence, $(\psi \blacklozenge \mu) \wedge \mu$ is equivalent to $\psi \wedge \mu$. Therefore, $(\psi \blacklozenge\!\!\!\!/ \mu) \wedge \mu$ is equivalent to $(\psi \blacklozenge \mu) \wedge \mu$.

Next, we show that $(\psi \blacklozenge\!\!\!\!/ \mu) \wedge \neg\mu$ is equivalent to $(\psi \blacklozenge \mu) \wedge \neg\mu$. By (E1), $\psi \wedge \neg\mu$ implies $(\psi \blacklozenge \mu) \wedge \neg\mu$. Hence, $(\psi \blacklozenge\!\!\!\!/ \mu) \wedge \neg\mu$ is equivalent to $(\psi \blacklozenge \mu) \wedge \neg\mu$.

REFERENCES

Alchourrón C,E., P. Gärdenfors and D. Makinson. (1985): "On the logic of theory change: partial meet contraction and revision functions", *Journal of Symbolic Logic 50*, 510–530.

Arló Costa, H.L. (1989): "Conditionals and monotonic belief revisions: the success postulate", *VI Simposio Latinoamericano de Lógica Matemática*.

Dalal, M. (1988): "Investigations into a theory of knowledge base revision: Preliminary Report", *Proceedings of the Seventh National Conference on Artificial Intelligence*, 475–479

Gärdenfors, P. (1978): "Conditionals and changes of belief", *Acta Philosophica Fennica*, Vol. XXX, 381–404.

Gärdenfors, P. (1981): "An Epistemic Approach to Conditionals", *Americal Philosophical Quarterly 18*, 203–211.

Gärdenfors, P. (1988): *Knowledge in Flux: Modeling the Dynamics of Epistemic States*. Bradford Books, Cambridge, MA: The MIT Press, Bradford Books.

Ginsberg, M.L., and D.E. Smith. (1987): "Reasoning about action I: a possible worlds approach", *Readings in Nonmonotonic Reasoning*, M.L. Ginsberg, ed., Los Altos: Morgan Kaufmann, 434–463

Grahne, G. (1991): "Updates and counterfactuals", *Principles of Knowledge Representation and Reasoning: Proceedings of the Second International Conference*, Allen, J.A., Fikes, R., and Sandewell, E. (eds.), San Mateo, California: Morgan Kaufmann, 269–276.

Grahne, G. and A.O. Mendelzon. (1991): "Updates and Subjunctive Queries", *Proceedings of the Workshop on Non-Standard Queries and Non-Standard Answers*, Toulouse, to appear in 1991.

Katsuno, H. and A.O. Mendelzon. (1989): "A unified view of propositional knowledge base updates", In *Proceedings of the 11th International Joint Conference on Artificial Intelligence*, 1413–1419, 1989.

Katsuno, H. and A.O. Mendelzon. (1990): "Propositional knowledge base revision and minimal change", Technical Report KRR-TR-90-3, Department of Computer Science, University of Toronto, March 1990. Revised version to appear in *Artificial Intelligence*.

Katsuno, H. and A.O. Mendelzon. (1991): "On the difference between updating a knowledge base and revising it", *Principles of Knowledge Representation and Reasoning: Proceedings of the Second International Conference*, Allen, J.A., Fikes, R., and Sandewell, E. (eds.) San Mateo, California: Morgan Kaufmann, 387–394.

Katsuno, H. and K. Satoh. (1991): "A unified view of consequence relations, belief revision, and conditional logic", *Proceedings of the 12th International Joint Conference on Artificial Intelligence*, 406–412

Keller, A.M. and M. Winslett Wilkins. (1985): "On the use of an extended relational model to handle changing incomplete information", *IEEE Trans. on Software Engineering*, SE-11:7, 620–633.

Lewis, D.K. (1973): *Counterfactuals.* Blackwell, Oxford.

Makinson, D. (1985): "How to give it up: A survey of some formal aspects of the logic of theory change", *Synthèse 62*, 347–363.

Makinson, D. (1989): "The Gärdenfors impossibility theorem in non-monotonic contexts", Unpublished. To appear in *Studia Logica*.

McCarthy, J.M. and P.J. Hayes (1969). "Some philosophical problems from the standpoint of artificial intelligence", In *Machine Intelligence 4*, B. Meltzer and D. Mitchie eds, Unversity of Edinburgh Press.

Nebel, B. (1989): "A knowledge level analysis of belief revision", *Proceedings of the First International Conference on Principles of Knowledge Representation and Reasoning*, 301–311.

Nute, D. (1984): "Conditional logic", In Dov M. Gabbay and Franz Guenthner, editors, *Handbook of Philosophical Logic*, D. Reidel, Dordrecht, 1984.

Rao, A.S. and N.Y. Foo. (1989): "Minimal change and maximal coherence: A basis for belief revision and reasoning about action", *Proceedings of the 11th International Joint Conference on Artificial Intelligence*, 966–971.

Winslett, M. (1988): "Reasoning about action using a possible models approach", In *Proceedings of the Seventh National Conference on Artificial Intelligence*, 89–93.

Winslett, M. (1989): "Theory revision semantics for use in reasoning about action", Unpublished manuscript.

Winslett, M. (1990): *Updating Logical Databases*. Cambridge, Cambridge University Press.

Planning from First Principles

MICHAEL MORREAU

Institut für maschinelle Sprachverarbeitung,
Keplerstrasse 17, 7000 Stuttgart 1, Germany

1 INTRODUCTION

Since the beginning of artificial intelligence research on action, researchers have been concerned with reasoning about actions with preconditions and postconditions. Through the work of Moore (1980), Pratt's (1980) *dynamic semantics* soon established itself in artificial intelligence as the appropriate semantics for action. Mysteriously, however, actions with preconditions and postconditions were not given a proper treatment within the modal framework of dynamic logic. This paper offers such an analysis. Things are complicated by the need to deal at the same time with the notion of *competence*, or an actor's ability. Below, a logic of actions with preconditions and postconditions is given a sound and complete syntactic characterization, in a logical formalism in which it is possible to express actor competence, and the utility of this formalism is demonstrated in the generation and evaluation of plans.

The notion of actions with pre- and postconditions arose in artificial intelligence in the field of planning. In formulating a plan to reach some particular goal, there are a number of things which a planning agent must take into account. First, he will have to decide which actions can and may be undertaken in order to reach the goal. The physical, legal, financial and other constraints under which an actor must act will be lumped together below, since we will be interested in what is common to them all, namely that they restrict available options. The options which remain open to the actor will be said to *lie within his competence*, or to be *allowed*.

Second, the planning agent will have to distinguish between those propositions which he takes to be generally true, independently of these allowed actions, and those other propositions which he takes to be true, but whose truth could be affected. In any planning situation this distinction is quite essential. In planning a journey which involves say first taking a bus and then a train, for example, one has to be sure that the train timetables are not among the things which could be changed by the kinds of actions which travelling involves, like taking the bus. They are, it is said in the planning literature, *protected* from the effects of such actions. One's location, by way of contrast, is something which taking the bus is not only allowed to change, but must change. Among ones protected propositions there will in general be both *frame* axioms constraining actions to leave some things, like the train timetables, as they are, and *ramifications* axioms describing changes which actions do bring about.

2 INFORMATION ABOUT ACTIONS

In this next section, possible worlds structures are used to model first an actor and his actions, and second a planning agent's partial information about these actions and their effects. To this end we now define two kinds of modal frames: actor frames and agent frames. These frames enable us to model formally the above notions of competence and protected propositions.

2.1 Actor and Agent Frames

In defining our frames, we presuppose a nonempty set W of possible states of the world. *Goals* are identified with *propositions*, or subsets of W; intuitively, to reach a goal g is just to bring it about that the actual state of the world is in g. To act, intuitively speaking, is to effect a transition from one possible state of the world to another. This makes it reasonable, in this simple setting, to interpret particular actions, or *action tokens*, as ordered pairs in W×W. For example, the particular action in which the actor eats a particular ice-cream at a particular speed on a particular day is modelled as the pair (u,v), where u models the state of the world on that particular day before, and v its state after, the ice-cream is eaten.

Action types may then be identified with subsets of W×W, the idea being that to carry out an action of type α is to effect some transition $(u,v) \in \alpha$. That is, an action type consists of the set of all particular actions the carrying out of which would count as carrying out an action of that type. So the action type of eating an ice-cream, for example, would be identified with the set of all transitions to states where an ice-cream has been eaten. The set $\wp$(W×W) of all action types is called A. The set of finite sequences of such action types is called A+ Such sequences $\underline{\alpha}$ are referred to as *courses of action*.

1 DEFINITION: An *actor frame* is a triple <W, $\mathcal{R}$, γ> where
(i)   W is a non-empty set of possible states of the world,
(ii) $\mathcal{R}$ is a distinguished action type, representing the actor's *competence*,
(iii) γ: W×A → W is a selection function.

The actor's competence, $\mathcal{R}$, contains all transitions which the actor is able to effect. It represents the constraints, whether physical, legal, financial or whatever, within which the actor must operate. We place the following constraint on our frames: for each $u \in$ W there is $v \in$ W such that $(u,v) \in \mathcal{R}$. The actor is assumed always to be able to change the state of the world in one way or other - even when doing "nothing" time passes.

As for γ, by definition there are in general a number of different ways of carrying out an action of any given type. But in any particular situation u our actor would, on undertaking some type α of action, do some particular thing. It is the business of the selection function γ to say what. In an actor frame, then, $\gamma(u,\alpha)$ stands for the way that u would end up if the actor were to undertake to carry out an action of type α. What the actor does will of course depend not only on u and α, but also on his competence. It is required that always $(u,\gamma(u,\alpha)) \in \mathcal{R}$; that is, the actor never effects transitions which go beyond his competence. It is *not* required that always $(u,\gamma(u,\alpha)) \in \alpha$. This is because even if the actor does his best to perform α, this action will not in general lie within his competence. The actor is not omnipotent.

Even so, the actor may be assumed to do his best within his limited competence. Formally, we require that for all α, u: if there is some v such that $(u,v) \in \alpha \cap \mathcal{R}$, then $(u, \gamma(u,\alpha)) \in \alpha$. In the following, all actor frames will be taken to satisfy this assumption that the agent *tries hard*. On undertaking to perform α, he does indeed perform α if this is within his competence.

It is useful to extend γ from individual action types to sequences of these, or *courses of action*. In the obvious recursive way, we set $\gamma(u,<\alpha>) := \gamma(u,\alpha)$, and $\gamma(u,<\alpha_1,\dots \alpha_{n+1}>) := \gamma(\gamma(u,<\alpha_1,\dots \alpha_n>, \alpha_{n+1})$.

We have the following important notion:

2 DEFINITION: An action type α lies *within the actor's competence*, in an actor frame $<W, \mathcal{R}, \gamma>$, just in case for each $u \in W$ there is some $v \in W$ such that $(u,v) \in \alpha \cap \mathcal{R}$.

Note that according to this definition, an action type lies within the actor's competence not if he is always able to carry out each and every particular action of that type, but instead if he is always able to carry out *some* particular action of that type. To say that someone is capable of eating an ice-cream is not to say that he is capable of doing so while standing on his head, for example, even though this would be one way of eating an ice-cream. Note also that given the assumption that the actor tries hard, the notion of competence can be reformulated in a manner which leaves out any reference to $\mathcal{R}$:

3 FACT: Let $\mathcal{F}$ be an action frame. Then α lies within the actor's competence in $\mathcal{F}$ just in case for each $u \in W$: $(u, \gamma(u,\alpha)) \in \alpha$.

4 DEFINITION: A proposition $p \subseteq W$ *is protected from an action type* α, in an actor frame $<W, \mathcal{R}, \gamma>$, just in case for each $u \in W$, if $u \in p$ then $\gamma(u,\alpha) \in p$.

Intuitively, a proposition is protected from an action just in case the actor in carrying out that action will never make that proposition false.

Actors have been assumed to act deterministically, in the sense that their actions always have unique outcomes. That is, $\gamma(u,\alpha)$ is always a unique possible world. One's *information* about these outcomes, on the other hand, is generally incomplete. In any given situation there may be, to the best of one's knowledge, several different outcomes which carrying out an action of any particular type might have. So, for example, each time an actor gets up out of bed, he will get out either on the left hand side, or on the right hand side. His action has a unique outcome. But on hearing that the actor has just completed an action of this type, one will in general not know exactly what this outcome is: whether he ends up to the left of the bed, or to the right. Any number of other details may also be unknown, even if, as modelled in our deterministic γ functions, the actual outcome of the action is perfectly specific.

In modelling reasoning agents' partial information about the outcomes of actions, Moore (1980) introduces indeterministic γ functions. On his approach, $\gamma(u,\alpha)$ becomes the set of those possible worlds which, as far as the agent can tell, might be the outcome of the actor's performing α in possible world u. To my mind, equating indeterminacy with partiality of information in this manner can only confuse the issue. In particular, there are good reasons for not confusing partial information about a deterministic world with total information about an indeterministic world. I opt instead for a broadly supervaluational approach: just as partial information about the world is commonly modelled by taking as information states sets of possible worlds, here partial information about the actor will be modelled by means of a set of "possible actors." Thus the epistemic predicament of our reasoner about action is modelled as not being able to say which of a number of alternative γ functions accurately represents the actor:

5 DEFINITION: Let $\mathcal{F}_1 = \langle W,\mathcal{R},\gamma_1 \rangle$, $\mathcal{F}_2 = \langle W,\mathcal{R},\gamma_2 \rangle$ etc. be actor frames. The *agent frame $\mathcal{F}$ based on* $\mathcal{F}_1$, $\mathcal{F}_2$, ... is the structure $\langle W,\mathcal{R},\Gamma \rangle$, where Γ is the set $\{\gamma_1, \gamma_2,...\}$.

Uncertainty about the effects of actions, as represented in Γ, is one way in which our planning agent can be ignorant, and it will lead to his being unsure about about the state in which action will leave the world. Uncertainty about what the world was like in the first place, before action was taken, will in general have the same effect. Uncertainty about the state of the world is now modelled in the same broadly supervaluational way as uncertainty about the actor, by representing information states as sets of possible worlds taken from agent frames. Intuitively, an agent's information state contains all those possible worlds which, as far as he can tell, might yet turn out to be the real world.

6 DEFINITION: The elements of $\wp W$ are in the case of agent frames referred to as *information states* σ, τ,...

We can now say how information states should be adapted to incoming information that the actor has followed a course of action $\underline{\alpha}$:

7 DEFINITION: Given an agent frame $<W,\mathcal{R},\Gamma>$ the *update function*
$$\Diamond: \wp W \times A^+ \to \wp W$$
is defined such that for each information state σ and each $\underline{\alpha} \in A^+$:
$$\sigma \Diamond \underline{\alpha} = \bigcup_{w \in \sigma} \bigcup_{\gamma \in \Gamma} \gamma(w, \underline{\alpha})$$

Intuitively, $\sigma \Diamond <\alpha_1,... \alpha_n>$ stands for the information state an agent would end up in if, while in information state σ, he were to hear that the actor has set out to perform first an action of type α_1, then an action of type α_2, and so on up to type α_n. According to this definition, the ways the agent thinks the world might end up after such a sequence of actions has been performed are just all the ways he thinks it could end up given his two uncertainties, both about the actor, and about what the world was like in the first place, before action was taken.

It is worth noting that updating, defined this way, may be thought of as a qualitative version of the notion of *imaging,* an update function on probability functions introduced by Lewis (1976). Further discussion of imaging is to be found in Gärdenfors (1988) and in Morreau (1991); it is also briefly mentioned in the introduction to this volume. Although it has received little attention in what has come to be known as the area of Belief Revision, imaging is nothing new in reasoning about action. Moore (1980) defines update functions for reasoning about the effects of actions which are based on a similar idea, as do Winslett (1988), and Katsuno and Mendelzon in their paper in this volume. One difference between the above definition and earlier ones is however worth mentioning: here updates are defined for iterated courses of action, instead of individual actions. It might be thought that the first of these should reduce to the second. In fact however, it is not difficult to think up examples which show that, in the context of partial information about the actor, it does not.

Suppose for example that there are before you two bedrooms, with somebody in each. About the person in the first room you know only that he consistently gets out of bed on the same side, but you do not know which side. About the second person you know nothing at all. Now suppose one night passes, and in each room somebody wakes and gets out of bed. What do you know about the two bedrooms? Just the same thing: in each bedroom somebody got out of bed, either on the left or on the right. Now let another day and night pass, so that everybody has woken and risen for a second time. Now you know more about what has gone on in the first room than in the second. There are essentially two possibilities: either somebody got out of bed twice on the right, or they got out twice on the left. In the case of the second room however there is an additional possibility that you must reckon with, namely that whoever is in there has gotten up once on the left, and once on the right of the bed. Apparently, in the context of partial information about the actor, reasoning about acting twice does not equal two times reasoning about acting once.

The notions of competence and protection may be extended from actor frames to agent frames in the obvious way: an agent frame is said to *assume that α lies within the actor's competence* just in case α lies within the actor's competence in each of the actor frames on which it is based. Analogously, a proposition p is *assumed protected from* α in an agent frame just in case p is protected from α in each of the actor frames of the base.

2.2 Actor and Agent Models
We now introduce a formal language and interpret it in the frames of the previous section, so as to obtain models of actors and agents.

8 DEFINITION: L is a language for classical propositional logic, with the standard connectives ¬, ∨, ∧. The set of its proposition letters p, q, r... is called *prop*. It is convenient to have a distinguished propositional letter T, to be interpreted as invariably true. The sentences of L are defined in the normal manner to include *prop* and anything obtained by conjoining sentences with connectives.

We now define a more expressive language in which to express propositions about actions and their effects, by introducing a non-empty set TERMS of *action terms*. These will be used to refer to types of action, like driving a car, or eating an ice-cream. Below, α is allowed to range not only over action types, as it did up until now, but also over action terms in TERMS. Similarly, $\underline{\alpha}$ ranges over finite sequences of such terms.

We also introduce a binary conditional connective >. For any action term α ∈ TERMS , the conditional sentence α>ψ will presently be interpreted in such a way as to express that if the agent were to carry out an action of type α, then this would result in the truth of ψ.[1]

9 DEFINITION: The set $L_>$ of sentences is the smallest set closed under the following clauses:
(i) If ϕ ∈ L, then ϕ ∈ $L_>$, and

---

[1] Actions are performed by actors, and conditional sentences might be expected to have sentences as their antecedents instead of actions. For these two reasons it would be better to write PERFORMS(a,α)>φ instead of α>φ, where PERFORMS is an operator which takes an agent a and an action α and returns the sentence PERFORMS(a,α) which means, intuitively, that a has performed α. Since we are keeping the agent constant in the following we have no real need for this notation, however, so in the interest of readability the PERFORMS operator has been left out. Readers troubled by this are free to imagine that it is there.

(ii) If $\alpha \in$ TERMS and $\phi \in L_>$ then $\alpha{>}\phi \in L_>$.

Note that the sentence ϕ in $\alpha{>}\phi$ is allowed to be logically complex. In particular it may refer, by means of $>$, to actions and their consequences. For any course of action $\underline{\alpha} = <\alpha_1, \alpha_2, \dots \alpha_n>$, $\underline{\alpha}{>}\phi$ is shorthand for the sentence $\alpha_1{>}(\alpha_2{>}\dots{>}(\alpha_n{>}\phi)\dots)$.

10 DEFINITION: An *actor model* M for $L_>$ is a tuple $<W, \mathcal{R}, \gamma, I>$ where
(i) $<W, \mathcal{R}, \gamma>$ is the (actor) frame of M,
(ii) I: WXProp $\rightarrow \{1, 0\}$ is an interpretation function assigning:
    a) to each proposition letter, in each possible world, either the
    truth value 1 or the truth value 0. These stand for true and false
    respectively. Furthermore, for every world w: $I(w, \mathrm{T}) = 1$.
    b) to each action term $\in$ TERMS some action type $\in$ A.

The recursive definition of truth relative to possible worlds in an actor model M is completely standard except for the following clause interpreting conditionals:
$$w \vDash_M \alpha{>}\phi \Leftrightarrow \gamma(w, I(\alpha)) \vDash_M \phi.$$
As elsewhere, the subscript M is dropped where possible. According to this truth condition, $\alpha{>}\phi$ is true at a possible world of an actor model if and only if the actor's carrying out α would transform w into a world where ϕ holds.

11 DEFINITION: An *agent model* M for $L_>$ is a tuple $<W, \mathcal{R}, \Gamma, I>$ where
(i) $<W, \mathcal{R}, \Gamma>$ is the (agent) frame of M, and
(ii) I is as in the definition of actor models.

The truth definition in agent models is essentially supervaluational. For any agent model $M = <W, \mathcal{R}, \Gamma, I>$, we set $w \vDash_M \phi$ just in case for each $\gamma \in \Gamma$: $w \vDash_{<W, \mathcal{R}, \gamma, I>} \phi$.

Thus $\underline{\alpha}{>}\phi$ is true at a possible world of an agent model just in case no matter which of the possible actors turns out to be the real actor, his carrying out the course of action $\underline{\alpha}$ would change the world into a place where ϕ holds. This truth definition is supervaluational in that the truth value of a sentence in an agent model is determined by referring back to all of the actor models on which that agent model is based.

Agent models contain information states, and the information supported by such a state is just everything which is true at each world which it contains:

12 DEFINITION: $\sigma \vDash_M \phi$, just in case for all $w \in \sigma$: $w \vDash_M \phi$.

Let the update functions $\Diamond$ of (the frames underlying) our agent models be extended to TERMS in the following obvious way: for each information state σ and each sequence of action terms $\underline{\alpha} = <\alpha_1, \alpha_2, \dots \alpha_n>$, $\sigma\Diamond\underline{\alpha}$ is set equal to $\sigma\Diamond<I\alpha_1, I\alpha_2, \dots I\alpha_n>$. Then it is not difficult to demonstrate the following intimate connection between updates and conditionals:

13 FACT: For all σ, $\underline{\alpha}$, and >-free sentences ϕ: $\sigma \vDash \underline{\alpha}{>}\phi$ $\Leftrightarrow$ $\sigma\Diamond\underline{\alpha} \vDash \phi$.

In philosophy, the name of Frank Ramsey is associated with this kind of relation between updates of information states and conditionals, since Ramsey once proposed something along these lines as an empirical hypothesis about the meaning of natural language conditionals. Here, we should rather think of this equivalence as stating that our conditional sentences are behaving as we intended: they express facts about the effects which courses of action would have. By the truth definition for >, a sentence $\underline{\alpha}{>}\phi$ is true at a possible world of an actor frame just in case the actor's successively carrying out the actions in $\underline{\alpha}$ would in fact change that world into a place where ϕ holds. Clearly this must be reflected in the reasoning about action which is supposed to be modelled by our update functions, and indeed what the above fact means is that the update functions which we have defined do succeed in this respect. For by the above fact, an agent has the information $\underline{\alpha}{>}\phi$ just in case on every way of resolving his uncertainties, both with respect to the actor and with respect to the initial state of the world, the course of action $\underline{\alpha}$ is guaranteed to turn the world into a place where ϕ is true.

3 PRECONDITIONS AND POSTCONDITIONS

In the previous section we spoke very generally about action types as sets of state transitions, but of course most of these will be pretty uninteresting. So as to be able to pick out those types which interest us, we have in our object language primitive action terms. In the much more expressive languages of dynamic logic, action types are described by action terms which are composed from such primitive action terms by means of dynamic connectives, such as concatenation (;), nondeterministic choice ($\cup$), and the Kleene star operation (*).

In artificial intelligence, action types have often been picked out in terms of the states of affairs which come to hold whenever they are successfully performed, or their *postconditions*. The examples we have been using have all been of this kind. The action type of eating an ice-cream could be thought of as the set of all particular actions which would bring about the truth of the sentence *an ice-cream is to be found in the stomach*, while the action type of an actor's getting out of bed can be identified with the transitions which end up with him out of bed. Indeed, Belnap (1989) recently argued that *all* actions that we talk about in natural language may be picked out in terms of what comes to hold as a result of their being performed.

In artificial intelligence, however, not just postconditions are held to be of importance in individuating action types, but also *preconditions*. The precondition of an action is the condition under which an actor who is capable of carrying out that action is able to bring about its postcondition. The following definition concerns action types which may be described by means of sentences of $L_>$:

14 DEFINITION: The $L_>$ sentences ϕ and ψ and the boolean expression B together define in M the action type α, just in case $\alpha = \{(u,v) : B(u \in [\![\phi]\!]^M, v \in [\![\psi]\!]^M\}$.

Here $[\![\phi]\!]^M$, the proposition expressed by ϕ in M, is defined to be $\{u : u \vDash_M \phi\}$. Again, sub- and superscripts M are dropped where possible.

The action type with precondition ϕ and postcondition ψ is here modelled as that type which is defined by ϕ and ψ together with the boolean expression *if...then...*. That is, a transition from u to v counts as a successful performance of the action with precondition ϕ and postcondition ψ just in case ψ is true at v if ϕ is true at u.

By way of motivation, it is worth verifying that an action with precondition ϕ and postcondition ψ lies with the actor's competence in an actor model just in case for each ϕ world u of that model there is some ψ world v such that the actor is able to make the transition from u to v. Or, in other words, if whenever ϕ holds the actor is able to bring it about that ψ holds.

In order to refer to action types defined by pre- and postconditions, which will turn up a lot soon, it is convenient to introduce special action terms $[\phi;\psi]$. To keep things simple, however, we do so only for >-free sentences ϕ and ψ. I is then required to respect the convention, by satisfying

$$I([\phi;\psi]) = \{(u,v) : if \; u \in [\![\phi]\!] \; then \; v \in [\![\psi]\!]\}.$$

Given the restriction to >-free ϕ and ψ, it will be clear that it does not matter whether the $[\![\phi]\!]$ and $[\![\psi]\!]$ of this definition are evaluated in an agent model or in any of the actor models on which it is based.

Let us say that an agent model M assumes $\alpha \in$ TERMS to lie within the actor's competence if the frame of M assumes $I\alpha$ to lie within the actor's competence, and that M assumes ϕ to be protected from α if the frame of M assumes $[\![\phi]\!]$ to be protected from $I\alpha$. Then we can state the following FACTS concerning the expressibility in agent models of assumptions concerning the actor's competence and the protection of propositions:

15 FACT: For >-free ϕ and ψ the following two statements are equivalent:
(1) M *assumes* $[\phi;\psi]$ *to lie within the actor's competence.*
(2) M $\vDash \phi \rightarrow ([\phi;\psi]>\psi)$.

16 FACT: For >-free ϕ, the following two statements are equivalent:
(1) M *assumes ϕ to be protected from α*.
(2) M $\vDash \phi \rightarrow (\alpha > \phi)$.

4 PLANNING FROM FIRST PRINCIPLES

Up until now the agent's reasoning about action has been implicit in the update functions + of our epistemic model of his reasoning, and we didn't care how this reasoning might actually be performed. In this section an algorithm is given for reasoning about actions, and its utility is demonstrated in plan formation and verification. Let Φ be a set of $L_>$ sentences, and let $\aleph$ be a set $\{[\phi_1;\psi_1], [\phi_2;\psi_2], [\phi_3;\psi_3], ...\}$ of actions with pre- and postconditions. Furthermore, let S be the class of agent models M such that M assumes each $\alpha \in \aleph$ to lie within the competence of the actor, and M assumes each $\phi \in \Phi$ to be protected from each $\alpha \in \aleph$. Then for sets K of sentences, and for individual sentences ψ, a notion of logical entailment may be defined as follows:

17 DEFINITION: K $\vdash_{\Phi|\aleph} \psi$, just in case for each model M $\in$ S and information state s of M: if $\sigma \vDash_M$ K, then $\sigma \vDash_M \psi$.

Restricting ourselves to the language $L_>$ which has only action terms of the form $[\phi;\psi]$, this notion of entailment turns out to correspond to the syntactic notion which is the subject of the following definition:[2]

18 DEFINITION: We define $\vdash_{\Phi|\aleph} \psi$ iff ψ may be derived using the following axioms and rules:

(A0)   All truth-functional tautologies in $L_>$
(A1) $\alpha > T$
       $\neg(\alpha > \neg T)$ for each $\alpha \in$ TERMS
(A2) $\phi \rightarrow ([\phi;\psi] > \psi)$ for each $[\phi;\psi] \in \aleph$ ("competence")
(A3) $\phi \rightarrow \alpha > \phi$ for each $\phi \in \Phi$ and for each $\alpha \in \aleph$ ("protection")
(A4) $(\phi \wedge \alpha > \psi) \rightarrow ([\phi;\psi] > \psi)$ for each $\alpha \in$ TERMS   ("trying hard")
(A5) $\alpha > \phi \vee \psi \rightarrow \alpha > \phi \vee \alpha > \psi$ ("determinism")
(A6) $[\phi;T] > \chi \leftrightarrow [F;\psi] > \chi$
       $[\phi;T] > \chi \leftrightarrow [\psi;T] > \chi$
       $[F;\phi] > \chi \leftrightarrow [F;\psi] > \chi$

(R1)   If $\vdash_{\Phi|\aleph} \phi_1 \leftrightarrow \phi_2$ and $\vdash_{\Phi|\aleph} \psi_1 \leftrightarrow \psi_2$, then

---

[2]The completeness should generalize to languages with other terms too, and to languages which allow action terms to be combined with various constructs familiar from programming languages and dynamic logic, such as *while* loops. But proofs have yet to be given.

$$\vdash_{\Phi|\aleph} [\phi_1;\psi_1]>\chi \leftrightarrow [\phi_2;\psi_2]>\chi.$$

(R2)   If $\vdash_{\Phi|\aleph} \psi$ and $\vdash_{\Phi|\aleph} \psi\rightarrow\chi$, then

$$\vdash_{\Phi|\aleph} \chi. \qquad \text{("modus ponens")}$$

(R3)   If $\vdash_{\Phi|\aleph} (\psi_1\wedge\psi_2\wedge..\psi_n)\rightarrow\chi$ then

$$\vdash_{\Phi|\aleph} (\alpha>\psi_1 \wedge \alpha>\psi_2 \wedge... \alpha>\psi_n) \rightarrow \alpha>\chi.$$

We can then define $K \vdash_{\Phi|\aleph} \psi$ iff there is a finite set $K_e \subseteq K$ such that $\vdash_{\Phi|\aleph} \wedge K_e\rightarrow\psi$.

Where it is clear which Φ and $\aleph$ are meant, and where it makes no difference which are meant, subscripts $\Phi|\aleph$ are conveniently dropped. Note that the compactness and deduction theorems are trivial for this notion of derivability from premises K. Together these theorems give us a Lindenbaum lemma and with it a fairly straightforward Henkin-style proof of the completeness theorem:

19 THEOREM: $K \vdash \psi \Leftrightarrow K \vDash \psi$.

The soundness part is trivial. The proof that $K \vdash \psi \Leftarrow K \vDash \psi$ involves a canonical model construction which makes use of the following lemma:

20 LEMMA: Let W be the set of all maximal, $\vdash$-consistent sets of sentences. And for any two sentences ϕ,ψ, let $(\phi;\psi)$ be the set $\{(u,v) \in W\times W: \phi \in u \Rightarrow \psi \in v\}$. Then the following two statements are equivalent:

i) $(\phi_1;\psi_1) = (\phi_2;\psi_2)$.

ii)   either a) $\vdash\phi_1\leftrightarrow\phi_2$ and $\vdash\psi_1\leftrightarrow\psi_2$

        or   b) $\vdash\phi_1\leftrightarrow F$ and $\vdash\phi_2\leftrightarrow F$

        or   c) $\vdash\psi_1\leftrightarrow T$ and $\vdash\psi_2\leftrightarrow T$

        or   d) $\vdash\phi_1\leftrightarrow F$ and $\vdash\psi_2\leftrightarrow T$

        or   e) $\vdash\phi_2\leftrightarrow F$ and $\vdash\psi_1\leftrightarrow T.$

For details of the proofs of this lemma and the rest of the completeness theorem, the reader is referred to Morreau (1992).

We now come to the main point, which is to demonstrate, first by a theorem and then in the next section by an example, the interest of the above derivability notion when it comes to the formation and verification of plans. Together with FACT 13, the completeness THEOREM 20 has the following corollary:

21 COROLLARY: For all K, Φ, $\aleph$, $\underline{\alpha}$ and $>$-free ϕ, the following two statements are equivalent:

(i) $K \vdash_{\Phi|\aleph} \underline{\alpha}>\phi$.

(ii)   For any M which assumes all $\alpha \in \aleph$ to lie within the agent's competence, and all $\phi \in \Phi$ to be protected from all $\alpha \in \aleph$, and for all information states σ of M:

$$\sigma \vdash_M K \Rightarrow \sigma \Diamond \underline{\alpha} \vdash_M \phi.$$

Suppose that action must be taken so as to transform the world into a place where ϕ is true. Then according to this corollary, the following two steps are the appropriate way to proceed:

(a)   Let $\aleph$ be the set of actions which may (physically, financially, legally) be taken in order to bring about ϕ. Further, let Φ contain those things which you take to be not only true but also unaffected by the actions in $\aleph$, and let K contain those things which you take to be true but not unaffected by the actions in $\aleph$.

(b)   By doing theorem proving in $\vdash_{\Phi|\aleph}$ search for some course of action $\underline{\alpha}$ in $\aleph$ such that $K \cup \Phi \vdash_{\Phi|\aleph} \underline{\alpha} > \phi$ (a course of action α is *in* $\aleph$ just in case each α_i is $\in \aleph$). Any such course of action which is found is a plan for bringing about ϕ.

Why is this the right way to proceed? Assume that you were right about each of the actions in $\aleph$ being within the competence of the actor, about Φ being true and protected from these actions, and about K being true. The implication from (i) to (ii) says that if such a course of action is found, then following it is guaranteed to result in the truth of ϕ, which was the goal. Furthermore, the implication from (ii) to (i) says that if there is a course of action which is guaranteed to bring about the truth of ϕ, then the above procedure of theorem proving in $\vdash_{\Phi|\aleph}$, is guaranteed to find it. Thus, this two step procedure generates only plans which are effective, and of these all are generated.

Here are some derived rules for $\vdash_{\Phi|\aleph}$ which are useful when it comes to generating and verifying plans. The first might be called *necessitation*: If $\vdash_{\Phi|\aleph} \phi$, then for any course $\underline{\alpha}$ of action whatsoever, $\vdash_{\Phi|\aleph} \underline{\alpha} > \phi$. Logical truths are stronger than actions. The following derived rule, call it *protection*, is related to necessitation. It says that true protected sentences are as good as theorems when it comes to the actions from which they are protected:

(R4)   If $\phi \in \Phi$ and $\underline{\alpha}$ is a course of action in $\aleph$, then
            $\phi \vdash_{\Phi|\aleph} \underline{\alpha} > \phi$.

Another derived rule which will be of use is this generalization of (R3):
(R5)   If for each $\phi \in K^*$: $K \vdash_{\Phi|\aleph} \underline{\alpha} > \phi$, and if furthermore $K^* \vdash_{\Phi|\aleph} \psi$, then $K \vdash_{\Phi|\aleph} \underline{\alpha} > \psi$.

5 A PLANNING EXAMPLE

You are in your counting house counting all your money when a messenger comes. He informs you that princess Merideth, who doesn't like boys, is complaining that another prince has climbed into the tree outside her window, and that she wants him shot. You are not so sure that there is a prince in the tree. But since you are looking forward to a quiet evening pottering around in the royal armory you decide it is better to make sure that there isn't one. So you form as your goal for that evening IA∧¬PIT. You want to be In the Armory, and you want no Prince In the Tree. Your unprotected beliefs include, in this situation, ¬IA, since at that time you are not in the armory.

We assume that, in order to reach your composite goal, you are able and willing to do things like go to the tree, move away from the tree, go home, etc. Such movement actions are assumed furthermore to be without preconditions, so ℵ, the set of actions which you are willing to undertake in order to reach your goal, includes at least [AT] , [¬AT] , [IA] etc., which stand for the actions with postconditions At Tree (the trivial precondition T being omitted), with postcondition not At Tree, with postcondition In Armory, etc. Another action you are assumed to be able to do without precondition is to start Looking for the royal Blunderbuss, [LB] . Note that the postcondition of this action is that you are looking for the blunderbuss, not that you have found it. Furthermore, we assume you to be willing and able to pick up a blunderbuss if you find one ([HB;CB], with as its precondition Have Blunderbuss and as its postcondition Carrying Blunderbuss), and say to put down a blunderbuss ([CB;¬CB]). Furthermore, provided you are At the Tree and Have a Blunderbuss, we assume you to be able to persuade the prince out of the tree. So the action [AT∧HB;¬PIT], like the above lot, is in ℵ too. For the example lots of unnecessary actions have been included, just to make things a little more realistic. Others could be added; little below depends on which others.

We have had some of your unprotected beliefs. Now for some beliefs which you take to be protected from the above actions (and any others you would be prepared to engage in order to achieve your goal). Among these, let us suppose, are at least the following axiom schemes. The first of these is a ramifications axiom:

P_1: IA→ [LB]>HB.

Provided you are In the Armory, if you Look for the Blunderbuss then you will end up Having the Blunderbuss.[3] The next one is a frame axiom scheme:

P_2: CB→ α>CB,   for each α ∈ {[IA] , [¬IA] , [AT],...}.

If you are Carrying something (in this case, the Blunderbuss) then performing a movement action (going to the armory, going out of the armory, going to the tree, etc...) doesn't affect this. Here is a logical truth which won't be effected by the actions:

P_3: CB→HB.

To Carry a Blunderbuss is to Have a Blunderbuss. A geographical truth which won't be affected by any actions you are considering is

P_4: AT→¬IA.

---

[3]To make this a non-linear planning example we are assuming that you are guaranteed to find the blunderbuss only if you are in the armory. It is not too difficult to contrive some reason why this constraint might be realistic: say because that is the only place where it is allowed to leave it.

You can't be both At the Tree and In the Armory. Finally, we assume the following protected scheme:

P$_5$: $\neg$PIT $\rightarrow$ α>$\neg$PIT, for all $\alpha \in \aleph$.

None of the actions under consideration will drive the Prince In the Tree.

Note well that it is not assumed that no actions which one could *conceivably* take, say to reach other goals, would affect the truth of these sentences. Locking yourself into the bathroom would affect your ability to move around at will; instituting a comprehensive language reform throughout your kingdom might well make untrue some previously analytically true sentences, and surely there are things which would drive a successfully extracted prince back up his tree again. What is being assumed is that you are not considering doing these things in order to get the prince out of the tree.

Let K contain your unprotected belief $\neg$IA and any others you like. Let Φ contain all of the other protected schemes, and any others you like. And let $\aleph$ contain all of the above action terms. Now we let the logic $\vdash_{\Phi|\aleph}$ prove theorems from the premises K$\cup\Phi$, and find that it proves the theorem:

[IA]>([LB]>([HB;CB]>([AT]>([HB$\wedge$AT;$\neg$PIT]>([IA]> IA$\wedge\neg$PIT))))).

To see this, it is sufficient, with propositional reasoning, to see that that both of the following are derived:

PIT$\rightarrow$[IT]>([LB]>([HB;CB]>([AT]>([HB$\wedge$AT;$\neg$PIT]>([IT]>IA$\wedge\neg$PIT))))

$\neg$PIT$\rightarrow$[IT]>([LB]>([HB;CB]>([AT]>([HB$\wedge$AT;$\neg$PIT]>([IT]>IA$\wedge\neg$PIT))))).

The second sentence follows with repeated application of P$_5$, preservation and (R5); the derivation is similar to that of the following abbreviated derivation of the first sentence and is left to the reader. Here is (a summary of) a derivation of the first sentence. The following sentences may be be derived from $\Gamma\cup\Phi$ with $\vdash_{\Phi|\aleph}$:

1	[IA]>IA	(A2), truth functional logic
2	[IA]>(IA$\rightarrow$([LB]>HB))	P$_1$, protection
3	[IA]>([LB]>HB)	1, 2, R5
4	[IA]>([LB]>(HB$\rightarrow$([HB;CB]>CB)))	3, 4, R5
6	[IA]>([LB]>([HB;CB]>(CB$\rightarrow$([AT]>CB))))	P$_2$, protection
7	[IA]>([LB]>([HB;CB]>([AT]>CB)))	5, 6, R5
8	[IA]>([LB]>([HB;CB]>([AT]>(CB$\rightarrow$HB))))	P$_3$, protection
9	[IA]>([LB]>([HB;CB]>([AT]>HB)))	7, 8, R5
10	[IA]>([LB]>([HB;CB]>([AT]>AT)))	(A2), necessitation, R5
11	[IA]>([LB]>([HB;CB]>([AT]>HB$\wedge$AT)))	9, 10, R5
12	[IA]>([LB]>([HB;CB]>([AT]>(HB$\wedge$AT$\rightarrow$([HB$\wedge$AT;$\neg$PIT]>$\neg$PIT)))	(A2), necessitation
13	[IA]>([LB]>([HB;CB]>([AT]>([HB$\wedge$AT;$\neg$PIT]>$\neg$PIT))))	11, 12, R5
14	[IA]>([LB]>([HB;CB]>([AT]>([HB$\wedge$AT;$\neg$PIT]>($\neg$PIT $\rightarrow$([IA]>$\neg$PIT))))))	P$_5$, protection
15	[IA]>([LB]>([HB;CB]>([AT]>([HB$\wedge$AT;$\neg$PIT]>([IA]>$\neg$PIT))))))	13, 14, R5
16	[IA]>([LB]>([HB;CB]>([AT]>([HB$\wedge$AT;$\neg$PIT]>([IA]> IA))))	(A2), necessitation, R4

17   [IA]>([LB]>([HB;CB]>([AT]>([HB∧AT;¬PIT]>([IA]> (IA∧¬PIT))))))   15, 16 , R5

18   PIT→([IA]>([LB]>([HB;CB]>([AT]>([HB∧AT;¬PIT]>([IA]> IA∧¬PIT)))))))   17

Q.E.D.

So how do you achieve your goal of getting the prince out of the tree and yourself into the armory? Since the theorem

[IA]>([LB]>([HB;CB]>([AT]>([HB∧AT;¬PIT]>([IA]>IA∧¬PIT))))))

has been proved, it seems that our theorem prover recommends the following course of action: <[IA], [LB], [HB;CB], [AT], [HB∧AT;¬PIT], [IA]>. That is, first go to the armory. Then look for the royal blunderbuss. Then pick it up. Then go to the tree. Then get the prince out. Then go back to the armory. Note that the plan is *non-linear* in the sense that by first going home and then later to the tree, you "undo" your achievement of part of your goal, namely IA, in order to make sure that ultimately the whole goal is reached.

6 CONCLUSION

A dynamic semantics for actions with preconditions and postconditions has been given, together with a model theoretic account of the notion of ability, or competence. Then, combining ideas from philosophical logic and the theory of belief revision, this dynamic semantics gave rise to a theory of reasoning about action. The update functions defined here differ from those of earlier applications of belief revision to reasoning about action in two ways. First, they are inspired by the notion of imaging introduced by Lewis (1976), rather than being based on the theory of belief revision developed of Alchourrón and others (1985). It has repeatedly been pointed out, by Winslett, and by Gärdenfors and Katsuno and Mendelzon in this volume, that this theory is unsuitable for reasoning about action. But, and second, the update functions defined here also differ from other approaches to reasoning about action based on imaging, such as those of Moore (1980), of Winslett (1988), and of Katsuno and Mendelzon in this volume, in being irreducibly defined for sequences of actions instead of individual actions. An example made clear that this is necessary if, realistically, we allow for reasoning agents to have only partial information about the effects of actions.

This paper does not solve the frame problem. A syntactic algorithm for generating and verifying plans is defined above. But anybody who wanted to implement it in a computer system would have to provide the theorem prover with all of the frame axioms stating which properties of the world are unaffected by which actions. The frame problem is usually thought of as the problem of saying which such sentences are true, and which are false. This is not a problem to be solved by analyzing concepts, it is an empirical one. And, as far as I know, there is no special reason to believe that it can be solved. That is, I can't think of any reason for believing that the collection of frame axioms which are true in our world can be characterized in a clean way, by being axiomatized.

ACKNOWLEGEMENT

I would like to express thanks to Johan van Benthem and Hans Kamp for helpful comments and suggestions, and to Keith van Rijsbergen for bringing the concept of imaging to my attention several years ago.

REFERENCES

Alchourrón and others (1985): Alchourrón, Gärdenfors and Makinson, "On the Logic of Theory Change." *Journal of Symbolic Logic, 50.*

Belnap, N. (1989): "Seeing to it that: a canonical form for agentives." *Theoria,* Vol. 54.
Gärdenfors, P. (1988): *Knowledge in Flux.* Bradford Books, MIT Press.

Gibbard and Harper, (1978): "Counterfactuals and Two Kinds of Expected Utility." C. Hooker and others (eds.) *Foundations and Applications of Decision Theory.* Western Ontario Series in the Philosophy of Science, Vol. 13, Dordrecht, Reidel.
Also appears in Harper and others (eds.) *Ifs,* Western Ontario Series in the Philosophy of Science, Vol. 15, Dordrecht, Reidel, 1981.

Lewis, D. (1976): "Probabilities of Conditionals and Conditional Probabilities." *Philosophical Review,* 85.

Moore, R. (1980): *Reasoning about Knowledge and Action.* PhD Thesis, published as SRI Technical note 191, October 1980, SRI International.

Morreau, M. (1991): "Epistemic Semantics for Counterfactuals." Forthcoming in the *Journal of Philosophical Logic,* 1991.

Morreau, M. (1992): "Actions with Preconditions and Postconditions." Forthcoming in Pearce and Wansing (eds.), *Non Classical Logics and Information Processing,* Lecture Notes in Artificial Intelligence, Springer Verlag, Heidelberg.

Pratt, V. (1980) "Application of Modal Logic to Programming." *Studia Logica,* Vol. 39, pp. 257 - 274.

Winslett (1988): "Reasoning about Action Using a Possible Models Approach." In the *Proceedings of AAAI,* Vol 1., Morgan Kaufmann Publishers.

Autonomous belief revision and communication

JULIA ROSE GALLIERS

University of Cambridge Computer Laboratory, Cambridge CB2 3QG,
ENGLAND

1 INTRODUCTION

This chapter describes a model of autonomous belief revision (ABR) which discriminates between possible alternative belief sets in the context of change. The model determines preferred revisions on the basis of the relative persistence of competing cognitive states. It has been implemented as ICM (increased coherence model); a belief revision mechanism encompassing a three-tiered ordering structure which represents a blend between coherence and foundational theories of belief revision.

The motivation for developing the model of ABR is as a component of a model of communication between agents. The concern is choice about changing belief. In communication, agents should be designed to choose *whether* as well as *how* to revise their beliefs. This is an important aspect of design for multi-agent contexts as open environments (Hewitt, 1986), in which no one element can be in possession of complete information of all parts of the system at all times. Communicated information cannot therefore be assumed to be reliable and fully informed. The model of ABR and system ICM, represent the first phase in the development of a computational model of cooperative, yet autonomously determined communication. The theory of ABR and communication is explicated in section 2.

Section 3 follows with an outline of the problem of multiple alternative revisions, and a discussion of preference and strength of belief issues from an AI perspective. This section includes the relevant comparative and theoretical background for understanding the model of ABR described in section 4.

Section 4 begins with a logical framework for describing alternative theories of belief revision. These are presented as various different ordering relations. A new ordering relation mc, is then proposed as particularly suited to the requirements of ABR. In addition to this logical basis, a heuristic method of ordering is described as a component of ABR.

Section 5 comprises a practical illustration of the ordering relations of ABR as implemented in ICM.

BELIEF REVISION AND COMMUNICATION

Many researchers in AI are concerned with the design of automated systems which can plan and execute actions. These actions should be appropriate to the goals of the system, and its context or environment. In this sense they are rational behaviours, and the system a rational 'agent'. Being an autonomous as well as a rational agent, means having the ability to reason about relations and behaviour appropriate to self and the world. And the world includes other agents, who similarly reason in order to act autonomously and rationally. Primary in this reasoning are representations, beliefs or cognitive states generated through perception and inference, and related to desires and action according to the rules of rationality encoded into the system. But these cognitive states are inevitably constantly changing. The world is dynamic. Expansion and contraction of a belief set occurs as new data is perceived or inferred, and old data is lost over time or in the light of new evidence. Often expansion and contraction occur together. This is belief revision as described by Gärdenfors in the introduction to this volume; changing one's cognitive state.

New data can be perceived directly from the world. It can also be communicated via another agent. According to Grice (1957, 1969), an utterance is a perceived event that conveys an intention; the speaker's intention that the hearer recognise an intention on the part of the speaker to cause a certain effect in the hearer's mental state. Since agents can be assumed to always have some mental state, then this can be alternatively stated as the recognition of a speaker intention for a particular *change* in the attendee's cognitive states. Any perceived change in the environment, including the recognition of a communicative intention via an utterance, changes the mental state, and can be dealt with as an incidence of revision. Communication is an incidence of belief revision.

Viewed in this way, a particular revision of another's cognitive state is the motivating force for communicative behaviour. Utterance planning concerns desired change, not simply a desired effect. Utterance planning therefore involves an understanding of the principles of belief revision; how beliefs are gained and lost in order to accomodate new evidence. One important issue associated with this is *preference* between alternative potential revisions. Section 3.1. describes the 'multiple extension' problem, where new evidence results in contradiction which can be resolved in alternative ways, all of which are logically equivalent. Various solutions and associated issues are discussed in section 3. For the moment, to follow the line of argument through, we need only say that whatever the system of preference, it is applicable to communication as an incidence of revision. There is a basis upon which one belief set is considered preferable to another. The suggestion here and described in full in section 4 relates this to maximising coherence with other beliefs. On recognition of a speaker's intention via an utterance, the hearer can apply this general principled basis of maximal coherence, not only to determine how to accomodate the new evidence, but also whether to accomodate it at all.

One important implication of this is that there is no need for separate axioms describing helpful agents as those that always adopt other's recognised goals, for example to believe P, unless they conflict with one in existence, such as already believing not P (Cohen and Levesque, 1987, Perrault, 1987). There is no need to dictate either adoption or persistence of belief, or to treat contradictions in any way as a special case. A basic system of preference is laid down and understood, general enough to encompass change of beliefs as expansion, contraction or revision wherever in the world the new evidence comes from. What is being considered is: Which is the more coherent state given my current cognitive state and this change in the environment which has just occurred?

The principle of rationality or property of agents which is embodied within this, is that agents are autonomous over their mental states. Changes of mental state are guided by general principles of belief change, relevant to communicative and non-communicative contexts. Autonomous agents may or may not comply with the recognised intended effects of an utterance on their cognitive states. There are no specialised rules dictating what is a cooperative response. Rational communicative action must therefore be planned not only as purposive, but as *strategic* (Galliers, 1989, 1991).

Strategic interaction acknowledges all participants as sharing control over the effects of a communication. Strategic action is that which maximises one's own outcome. Maximising one's own outcome in a situation of shared control, is a matter of it being maximal for the other party(s) also. Achieving a desired change in another's belief states is therefore a matter of creating a context such that the general rules of rational belief revision would dictate that change anyway. The aim in utterance planning, is to determine one's own actions according to one's own goals and the context. This context includes the other agent and her presumed existing mental states, and a prediction of the changed context which will result in her preferring the intended belief state according to the principles of rational, autonomous belief revision. Cooperative behaviour can emerge autonomously, without being imposed from explicitly stated descriptions of how to behave 'helpfully'. However, is this just replacing prescribed acceptance with cooperation as artful persuasion; strategically getting another to want (autonomously) to agree? The answer is 'no'. All agents have autonomy over their belief states; all employ preference orderings based in maximal coherence in contexts of choice. If an utterance is unsuccessful, it may be that there is insufficient evidence for its adoption on the part of the hearer to result in as coherent a belief state as not adopting it. In this case the speaker may offer the extra evidence, to persuade. But on the other hand, it may be the case that there is some evidence which the hearer has and the speaker does not, which causes the difference in coherence of this item of evidence with other beliefs. A conversation aimed at achieving some joint or collaborative venture which presumably at this point is not yet achieved, would then continue with an appropriate contribution by the hearer. This is *adaptive* cooperation in a distributed environment. It is a model of cooperation which does not shy away from the positive role of conflicts and their resolution (Galliers, 1989, 1990). Cooperation is achieved over a series of utterances, motivated by this as an ultimate joint goal and an understanding that all concerned are operating according to a rationality specified by general principles of *autonomous* belief change.

The need for the proposed lack of imposed 'helpfulness' and associated assumptions about agents as reliable and informed and hence 'knowing what they are talking about', is because multi-agent environments are 'open environments' (Hewitt, 1986). No agent can know everything about its environment. No agent can *know* another's belief states. Such a state of affairs would not even be desirable as there would be unnecessary bottlenecks of information processing (Hewitt, 1986, Gasser, 1989, Galliers, 1990). Hence the use above of words such as 'presumed' and 'predicted' in phrases referring to others' mental states. This lack of complete information, together with the dynamic nature of both the physical and multi-agent world, is the background within which belief revision is viewed as fundamental to rational interaction. It is also the background to collaborative dialogue as a series of negotiated or mutually accepted belief revisions.

To summarise the main points:
(1) An agent always has a cognitive state. Perceiving and inferring new beliefs changes this state by expansion, contraction and revision. There are principles which determine how this takes place; principles of rational belief change.
(2) Communication is a special case of belief change which involves other agents. Agents plan to revise, and perceive (recognise) other's plans as such.
(3) Agents are autonomous. They determine their own cognitive states according to the principles of rational belief change. There are no special axioms dictating helpfulness and promoting cooperation when in a multi-agent context.

(4) Multi-agent communication must therefore be strategically driven. Plans to effect changes to another's cognitive state can only be successful if they take into account the principles whereby rational and autonomous agents change their beliefs. Maximising one's own outcome with respect to another agent is dependent upon them maximising theirs.

(5) Cooperative behaviour can emerge from general principles of belief revision and agent autonomy.

This chapter investigates the nature of autonomous belief revision.

3 BELIEF REVISION AND STRENGTH OF BELIEF

3.1 Belief revision in AI

Belief revision in AI is associated with nonmonotonic reasoning; reasoning with inferences potentially withdrawable at some later stage. Doyle specifies two aspects of nonmonotonicity. Firstly, temporal nonmonotonicity in which attitudes are lost and gained over time, and secondly logical nonmonotonicity, in which unsound inferences are made but as a product of sound reasoning, incomplete information and a 'will to believe' (Doyle, 1988). An example of the latter is default reasoning.

Reason maintenance systems (RMS's) are AI's mechanisms for belief revision. They maintain consistent sets of beliefs in the light of new evidence. DeKleer's ATMS (1986) maintains various consistent sets of beliefs appropriate to different assumptions or contexts, whereas the RMS's of Doyle (1979) and McAllester (1980) maintain just one.

But new evidence may be accomodated into a belief set in alternative ways, and all of these maintain consistency. This is known as the 'multiple extensions' problem. For example:

$$(a) P \lor Q \qquad (b) R \supset Q \qquad (c) P \lor R$$

$$\text{new evidence:} \quad \neg P \land \neg Q$$

Incorporating the new evidence results in two logically equivalent extensions. These are (b) and the new evidence, or (c) and the new evidence, because (a) is inconsistent with the new evidence, and *either* (b) *or* (c) are consistent with it, but not both (Rescher, 1964).

Alternatively again, the new evidence can be rejected if it is not assumed as 'truth' in which case the third possible extension is (a), (b) and (c). This latter alternative is a possibility for example in communication, as long as there are no assumptions regarding the communicator's omniscience and/or sincerity.

The only way of determining a preferred option from these kinds of possibilities is to incorporate some factor other than consistency. This factor should be the basis for *ordering or prioritising the various alternative combinations of belief.* The following section deals with various aspects, problems and solutions to this issue of preference in belief revision.

3.2 Preference in belief revision

This section comprises various parts, each directed at some aspect of the problem of incorporating ordering or assigning priorities in the belief revision context. This is discussed under the heading *strength of belief.* Advantages and disadvantages of different approaches are considered. Section 4 then follows with a description of the proposed model of autonomous belief revision, in which a particular stand has been taken on each of the issues raised here.

Strength of belief.

In general, AI approaches to non-monotonic reasoning do not consider beliefs to vary in strength. All beliefs are equal for the purposes of inference and decision. Strength of belief is an accepted notion within inductive logic, however. It can involve acceptance theories comprising sets of confirmation functions and acceptance rules. Alternatively, Jeffrey's theory of partial belief (Jeffrey, 1983) assigns degrees to beliefs as subjective probabilities computed using Bayes' theorem from a set of evidence hypotheses. Some AI approaches similarly assign numbers as probabilities to every belief. For example, certainty factors in expert systems, and Dempster/Shafer theory (Shafer, 1976). In these cases, individual beliefs are differentiated in a manner which provides a ranking or order. The values assigned to new beliefs inferred from old or as evidence is gained or lost, reflects the combinations of values from their multiple sources.

Some AI approaches maintain beliefs as equal but differentiate the rules which generate those beliefs. It is a kind of preemptive approach whereby beliefs that would be inferred on the basis of less preferred rules are not inferred in the first place. Examples are systems employing prioritised competing default rules, such as in HAEL (Hierarchic AutoEpistemic Logic) (Konolige, 1988). In this, the belief set is divided into a hierarchy of evidence spaces. Sentences in lower spaces are considered stronger evidence in being more specific, than those higher up. Inferences drawn from rules situated lower in the hierarchy override potential inferences higher up. An individual bat for example, can be inferred to fly even though the following two default rules contradict each other:

(1) Normally mammals do not fly

(2) Bats are mammals which do fly

The latter default rule relies on the more specific information, and is thus placed lower in the hierarchy. The bat as a mammal that cannot fly is not less preferred; it is never inferred in the first place. The issues involved in structuring priorities into the belief set in this way are discussed below.

Reasoning about strength of belief.

In the example of HAEL above (Konolige, 1988), priorities are structured into the belief system. The priorities are therefore reasoned with, but not something to be reasoned *about*. Alternative ordering schemes such as Gärdenfors' ordering of sentences in a belief set according to their 'epistemic entrenchment', Nebel's 'epistemic relevance' (Nebel, 1989, this volume), Doyle's system of rational revision (Doyle, 1991) and this author's *mc* relation described in section 4 (Galliers and Reichgelt, 1990) provide a qualitative basis for assessment, as opposed to a fixed measurement or structure. Cohen (1985) deals explicitly with this issue; he discusses the importance of being able to reason about uncertainty.

The primary limitations of fixed structural ordering are inaccessibility and inflexibility. Doyle and Wellman (1989) refer to Konolige's specification of the hierarchy in HAEL as 'dictatorial' in its inflexibility. It violates the modularity principle, critical to successful construction of complex structures such as commonsense knowledge bases. Modularity offers general rules of combination applied as the need arises, as opposed to employing a 'sovereign authority' whose task of resolving all potential conflicts is in any case infeasible with a large set of criteria. In addition, new criteria would necessitate a complete restructuring of the preference order. And with respect to the inaccessibility issue, Carver(1988) and Cohen (1985) argue that if it is impossible to reason why a particular fixed ordering has been set, it is impossible to revise satisfactorily and flexibly in the light of new evidence. This is especially the case with numeric representations.

Representing strength of belief.

Numeric representations of strength of belief are used with Bayes' theorem to provide a means of computing the probability of a conclusion given the numeric probability or degree of belief attached to each evidence hypothesis. There are various problems with this 'conditionalization' approach (Jeffrey, 1983). Firstly, for every proposition whose probability is to be updated in the light of new evidence, there must be already assigned probabilities to various conjunctions of the proposition and one or more of the possible evidence propositions and/or their denials. This leads to a combinatorial explosion. The number of conjunctions is an exponential function of the number of possibly relevant evidence propositions (Harman, 1986).

In addition, once the number has been set, its rationale in terms of the multitude of factors from which it is comprised, is submerged. There is no means of distinguishing between ignorance and uncertainty, for example (Carver, 1988). A low number could imply a lack of evidence or alternatively plenty of dubious evidence. Dempster/Shafer is a numeric approach which does not suffer from this latter problem in representing both a belief's support and its plausibility (Shafer, 1976). Cohen (1985) and Carver (1988) prefer non-numeric representations attached both to data and to rules, to represent all the various aspects appropriate to reasoning about uncertainty. Cohen refers to these as *endorsements.*

The advantage of numbers is ease of manipulation and combination. But for determination of preferred belief states for 'real' problems, the calculation must be based on more than probabilities of truth. As pointed out by both Doyle (1988) and Harman (1986), however probable and well supported or plausible a tautology is, it has little utility. In contrast, epistemic entrenchments are an indication of *explanatory power and informational value* (Gärdenfors 1988, 1989). Associated with such an emphasis on the utility of belief as opposed to its certainty, is a very particular viewpoint on the nature of strength of belief, described below.

The nature of strength of belief.

The probability approach described above considers beliefs as variably certain. Only fully accepted or certain beliefs have a probability of 1. An alternative viewpoint is to consider all beliefs as accepted sentences, fully believed with a probability of 1, but not all of these may be equally *corrigible* in the sense of being more or less 'vulnerable to removal' (Levi, 1984). What distinguishes them is their persistence; their relative ease of disbelief. Harman and Gärdenfors take this view. For Gärdenfors (1988) corrigibility is related to usefulness in inquiry and deliberation. He offers an example from modern chemical theory. Knowledge about combining weights is more important than colour or taste; it has more explanatory power. If chemists change their opinion over the combining weight of two substances, this would have more radical effects on chemical theory than if they changed their opinions over tastes. Beliefs about weights are therefore less corrigible or more entrenched than knowledge about tastes, although knowledge about both is certain.

This view that accepted beliefs are certain but variably corrigible, as opposed to all beliefs being variably certain, is an important component of the model of autonomous belief revision described in the next section. In this model of ABR, beliefs are held or not held in a yes/no fashion, but strength as a pragmatic and purely comparative notion is entertained at the point when held beliefs are challenged. It is a facet of revision. It also relates to *entire belief sets.* Preference of cognitive *state* in the light of a particular change is assessed according to relative persistence or comparative *'hardness of revision'* of alternative combinations of belief. Which set or sets are the most persistent or hardest to revise? Doyle similarly considers the ordering of entire belief sets to be more appropriate than for example, Gärdenfors' ordering of individual propositions. And in Doyle's work as well as our model of autonomous belief revision, there may be alternative, equally preferred revisions. Again this differs from Gärdenfors' epistemic entrenchments which determine a unique and correct revision.

The origins of strength of belief.

In the discussion above, it is suggested that 'hardness of revision' does not relate to varying certainty or probability of truth, but perhaps to utility in terms of explanatory power and informational value. What is the basis of this explanatory power or informational value?

For Gärdenfors (1988, 1989) more useful beliefs are more entrenched. He offers various postulates for epistemic entrenchment which maintain individual beliefs as more entrenched than others on purely logical grounds.

Nebel (1989, this volume) talks about particular sets of beliefs as more 'valuable' than others, these being more epistemically *relevant.* He describes epistemic relevance as a generalisation of epistemic entrenchment, but representing some 'extra-logical, pragmatic preference'.

The specificity/generality distinction referred to above as the basis of HAEL (Konolige, 1988) could be one such pragmatic preference candidate. A specific belief is preferable over a generality (Poole, 1985). It has more explanatory power and informational value. This notion is also incorporated into inferential distance algorithms for inheritance systems (Etherington, 1987, Touretzky, 1986).

A wider approach in this latter vein is to look generally at the source of beliefs or the evidences from which they were concluded. As well as being specific or general, perceived beliefs can be the result of first hand experience via sensory apparatus, or they may be the result of second hand communications via other agents or documentation. Cohen (1985) attaches various endorsements to data, one type of which is based on source information. A representation of such endorsements and related set of heuristics regarding combinations of endorsements is outlined in the following sections's description of ABR. The intuition is that there are general rules with respect to sources of assumptions underpinning beliefs, such as whether information came from a reliable source or was the subject of gossip for example, which are an important factor in determining relative persistence as relative explanatory power and informational value.

Doyle (1991) uses decision theory to determine preferred revisions. Assessments of preference involve expected utilities of belief or utility of their consequences, whilst taking the probability of their occurence into account.

One question is whether it is feasible to deploy general domain-independent principles such as entrenchment, utility, specificity or endorsement to determine preferred revision. Some recent work by Konolige (1989) refutes the use of generalities in favour of 'knowledge-intensive heuristics tailored to a domain'.

The context for strength.

There are currently two theories of rational belief change. They are *foundation theory* and *coherence theory*. These form alternative contexts within which any ordering or system of priorities for revision is to be accomodated. Generally these are described as competing theories, although Doyle (this volume) suggests that on close examination, the differences and corresponding pros and cons are certainly not as clear cut as has been previously suggested, and perhaps not even that significant.

Foundation theory focusses on justified belief. New beliefs are only added on the basis of other justified beliefs, and beliefs no longer justified are abandoned. An example of this approach in practice is the truth (reason) maintenance system of Doyle (1979). Foundation theory takes its name from the emphasis on justification for belief, which obviously is not infinite. Where it ends up is in beliefs which are justified by themselves, and which then justify or are *foundational* to others. These are self-evident beliefs, for example an observation.

Coherence theory on the other hand, represents a conservatism whereby justification is only a requisite condition of believing if there is a special reason to doubt a belief:

The Principle of Conservatism:

current fully accepted beliefs are justified in the absence of any challenge to them (Harman, 1986).

If there is such a challenge, for example a new belief making one's belief set inconsistent, the guiding principles are those of *minimal change* and *maximal coherence*:

The Principle of Minimal Changes:

In revising one's view one should make minimal changes in both adding new beliefs and eliminating old ones (Harman, 1986).

The notion of changes of state being restricted to keep as much as possible of the previous state, is generally accepted as a good thing, both in philosophy and AI. The competing notion is coherence. This prevents such conservatism resulting in tenacity of belief regardless of evidence to the contrary:

'...changes are allowed only to the extent that they yield sufficient increases in coherence' (Harman,1986).

Coherent beliefs are mutually supporting. P can be justified because it coheres with Q and Q be justified because it coheres with P. But the *nature* of this mutual support is of interest. According to Harman, coherence includes not only a consistency relation, but relations of implication and explanation too. Coherence is connections, and the connections are of *intelligibility*, in particular intelligible deductive and non-deductive explanation of why or how it is that something is the case. For example, if one believes P, Q and R, but also R *because P and Q*. Part of one's view makes it intelligible why some other part should be true. The 'because' can be deductive in P and Q implying R, or it could be statistical as in P and Q generally implies R 'if other things are equal', or it could be based in commonsense psychology (Harman, 1986). Believing R is explained by the beliefs P and Q. The connection offers intelligibility and makes the set more coherent than if P, Q and R were consistent but unrelated.

Modelling the context.

Associated with a choice of context or theory for revision, is the issue of how these are to be modelled. There are various computational examples of foundation theory in the form of reason maintenance systems, such as those of de Kleer (1986), Doyle (1979), and McAllester (1980). There is only one computational example of coherence theory (Georgeff and Lansky, 1986), but several formal models, the foremost of which is AGM-theory (Alchourron, Gärdenfors and Makinson, 1985). One formal hybrid model is described by Rao and Foo (1989), Rao (1990).

Models of coherence theory generally model minimal change amongst sets of consistent beliefs with no justification relations. Maximal coherence is the retention of the maximum possible *logically consistent* beliefs during belief change. These approaches therefore leave out much of Harman's intuitions on the nature and role of coherence. They cannot express that some beliefs are reasons for or explanations of others. However, Gärdenfors' epistemic entrenchments are an attempt to include some of the justificational information available in foundation theory into a formal coherence model. He describes how epistemic entrenchments can be used to reconstruct justifications when needed (Gärdenfors, 1990).

The major criticism of foundation based theories concerns the maintenance or explicit representation of justifications for beliefs, and also then the propagation of disbelief. Harman (1986) and Gärdenfors (1989) cite debriefing studies which demonstrate experimentally that people do not keep track of the justifications for their beliefs. It may therefore not be known when sole reasons for a belief have been discredited, and as a consequence unjustified beliefs are retained. Doyle (this volume) criticises this as a psychological argument against foundation models. He distinguishes well-founded support from all arguments as well-founded, and separates the issue of recording reasons from that of their use. He also counters the economic arguments raised by Gärdenfors (1990) who suggests that regardless of the psychological plausibility issue, the benefits from keeping track of justifications are outweighed by the computational costs. Gärdenfors' view in this matter is echoed by Rao and Foo (1989b), who justify their own model by claiming RMS's as very inefficient.

All sides agree that justifications as reasons for belief are important, however. The conclusions from the debriefing studies were that in people, beliefs will eventually be abandoned, but not on thew basis of a lack of justification. Disbelief occurs only on the basis of *positive* beliefs about lack of good reasons for believing. Harman correspondingly expands the principle of conservatism as follows:

The Principle of Positive Undermining:
only stop believing a current belief if there are positive reasons to do so, and this does not include an absence of justification for that belief (Harman, 1986).

Positive reasons are believing one's reasons for believing the belief to be nogood. This is stated as:

'It is incoherent to believe both P and also that all one's reasons for believing P

relied crucially on false assumptions' (Harman,1986).

It is this particular version of conservatism, (discussed also by Doyle in this volume) which has been adopted in the model of autonomous belief revision. The following sections describe firstly the logical framework and then the computational model for ABR. The latter is implemented as a system called ICM (increased coherence model). It represents a blend of coherence and foundation theories.

4 A MODEL OF AUTONOMOUS BELIEF REVISION (ABR)

The model of autonomous belief revision described here, determines preferred cognitive states at times of change. Of particular interest are instances of change caused by communicative acts, and where the content of an utterance contradicts an existing belief. In such cases, the principles upon which preferred cognitive states are determined from the logically equivalent possibilities are employed to reason about *whether* to adopt the recognised intended belief via an utterance, as well as *how* to do this. The model is implemeted as ICM. It embodies a qualitative approach to the strength of belief issue. All-or-nothing beliefs comprise belief sets. If the world changes, new evidence is incorporated such that the resulting belief state is the most persistent of the logically equivalent alternatives. And this includes the belief state where the new evidence is not incorporated. In a context of communication in open systems, agents are autonomous in revision. The preferred belief set(s) after revision are those retained, and beliefs in all of these are believed. The mechanisms for reasoning about preferred revisions are described below. Note, the concern is with whole belief states and not individual beliefs. The preferred state(s) are the most coherent or most persistent or 'hardest to disbelieve'.

Firstly, a general logical framework for belief revision is introduced, within which ordering relations for preferred revisions can be discussed.

4.1 A logical framework for ABR

In Galliers and Reichgelt (1991), we present a general logical framework for a theory of autonomous belief revision. The framework supports both coherence and foundation theories of belief revision. It can be compared with epistemic entrenchments (Gärdenfors, this volume) and epistemic relevance (Nebel, 1989, this volume) as well as with Doyle's framework for rational revision (Doyle 1991). Primarily, it differs from these in allowing revision to be no revision at all; the preferred revision may not include the new evidence. We follow Nebel in assuming finite belief sets of consistent propositions, or belief bases in the sense in which Gärdenfors uses the notion (this volume). However, our more-coherence ordering relation or *mc* compares these as whole entities, as opposed to either epistemic entrenchments or epistemic relevance which are local notions and order the different propositions within belief sets (or bases). In addition, we agree with Doyle's (1991) criticism of epistemic entrenchments and epistemic relevance in their requirement for unique revisions; we permit equally acceptable alternative revisions.

We assume that an agent has a finite set of beliefs K, which is consistent but not necessarily closed under deduction. Our framework postulates two operations on belief sets, addition and deletion. The addition of a proposition ϕ to K, $K^+\phi$, is then defined as:

$$K^+\phi = \{K' | K' \subseteq K \cup \{\phi\} \text{ and } cons(K') \text{ and } K' \vdash \phi\} \cup \{K\}$$

where $cons(K)$ intuitively means "K is consistent" and can be defined as "there is a ψ such that $K \not\vdash \psi$". Thus, the addition operator defines a set of possible revised belief sets. Note that, because $K \in K^+\phi$, $K' \in K^+\phi$ does not always imply that $K' \vdash \phi$. This is because we are interested in autonomous belief revision in which an agent may decide to ignore a new piece of evidence. Also, the members of $K^+\phi$ are not necessarily maximal subsets of K. This reflects the intuition expressed by Doyle (1991) that belief revision is not always minimal in the sense that we keep as many of our old beliefs as possible. The only restriction that we have is that, if one decides not to engage in belief revision, nothing changes.

The deletion of a proposition ϕ from a belief set K, $K \dot{-} \phi$, can be defined in a similar vein as:

$$K \dot{-} \phi = \{K' | K' \subseteq K \text{ and } cons(K') \text{ and } K' \not\vdash \phi\} \cup \{K\}$$

Our addition and deletion operator define a set of potential new belief sets. In order to decide which belief set will actually be adopted, our logic requires an ordering relation between belief sets. Different orderings can be regarded as defining different logics for autonomous belief revision. Ideally, these orderings should define, for every set of belief bases, one maximal member. This belief base is the one that will be adopted after revision.

4.2 Ordering relations for ABR
In the terms of our framework, we can reconstruct the difference between the two types of belief revision theories, foundation and coherence, as a difference between the types of ordering between belief sets imposed by the different approaches. For example, in a foundational approach, the ordering relies on some notion of well-founded support. First, we restrict ourselves to set-theoretically maximal members of $K^+\phi$ or $K \dot{-} \phi$ minus K. Moreover, we assume that there is a set of self-evident beliefs, E. We then say that K is foundationally preferred to K', $K' <_f K$, if for

all $\phi \in K, K \cap E \vdash \phi$, and there is a $\psi \in K', K' \cap E \nvdash \psi$. This means that K is foundationally preferred to K' if all sentences in K ultimately depend on self-evident beliefs, whereas there is at least one sentence in K' that is not supported in this way. It is unlikely that this ordering will produce one maximal member in $K^+\phi$ or $K \dotdiv \phi$, and in general it will therefore have to be combined with some other ordering. One such additional ordering is McAllester's proposal to divide propositions into likelihood classes and to prefer those belief sets whose members are in the higher likelihood class (McAllester, 1980).

The criteria used in coherence theories are described earlier. Firstly there is minimal change. The belief sets in $K^+\phi$ or $K \dotdiv \phi$ that maintain as much of K as possible are preferred to those that make more radical changes. The competing notion is maximal coherence. The tension between the principles of minimal change and maximal coherence is most clearly illustrated in our general framework. Since $K^+\phi$ includes K, the principle of minimal change would produce K itself as the maximal member of $K^+\phi$. However, the coherence principle may produce other results, depending what factor is chosen as the operationalization of the notion of coherence. For example, another member of $K^+\phi$ may have greater explanatory power than K. Harman provides a synthesis out of this clash in his principle of Positive Undermining.

4.3 Increased coherence

We suggest a new coherence ordering, particularly suited to ABR for modelling communication. This is increased or more-coherence, hereafter referred to as mc. mc orders logically consistent sets according to maximal derivability of core beliefs. This is based on the intuition that for a particular context, an agent has a number of central beliefs and that any piece of evidence that increases the agent's confidence in these central beliefs will be adopted.

We say that a proposition ϕ increases the coherence of K with respect to some core belief ψ if adding ϕ to K would generate a new proof of ψ. In order to establish whether this is the case, we first remove ψ from K, after which we add ϕ to each resulting belief set. The aim is to establish whether ψ can then be proved in at least one of the resulting belief sets. Thus, we define $mc(K, \psi, \phi)$ (ϕ increases the coherence of K with respect to ψ) as

$$mc(K, \psi, phi) \text{ iff there is a } K' \in (K \dotdiv \psi)^+\phi, K' \vdash \psi$$

We can then start preferring belief sets that have an increased coherence with respect to some core belief ψ. Thus, we define the ordering $\leq_\psi$ as

$$K' \leq_\psi K \text{ iff for all } \phi, \text{ if } mc(K', \psi, \phi) \text{ then } mc(K, \psi, \phi)$$

We can then define a strict ordering in the normal way as $K' <_\psi K$ iff $K' \leq_\psi K$ and $K \not\leq_\psi K'$.

The above describes a more-coherent belief base relative to some core belief, as the harder to disbelieve because there are more justifications, more *proofs* of that core belief. For example, I believe that I have to pay 50 pounds for the repairs to my car when I collect it from the garage. This is a core belief; it is central to my concerns at the time of collection. I believe it as a self-evident belief because I was told so by the mechanic when I left the car. In addition I believe that if I believe the mechanic has completed the job, and also that there is a bill for 50 pounds, then I do indeed have to pay 50 pounds. When I get to the garage I can directly perceive that the mechanic has completed the job and I therefore believe he has completed the job. However, there is no bill evident as yet. At this point I believe that I will have to pay 50 pounds for the one, self-evident reason as above. However, then I am given some new communicated evidence. I am told there is a bill going in the post for 50 pounds. If I believe this, then I have additional proof of my core belief. By taking on the belief that there is a bill for 50 pounds, it is 'harder' to disbelieve that I have to pay 50 pounds, given I believe the job has been completed and I believe the rule above. This is because, in order to *now* disbelieve that I have to pay 50 pounds, either I would have to disbelieve both what the mechanic said to me earlier and the fact that the job has been completed, OR I would have to disbelieve both what the mechanic had said earlier and the existence of a 50 pound bill, OR I would have to disbelieve both what the mechanic had said earlier and the rule that if the mechanic has completed the job, and there is a bill for 50 pounds, then I do indeed have to pay 50 pounds. On the other hand, before hearing about the bill, I would only have had to disbelieve what the mechanic had said to me earlier in order to disbelieve that I have to pay 50 pounds. So, it is more coherent for me to revise my belief set by adopting the communicated belief. I believe that there is a bill in the post for 50 pounds.

The more-coherent set does not have to be one including the new evidence. Each potential state is compared equally and autonomously. For example, another time maybe I also believe that if the mechanic has completed the job but there is no bill, then I just pay the 50 pounds he quoted earlier. So, when I get to the garage and there is no bill I still have additional proof of my owing 50 pounds. A belief that there is no bill is inconsistent with the belief that there is a bill. When I get told there is a bill in the post, do I adopt this new belief or not? Is the preferred belief state one where there is a bill and I believe the new evidence, or one where I reject the new evidence and stay believing there is no bill? In fact, both are preferred, more coherent states according to the definition of *mc*. They both offer additional proof of the core belief. I still have to pay 50 pounds. The only issue here is whether I also believe there is a bill for 50 pounds or not.

In reality we have good heuristic and intuitive guides which may assist in discriminating between such alternative belief states. In general, if we are told something by someone considered knowledgeable about the matter in hand and who is also considered to be reliable, we will tend to believe it in preference to something contradictory that may have been believed on the basis of less 'persistent' evidence. In the example above, all else being equal, evidence communicated from an employee of the garage is more persistent than contradictory evidence based upon what has generally happened in such instances. The suggestion is that there are other ordering relations which can be employed in conjunction with mc and which play their part in the relative persistence of one belief state over another. These are described below.

4.4 Endorsements and the role of foundational assumptions

We employ an aspect of foundationalism adapted to encompass also a heuristically based ordering, to assist mc with the determination of preferred revisions. This is described below.

The foundational approach was described in the terms of our logical framework in section 4.2 as an ordering relation in which one belief state is foundationally preferred to another only if there is some sentence in the latter unsupported by some self-evident or self-justified belief(s). Self-evident beliefs are foundational beliefs from which others are derived, referred to as *assumptions* as in de Kleer's ATMS (de Kleer,1986). As in the ATMS, ICM operates on beliefs stored as a nodes comprising a description along with a label (sets of assumptions) and justifications from which the description may be derived. Assumptions are belief nodes, distinguished by being beliefs justified by their own existence.

Assumptions in ICM have an additional component over their ATMS counterparts. They are *endorsed* according to their source. The intuition is that there are general rules related to the sources of information which are relevant when considering how relatively 'hard' that information is then to give up. For example, whether they came from a reliable source such as directly from sensory apparatus, or alternatively, indirectly via another agent, or if they were assumed on the basis of generalised knowledge in the absence of anything more specific, and so on. Other works concentrating on the role of the source of evidence when reasoning in situations of uncertainty are Thost (1989) and Garigliano (1988).

Each founding assumption is endorsed as:

(1) *communicated*, either *first-hand* (sensory information) or *second-hand* (via another agent or text). These assumptions are also very roughly graded as 'pos' if they are communicated with conviction or from a very reliable source, or 'neg' if they are communicated from a spurious source or without conviction: [1c-pos], [1c-neg], [2c-pos] or [2c-neg].

(2) *given*, either as *specific* information widely believed and without any particular source, for example 'James Dean was a film star', or as *default* generalities similarly widely believed. For example, 'birds fly'. Alternatively, given assumptions may be *values* denoting a notion of goodness which may be linked with desires. Values can also be 'pos' or 'neg' as a rough grading scheme between those more persistent in being considered a 'very good thing' and those just considered 'a good thing'. These are obviously subjective to the individual being modelled, although generally accepted (culturally held) values such as it being good to have money or to be conscientious or trustworthy can be incorporated as defaults. The possibilities are: [spec], [def], [value-pos] or [value-neg].

(3) *hypothetical*, with no evidence at all other than as a possible grounding for a belief under consideration [hypoth].

In ICM, any belief added has its negation automatically added too, and if without any other endorsement, this is endorsed as a [hypoth]. The inconsistency is recorded as a 'nogood' as in the ATMS. Other inconsistencies are given explicitly.

Combinations of endorsed assumptions underlying competing revisions can then be compared using a set of very simple guiding heuristics:

(1) Belief states founded upon first-hand evidence are harder to disbelieve than those founded on any other combination of assumptions. (This does not take the possibility of faulty sensors into account). Prefer belief states grounded with more [1c-pos] assumptions.

(2) The more positive communicated assumptions or specific assumptions, that ground a belief state, the harder the process of disbelief, regardless of the number of 'neg' or default or value assumptions. Prefer belief states grounded with more [2c-pos] and [spec] assumptions.

(3) Combinations of 'neg' endorsed assumptions and defaults can be relatively ranked, and values can enhance these. Believing it would be good to believe something does additionally endorse its belief. However, values are only compared when in conjunction with other endorsements. For example, however much it may be believed that it is good to win the pools, this can only endorse and make more persistent the belief state in which I believe I have won the pools if I have some other even vague, evidence for this. Prefer belief states with more [1c-neg] over [2c-neg] or [def]. And [value-pos] offers more persistence

support than [value-neg] but only when in conjunction with others.

In our model, preferred belief states on revision comprise only self-evident beliefs and beliefs derived from these. In this sense our model employs foundationalism as an ordering relation. The foundational ordering is the first layer upon which *mc* is then employed. In addition, assumptions are endorsed and comparisons can be made between states on the basis of these endorsements and the heuristics above. This is then a third ordering relation. The three-tiered ordering as implemented in ICM is demonstrated in the description of the example in section 5.

It is important to note that there is a difference in the foundationalism implemented within ICM from that found in the ATMS or other RMS's. When beliefs are unsupported in ICM their disbelief is only propagated backwards to founding assumptions so that a disbelieved belief cannot immediately be rederived. Disbelief propagation does not occur forward. Beliefs justified by the removed beliefs are retained in ICM, unless they are themselves the subject of challenge. This is the conservatism of coherence models in which beliefs are retained unless there is reason to not believe them, which is different from saying there is an absence of justification. This is Harman's principle of positive undermining or positive disbelief. In ICM, beliefs left without justification in this way become new assumptions, although endorsed only as [hypoth]. ICM and the model of ABR described here represents a blend of coherence and foundationalism.

5 AN EXAMPLE. THE GARAGE.

This section describes the modelling of autonomous changes in an agent's belief state as a result of particular changes in that agent's environment, according to the principles of ABR and as implemented in ICM. The example scenario concerns a car owner with a faulty car in a garage. The changes occur when she returns to pick up the car. She is told by a mechanic's assistant that she can take the car, and the mechanic has left no bill. Previously she had believed that she would have to pay, given all she knows about getting faulty cars mended at garages and also what she knows about this particular car and mechanic. The beliefs which go towards the determination of the initial belief state are shown in Figure 1 and described below. There are two changes in two brief conversations, one with the mechanic's assistant, and one with the mechanic himself. These are also described below.

In order to set up the ICM to determine the agent's initial belief state on leaving the car and before the conversations with mechanic's assistant and mechanic, the ICM is given information. This includes firstly a set of assumptions relating to the context of the agent as car owner, car and mechanic. These assumptions are believed

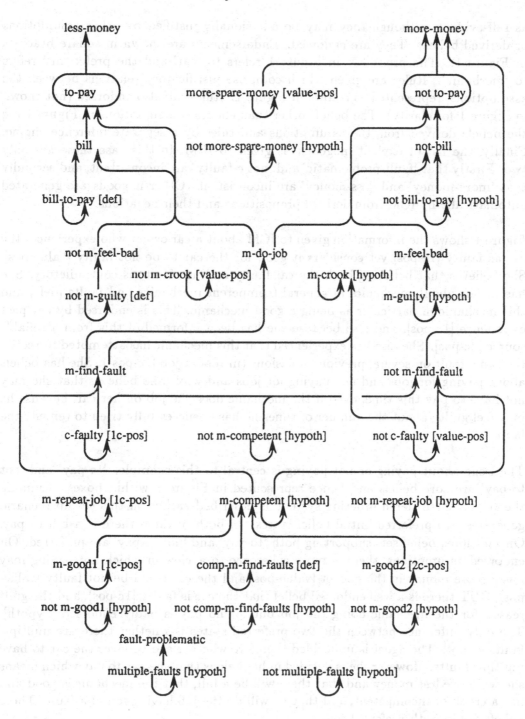

less-money

to-pay   more-spare-money [value-pos]   not to-pay

bill   not more-spare-money [hypoth]   not-bill

bill-to-pay [def]   not bill-to-pay [hypoth]

not m-feel-bad   m-do-job   m-feel-bad

not m-crook [value-pos]   m-crook [hypoth]

not m-guilty [def]   m-guilty [hypoth]

m-find-fault   not m-find-fault

c-faulty [1c-pos]   not m-competent [hypoth]   not c-faulty [value-pos]

m-repeat-job [1c-pos]   m-competent [hypoth]   not m-repeat-job [hypoth]

m-good1 [1c-pos]   comp-m-find-faults [def]   m-good2 [2c-pos]

not m-good1 [hypoth]   not comp-m-find-faults [hypoth]   not m-good2 [hypoth]

fault-problematic

multiple-faults [hypoth]   not multiple-faults [hypoth]

more-money

Figure 1:   The garage example

as self-evident, although they may be additionally justified by other assumptions or derived beliefs. They are endorsed. Endorsements are shown in square brackets in Figure 1. The prefix 'c-' in Figure 1 refers to 'car' and the prefix 'm-' refers to 'mechanic'. Rules are given which comprise justificatory relations between the assumptions, represented as arrows in Figure 1. Rules are also endorsed (not shown in Figure 1 for clarity). The beliefs other than endorsed assumptions in Figure 1 are the beliefs derived from the assumptions and rules by a separate inference engine. Finally, the list of explicit 'nogoods' is given to ICM. In this case these are only two. Firstly that 'fault-problematic' and 'not c-faulty' are inconsistent, and secondly that 'more-money' and 'less-money' are inconsistent. Other nogoods are generated automatically by ICM from derived propositions and their negations.

Figure 1 shows the information given to ICM about a car owner who experiences the car as faulty [1c-pos] yet considers it good for the car to be not faulty [value-pos]. She believes that believing both the car faulty and not faulty is contradictory. She has beliefs about mechanics in general (competent mechanics find faults [def]) and this mechanic in particular as being a good mechanic. This is endorsed by her past experience [1c-pos], and also because she has been informed of this from a reliable source [2c-pos]. She also has experienced that this mechanic has attempted to rectify the same fault on several previous occasions (m-repeat-job [1c-pos]). She has beliefs about paying for jobs and not paying for jobs and why. She believes that she may not have to pay this time, even if the mechanic does the job on her car, because he may feel guilty about the number of times he has unsuccessfully tried to remedy the fault.

The issue about paying or not paying is central to this example. 'to-pay' and 'not to-pay' are core beliefs and hence represented in Figure 1 within boxes. Running the ICM's three tiered ordering system as described earlier on this set up scenario generates two preferred initial belief states. In both of these there is a bill to pay. On *mc* alone, belief sets supporting both 'to-pay' and 'not to-pay' are preferred. On endorsed assumptions, there is more coherence to a view in which not paying may mean more money in the pocket [value-pos] and the car could be not faulty [value-pos], BUT there is a well endorsed belief that the car is faulty [1c-pos], and the guilt reason for the mechanic doing the job but for no pay is badly endorsed [hypoth]. The only difference between the two preferred states is whether there are multiple faults or not. The agent is undecided therefore whether she believes the car to have multiple faults. However she is decided in her beliefs that she has to pay which means she will have less money and that there will be a bill, that the mechanic is good and not a crook or incompetent, and that he will do the job having found a fault. These beliefs are in both preferred sets.

On turning up at the garage to collect the car, the agent experiences a change to this scenario. There is an exchange between the agent (A) and the mechanics assistant (MA):

(MA:) The car is ready for you.
 (A:) Is there a bill?
(MA:) I don't think so, but I'm not sure and the mechanic's at lunch.

The above change to be accomodated with respect to the issue of payment can be considered as an utterance, the propositional content of which is that there is no bill to pay. The assumption 'not bill-to-pay' [1c-neg] is introduced to ICM as more than a [hypoth] now. It is a self-evident assumption, experienced by the agent as communicated yet without confidence. 'to-pay' and not 'to-pay' are still core beliefs. The utterance is initially accepted according to *mc* because of its additional support for the core belief 'not to-pay'. But on incorporating it into the two previously preferred sets, an inconsistency is detected. It is therefore incorporated into the original set up of beliefs which represents all that may be and may have been known about this context. (Referring back to such a database allows beliefs to be retrieved which may have become disbelieved at some stage. It allows for repair.) The labels of all sets that are to be disbelieved in order for a consistent set to be constructed, are created. Of these, those whose sets contain the maximum number of core beliefs are returned. And of these, only the maximally endorsed sets (according to the combination heuristics) are retained as preferred sets. At this stage there are 10 preferred sets. In some of these there is a bill to pay and in some there is no bill to pay. In other words the agent is undecided about whether she has to pay or not.
To limit these options and achieve some result about the beliefs 'to-pay' or 'not to-pay', a minimal change mechanism can be employed. The 10 preferred states are compared with the the 2 states prior to the current change and those best endorsed and closest to the previous state(s) are selected. In other words, those sets with the greatest intersection with the previous state are preferred. So, running the ICM in this manner to decide whether and how to accomodate the utterance, ultimately generates five preferred belief states, and in all of these the belief that there is a bill to pay is retained; the new 'evidence' that there is no bill to pay is rejected. The original belief is persistent in being more coherent with all else believed than the new belief that there is no bill to pay. However, it is a close thing, decided only via the incorporation of a minimal change mechanism.

The reason for the result of 5 alternative yet preferred belief states at this stage is because of the employment of positive disbelief as described in section 4.4. The differences relate to the issue of multiple faults and this as justification for a belief that the finding of the 'fault' with the car is problematic (see Figure 1). Because disbelief is not propagated from disbelieved beliefs to the beliefs they justify, 'fault-problematic' may remain even after the belief that there are multiple faults has been disbelieved.

The final change to the scenario is a conversation between the agent and the mechanic (M) himself, because the agent still believes there is a bill to pay:

(A:) So, what do I owe you?
(M:) M : Nothing. It's ok. And the car's fine.

The above change now to be accomodated with respect to the issue of payment is another utterance, the propositional content of which is also that there is no bill to pay. The assumption 'not bill-to-pay2' [2c-pos] is introduced to ICM. The assumptions 'not bill-to-pay'[1c-neg] and 'not bill-to-pay2' [2c-pos], are the result of the two utterances, both now justifying 'not-bill'. 'to-pay' and 'not to-pay' are still core beliefs. Running the ICM to decide whether and how to accomodate the new utterance with the maximal coherence mechanisms of *mc* and endorsements, and the minimal change mechanism as described above, generates three preferred belief states. In all of these there is now *no* bill to pay. The agent has 'changed her mind' about the payment issue, following this second change in her environment making it more coherent for her. Again, the distinction between the three preferred states is in the beliefs about the fault being problematic. The agent is still undecided whether she believes the fault was problematic or not problematic.

6. CONCLUSIONS

This chapter has described a model of autonomous belief revision. It is offered as the basis of a theory of communication. Belief revision is considered a fundamental property of rationality, communication being a special case of this. Communicating agents recognise each others intentions to *change* their cognitive state. Such observed communicative actions alter a cognitive state which already exists, as do observations of the natural world. Agents which are autonomous in their actions and reactions to the world, then share control over these changes. This is an important aspect of interaction in open, multi-agent environments where no one agent can be in possession of the 'truth' and prescribed behaviours imposing cooperation as benevolence, may therefore be inappropriate. Modelling cooperative communicative behaviour fundamentally involves a model of autonomous belief revision, for the autonomous attainment of mutually satisfactory belief states.

The model of autonomous belief revision, ABR, determines preferred sets of belief on recognition of new communicated evidence, with no requirement for a unique revision. There is also no requirement that the preferred revision incorporate the new communicated evidence. Agents can decide not to revise. Preference is established as a qualititative ordering between alternative sets in which the preferred sets are maximally persistent. This means the 'hardest to revise' in being maximally coherent or offering maximal derivability of core beliefs and having maximally endorsed founding assumptions. The model therefore represents a blend of coherence and foundation theories of belief revision. It is also a part logical and part heuristic solution to the problem of discrimination between alternative, logically equivalent revisions. Its implementation as ICM is an integral component of a strategic planner for cooperative dialogue currently being developed at the University of Cambridge Computer Laboratory (ESRC/MRC/SERC Cognitive Science/HCI Initiative Project ID: 90/CS42).

ACKNOWLEDGEMENTS

I would like to thank Han Reichgelt for his development of the formal framework of ABR, and Steven Reece for his implementation of ICM. This research was funded by a SERC IT fellowship.

REFERENCES

Alchourron, C., Gärdenfors P. and Makinson D. (1985): "On the Logic of Theory Change: Partial meet Contraction Functions and their Associated Revision Functions." *Journal of Symbolic Logic,* 50, pp510-530.

Carver N. (1988): "Evidence-Based Plan Recognition." COINS Tech. Report 88-13, Computer and Information Science Dept., University of Massachusetts at Amherst.

Cohen P.R. (1985): *Heuristic Reasoning about Uncertainty: an Artificial Intelligence Approach*, Pitman, Boston.

Cohen, P. and Levesque H. (1987): "Rational Interaction as the basis for Communication." Technical report No. 89. Centre for the Study of Language and Information, Stanford University, California, U.S.A.

De Kleer J. (1986): "An Assumption-based TMS." *Artificial Intelligence* Vol 28 No. 2 pp127-162.

Doyle J. (1979): "A Truth Maintenance System." *Artificial Intelligence* Vol. 12, pp232-272.

Doyle J.(1985): "Reasoned Assumptions and Pareto Optimality." *Proceedings of IJCAI*, Los Angeles.

Doyle J. (1988): "AI and Rational Self-Government." Tech Report CMU-CS-88-124, Carnegie-Mellon, Computer Science Dept.

Doyle J. (1988): "On Universal Theories of Defaults." Carnegie-Mellon Computer Science Tech. Report. No. CMU-CS-88-111. .

Doyle J. (1991): "Rational Belief Revision: Preliminary report." In eds: Fikes R.E. and Sandewall E. *Proceedings of the second conference on principles of knowledge representation and reasoning*, San Mateo, CA.

Doyle J. and Wellman M. P. (1989): "Impediments to Universal Preference-Based Default Theories. " *Proceedings of First International Conference on Knowledge Representation and Reasoning.* Toronto.

Etherington D.W. (1987): "Formalizing Nonmonotonic Reasoning Systems, Artificial Theories and Inferential Distance." *Proceedings AAAI.*

Galliers, J.R. (1991): "Cooperative interaction as strategic belief revision." In ed: Deen S.M. *Cooperating Knowledge Based Systems 1990.* Springer-Verlag, London.

Galliers J.R. (1990): "The Positive Role of Conflict in Cooperative Systems. In eds: Demazeau Y. and Muller J-P. *Decentralized Artificial Intelligence.* Elsevier, Amsterdam.

Galliers, J.R. (1989): "A Theoretical Framework for Computer Models of Cooperative Dialogue, Acknowledging Multi-Agent Conflict." PhD thesis. Cambridge University Computer Lab. Tech Report No. 172, and HCRL, Open University Tech Report No. 51.

Galliers, J.R. and Reichgelt, H (1990): "A Framework for Autonomous Belief Revision." University of Cambridge Computer Laboratory, Working paper.

Gärdenfors P. (1988): *Knowledge in Flux: Modeling the Dynamics of Epistemic States.* MIT Press.

Gärdenfors P. (1989): "The Dynamics of Belief Systems: Foundations vs Coherence Theories." *Revue Internationale de Philosophie*, Vol. 172, pp24-46.

Gasser L. et al. (1989): "Representing and Using Organizational Knowledge in Distributed AI Systems." In eds: Gasser and Huhns. *DAI* Volume 2. Pitman, London.

Georgeff M.P. and Lansky, A. (1986): "A System for Reasoning in Dynamic Domains: Fault diagnosis on the Space Shuttle." SRI Technical Note No. 375.

Grice, H.P. (1957): "Meaning." *Philosophical Review*, Vol. 66, pp.377-388.

Grice, H.P. (1967): "Utterer's Meaning and Intentions." *Philosophical Review* Vol 78, No. 2, pp147-177.

Harman G. (1986): *Change in View - Principles in Reasoning*. Bradford Book, MIT Press, Camb., Mass

Hewitt, K. "Offices are Open Systems." *ACM Transactions on Office Information Systems*, 4(3): pp 271-287.

Jeffrey R.C. (1983): *The Logic of Decision*. Univ. of Chicago Press, Chicago.

Kelleher G. (1988): "An Overview of Assumption Based Reason Maintenance." Technical Report CBLU-ULE/043, Computer Based Learning Unit, Univ. of Leeds.

Konolige K. (1988): "Hierarchic Autoepistemic Theories for Nonmonotonic Reasoning." Tech. Note 446, SRI International, California.

Konolige K. (1989): "Defeasible argumentation in reasoning about events." *Proceedings of the International Symposium on Machine Intelligence and Systems*. Italy.

Levi I. (1984): "Truth, Fallibility and the Growth of Knowledge." in *Decisions and Revisions*, Cambridge University Press.

Martins J.P. and Shapiro S.C. (1988): "A Model for Belief Revision." *Artificial Intelligence* Vol. 35 No. 1, pp 25-79.

McAllister D.A. (1980): "An Outlook on Truth Maintenance." AI Lab, AIM no. 551, MIT, Camb. Mass.

Nebel. B. (1989): "A Knowledge Level Analysis of Belief Revision." *Proceedings of 1st Conference on Principles of Knowledge Representation and Reasoning*. Toronto, Canada.

Perrault, C.R. (1987): "An application of Default logic to Speech Act Theory." Report No. CSLI 87-90, CLSI, SRI International, California, U.S.A.

Poole D.L. (1985): "On the Comparison of Theories; Preferring the most Specific Explanation." *Proceedings IJCAI*, Los Angeles, pp144-147.

Rao A.S. and Foo N.Y. (1989a): "Minimal Change and Maximal Coherence: A Basis for Belief Revision and Reasoning about Actions." *Proceedings IJCAI '89*, Detroit, U.S.A.

Rao A.S. and Foo N.Y. (1989b):" Formal Theories of Belief Revision." *Proceedings of 1st Conference on Principles of Knowledge Representation and Reasoning.* Toronto, Canada.

Reichgelt H. (1988): "The Place of Defaults in a Reasoning System." in eds: Kelleher G. and Smith B. *Reason Maintenance Systems and Their Applications.* Ellis Horwood.

Reiter R. (1980): "A Logic for Default Reasoning." *Artificial Intelligence Vol. 13, pp81-132.*

Reiter R. and de Kleer J. (1987): "Formal foundations of assumption-based truth maintenance systems: preliminary report." *Proceedings of 6th AAAI, pp183-187, Seattle, Washington.*

Rescher N. (1964): *Hypothetical Reasoning.* North-Holland Publ. Co., Amsterdam.

Shafer G. (1976): *A Mathematical Theory of Evidence.* Princeton Univ. Press, Princeton, NJ.

Swain M. (1970): *Induction, Acceptance and Rational Belief,* Reidel, Dordrecht, 1970.

Thagard P. (1989): "Explanatory Coherence." *Behavioural and Brain Sciences Vol. 12 No. 3.*

Thost M. (1989): "Generating facts from Opinions with Information Source Models." *Proceedings of IJCAI*, Detroit, U.S.A.

Touretzky D.S. (1986): *The Mathematics of Inheritance Systems.* Pitmans Research Notes in Artificial Intelligence, Pitman Publ. Ltd., London.

Conditionals and Knowledge-Base Update[*]

CHARLES B. CROSS
Department of Philosophy
University of Georgia

RICHMOND H. THOMASON
Intelligent Systems Program
University of Pittsburgh

Knowledge update has been a matter of concern to two quite separate traditions: one in philosophical logic, and another in artificial intelligence.[1] In this paper we draw on both traditions to develop a theory of update, based on conditional logic, for a kind of knowledge base that has proven to be of interest in artificial intelligence. After motivating and formulating the logic on which our theory is based, we will prove some basic results and show how our logic can be used to describe update in an environment in which knowledge bases can be treated as truth-value assignments in four-valued logic. In keeping with Nuel Belnap's terminology in Belnap (1977a) and Belnap (1977b), we will refer to such truth-value assignments as *set-ups* or as *four-valued set-ups*.

1. Paraconsistency, primeness, and atomistic update

For the moment we will not say exactly what a four-valued set-up is. Instead we will describe informally some conditions under which it would be natural to structure one's knowledge base as a four-valued set-up. One of these conditions has to do with the treatment of inconsistent input; a second has to do with the representation of disjunctive information; the third concerns what kinds of statements can be the content of an update.

1.1. Inconsistent input

A logical calculus is *paraconsistent* if it cannot be used to derive arbitrary conclusions from inconsistent premises. Belnap argues[2] in general terms that paraconsistent reasoning is appropriate any context where an automated reasoner must operate without any guarantee that its input is consistent, and where nondegenerate performance is desirable

---

[*] The authors acknowledge the support of the National Science Foundation under grants IST-8516313 and IRI-8700705.
[1] Of course, it is also a concern to other traditions as well, and in particular to decision theory. Though the results we will present here are relevant to probabilistic approaches, the present study is restricted to a qualitative setting.
[2] See Belnap (1977a), p. 30-32, and Belnap (1977b), pp. 8-9.

even if inconsistency is present. Knowledge bases used in AI applications are cases of this sort.

There is a more specific and technical reason for our choice of a mildly paraconsistent logic in this paper: we have models in mind of our conditional theories that involve path-based inheritance reasoning. In fact, the results of this paper were motivated by noticing that update in such inheritance networks yielded, by means of the Ramsey test, a simple theory of conditionals with many of the properties of the more familiar conditional logics. But the logic of inheritance networks is paraconsistent; see Thomason, Horty, & Touretzky (1986) for details.

1.2. Disjunction completeness and prime knowledge bases

Let T be a deductively closed set of statements (a theory) in a given logical system. T is *disjunction complete* iff whenever it contains a disjunctive statement $\phi \vee \psi$, it contains either ϕ or ψ. Suppose that we have interpreted a knowledge base K in some logical system, so that K is identified with a certain deductively closed theory T. If so, then K is *prime* (with respect to this interpretation) iff T is disjunction complete. Set-ups pick out disjunction complete theories in four-valued logic, and our use of set-ups to represent knowledge bases is motivated in part by the assumption that prime knowledge bases are at least interesting enough to provide a reasonable initial theory of knowledge update.

We will take some care to make this approach seem sensible, arguing (in Section 1.4) that prime knowledge bases have some independent interest. We should point out immediately, though, that the sort of update theory we wish to develop is a conditional-based account that postulates the "Ramsey rule." And, of course, we hope to obtain a semantics that is plausible and that provides a large number of interesting models for update. Since (as we explain below in Section 4), impossibility proofs have been provided for a number of theories of this kind, it has to be understood at the outset that we can expect difficulties, and that simplifying assumptions may well be in order. It is in this spirit that we propose limiting our attention to prime knowledge bases. We hope, however, that the results of this paper can be extended to more general cases.

Note that a prime knowledge base need not itself have a way of expressing disjunction. On the contrary, restricting oneself to prime knowledge bases seems most natural if one's knowledge representation system does *not* provide a syntax for disjunction. For example, the semantic network knowledge bases to which we will apply our theory do not possess such a syntax. We *will* make disjunction available in our theory of update, however, and so it must be kept firmly in mind that we are developing a knowledge representation *metatheory*.

For knowledge bases that do contain disjunction, disjunctive completeness is unnatural. The techniques of this paper can be generalized to deal with such cases by relaxing the account of truth values from the four-valued case that we assume here to the more general case of *bilattices*.[3] In future work we wish to explore the theory of knowledge update for

---

[3] See Ginsberg (1988) and Ginsberg (1990).

bilattice-based knowledge representation; we hope that bilattice techniques will provide an account of knowledge bases with disjunction, and of disjunctive updates.

1.3. Atomistic update

What sort of constraints would motivate or justify the need to use prime knowledge bases? The content of a knowledge base depends primarily on the kinds of information that can be entered, i.e. on the kinds of updates that can be made. Clearly, if purely disjunctive updates can be made, then the knowledge base should fail to be prime. Our use of set-ups to represent knowledge bases will therefore also be motivated in part by the assumption that the knowledge representation problem at hand calls for a system in which purely disjunctive updates are not permitted. We will go even further, however, and assume that the given knowledge representation problem calls for knowledge bases that can be updated only with atomic and negated atomic statements. In short, we will restrict ourselves to *atomistic update*.[4]

1.4. The importance of set-up-based knowledge representation

We have identified three requirements on a knowledge representation system that jointly suffice to motivate the use of four-valued set-ups to represent knowledge bases: a requirement of paraconsistency, a requirement of primeness, and an associated restriction to atomistic update. Let us call a knowledge representation system that satisfies all three requirements a *set-up-based knowledge representation system*.

Set-up-based knowledge representation is distinctive in the way it handles incomplete information: a set-up-based knowledge base may be *globally* incomplete, but it must always be *locally* specific. That is, even though it may contain no information about some events, it always contains fully specific information about the events it does describe. This makes set-up-based knowledge representation attractive as a conceptual framework for modelling perception. As Barwise and Perry have argued,[5] the logic of naked infinitive visual reports indicates that what an agent sees is incomplete and yet specific in just this way. For example, I may not have seen Smith put on his hat or leave it on the table, but if I saw Smith or Jones get into a car, then either I saw Smith get into a car or I saw Jones get into a car.[6]

---

[4] Such a decision, of course, must be accompanied by a restriction that limits the constraints applicable to update. It is useless to rule out disjunctive updates if we allow meaning postulates like

$$\forall x[\textit{In-Carolina}(x) \equiv [\textit{In-North-Carolina}(x) \lor \textit{In-South-Carolina}(x)]].$$

[5] See Barwise & Perry (1983), Chapter 8.

[6] As a corollary to this point we note that situation semantics itself is an example of set-up-based knowledge representation.

1.5. Knowledge update in a set-up-based environment

Having argued for the importance of set-up-based knowledge representation, we turn now to consider the problem of characterizing update in this context. We will be investigating a revision operation which, given a set-up-based knowledge base and a statement ϕ, yields a new set-up-based knowledge base: the result of revising the original knowledge base by incorporating the information ϕ.

2. Logical approaches to theory revision

Independently of any computational applications, logicians have developed an account of the revision operation for first-order theories. The work of formulating and developing this theory has carried out by Carlos Alchourrón, Peter Gärdenfors, and David Makinson; since much of the work is joint, we will refer to it as the "AGM theory."[7]

The central notion of this work is a notion of *logical contraction* which involves the production from a theory T and a formula ϕ of a theory $T \dotminus \phi$, which is to be thought of as a minimal modification of T designed to render it consistent with ϕ. Of course, if T is already consistent with ϕ, then $T \dotminus \phi$ is T; the nontrivial case is the one in which ϕ is inconsistent with T, and so some things in T must be "given up." In general, there is no plausible way of using logical criteria alone to find a unique value for $T \dotminus \phi$.[8] Therefore, the AGM approach simply lays down abstract postulates for the operation $\dotminus$.

A *revision* operation can be defined in terms of $\dotminus$: to add ϕ to T, first make T consistent with ϕ and then add ϕ to the resulting theory and take the logical closure.

$$T \dotplus \phi \;=\; Cn((T \dotminus \neg\phi) \cup \{A\})^9$$

Notice that revision, on the AGM approach, decomposes into two discrete operations: contraction followed by a second operation. Following the AGM theorists, we will refer to this second operation, that of adding a formula to a theory and taking the logical closure, as *expansion*; i.e. the expansion of T to include ϕ is the theory $Cn(T \cup \{\phi\})$.

Abstract postulates for revision are given in Makinson (1987); they are as follows.

1   $T \dotplus \phi$ must be a theory.[10]
2   $\phi \in T \dotplus \phi$.
3   If $\neg\phi \notin Cn(T)$ then $T \dotplus \phi = Cn(T \cup \{A\})$.
4   If $\neg\phi \notin Cn(\emptyset)$ then $T \dotplus \phi$ is consistent if T is consistent.
5   If $Cn(\{\phi\}) = Cn(\{\psi\})$ then $T \dotplus \phi = T \dotplus \psi$.

These postulates, which are minimal for a revision policy that preserves consistency at all costs, make revision nonmonotonic, in a certain sense.

---

[7] See especially Makinson (1986) and Gärdenfors (1988).
[8] For instance, let T consist of the logical consequences of $\{Fa \wedge Fb\}$, and let ϕ be $\{\neg Fa \vee \neg Fb\}$; there is no way in principle to see whether Fa or Fb should be given up.

3. Two kinds of nonmonotonicity

In the computational literature, "nonmonotonic" reasoning is generally taken to originate in a nonmonotonic logical consequence relation, in that the following principle of *deductive monotonicity* fails.

If $\Gamma \vdash \phi$ then $\Gamma \cup \{\phi\} \vdash \psi$.

On the other hand, nonmonotonic reasoning is often informally explained as reasoning in which the process of *update* is nonmonotonic: if new information is added to the knowledge represented by a system, information that previously was obtainable may no longer be forthcoming. Where S is a knowledge base of some sort (either an axiomatic basis in first-order logic, or a database), and ϕ is a formula, suppose the result $U(S, \phi)$ of updating S by adding the information ϕ to S to be defined.

The principle of *revisionary monotonicity* that is violated in this case, then, is stated as follows.

If S yields ψ then $U(S, \phi)$ yields ψ.

In the previously described AGM theory we have the following example of revisionary nonmonotonicity: if $T = Cn(\{Pa, Pb\})$ then $Pa \in T$ but $Pa \notin T \dotplus \neg Pa$, where a and b are different constants.

It follows from these distinctions that it is theoretically possible for a reasoning system to exhibit revisionary *nonmonotonicity* while exhibiting deductive *monotonicity*. We could imagine a system whose deductive component relies on a first-order theorem prover, and that somehow implements an approximation of the AGM revision operator for update. Such a system would achieve nonmonotonicity in its update performance, but instead of employing any form of nonmonotonic logic, its nonmonotonic learning behavior would follow from the nonmonotonicity of AGM update operators.

As a system of this kind is exposed to inputs, an original theory T_0 will be revised successively, yielding a succession of theories $T_0, T_1, \ldots$ in response to inputs $\phi_1, \phi_2, \ldots$. It follows from the postulates for revision that the system is totally trusting at each stage about the input information; it is willing to give up whatever elements of the background theory must be abandoned to render it consistent with the new information. Once this information has been incorporated, however, it at once is as susceptible to revision as anything else in the current theory.

Such a rule of revision seems to place an inordinate value on novelty, and its behavior towards what it learns seems capricious. What is unquestioned at the time it is introduced may be discarded at the very next turn. Nor does the rule fit either a *selective fact-finding* view or a *suppositional* view of belief revision.

On the first view, inputs are not always reliable, and have to pass certain tests before they are adopted. It is hard to see how to provide qualitative axioms for such a view; the revision process is complicated by the fact that, on the basis of new information, it may be discovered that some input that was incorporated earlier did not in fact pass the tests. Nevertheless, it is clear that this sort of revision does not satisfy the AGM postulates.

On the second view, an input is something *supposed* for certain purposes—for the sake of argument for instance, or (what is much the same thing) for storage in a knowledge base which is intended to make available the consequences of what it is told to suppose.

The suppositional picture fits the rules of revision better, since it accounts for the feature that inputs are accepted. However, supposition appears to be cumulative. If I believe initially that a light switch is off (because the light is off), then supposing that the switch is on causes the original belief to be retracted; perhaps I conclude that the bulb is broken. So far, so good. But if I then suppose that the switch is off I have a contradiction, not a case in which the first supposition is retracted in view of the new one. It is, of course, possible to withdraw a supposition and return to the previous belief state, as in reasoning by cases; but this is not the same as input-driven AGM revision. Even in our simple example of the light, there is a difference. If the supposition that the switch is on is withdrawn before supposing that it is off, then the conclusion that the bulb is broken will be withdrawn as well in returning to the original belief state. A process of successive revisions does not work like this; in fact, it would be difficult to avoid the retention of the conclusion that the bulb is broken on this approach.

On a suppositional view of revision, then, it is natural to retain entrenched portions of the background theory, even when new suppositions contradict them. If we imagine that this sort of revision is implemented in a knowledge management system, there is a clear reason for this strategy; this will enable the system's user (or the system itself) to detect inconsistencies.[11]

These reflections provide a strong argument for combining revisionary nonmonotonicity with deductive nonmonotonicity. The reason for this is that nonmonotonic formalisms enable us to distinguished entrenched from nonentrenched conclusions in a way that relates naturally to suppositional models of update. That is, in a nonmonotonic deductive system we can distinguish between (i) what the system can conclude monotonically from what it has been told, and (ii) conclusions it has reached defeasibly from what it has been told. The former knowledge corresponds to cumulated suppositions which are not subject to revision under further updates; the latter (being defeasible) corresponds to what a rational agent should be willing to give up on learning more material. Moreover, as we will see, a nonmonotonic deductive apparatus can provide much of the information that is needed for revision.

Though, as we said, a combination of deductive monotonicity and revisionary non-monotonicity is theoretically coherent (and may, for all we know, even be implemented in a way that yields acceptable performance), we advocate a dual nonmonotonicity, as better motivated and more promising as an account of theory management.

Other, more direct arguments for this position follow from quite different considerations having to do with the *Ramsey rule*—we now turn to these.

---

[11] Once such inconsistencies have been detected, it of course may be desirable to make repairs by retracting some beliefs. Procedures for making such repairs are an important part of theory management. But, on our view, these procedures are different from procedures for update, which we regard as suppositional. Note, by the way, that a suppositional update followed by a consistency repair is not the same as an AGM revision; it may be that the best repair is to refuse the update.

4. Conditionals and update

Another tradition in the logical literature on update is concerned with (indicative) conditionals and the so-called "Ramsey rule," which may be stated, for our purposes, as follows:[12]

> A database contains the information **If** ϕ, **then** ψ if and only if updating it with the information ϕ produces a database that contains the information ψ.

As originally formulated, the Ramsey rule refers not to a database but to a *belief set*, the set of propositions that represents what a given thinking agent believes. In the context of that formulation it is relevant to ask whether the conditional propositions that a given idealized agent believes really do express constraints on his belief revision, and, if so, which classes of conditional propositions express such constraints. There is a tremendous difference, for example, between saying that belief revision depends on *indicative* conditionals like "If Tolstoy did not write *War and Peace*, then someone else did" or on so-called subjunctive conditionals[13] like "If Tolstoy had not written *War and Peace*, then someone else would have." These two sentences about Tolstoy illustrate the fact that corresponding indicative and subjunctive conditionals differ somehow in what they say, and also show that only the indicative conditionals can be regarded as expressions of willingness to update beliefs. Briefly, the general rule is that subjunctive conditionals are *causal*, while *indicative* conditionals are epistemic.

The Ramsey rule provides an attractive formal framework for investigating update because, within the logical theory of conditionals, one can state very abstract constraints on the update operation. These constraints can be applied to specific cases because individual sets of conditional formulas can be used to identify particular update operations. It is even possible to use the symbolic notation of conditional logic, in conjunction with a theorem prover, to implement an update system.[14]

Unfortunately, despite its intuitive appeal and theoretical promise, the Ramsey rule approach faces major difficulties. In Lewis (1976), David Lewis showed that a straightforward probabilistic interpretation of the Ramsey rule was unacceptable, because the associated probability spaces are trivialized. Lewis' result establishes that attempts to relate the Ramsey rule to Bayesian updates in the spirit of Jeffrey (1983) were doomed to failure. Such attempts, however, rest on a strong *quantitative* foundation. Propositions (including indicative conditionals) are assigned probabilities, which are to be thought of as degrees of belief, and the update operation takes a probability function p and sentence ϕ into a probability function p_ϕ. In this quantitative context, the Ramsey rule states that $p(\phi > \psi) = p_\phi(\psi)$: the degree of belief in a conditional is identical to the degree of belief in its consequence in the belief-state that results from supposing its antecedent.

Lewis' proof is thoroughly numerical, and so his result leaves open the possibility that

---

[12] See Harper, Stalnaker & Pearce (1980) for the best collection of references to this tradition, and Harper (1980) and Stalnaker (1968) in particular.

[13] We say "so-called" because these conditionals are not grammatically subjunctive; but this is how 'had'-'would' conditionals are usually characterized in the logical literature.

[14] See Nute (1985), for example.

qualitative versions of the Ramsey rule, such as ours, might be viable. In fact, the Ramsey rule could be used as a criterion for constructing an appropriate qualitative framework for belief revision.

However, recent work of Peter Gärdenfors' presents a challenge even to very weak formulations of the Ramsey rule.[15] And whereas Gärdenfors' results apply only in the context of purely deductive reasoning, David Makinson has shown that problems with the Ramsey rule extend to the context of nonmonotonic reasoning, as well.[16]

Despite these difficulties, it is possible to work out a Ramsey rule theory of update, at least in the context of set-up-based knowledge representation, because at least in cases where only atomistic update is allowed. Speaking more generally, we must distinguish information that is allowed to be the content of an update (update-eligible information) from information that is not allowed to be the content of an update (update-ineligible information). This distinction, of course, has to be provided with a plausible account, based on general properties of belief management. We will not try to do that here, and will only remark that propositions whose purpose is to *restructure* beliefs can indeed have a dynamic effect on beliefs; but these effects need not in general be updates.

Inheritance networks provide an example of the distinction. In these networks, individual links of the form $x \rightarrow y$ and $x \not\rightarrow y$, where y is a class term and x is an individual term, are the only update-eligible units of information.[17] An inheritance network may implicitly contain other sorts of information, including disjunctive or conditional information, but only individual links may be manipulated. Accordingly, when we formulate our Ramsey rule theory of update, we will restrict the kinds of statements that may appear as the antecedents of conditionals.[18]

The constraints on update-eligible information used in this paper are overly restrictive. (For instance, the fact that many indicative conditionals with disjunctive antecedents are perfectly natural suggests that some disjunctions should be update-eligible.) But the constraints admit a nontrivial range of cases, and provide, we feel, a good beginning. We are confident that the results of this paper can be extended to more general accounts of update-eligibility; it is an open question, however, whether results like those of Lewis, Gärdenfors, and Makinson will impose unwelcome limitations on the possibilities for extending the current theory in this direction.

5. The four-valued logic of conjunction, disjunction, and negation

We will begin the presentation of our theory by spelling out the four-valued background logic on which our conditional logic is built.

---

[15] See Gärdenfors (1986) and Gärdenfors (1987).
[16] See Makinson (1990).
[17] For explanation, see the remarks in Horty, Thomason & Touretzky (1990) concerning the Stability Theorem.
[18] We will appear to have adopted the proposal of Isaac Levi in Levi (1988) to exclude conditional propositions themselves from the antecedents of Ramsey rule conditionals, but Levi defends this proposal on the basis of philosophical claims with which we disagree. We adopt this proposal here only because it can be motivated by the particular knowledge representation context in which we are working.

In four-valued logic, formulas are assigned values from the set

$$\mathcal{T} = \{\{T\}, \{F\}, \emptyset, \{T, F\}\}.$$

The members of $\mathcal{T}$ should be understood not as truth values but as the possible epistemic states of a system with respect to a statement. A statement ϕ is assigned the value $\{T\}$ provided that the system has been told that ϕ is true but not that ϕ is false. ϕ is assigned the value $\{F\}$ if the system has been told that ϕ is false but not that ϕ is true. ϕ is assigned the value $\emptyset$ if the system has been told nothing regarding ϕ's truth. ϕ is given the value $\{T, F\}$ provided that the system has been told both that ϕ is true and that ϕ is false.

Definition 1. A four-valued valuation, a *set-up*, for a propositional language $\mathcal{L}$ (with $\wedge$, $\vee$, and $\neg$ as primitive) is a function v that assigns a member of $\mathcal{T}$ to each atomic formula of $\mathcal{L}$. Each valuation v is extended to a full assignment of values $[\![\phi]\!]$ to formulas ϕ by the following rules.

> **(1-1)** If ϕ is atomic, then $[\![\phi]\!] = v(\phi)$;
>
> **(1-2)** T$\in [\![\neg\phi]\!]$ iff F$\in [\![\phi]\!]$, F$\in [\![\neg\phi]\!]$ iff T$\in [\![\phi]\!]$;
>
> **(1-3)** T$\in [\![\phi \wedge \psi]\!]$ iff T$\in [\![\phi]\!]$ and T $\in [\![\psi]\!]$, F$\in [\![\phi \wedge \psi]\!]$ iff F$\in [\![\phi]\!]$ or F$\in [\![\psi]\!]$;
>
> **(1-4)** T$\in [\![\phi \vee \psi]\!]$ iff T$\in [\![\phi]\!]$ or T$\in [\![\psi]\!]$, F$\in [\![\phi \vee \psi]\!]$ iff F$\in [\![\phi]\!]$ and F$\in [\![\psi]\!]$.

Where Γ is a set of formulas, Γ *implies* ϕ iff for every valuation, T $\in [\![\phi]\!]$ provided T $\in [\![B]\!]$ for all $\psi \in \Gamma$. ϕ is *valid* iff $\emptyset$ implies ϕ.

The semantics of four-valued logic provides a formal framework for set-up-based knowledge representation.[19]

5.1. *Proof theory, soundness, and completeness*

For a language with just the connectives $\wedge$, $\vee$, and $\neg$ there will be no valid formulas. Though validity is trivial for such a language, the consequence relation $\Gamma \vdash \phi$ between a set of formulas Γ and a formula ϕ is not. For this reason, a natural deduction approach to axiomatization is appropriate. Since it is not clear how to obtain cut free formulations of conditional logics, and since we will extend this logic to include a conditional connective, we will take cut to be a primitive rule of inference.

The following rules yield a complete axiomatization of the $\{\wedge, \vee, \neg\}$ fragment.

Structural rules:

$$\phi \in \Gamma \Rightarrow \Gamma \vdash \phi \qquad \frac{\Gamma \vdash \phi}{\Gamma, \Delta \vdash \phi} \qquad \frac{\Gamma \vdash \phi \quad \Delta, \psi \vdash \psi}{\Gamma, \Delta \vdash \psi}$$

---

[19] Bilattice theory provides a more general framework, since the four truth values of four-valued logic form a bilattice; see Ginsberg (1988) and Ginsberg (1990).

Logical rules:

$$\frac{\Gamma \vdash \phi \wedge \psi}{\Gamma \vdash \phi} \qquad\qquad \frac{\Gamma \vdash \phi \wedge \psi}{\Gamma \vdash \psi} \qquad\qquad \frac{\Gamma \vdash \phi \quad \Gamma \vdash \psi}{\Gamma \vdash \phi \wedge \psi}$$

$$\frac{\Gamma \vdash \neg(\phi \wedge \psi) \quad \Delta_1, \neg\phi \vdash \chi \quad \Delta_2, \neg\psi \vdash \chi}{\Gamma, \Delta_1, \Delta_2 \vdash \chi}$$

$$\frac{\Gamma \vdash \neg\phi}{\Gamma \vdash \neg(\phi \wedge \psi)} \qquad\qquad\qquad \frac{\Gamma \vdash \neg\psi}{\Gamma \vdash \neg(\phi \wedge \psi)}$$

$$\frac{\Gamma \vdash \phi \vee \psi \quad \Delta_1, \phi \vdash \chi \quad \Delta_2, \psi \vdash \chi}{\Gamma, \Delta_1, \Delta_2 \vdash \chi}$$

$$\frac{\Gamma \vdash \phi}{\Gamma \vdash \phi \vee \psi} \qquad\qquad\qquad \frac{\Gamma \vdash \psi}{\Gamma \vdash \phi \vee \psi}$$

$$\frac{\Gamma \vdash \neg(\phi \vee \psi)}{\Gamma \vdash \neg\phi} \qquad\qquad\qquad \frac{\Gamma \vdash \neg(\phi \vee \psi)}{\Gamma \vdash \neg\psi}$$

$$\frac{\Gamma \vdash \neg\phi \quad \Gamma \vdash \neg\psi}{\Gamma \vdash \neg(\phi \vee \psi)} \qquad \frac{\Gamma \vdash \neg\neg\phi}{\Gamma \vdash \phi} \qquad \frac{\Gamma \vdash \phi}{\Gamma \vdash \neg\neg\phi}$$

Define a *saturated* set of formulas to be a set $\overline{\Gamma}$ that is deductively closed, and is also *disjunction complete*. (Note: saturated sets need not be consistent.)

Theorem 1. If $\Gamma \vdash \phi$ is provable, then Γ implies ϕ.

Proof. The soundness of our rules with respect to the four-valued interpretation is established by checking that they are all validity-preserving. This is trivial for the first two structural rules. We include details for the third structural rule (Cut) and for the fourth logical rule. Other cases are left to the reader.

Cut: Assume that Γ implies ϕ and that $\Delta \cup \{\phi\}$ implies ψ, and let v be given so that $\mathrm{T} \in [\![\chi]\!]$ for all $\chi \in \Gamma \cup \Delta$. Then $\mathrm{T} \in [\![\phi]\!]$ and so $\mathrm{T} \in [\![D]\!]$ for all $D \in \Gamma \cup \{\phi\}$. Hence $\mathrm{T} \in [\![\psi]\!]$, as required.

Rule 4: Suppose that Γ implies $\neg(\phi \wedge \psi)$, $\Delta_1 \cup \{\neg\phi\}$ implies χ; and $\Delta_2 \cup \{\neg\psi\}$ implies χ, and let v be given so that $\mathrm{T} \in [\![D]\!]$ for all $D \in \Gamma \cup \Delta_1 \cup \Delta_2$. Then $\mathrm{T} \in \neg(\phi \wedge \psi)$, and so (i) $\mathrm{T} \in [\![\neg\phi]\!]$ or (ii) $\mathrm{T} \in [\![\neg\psi]\!]$. If (i), then $\mathrm{T} \in [\![D]\!]$, for all $D \in \Delta_1 \cup \{\neg\phi\}$, and so $\mathrm{T} \in [\![\chi]\!]$. Similarly, if (ii), then again $\mathrm{T} \in [\![\chi]\!]$. So $\Gamma \cup \Delta_1 \cup \Delta_2$ implies χ. ∎

Completeness is proved Henkin-fashion, by using saturated sets to construct a countermodel to the sequent $\Gamma \vdash \phi$ on the assumption that $\Gamma \nvdash \phi$. The following lemma is crucial for completeness.

Lemma 1. If $\Gamma \vdash \phi$ is not provable then there is a saturated extension $\overline{\Gamma}$ of Γ such that $\phi \notin \overline{\Gamma}$.

Proof. Following the method described in Thomason (1969), we construct a saturated extension $\overline{\Gamma}$ of Γ by selectively adding one disjunct to Γ from any disjunction that we can add one from.

Let $\{(\chi_1 \vee \chi_1'), \ldots, (\chi_n \vee \chi_n'), \ldots\}$ be an enumeration of all disjunctive formulas. Then we define a sequence of sets Γ_k as follows:

$$\Gamma_1 \quad = \quad \Gamma$$

$$\Gamma_{k+1} \quad = \quad \begin{cases} \Gamma_k, & \text{if } \Gamma \cup \{\chi_k \vee \chi_k'\} \vdash \phi; \\ \Gamma_k \cup \{\chi_k'\}, & \text{if } \Gamma \cup \{\chi_k\} \vdash \phi, \text{ but } \Gamma \cup \{\chi_k'\} \nvdash \phi; \\ \Gamma_k \cup \{\chi_k\}, & \text{if } \Gamma \cup \{\chi_k\} \nvdash \phi. \end{cases}$$

We let $\Gamma_\infty = \bigcup\limits_{n=1}^{\infty} \Gamma_n$, and we let $\overline{\Gamma}$ be the deductive closure of Γ_∞. It is straightforward to show that $\overline{\Gamma}$ is disjunction complete, and an easy induction argument shows that $\phi \notin \overline{\Gamma}$. ∎

Theorem 2. If Γ implies ϕ, then $\Gamma \vdash \phi$ is provable.

Proof. Suppose that $\Gamma \vdash \phi$ is not provable. By Lemma 1, let $\overline{\Gamma}$ be a saturated extension of Γ not containing ϕ. The required countermodel to $\Gamma \vdash \phi$ is obtained by letting $T \in v(\psi)$ iff $\psi \in \overline{\Gamma}$ and $F \in v(\psi)$ iff $\neg\psi \in \overline{\Gamma}$, for all atomic ψ. It then follows by induction that $T \in [\![\chi]\!]$ iff $\chi \in \overline{\Gamma}$ and $F \in [\![\chi]\!]$ iff $\neg\chi \in \overline{\Gamma}$, for all formulas χ. ∎

6. Four-valued conditional logic

Since the intended context of our logic is set-up-based knowledge representation, we will design a formal language with this context in mind. In particular, as noted above, we must pay attention to what sorts of statements can occur as the *antecedents* of conditionals in our Ramsey rule theory.

A set-up-based knowledge base may in some sense contain disjunctive information, but only indirectly. And since a purely disjunctive update is not possible in a set-up-based knowledge base, disjunctive statements will be excluded as the antecedents of conditionals. We also exclude conditional statements themselves from the antecedents of conditionals because, again, only atomistic update is allowed. Our purpose here is to focus on knowledge bases with *fixed* update procedures, i.e. knowledge bases in which the update procedure is not itself update-eligible.

We define a language $\mathcal{L}_{CL_4}$ as follows. Let some set of atomic statements be given, and note that a *literal* is an atomic or negated atomic statement. We will call a (possibly degenerate) conjunction of literals a *conjunctive clause*.

Definition 2. The set of formulas of $\mathcal{L}_{\mathbf{CL4}}$ is the smallest set S meeting the following conditions:

(2-1) if ϕ is atomic, then $\phi \in \mathcal{S}$;

(2-2) if $\phi, \psi \in \mathcal{S}$, then $(\phi \wedge \psi)$, $(\phi \vee \psi)$, $\neg\phi \in \mathcal{S}$;

(2-3) if $\phi, \psi \in \mathcal{S}$ and ϕ is a conjunctive clause, then $(\phi > \psi) \in \mathcal{S}$.

Note that the conditional connective $>$ *is* permitted to appear in the consequent of a conditional statement.

6.1. Semantics

Definition 3. A *model* $\mathcal{M}$ of $\mathcal{L}_{\mathrm{CL4}}$ is a triple $\langle W, v, f \rangle$ where W is a set of possible worlds; for each $w \in W$, v_w is a valuation assigning a member of $\mathcal{T}$ to each atomic formula; and γ is a function mapping each $w \in W$ and conjunctive clause ϕ to a member $\gamma(\phi, w)$ of W. The function γ must meet the following conditions, where $w_1 \simeq w_2$ iff $v_{w_1}(\phi) = v_{w_2}(\phi)$ for all atomic formulas ϕ, and $w_1 \approx w_2$ iff $[\![\psi]\!]_{w_1} = [\![\psi]\!]_{w_2}$ for all formulas ψ.

(3-1) If $\mathrm{T} \in [\![\phi]\!]_w$ and ϕ is a conjunctive clause, then $\gamma(\phi, w) \simeq w$;

(3-2) If $[\![\phi]\!]_w = \{\mathrm{T}, \mathrm{F}\}$ then $[\![\phi]\!]_{\gamma(\psi, w)} = \{\mathrm{T}, \mathrm{F}\}$;

(3-3) $\mathrm{T} \in [\![\phi]\!]_{\gamma(\phi, w)}$;

(3-4) $\gamma(\phi \wedge \psi, w) = \gamma(\psi, \gamma(\phi, w))$;

(3-5) If $\mathrm{T} \in [\![\phi]\!]_{\gamma(\psi, w)}$ and $\mathrm{T} \in [\![\psi]\!]_{\gamma(\phi, w)}$, then $\gamma(\phi, w) \simeq \gamma(\psi, w)$.

The satisfaction conditions for $\wedge, \vee$, and $\neg$ are obtained by relativizing the previous conditions to worlds. The clause for conditional formulas is as follows.

$$[\![\phi > \psi]\!]_w = [\![\psi]\!]_{f(\phi, w)}.$$

Semantic consequence is defined as follows.

Definition 4. A set Γ *entails* a formula ϕ iff for each w in each model $\mathcal{M}$ of $\mathcal{L}_{\mathrm{CL4}}$, $\mathrm{T} \in [\![\phi]\!]_w$ provided that $\mathrm{T} \in [\![\psi]\!]_w$ for all $\psi \in \Gamma$. A world w *satisfies* a set Γ in a model $\mathcal{M}$ to which w belongs iff $\mathrm{T} \in [\![\chi]\!]_w$ for each $\chi \in \Gamma$.

We state the following lemma without proof.

Lemma 2. If ϕ is conditional-free and $w_1 \simeq w_2$, then $[\![\phi]\!]_{w_1} = [\![\phi]\!]_{w_2}$.

6.2. Four-valued models and knowledge update

The structure of four-valued models and the formal properties of the selection function γ are specifically motivated by intuitive requirements of an update operation in the context of set-up-based knowledge representation. Each possible world belonging to W represents a set-up-based knowledge base, and so the function γ is to be thought of as mapping one knowledge base to another with respect to a given update-eligible statement. Since our theory is only intended to apply to set-up-based knowledge bases, we can exclude the possibility of having to make a purely disjunctive update. And since the update operation itself is not revisable in a set-up-based knowledge representation system we can exclude the possibility of having to make a conditional update. Thus γ can take only a conjunctive clause as its first argument.

First we must identify γ as an update operation, rather than as something else (such as a contraction operation). For this reason we impose condition (3-3), which is our "Postulate of Success."

Next we consider the treatment of redundant information. If a knowledge base already contains a given piece of update-eligible information, then, intuitively speaking, one would not expect the other update-eligible information contained in the knowledge base to change when this redundant information is added. It is a kind of closure condition on the knowledge base that supposing a fact that is known should neither cause retractions from or additions to the concluded facts. This principle is captured by condition (3-1). On the other hand, update-ineligible information may well be changed by redundant updates because, for instance, updates can change the status of conditionals. We discuss cases of this sort in detail below, in Section 8.1.

Third we consider the persistence of information in the knowledge base. We have already mentioned that one motivation for adopting a set-up-based knowledge representation system is that information that has been directly entered should not be masked or removed, even contradictory information. Condition (3-4) captures part of this requirement by ensuring that updates themselves, which involve the direct entering of information, are expansive. Not all of the information retrievable from a knowledge base need persist, however. If the knowledge base incorporates a nonmonotonic reasoning system, then as we have already noted, even a purely expansive update operation may exhibit revisionary nonmonotonicity.[20] But even in the case of a nonmonotonic reasoner, one kind of information should always persist, namely contradictory information. Why? Because it would be unreasonable for a paraconsistent reasoner to introduce contradictions gratuitously, so that we should not expect inconsistent conclusions that do not follow monotonically from inconsistencies that were directly entered.[21] Directly entered information is to be preserved under update, and so, in particular, contradictions already in a knowledge base are to be preserved under update. Condition (3-2) captures this requirement.

Condition (3-5) captures a version of what in Makinson (1986) is called the Stalnaker Property. The idea is that the result of an update should be a function of the content of the update proposition, not simply a function of its formulation. If adding ϕ to the current knowledge base would produce a knowledge base that yields ψ and vice-versa, then, as far as the current knowledge base is concerned, ϕ and ψ are equivalent. Condition (3-5) captures this.

---

[20] Our update model applies to nonmonotonic knowledge bases even though it does not explicitly include a nonmonotonic reasoning component.

[21] For an example of a nonmonotonic system satisfying this condition, see Horty, Thomason & Touretzky (1990), p. 325.

6.3. *Proof Theory*

Based on the theory of knowledge update presented just above, we obtain our system **CL4** of conditional logic by expanding the four-valued logic of $\wedge$, $\vee$, $\neg$ by the following rules.[22]

$$\textbf{FCP} \quad \frac{\Gamma \vdash \phi > \psi_1 \ldots \Gamma \vdash \phi > \psi_n \quad \{\psi_1, \ldots, \psi_n\} \vdash \chi}{\Gamma \vdash \phi > \chi}$$

$$\textbf{EDC} \quad \frac{\Gamma \vdash \phi > (\psi \vee \chi)}{\Gamma \vdash (\phi > \psi) \vee (\phi > \chi)}$$

ID $\quad \Gamma \vdash \phi > \phi$, if ϕ is a conjunctive clause.

$$\textbf{RMP} \quad \frac{\Gamma \vdash \phi \quad \Gamma \vdash \phi > \psi}{\Gamma \vdash \psi} \text{, if } \psi \text{ is conditional-free.}$$

$$\textbf{RCEN} \quad \frac{\Gamma \vdash \phi \quad \Gamma \vdash \psi}{\Gamma \vdash \phi > \psi},$$

if ϕ is a conjunctive clause and ψ is conditional-free.

$$\textbf{PC} \quad \frac{\Gamma \vdash \psi \wedge \neg\psi}{\Gamma \vdash \phi > (\psi \wedge \neg\psi)} \text{, if } \phi \text{ is a conjunctive clause.}$$

$$\textbf{NCE} \quad \frac{\Gamma \vdash \neg(\phi > \psi)}{\Gamma \vdash \phi > \neg\psi}$$

---

[22] The deductive system presented here differs from the system **INH4** that is described in Cross & Thomason (1987) in the treatment of disjunctive antecedents, which we now recognize as being unnecessary.

$$\text{NCI} \frac{\Gamma \vdash \phi > \neg\psi}{\Gamma \vdash \neg(\phi > \psi)}$$

$$\text{IMP} \frac{\Gamma \vdash \phi > (\psi > \chi)}{\Gamma \vdash (\phi \wedge \psi) > \chi}$$

$$\text{EXP} \frac{\Gamma \vdash (\phi \wedge \psi) > \chi}{\Gamma \vdash \phi > (\psi > \chi)}$$

$$\text{EQ} \frac{\Gamma \vdash \phi > \psi \quad \Gamma \vdash \psi > \phi \quad \Gamma \vdash \phi > \chi}{\Gamma \vdash \psi > \chi} \text{, if } \chi \text{ is conditional-free.}$$

6.4. Soundness and Completeness

Theorem 3. If $\Gamma \vdash \phi$ is provable, then Γ entails ϕ.

Proof. We verify each new rule in turn. As for rule **FCP**, suppose that Γ entails $\phi > \psi_i$ for $1 \leq i \leq n$ and that $\{\psi_1, \dots, \psi_n\}$ entails χ. Let a model $\mathcal{M}$ and a world w in $\mathcal{M}$ be given. Suppose that w satisfies Γ in $\mathcal{M}$. Then $\mathrm{T} \in [\![\psi_i]\!]_{\gamma(\phi,w)}$ for each i. But then $\mathrm{T} \in [\![\chi]\!]_{\gamma(\phi,w)}$, and so $\mathrm{T} \in [\![\phi > \chi]\!]_w$. Hence Γ entails $\phi > \chi$, as required. Next we consider rule **EDC**. Suppose that Γ entails $\phi > (\psi \vee \chi)$, and let a model $\mathcal{M}$ and a world w in $\mathcal{M}$ be given. Suppose that w satisfies Γ in $\mathcal{M}$; then $\mathrm{T} \in [\![\psi \vee \chi]\!]_{\gamma(\phi,w)}$, and so $\mathrm{T} \in [\![\psi]\!]_{\gamma(\phi,w)}$ or $\mathrm{T} \in [\![\chi]\!]_{f(\phi,w)}$. Hence $\mathrm{T} \in [\![\phi > \psi]\!]_w$ or $\mathrm{T} \in [\![\phi > \chi]\!]_w$, and so $\mathrm{T} \in [\![(\phi > \psi) \vee (\phi > \chi)]\!]_w$. Hence Γ entails $(\phi > \psi) \vee (\phi > \chi)$, as required. Entailment holds for rule **ID** because of condition (3-3): since $\mathrm{T} \in [\![\phi]\!]_{\gamma(\phi,w)}$, $\mathrm{T} \in [\![\phi > \phi]\!]_w$, whenever w satisfies Γ in $\mathcal{M}$, and so Γ entails $\phi > \phi$. Rule **RMP** (restricted *modus ponens*) preserves implication because of Lemma 1 and condition (3-1). Suppose that Γ entails ϕ and Γ entails $\phi > \psi$, where ψ is conditional-free, and let w satisfy Γ in $\mathcal{M}$. Then $\mathrm{T} \in [\![\phi]\!]_w$ and $\mathrm{T} \in [\![\psi]\!]_{\gamma(\phi,w)}$, and so $\mathrm{T} \in [\![\psi]\!]_w$. Hence Γ entails ψ. **RCEN** preserves implication because of Lemma 1 and condition (3-1):[23] suppose that Γ entails conjunctive clause ϕ and atomic formula ψ, and let w satisfy Γ in $\mathcal{M}$. Then $\mathrm{T} \in [\![\phi]\!]_w$, and so $\gamma(\phi,w) \simeq w$. But $\mathrm{T} \in [\![\psi]\!]_w$, and so $\mathrm{T} \in [\![\phi > \psi]\!]_w$, as required. **PC** preserves entailment because of Condition (3-2). Consider rule **NCE**. Suppose that Γ entails $\neg(\phi > \psi)$, and let w satisfy Γ in $\mathcal{M}$. Then

---

[23] Note that although $\gamma(\phi, w)$ may be distinct from w even when $\mathrm{T} \in [\![\phi]\!]_w$, $\gamma(\phi, w)$ and w will treat all atomic formulas in the same way, and so will treat all antecedents of conditionals alike. Note, however, that w and $\gamma(\phi, w)$ may treat conditional formulae differently.

$F \in [\![\psi]\!]_{\gamma(\phi, w)}$, and so $T \in [\![\phi > \neg\psi]\!]$, as required. Next, we consider rule **NCI**. Suppose that Γ entails $\phi > \neg\psi$, and let w satisfy Γ. Then $F \in [\![\psi]\!]_{\gamma(\phi, w)}$, and so $T \in [\![\neg(\phi > \psi)]\!]_w$, as required. Rules **IMP** and **EXP** preserve entailment because of condition (3-4), and rule **EQ** does so because of condition (3-5). ∎

Theorem 4. If Γ entails ϕ, then $\Gamma \vdash \phi$ is provable.

Proof. Suppose that $\Gamma \vdash \phi$ is not provable; we wish to show that Γ does not entail ϕ. Let $\overline{\Gamma}$ be a saturated extension of Γ that does not contain ϕ; let $\gamma(\phi, \overline{\Delta})$ be the set $\{\psi : \phi > \psi \in \overline{\Delta}\}$, for any conditional-free formula ϕ and any saturated $\overline{\Delta}$. Because of the rules **FCP** and **EDC**, $\gamma(\phi, \overline{\Delta})$ will itself be saturated. Let $\mathcal{W}$ be the closure of $\{\overline{\Gamma}\}$ under γ, and let $T \in v_{\overline{\Delta}}(\phi)$ iff $\phi \in \overline{\Delta}$ and $F \in v_{\overline{\Delta}}(\phi)$ iff $\neg\phi \in \overline{\Delta}$, for atomic formulas ϕ.

Completeness follows from the following facts: first, the structure we have defined is a model, and second, $T \in [\![\phi]\!]_{\overline{\Delta}}$ iff $\phi \in \overline{\Delta}$ and $F \in [\![\phi]\!]_{\overline{\Delta}}$ iff $\neg\phi \in \overline{\Delta}$, for all formulas ϕ. This implies that $\overline{\Gamma}$ satisfies each formula $\psi \in \Gamma$ in the structure defined above, since $\Gamma \subseteq \overline{\Gamma}$. Also, $T \notin [\![\phi]\!]_{\overline{\Gamma}}$, since $\phi \notin \overline{\Gamma}$, so that Γ cannot entail ϕ. We establish first that satisfaction coincides with set membership and then that the six conditions on models hold.

To show that satisfaction coincides with set membership we note that for the connectives $\wedge$, $\vee$, $\neg$, the corresponding part of the completeness proof for the logic of $\wedge$, $\vee$, $\neg$ applies here. We need only consider, then, the case of the conditional connective. Proof that $\phi > \psi \in \overline{\Delta}$ if $T \in [\![\phi > \psi]\!]_{\overline{\Delta}}$ is by induction on the number of occurrences of $>$ in ψ. Assume first that ψ contains no occurrences of $>$; then $T \in [\![\phi > \psi]\!]_{\overline{\Delta}}$ iff $T \in [\![\psi]\!]_{\gamma(\phi, \overline{\Delta})}$ iff $\psi \in \gamma(\phi, \overline{\Delta})$. But $\psi \in \gamma(\phi, \overline{\Delta})$ iff $\phi > \psi \in \overline{\Delta}$, by the definition of γ. Similarly, $F \in [\![\phi > \psi]\!]_{\overline{\Delta}}$ iff $F \in [\![\psi]\!]_{\gamma(\phi, \overline{\Delta})}$ iff $\neg\psi \in \gamma(\phi, \overline{\Delta})$. But $\neg\psi \in \gamma(\phi, \overline{\Delta})$ iff $\phi > \neg\psi \in \overline{\Delta}$, by the definition of γ. And $\phi > \neg\psi \in \overline{\Delta}$ iff $\neg(\phi > \psi) \in \overline{\Delta}$, by rules **NCE** and **NCI**. This establishes the base case; the inductive case is exactly similar.

Next we verify condition (3-1). Let $T \in [\![\phi]\!]_{\overline{\Delta}}$ and let ϕ be a conjunctive clause, and let ψ be atomic. Suppose that $T \in v_{\gamma(\phi, \overline{\Delta})}(\psi)$. Then $T \in [\![\phi > \psi]\!]_{\overline{\Delta}}$, so $\overline{\Delta} \vdash \phi$ and $\overline{\Delta} \vdash \phi > \psi$. Hence by rule MP, $\overline{\Delta} \vdash \psi$, and so $T \in v_{\overline{\Delta}}(\psi)$, as required. Conversely, let $T \in v_{\overline{\Delta}}(\psi)$. Then $\overline{\Delta} \vdash \phi > \psi$ by rule CEN, and so $T \in v_{\gamma(\phi, \overline{\Delta})}(\psi)$, as required. By an exactly similar argument, $F \in v_{\gamma(\phi, \overline{\Delta})}(\psi)$ iff $F \in v_{\overline{\Delta}}(\psi)$, and so $\gamma(\phi, \overline{\Delta}) \simeq \overline{\Delta}$.

Now consider condition (3-2). Let $[\![\phi]\!]_{\overline{\Delta}} = \{T, F\}$. Then $\overline{\Delta} \vdash \phi \wedge \neg\phi$, and so by rule **PC**, $\overline{\Delta} \vdash \psi > (\phi \wedge \neg\phi)$. Hence $\overline{\Delta} \vdash \psi > \phi$ and $\overline{\Delta} \vdash \psi > \neg\phi$, by rule **FCP**, and so $[\![\phi]\!]_{\gamma(\psi, \overline{\Delta})} = \{T, F\}$, as required.

Since $\overline{\Delta} \vdash \phi > \phi$, we have $\phi > \phi \in \overline{\Delta}$, and so $\phi \in \gamma(\phi, \overline{\Delta})$. Hence $T \in [\![\phi]\!]_{\overline{\Delta}}$, and so condition (3-3) is satisfied.

Next we consider condition (3-4). Let ϕ and ψ be conjunctive clauses, and let $\chi \in \gamma(\phi \wedge \psi, \overline{\Delta})$; then $(\phi \wedge \psi) > \chi \in \overline{\Delta}$, and hence $\phi > (\psi > \chi) \in \overline{\Delta}$, by rule **EXP**. So $\psi > \chi \in \gamma(\phi, \overline{\Delta})$ and therefore $\chi \in \gamma(\psi, \gamma(\phi, \overline{\Delta}))$. Hence $\gamma(\phi \wedge \psi, \overline{\Delta}) \subseteq \gamma(\psi, \gamma(\phi, \overline{\Delta}))$. By a similar argument, rule **IMP** implies that $\gamma(\psi, \gamma(\phi, \overline{\Delta})) \subseteq \gamma(\phi \wedge \psi, \overline{\Delta})$, and so $\gamma(\phi \wedge \psi, \overline{\Delta}) = \gamma(\psi, \gamma(\phi, \overline{\Delta}))$, as required.

Finally we consider condition (3-5). Let $T \in [\![\phi]\!]_{\gamma(\psi, \overline{\Delta})}$ and $T \in [\![\psi]\!]_{\gamma(\phi, \overline{\Delta})}$. Then $\overline{\Delta} \vdash \psi > \phi$ and $\overline{\Delta} \vdash \phi > \psi$. Let χ be any atomic formula, and suppose that $T \in$

$[\![\chi]\!]_{\gamma(\phi,\overline{\Delta})}$. $\overline{\Delta} \vdash \phi > \chi$. Hence by rule **EQ**, $\overline{\Delta} \vdash \psi > \chi$, and so $\mathrm{T} \in [\![\chi]\!]_{\gamma(\psi,\overline{\Delta})}$. By a similar argument, if $\mathrm{F} \in [\![\chi]\!]_{\gamma(\phi,\overline{\Delta})}$ then $\mathrm{F} \in [\![\chi]\!]_{\gamma(\psi,\overline{\Delta})}$. Since the converses obviously hold as well, we have $\gamma(\phi,\overline{\Delta}) \simeq \gamma(\psi,\overline{\Delta})$, as required. ∎

7. Multiple inheritance with exceptions

As an example to illustrate our theory, we repeat the main definitions from the theory of nonmonotonic inheritance that is presented in Horty, Thomason & Touretzky (1990), which should be consulted for motivation and detailed explanation. We begin with some general preliminaries.

We introduce for our primitive vocabulary a set of terms a, b, c, d to represent *individuals*, and a set of terms p, q, r, s, P, Q, R, S to represent *kinds*. (We use upper case when kinds are identified with predicates.) Where y is a kind term and x is either a kind term or an individual term, the *links* $x \rightarrow y$ and $x \not\rightarrow y$ will represent the statements x IS-A y and x IS-NOT-A y, respectively. If x is an individual term, then we call $x \rightarrow y$ and $x \not\rightarrow y$ *particular links*.

A *net* is defined to be any set of links. We use the notation $u \succ v$ to denote any link of the form $u \rightarrow v$ or $u \not\rightarrow v$, and we define a *pseudo-path* from x to y in a net $\mathcal{G}$ to be any sequence $x \succ u_1 \succ \ldots \succ u_m \succ y$, where $x \succ u_1, u_m \succ y \in \mathcal{G}$, and for all i such that $1 \leq i < m$, $u_i \succ u_{i+1} \in \mathcal{G}$. A *path* from x to y in a net $\mathcal{G}$ is defined to be a sequence of the form $x \rightarrow u_1 \rightarrow \ldots \rightarrow u_m \rightarrow y$ (or $x \rightarrow u_1 \rightarrow \ldots \rightarrow u_m \not\rightarrow y$), where $x \rightarrow u_1, u_m \rightarrow y$ (or $u_m \not\rightarrow y$) $\in \mathcal{G}$ and for each i such that $1 \leq i < m$, $u_i \rightarrow u_{i+1} \in \mathcal{G}$. A *basic* path is a path of length 1. We use lower case Greek letters $\sigma, \tau, \xi, \pi, \omega$ to range over paths. We will use calligraphic capital letters $\mathcal{D}, \mathcal{E}, \mathcal{F}, \mathcal{G}$ to range over nets.

We restrict our attention to *acyclic* nets, i.e. nets in which no there are no pseudo-paths from x to x. Where $\mathcal{G}$ is an acyclic net, and where σ is a path from x to y in $\mathcal{G}$, $\deg_{\mathcal{G}}(\sigma)$ (the degree of σ in $\mathcal{G}$) is defined to be the length (number of arrows) of the longest pseudo-path from x to y in $\mathcal{G}$. Since we concern ourselves only with acyclic nets, every path in a net will have a well-defined degree.

Consequence is specified in nets by an inheritance definition, which characterizes the paths that are permitted by the net.

Definition 5. Let an acyclic net $\mathcal{G}$ be given, and let σ be a path from x to y. Permission is defined inductively as follows.

(5-1) If σ is basic, then $\mathcal{G}$ permits σ iff $\sigma \in \mathcal{G}$; this defines permission for all paths of degree 1.

(5-2) Suppose that permission is defined for all paths in $\mathcal{G}$ of degree less than n, and let $\deg_{\mathcal{G}}(\sigma) = n$. If $\sigma = x \rightarrow \xi \rightarrow u \rightarrow y$, then $\mathcal{G}$ permits σ iff

   (5-2-1) $\mathcal{G}$ permits $x \rightarrow \xi \rightarrow u$ and $u \rightarrow y \in \mathcal{G}$.

   (5-2-2) $x \not\rightarrow y \notin \mathcal{G}$;

   (5-2-3) If $\mathcal{G}$ permits $x \rightarrow \tau \rightarrow v$ and $v \not\rightarrow y \in \mathcal{G}$, then there exists a z such that $\mathcal{G}$ permits $x \rightarrow \tau_1 \rightarrow z \rightarrow \tau_2 \rightarrow v$ and $z \rightarrow y \in \mathcal{G}$.

If $\sigma = x \rightarrow \xi \rightarrow u \not\rightarrow y$, then $\mathcal{G}$ permits σ iff

(5-2-4) $\mathcal{G}$ permits $x \to \xi \to u$ and $u \not\to y \in \mathcal{G}$.

(5-2-5) $x \to y \notin \mathcal{G}$;

(5-2-6) If $\mathcal{G}$ permits $x \to \tau \to v$ and $v \to y \in \mathcal{G}$, then there exists a z such that $\mathcal{G}$ permits $x \to \tau_1 \to z \to \tau_2 \to v$ and $z \not\to y \in \mathcal{G}$.

We abbreviate "$\mathcal{G}$ permits σ" as follows: $\mathcal{G} \models \sigma$. Some examples of networks and permitted paths are given in Sections 8.1 and 8.2 below; more can be found in Horty, Thomason & Touretzky (1990).

7.1. Models of CL4 in inheritance nets

We now show how to generate a CL4 model from a single inheritance net $\mathcal{G}$. (Note that $\mathcal{G}$ may contain nodes that are not linked to any other nodes.) Let $\mathcal{P}_{\mathcal{G}} = \{P_1, \ldots, P_n\}$ consist of all the kind terms appearing in $\mathcal{G}$, and let $\mathcal{A}_{\mathcal{G}} = \{a_1, \ldots, a_m\}$ consist of all the individual terms appearing in $\mathcal{G}$. Let $\mathcal{G}^+ = \{a \to P : a \in \mathcal{A}_{\mathcal{G}}, P \in \mathcal{P}_{\mathcal{G}}\}$, let $\mathcal{G}^- = \{a \not\to P : a \in \mathcal{A}_{\mathcal{G}}, P \in \mathcal{P}_{\mathcal{G}}\}$.

A *positive literal* over a net $\mathcal{G}$ is a formula Pa, where $a \to P \in \mathcal{G}^+$; a *negative literal* over $\mathcal{G}$ is a formula $\neg Pa$, where $a \not\to P \in \mathcal{G}^-$. A *conjunctive clause* is a conjunction of literals. We define a translation function f from conjunctive clauses to corresponding sets of links by the following induction:

$$
\begin{aligned}
f(P_j a_k) &= \{a_k \to P_j\}; \\
f(\neg P_j a_k) &= \{a_k \not\to P_j\}; \\
f(\phi \wedge \psi) &= f(\phi) \cup f(\psi).
\end{aligned}
$$

Nets can be likened to postulates, and permitted paths to proofs. It is natural, then, to define a relation like provability between nets and conjunctive clauses, which holds in case some paths expressing these clauses are permitted in the net. We call this provability relation "support."

Definition 6. Where $\mathcal{G}$ is an acyclic net and ϕ is a positive literal Pa over $\mathcal{G}$, we say that $\mathcal{G}$ *supports* ϕ in case $\mathcal{G}$ permits a positive path from a to P; similarly, where ϕ is a negative literal $\neg Pa$, $\mathcal{G}$ supports ϕ in case $\mathcal{G}$ permits a negative path from a to P. $\mathcal{G}$ supports a conjunctive clause ϕ in case $\mathcal{G}$ supports every conjunct of ϕ. We abbreviate "$\mathcal{G}$ supports ϕ" as follows: $\mathcal{G} \models \phi$.

Turning now to the **CL4** model corresponding to $\mathcal{G}$, let $W = \{\mathcal{G} \cup X \cup Y : X \subseteq \mathcal{G}^+, Y \subseteq \mathcal{G}^-\}$. We identify $\mathcal{G}$ as the *base world* of the model.

We define the valuation function on the positive literals (or atomic formulas) over $\mathcal{G}$ as follows: for each j and k, and for each $\mathcal{H} \in W$, let $\text{T} \in v_{\mathcal{H}}(P_j a_k)$ iff $\mathcal{H} \models P_j a_k$, and let $\text{F} \in v_{\mathcal{H}}(P_j a_k)$ iff $\mathcal{H} \models \neg P_j a_k$.

Finally we define the selection function γ: for every conjunctive clause ϕ and every $\mathcal{H} \in W$,

We have not defined the update operation on generic links, nor can we allow such links to be captured as formulas of our conditional logic. Our aim at this stage is to relate multiple inheritance with exceptions to systems of conditional logic of a more or less familiar sort (such as Stalnaker (1968)). In particular, this means looking at systems of conditional logic that have monotonic consequence relations. If we were to include generic links among the well-formed formulas of our conditional logic, the resulting consequence relation would be *non*monotonic.

7.2. Soundness and incompleteness

In this section we prove that the class of structures defined above are sound with respect to **CL4** but that not every inference valid in these structures is provable in **CL4**. We begin by proving that semantic net models indeed are models of **CL4**.

Lemma 3. If $T \in [\![\phi]\!]_w$ and ϕ is a conjunctive clause, then $\gamma(\phi, w) \simeq w$.

Proof: Theorem 5.2 (the Stability Theorem) of Horty, Thomason & Touretzky (1990), p. 327, states that if $\mathcal{G} \models \phi$, where ϕ is a positive literal Pa, then $\mathcal{G} \cup \{a \to P\} \models \psi$ iff $\mathcal{G} \models \psi$, for any literal ψ. The proof of this theorem is easily generalized to the case in which ϕ is any literal. The result follows from this generalization and the definition of γ. ∎

Lemma 4. If $[\![\phi]\!]_w = \{T, F\}$ then $[\![\phi]\!]_{\gamma(\psi, w)} = \{T, F\}$.

Proof: By Theorem 5.1 of Horty, Thomason & Touretzky (1990), p. 325, which states that if $\mathcal{G} \models \phi$ and $\mathcal{G} \models \neg\phi$, where ϕ is a positive literal Pa, then $a \to P, a \not\to P \in \mathcal{G}$. ∎

Lemma 5. For any conjunctive clause ϕ, $T \in [\![\phi]\!]_{\gamma(\phi, w)}$.

Proof: By inspection of the definition of γ. ∎

Lemma 6. If ϕ and ψ are conjunctive clauses, then $\gamma(\phi \wedge \psi, w) = \gamma(\psi, \gamma(\phi, w))$.

Proof: By inspection of the definition of γ. ∎

Lemma 7. If $T \in [\![\phi]\!]_{\gamma(\psi, w)}$ and $T \in [\![\psi]\!]_{\gamma(\phi, w)}$, then $\gamma(\phi, w) \simeq \gamma(\psi, w)$.

Proof: We wish to prove that for any net $\mathcal{G}$ and any sets Δ_1 and Δ_2 of particular links, if $\mathcal{G} \cup \Delta_1$ supports every formula in $f(\Delta_2)$ and $\mathcal{G} \cup \Delta_2$ supports every formula in $f(\Delta_1)$, then $\sigma, \mathcal{G} \cup \Delta_1 \models \phi$ iff $\mathcal{G} \cup \Delta_2 \models \phi$, for all literals ϕ.

We use the generalized Stability Theorem to which we appealed in the proof of Lemma 3. By repeated applications of this theorem, $\mathcal{G} \cup \Delta_1 \models \phi$ iff $\mathcal{G} \cup \Delta_1 \cup \Delta_2 \models \phi$, for any literal ϕ. But $\mathcal{G} \cup \Delta_2 \models \phi$ iff $\mathcal{G} \cup \Delta_2 \cup \Delta_1 \models \phi$. The result follows immediately. ∎

These lemmas suffice to establish that net-models are models, and so we conclude that

Theorem 5. Every inference that is derivable in **CL4** is valid with respect to net-models.

But **CL4** is not complete with respect to net-models. To prove this we note the following lemmas and theorem.

Lemma 8. $\{\neg\phi > \neg\psi, \psi\}$ does not entail $\phi \vee \neg\psi$.

Proof: Define a countermodel as follows: $W = \{i, j, k\}$; $v_i(\phi) = \emptyset$, $v_j(\phi) = \{F\}$, $v_k(\phi) = \{T, F\}$, $v_i(\psi) = \{T\}$, $v_j(\psi) = \{F\}$, $v_k(\psi) = \{T, F\}$; γ is defined with respect to the following well orderings $\prec_i$ and $\prec_j$:

$$w_1 \prec_i w_2 \text{ iff } \langle w_1, w_2 \rangle \in \{\langle i, j \rangle, \langle j, k \rangle \langle i, k \rangle\};$$
$$w_1 \prec_j w_2 \text{ iff } \langle w_1, w_2 \rangle \in \{\langle j, i \rangle, \langle i, k \rangle \langle j, k \rangle\}.$$

Where Q is any conjunctive clause and $w \in W$, let

$$\gamma(Q, w) = \begin{cases} k, & \text{if } w = k; \\ \inf_{\prec_w} \{v \in W : T \in [\![Q]\!]_v\}, & \text{if } w \neq k. \end{cases}$$

In this model, $T \in [\![\neg\phi > \neg\psi]\!]_i$, $T \in [\![\psi]\!]_i$, but $T \notin [\![\phi \vee \neg\psi]\!]_i$. ∎

Lemma 9. Suppose that $\mathcal{G} \not\models Pa$, that $\mathcal{G} \not\models \neg Pa$, and that $\sigma = b \to \tau \succ q$, where σ does not have the form $a \to \rho \not\to P$. Then $\mathcal{G} \cup \{a \not\to P\}$ permits σ iff $\mathcal{G}$ permits σ.

Proof: By induction on the degree of σ in $\mathcal{G} \cup \{a \not\to P\}$. Let $\mathcal{G} \cup \{a \not\to P\} = \mathcal{G}'$.

Let $\deg_{\mathcal{G}'}(\sigma) = 1$. If $\mathcal{G}'$ permits σ, then $\sigma \in \mathcal{G}'$, and so, since $\sigma \neq a \not\to P$, $\sigma \in \mathcal{G}$, so that $\mathcal{G}$ permits σ. Conversely, if $\mathcal{G}$ permits σ, then $\deg_{\mathcal{G}}(\sigma) \leq \deg_{\mathcal{G}'}(\sigma) = 1$, so $\sigma \in \mathcal{G}$, and so $\sigma \in \mathcal{G}'$, so that $\mathcal{G}'$ permits σ. So $\mathcal{G}'$ permits σ iff $\mathcal{G}$ permits σ, for all σ of degree 1.

Let $\deg_{\mathcal{G}'}(\sigma) = n$, with $n > 1$, and let $\sigma = b \to \pi \succ q$. First we assume, for *reductio*, that $\mathcal{G}'$ permits σ but $\mathcal{G}$ does not permit σ. Then, for some u, ξ, $\mathcal{G}$ permits $b \to \xi \to u$ and $u \not\succ q \notin \mathcal{G}$, and for all z, τ_1, and τ_2, if $\mathcal{G}$ permits $b \to \tau_1 \to z \to \tau_2 \to u$, then $z \succ q \notin \mathcal{G}$. There are two cases: (a) $\deg_{\mathcal{G}'}(b \to \xi \to u) = \deg_{\mathcal{G}}(b \to \xi \to u) < n$, or (b) $\deg_{\mathcal{G}'}(b \to \xi \to u) > \deg_{\mathcal{G}}(b \to \xi \to u)$. If (a), then, by the inductive hypothesis, $\mathcal{G}'$ permits $b \to u$, and of course $u \not\succ q \in \mathcal{G}'$. Let $\mathcal{G}'$ permit $b \to \tau_1 \to z \to \tau_2 \to u$. Then $\mathcal{G}$ permits $b \to \tau_1 \to z \to \tau_2 \to u$, so $z \succ q \notin \mathcal{G}$. If (b), then $a = b$ and, for some ω, $a \not\to P \to \omega \to u$ is a pseudo-path in $\mathcal{G}'$ and $P \neq u$. This pseudo-path cannot affect the permissibility of $b \to \tau_1 \to z \to \tau_2 \to u$ in $\mathcal{G}'$, so $\mathcal{G} \models b \to \tau_1 \to z \to \tau_2 \to u$, and so $z \succ q \notin \mathcal{G}$.

So in both cases (a) and (b), $z \succ q \notin \mathcal{G}$. Again we have two cases: if (i) $z \succ q = z \to q$, then $z \succ q \notin \mathcal{G}'$, since $z \to q$ cannot by $a \not\to P$. If (ii) $z \succ q = z \not\to q$, then again $z \succ q \notin \mathcal{G}'$. For otherwise $z = a$ and $q = P$, in which case $b = a$, and $\sigma = a \to \pi \not\to P$, contrary to assumption.

So, in both cases $z \succ q \notin \mathcal{G}'$, and so $\mathcal{G}'$ does not permit $b \to \pi \succ q$, contrary to hypothesis. Hence if $\mathcal{G}'$ permits σ, then $\mathcal{G}$ permits σ.

Conversely, suppose for *reductio* that $\mathcal{G}$ permits σ but $\mathcal{G}'$ does not permit σ. Then, for some u, ξ, $\mathcal{G}'$ permits $b \to \xi \to u$ and $u \not\succ q \in \mathcal{G}'$, and for all z, τ_1, and τ_2, if $\mathcal{G}'$ permits $b \to \tau_1 \to z \to \tau_2 \to u$, then $z \succ q \in \mathcal{G}'$. Since $\mathcal{G}'$ permits $b \to u$, it follows by the inductive hypothesis that $\mathcal{G}$ permits $b \to \xi \to u$. And since $u \not\succ q = a \not\to P$ is impossible, $u \not\succ q \in \mathcal{G}$. So let $\mathcal{G}$ permit $b \to \tau_1 \to z \to \tau_2 \to u$. Then $\deg_{\mathcal{G}'}(b \to \xi \to u) < n$, so $\mathcal{G}' \models b \to \tau_1 \to z \to \tau_2 \to u$, and so $z \succ q \notin \mathcal{G}'$, and so $z \succ q \notin \mathcal{G}$. Consequently, $\mathcal{G}$ does not permit $b \to \pi \succ q$, contrary to hypothesis. ∎

Theorem 6. For any atomic statements ϕ and ψ, the inference from $\{\neg\phi > \neg\psi, \psi\}$ to $\phi \vee \neg\psi$ is valid in net-models.

Proof: Let Pa and Qb be atomic formulas. Let a net-model be given, and let $\mathcal{G}$ be a world thereof in which Qb and $\neg Pa > \neg Qb$ are both true but Pa is not true. Then, by the construction of the selection function γ, $\gamma(\neg Pa, \mathcal{G}) = \mathcal{G} \cup \{a \to P\}$.

If $\neg Pa$ is already true in $\mathcal{G}$, then by restricted *modus ponens* we are done, so suppose that $\neg Pa$ is not true at $\mathcal{G}$. And if $Pa = Qb$, then again we are done, by four-valued logic, so suppose that $Pa \neq Qb$. Then we know that (i) $\mathcal{G} \not\models Pa$, (ii) $\mathcal{G} \not\models \neg Pa$, (iii) $\mathcal{G} \cup \{a \not\to P\} \models \sigma_{Qb}$, for some path σ_{Qb} that enables Qb and (iv) $\sigma_{Qb} \neq \sigma_{Pa}$, for any path σ_{Pa} that enables Pa. Hence by Lemma 9, $\mathcal{G} \models \sigma_{Qb}$, and so $\neg Qb$ is true at $\mathcal{G}$, as required. $\blacksquare$

It is problematic whether the "validity" that is established in Theorem 6 is intuitively incorrect. This is related to the validity of contraposition, which, though it is generally regarded as invalid for arbitrary conditionals, is controversial for indicatives. In any case, we do not feel that the very simple inheritance networks we consider here, though they are capable of generating some interesting models of conditional logic, are sufficiently strong to yield nearly enough of these models. It is possible that reasonable extensions of the inheritance system of Horty, Thomason & Touretzky (1990) would yield a complete interpretation of a well-motivated conditional logic; in fact, this might be used as a way to motivate inheritance systems, and to investigate extensions of **CL4**. However, we have not yet pursued this idea in detail.

8. CL4 as a system of conditional logic

Several things about **CL4** make it unusual as a system of conditional logic. In the systems of Stalnaker, Lewis, and others, for example, the rules of *modus ponens* and Centering are unrestrictedly valid, whereas the rules of Exportation and Importation are not. In **CL4** the situation is reversed. We turn now to consider why this is so; the discussion shows how principles of knowledge update express themselves as principles of conditional logic.

8.1. *Exportation and* modus ponens

As we have just noted, one peculiarity of the system **CL4** is that *modus ponens*

$$\frac{\Gamma \vdash \phi \qquad \Gamma \vdash \phi > \psi}{\Gamma \vdash \psi}$$

is valid in **CL4** only for conditional-free ψ. Why the restriction? It has to do with the fact that in a set-up-based knowledge base, update is purely expansive—a fact which is captured by the rule of Exportation (**EXP**). Unrestricted *Modus ponens* interacts with Exportation to produce several theorems that would incorrectly characterize knowledge update in any *nonmonotonic* knowledge base.

For example, if unrestricted *modus ponens* were added to **CL4**, the following principle of *Unrestricted Persistence* would become derivable:

$$\frac{\Gamma \vdash \psi}{\Gamma \vdash \phi > \psi}$$

where ϕ and ψ are conjunctive clauses. Here is a derivation of this inference, using (in order) a structural rule, the rules Conjunction Elimination and **ID**, **FCP**, **EXP**, and unrestricted *modus ponens*.

$$\cfrac{\cfrac{\Gamma \vdash (\psi \wedge \phi) > (\psi \wedge \phi) \qquad \cfrac{\psi \wedge \phi \vdash \psi \wedge \phi}{\psi \wedge \phi \vdash \psi}}{\Gamma \vdash (\psi \wedge \phi) > \psi}}{\cfrac{\Gamma \vdash \psi \qquad \Gamma \vdash \psi > (\phi > \psi)}{\Gamma \vdash \phi > \psi}}$$

where ϕ and ψ are conjunctive clauses. Under its Ramsey rule interpretation, this derived rule is not intuitively valid for nonmonotonic knowledge bases. One can easily imagine, for example, being in the following situation: you have enough evidence to justify the belief that Herman is well-fed, but your evidence is defeasible. Learning that Herman is a beggar would undermine the evidence that Herman is well-fed.

A second illustration of the same point is provided by the fact that adding unrestricted *modus ponens* to **CL4** would allow us to derive a version of the principle of Left Monotonicity:

$$\frac{\Gamma \vdash \chi > \psi}{\Gamma \vdash (\chi \wedge \phi) > \psi}$$

where ϕ, ψ and χ are conjunctive clauses. Again, this inference, under its Ramsey rule interpretation, is simply not a valid principle of knowledge update for a nonmonotonic knowledge base. In the context of nonmonotonic semantic nets, we can illustrate the problem in a particularly vivid way, since in this context unrestricted *modus ponens* implies the following implausible principle.

> If $\mathcal{G}$ is a net, $\mathcal{A}$, $\mathcal{B}$, and $\mathcal{C}$ are sets of particular links, $\mathcal{G}$ supports every member of $f(\mathcal{A})$, and $\mathcal{G} \cup \mathcal{A} \cup \{a \succ P\}$ supports every member of $f(\mathcal{C})$, then $\mathcal{G} \cup \{a \succ P\}$ supports every member of $f(\mathcal{C})$.

This principle would require every particular link supported by a net to belong to the net. In fact, suppose that $\mathcal{G}$ supports Pa. Then $\mathcal{G} \cup \{a \to P\} \cup \{a \not\to P\}$ supports every member of $\{Pa\}$. Then (by the unrestricted *modus ponens* principle) $\mathcal{G} \cup \{a \not\to P\}$ would support Pa. But this can happen only if $a \to P \in \mathcal{G}$.[24]

The upshot of these points seems to be this: in the context of a knowledge repre-

---

[24] We appeal here to Theorem 5.1 of Horty, Thomason & Touretzky (1990), p. 325. According to this theorem, $\mathcal{G}$ supports Pa and $\neg Pa$ only if $a \to P$ and $a \not\to P \in \mathcal{G}$.

sentation system in which update is expansive, unrestricted *modus ponens* holds if and only if the system implements purely monotonic reasoning. The broad interest of this point is illustrated by intuitive evidence that *modus ponens* is invalid even in everyday contexts. Vann McGee, in particular, has argued (in McGee (1985)) that unrestricted *modus ponens* is simply not valid for the English indicative conditional. The class of cases where *modus ponens* fails in **CL4** is exactly the class of cases for which McGee claims (on intuitive grounds) that it fails, namely those cases where the conclusion of *modus ponens* is itself a conditional. If McGee is right and if even a very restricted form of the Ramsey rule holds for the English indicative conditional, it follows that everyday reasoning *must be*, as some members of the AI community have long insisted, fundamentally nonmonotonic.

McGee offers this example.[25]

> Opinion polls taken just before the 1980 election showed the Republican Ronald Reagan decisively ahead of the Democrat Jimmy Carter, with the other Republican in the race, John Anderson, a distant third. Those apprised of the poll results believed, with good reason:
>
> > If a Republican wins the election, then if it's not Reagan who wins it will be Anderson.
> > A Republican will win the election.
>
> Yet they will not have good reason to believe
>
> > If it's not Reagan who wins, it will be Anderson.

The hypothetical believers of this example believe (with good reason) that a Republican will win because they believe (with good reason) that Reagan will win. And since Anderson is the only other Republican with a chance of winning, they believe (with good reason) that if a Republican *other* than Reagan wins, it will be Anderson. But since Carter is far ahead of Anderson in the polls, they have no good reason to believe that if Reagan does not win, then Anderson will. On the contrary, the presumption is that if Reagan does not win, then Carter will. So far so good, but so far we have not described a counterexample to *modus ponens*. We *have* described a situation in which ϕ' and $(\phi \wedge \psi) > \chi$ are reasonable things to believe, but in which $\psi > \chi$ is not a reasonable thing to believe. What we need is a situation in which ϕ and $\phi > (\psi > \chi)$ are *true*, but $\psi > \chi$ is not *true*. In order to get a real counterexample to *modus ponens* out of McGee's story we need two assumptions: (i) that exportation is logically valid, and (ii) that logically valid inferences preserve positive justification status (the property of being a justified belief). If these are granted, then the good grounds for believing ϕ' (that Reagan will win) become good grounds for believing ϕ (that a Republican will win). And the good grounds for believing $(\phi \wedge \psi) > \chi$ (that if a Republican other than Reagan wins, it will be Anderson that wins) become good grounds for believing $\phi > (\psi > \chi)$ (that if a Republican wins, then if it is not Reagan, it will be Anderson). And, finally,

[25] McGee (1985), p. 462.

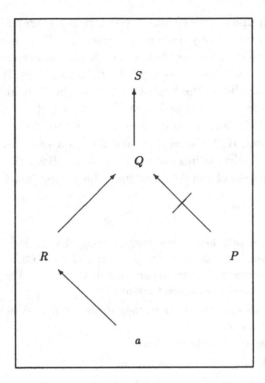

Fig. 1. A net counterexample to *modus ponens*

the fact that justification is not preserved by the inference from ϕ and $\phi > (\psi > \chi)$ to $\psi > \chi$ implies that it is possible for ϕ and $\phi > (\psi > \chi)$ to be *true* although $\psi > \chi$ is *not true*.

McGee's counterexamples to *modus ponens* are all of the following form: ϕ and $\phi > (\psi > \chi)$ are true, but $(\psi > \chi)$ is not true. Semantic nets provide a class of counterexamples to *modus ponens* of precisely this form. Consider the net in Figure 1, for example.   This net supports the statements Qa and $Qa > (Pa > Sa)$, but it does not support the statement $Pa > Sa$. We obtain a concrete example by letting S stand for the predicate *malnourished*, Q for the predicate *ill-fed*, P for the predicate *wealthy*, and R for the predicate *beggar*. The name a will stand for *Alfred*. The net then tells us this: *Alfred is a beggar and can therefore be presumed to be ill-fed* (and hence malnourished). Indeed, *if it turns out that Alfred is ill-fed, then even if it turns out that he is wealthy, we can still presume that he is malnourished*. But it does not follow that *if it turns out that Alfred is wealthy, then we can presume that he is malnourished!* On the contrary, if, in our present state of knowledge, we learn *only* that Alfred is wealthy, we will be unable to make any presumption about whether he is malnourished, for in that case we will have two pieces of evidence, one for and one against his being ill-fed, without any basis for deciding which evidence to base a presumption on (since *beggar* and *wealthy person* are incomparable nodes).

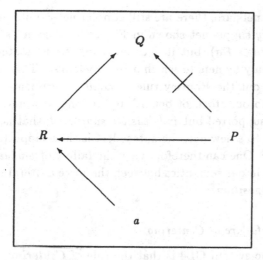

Fig. 2. A simpler net counterexample to *modus ponens*

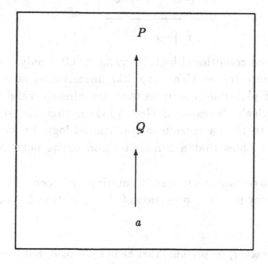

Fig. 3. The simplest net counterexample to *modus ponens*

We can find still simpler semantic net counterexamples to *modus ponens*. Consider the net in Figure 2, for example.

Let R stand for the predicate *teacher*, P for the predicate *computer science professor*, and Q for the predicate *underpaid*. Let the individual term a stand for *Alfred*. *Alfred is a teacher and can therefore be presumed to be underpaid*, and *if Alfred is underpaid, then even if he is a professor of computer science, he is nevertheless underpaid*. But it does not follow that *if Alfred is a professor of computer science, then he is underpaid!* On the contrary, if Alfred is a computer science professor, then (other things being equal) we should conclude that he is *not* underpaid. After all, computer science professors are generally not underpaid, and if we knew that Alfred was a computer science professor, that would be the most specific thing we would know about him.

But, as simple as these nets are, there are still simpler net-counterexamples to *modus ponens*. Consider the *very* simple net shown in Figure 3. This net supports the statements Pa and $Pa > (\neg Pa > Pa)$, but it does not support the statement $\neg Pa > Pa$. (The latter is supported only by nets to which $a \rightarrow P$ belongs.) This example highlights the fact that in carrying out the Ramsey rule thought experiment on a semantic net we "add the antecedent to our stock of beliefs" by moving to a new net in which the antecedent is not merely supported but *indefeasibly supported*; that is, when we assume the antecedent by moving to a new net, the antecedent is then supported by the new net *and all of its extensions*.[26] One can therefore view the failure of *modus ponens* as a consequence of the difference in our semantics between the force a literal has as a *supported link* and its force as a *supposition*.

8.2. Importation and the failure of Centering

A second peculiarity of the system **CL4** is that the rule of *Centering*,

$$\frac{\Gamma \vdash \phi \qquad \Gamma \vdash \psi}{\Gamma \vdash \phi > \psi}$$

which is valid in two-valued conditional logic, is valid in **CL4** only for conditional-free ψ.[27] The reason is that unrestricted Centering, like unrestricted *modus ponens*, would interact unfavorably with plausible principles that are already valid in **CL4**, such as Importation. One of McGee's theses in McGee (1985) is that his counterexamples to *modus ponens* show that there is a tension in conditional logic between *modus ponens* and Exportation. We can show that a similar tension exists between Centering and Importation.

One can point directly to certain instances of Centering that seem, on intuitive grounds, to be invalid given a Ramsey rule interpretation of the conditional. Consider this example.

> Since Alfred is a teacher, we presume that he is underpaid, but if it turns out that he is a computer science professor, then we should presume that he is not underpaid. This gives us no reason to believe (absurdly) that if Alfred is underpaid, then if he is a computer science professor, he is not underpaid.

Figure 4, which is identical to Figure 2, illustrates this example. Here, as before during the discussion of Figure 2, we let P stand for *computer science professor*, R for *teacher*, Q for *underpaid*, and a for *Alfred*. The net supports the statements Qa and $Pa > \neg Qa$, but it does not support the statement $Qa > (Pa > \neg Qa)$ (nor does it support $(Qa \wedge Pa) > \neg Qa$).

---

[26] This is easiest to see in cases where the antecedent is itself a literal, in which case we assume the antecedent by simply *adding it* to the net as a basic link!

[27] ϕ must also be conditional-free, but that is because *every* well-formed conditional in the language of **CL4** has a conditional-free antecedent.

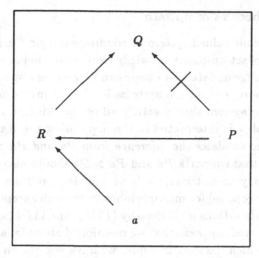

Fig. 4. A counterexample to centering

It seems that this example depends for its force on the validity of Importation. If I did believe $Qa > (Pa > \neg Qa)$ (if Alfred is underpaid, then if he is a computer science professor, then he is *not* underpaid), then by Importation I would believe $(Qa \wedge Pa) > \neg Qa$ (if Jack is an underpaid computer science professor then he is not underpaid). If we reject the former it is because we reject the latter. Our intuitions are, in other words, helped along by Importation, in the sense that Alfred's story gets its force as a counterexample to Centering from its force as a counterexample to the following *clearly* unreasonable inference.

$$
\text{(CEN+IMP)} \qquad \frac{\Gamma \vdash \phi \qquad \Gamma \vdash \psi > \chi}{\Gamma \vdash (\phi \wedge \psi) > \chi}
$$

where ϕ and ψ are conjunctive clauses. This inference is valid, however, if unrestricted Centering and Importation (as formulated in **CL4**) are both assumed to be valid.

Figure 4, which is identical to Figure 2, provides an even simpler counterexample to Centering (and to (CEN+IMP), of course). This net supports the statements Qa and $Pa > \neg Qa$, but it does not support the statement $Qa > (Pa > \neg Qa)$ (nor does it support $(Qa \wedge Pa) > \neg Qa$). Since Alfred is a teacher, we presume that he is underpaid, but if it turns out that he is a computer science professor, then he is not underpaid. But this gives us no reason to believe (absurdly) that if Alfred is an underpaid computer science professor, then he is not underpaid. (Here, as before during the discussion of Figure 2, we let P stand for *computer science professor*, R for *teacher*, Q for *underpaid*, and a for *Alfred*.)

9. Conditional-based theories of update

As we have just seen, the four-valued system of conditional logic **CL4** presented above can be used in the context of set-up-based knowledge representation as a formal device for stating principles of knowledge update. This logic can be used as a specification criterion for set-up-based knowledge representation systems implementing an update function—the criterion being that the system should satisfy all of the principles validated by this logic, when the conditional $>$ is interpreted in the logic using the Ramsey rule. Thus, for example, since the logic validates the inference *from Pa and Pa $>$ Qb to infer Qb*, any inheritance algorithm that supports Pa and $Pa > Qb$ should also support Qb.

Though this criterion may seem trivial, it is not; in fact, it rules out many of the algorithms that have been proposed for multiple inheritance with exceptions. Touretzky's criticism of shortest-path algorithms in Touretzky (1986), pp. 117-119, is an example in which the valid instance of *modus ponens* that we mentioned above fails. In presenting an inheritance algorithm for which the logic is sound, we have also shown that the criterion is not impractically strict.

Moreover, the use of conditionals allows one to specify *local* constraints on update; a conditional such as $Pa > Qa$ can be regarded as a constraint to the effect that Qa is to be concluded on learning Pa. This would correspond to a *specific* constraint, e.g., that we should conclude that Clyde is gray on learning that Clyde is an elephant.

The fact that we can state these constraints in a relatively tractable logic gives us the opportunity to design systems that can reason explicitly about update principles by means of the logic. So far, though, we have not taken this step and are employing the logic as an external criterion for inheritance algorithms.

REFERENCES

Barwise, J. and J. Perry (1983): *Situations and Attitudes*. Cambridge, MA: The MIT Press.

Belnap, N. (1977a): "How a computer should think", in *Contemporary Aspects of Philosophy*, ed. by G. Ryle, New York, NY: Oriel Press, 30–56.

Belnap, N. (1977b): "A useful four-valued logic", in *Modern Uses of Multiple-Valued Logic*, ed. by J. Dunn and G. Epstein, Dordrecht: D. Reidel, 8–37.

Cross, C.B. and R. H. Thomason (1987): "Update and conditionals", in *Methodologies for Intelligent Systems*, ed. by Z.W. Ras and M. Zemankova, Amsterdam: Elsevier, 392–399.

Gärdenfors, P. (1986): "Belief revisions and the Ramsey test for conditionals", *Philosophical Review 95*, 81–93.

Gärdenfors, P. (1987): "Variations on the Ramsey test: more triviality results", *Studia Logica 46*, 321–327.

Gärdenfors, P. (1988): *Knowledge in Flux: Modeling the Dynamics of Epistemic States*, Cambridge, MA: The MIT Press, Bradford Books.

Ginsberg, M.L. (1988): "Multivalued logics: a uniform approach to reasoning in artificial intelligence", *Computational Intelligence 4*, 265–316.

Ginsberg, M.L. (1990): "Bilattices and modal operators", in *Theoretical Aspects of Reasoning About Knowedge: Proceedings of the Third Conference*, ed. by R. Parikh, Los Altos, CA: Morgan Kaufmann, 273–287.

Harper, W.L., R.C. Stalnaker, and G. Pearce (1980): *Ifs: Conditionals, Belief, Decision, Chance, and Time*, Dordrecht: D. Reidel.

Harper, W.L (1980): "A sketch of some recent developments", in Harper, Stalnaker & Pearce (1980), 3–38.

Horty, J.F, R.H. Thomason, and D.S. Touretzky (1990): "A skeptical theory of inheritance in nonmonotonic semantic networks", *Artificial Intelligence 42*, 311–348.

Jeffrey, R.C. (1983): *The Logic of Decision*. Chicago, IL: University of Chicago Press.

Levi, I. (1988): "Iteration of conditionals and the Ramsey Test", *Synthese 76*, 49–81.

Lewis, D.K. (1976): "Probabilities of conditionals and conditional probabilities", *Philosophical Review 85*, 297–315, reprinted in Harper, Stalnaker & Pearce (1980), 129–147.

Makinson, D. (1986): "How to give it up: a survey of some formal aspects of the logic of theory change", *Synthese 62*, 347–363.

Makinson, D. (1987): "On the status of the postulate of recovery in the logic of theory change", *Journal of Philosophical Logic 16*, 383–394.

Makinson, D. (1990): "The Gärdenfors impossibility theorem in non-monotonic contexts", *Studia Logica 49*.

McGee, V. (1985): "A counterexample to *modus ponens*", *Journal of Philosophy 82*, 462–471.

Nute, D. (1985): "A non-monotonic logic based on conditional logic", Research Report 01-0007, Advanced Computational Methods Center, University of Georgia.

Sosa, E. (1975): *Causation and Conditionals*, Oxford: Oxford University Press.

Stalnaker, R.C (1968): "A theory of conditionals", in *Studies in Logical Theory*, number 2 in American Philosophical Quarterly Monograph Series, Oxford: Basil Blackwell, 98–112, reprinted in Harper, Stalnaker & Pearce (1980) and in Sosa (1975); page references are to Sosa (1975).

Thomason, R.H. (1969): "A semantical study of constructible falsity", *Zeitschrift für mathematische Logik und Grundlagen der Mathematik 15*, 247–257.

Thomason, R.H., J.F. Horty, and D.S. Touretzky (1986): "A calculus for inheritance in monotonic semantic nets", Technical Report CMU-CS-86-138, Carnegie Mellon University.

Touretzky, D.S. (1986): *The Mathematics of Inheritance Systems*. Los Altos, CA: Morgan Kaufmann.

Index

Printed in the United States
By Bookmasters